liberazione della donna

feminism in Italy

liberazione della donna feminism in Italy

Lucia Chiavola Birnbaum

 Wesleyan University Press
Middletown, Connecticut

Chapter 9 was originally published, in somewhat different
form, as "The Feminist Catholic Left in Italy," in the *Stanford
Italian Review*, Volume 3:1, Spring, 1983, published by Anima
Libri; Chapter 15, in somewhat different form, as "European
disarmament movement: the next steps," in the *Journal of
women and religion*, Volume 2:2.

Endsheet: Courtesy of *siamo in tante . . .* , © 1975

Library of Congress Cataloging in Publication Data

Birnbaum, Lucia Chiavola, 1924–
   Liberazione della donna.

   Includes index.
   1. Feminism—Italy.   2. Women—Italy—Social conditions.   I. Title.
HQ1642.B56   1986   305.4'2'0945   85–5390
ISBN 0-8195-5133-3 (alk. paper)

All inquiries and permission requests should be addressed
to the Publisher, Wesleyan University Press, 110 Mt. Vernon
Street, Middletown, Connecticut 06457.

Distributed by Harper & Row Publishers, Keystone Industrial Park, Scranton, Pennsylvania 18512.

Manufactured in the United States of America
FIRST EDITION

Dedicated to women of the United States. With especial love to my own earth mother, Kate Cipolla Chiavola, and to a many-faceted cluster of different women: Joie Mellenbruch, Dora Birnbaum, Elsa Polansky, Marge Lasky, Judith Skeldon, Barbara Birnbaum, Nancy Kimura, Eula Thomas, Delorease Grigsby, Ellen Setteducati, Lori and Kathy Chiavola, and Sabrina and Jessica Birnbaum. And to the three others named Lucia.

Non c'è rivoluzione senza liberazione della donna.
Non c'è liberazione della donna senza rivoluzione.
—Italian feminists

contents

part one: her story

illustrations

"... Vote the Italian Socialist Party," Psi postwar poster

"Mothers! Save your children from Bolshevism," Dc postwar poster

March of women of anti-Communist Catholic Action, Rome, 1948

"... Slay the vipers of divorce and free love," Dc postwar poster

"... Your future and your families are at stake," Dc poster, c. 1950

"... Vote yes against divorce to save the family," Msi poster, c. 1970

New left poster

"Women say no," *effe* cover, 1974

National Conference on Abortion, Rome, c. 1975

"Unedited Marxism," 1985 cartoon

"Pci advances again," headline from *l'Unità*, 1976

"... Vote Psi," Socialist party poster, c. 1975

"Women in struggle for the alternative," Psi poster, c. 1975

Militant posters from *le donne al muro*

following page 246

Woman as brooding hen, 1975 caricature

"Abortion Faced by Us"

"Feminist counter-information," *effe* logo

"The Alternative of self-management," 1975

"... A woman is owned by the man," drawing, 1974

"Patient" and "doctor" at rally for abortion, 1975

"Legal regulation of abortion," Udi rally, Rome, 1977

Patriarchal totem pole, drawing from *effe*, 1974

"When the cook knows how to govern...,"*effe*, 1974

"... The crutch of masculine power," photo, 1975

Casa della donna graffiti

Protest against unsafe conditions of women workers, from *noi donne*, 1980

Lavoro a domicilio, Sicily, 1975

Women embroidering, 1974

Women in Rome

Vigil protesting violence, Naples, 1976

Comiso rally, 1983 poster

Rally in Comiso, 1983

preface

The hope of sisterhood is global but culture may determine the contours of a particular women's movement. Italy, the seat of Roman catholicism and the nation with the largest communist party in the western hemisphere, has been the site in the last decade and a half of significant feminist advances and a pervasive women's consciousness.* Since these two institutions are often considered unsympathetic to women, this may be a paradox. Or dialectic may be at hand.

In the case of catholicism, conservative church doctrines may be considered negative for women, yet beliefs deriving from John XXIII and vatican council II have encouraged women's advancement. Today, feminist ideas are visible at the base of the church, if not at the top of the hierarchy. In the case of communism, a new left critique of the Italian communist party (Pci) combined with feminist confrontation produced a synthesis by the mid-eighties in which the Pci recognizes the women's movement as an agency of social transformation, the Dc (the christian democratic party, dominant since 1948 and aligned with constrictive views of women) has been dealt set-

---

* For an explanation of the use of capitalization in this book, see note at end of preface.

ITALY

Turin · Milan

Bologna·

Florence·

ADRIATIC
SEA

⊛ Rome

Naples

TYRRHENIAN
SEA

Palermo·

SICILY

Catania·

Comiso·

N

0   100
M

0   100
KM

Karen Wysocki

backs by women's vote, and feminists are intent on creating a women's movement autonomous of political parties.

A few decades ago Italian peasant women served men at table and then ate their supper on the rocks of the fireplace. A little boy was taught to be *bravo* (capable), a little girl was taught to be *buona* (good). In traditional Italian culture, a woman was good if she was a selfless wife and mother subordinating herself to husband, family, church, and society. Yet equal rights were written into Italy's 1948 constitution, and what may be the most advanced feminist legislation of Europe was placed into the Italian code after 1968. A milestone in cultural change was marked in the 1981 vote sustaining legal abortion with large majorities in every province of Italy but one (the alpine, German-speaking Alto Adige).

Iconoclastic to both traditional catholicism and traditional marxism is the insistence of Italian feminists that genuine equality includes recognition of differences: women's own definitions of their differences from men, the value of women's differences among themselves, and the integrity of differing interpretations of accepted truths—or what Italians describe as an "unedited gospel" and "unedited marxism." For the church (and its aligned party, the Dc) unsettling implications are inherent in the perspectives of feminist (and other) liberation theologies grounded on an unedited gospel. For world politics, the implications of unedited marxism are large. In the libertarian self-managed socialist society to which most Italian feminists aspire, equality would be enriched by a multiplicity of perspectives emerging from the self-confidence and release of creativity that accompany consciousness—and political and social guarantees—of the equal worth of every human being.

I am an Italian American woman, a historian whose field is the history of beliefs. Feminist and new left values predispose me to view the Italian women's movement with empathy. A generation ago, historians who did not identify their values were considered "objective" and free from bias. Today, students of history understand the sociology of knowledge and are skeptical of historians who claim to record facts but do not acknowledge their own assumptions. As a contemporary U.S. scholar has said, "All historiography is a selective view of the past. Historical interpretation is defined by contemporary questions and horizons of reality and conditioned by contemporary political interests and structures of domination. Historical 'objectivity' can only be approached by reflecting critically on and naming one's theoretical presuppositions and political allegiances."[1] In today's Italy discussions of epistemology by one school of philosophers underline that one can "know" anything only by participating in the phenomenon. Elsewhere, in a convergence of feminist epistemology with post-Cartesian philosophy, the importance of "participant observation" is recognized as indispensable for social science as public philosophy.[2] My participant observation in fifteen research stays in Italy since 1969 has been checked and balanced by traditional historical methodology, using documents accessible to the reader to corroborate findings.

Italians speak of the "world of catholicism" and the "world of communism" in their culture. This is a historical study of Italian women in relation to these two worlds. Because the two worlds are in rapid change in Italy, it is necessary to look outside, as well as inside, the institutions of the papacy and the Pci (e.g., in *comunità di base* and in parties of the new left) to see dynamics of change.

For specific focus I have chosen Sicilian women as a case and also as an evocative metaphor for Italian women. This choice was made not only because all four of my grandparents and my father emigrated from Sicily to Kansas City, Missouri but because the women of Sicily, that underdeveloped island of Italy, offer a mirror of *others* that can help in understanding a movement that was initially propelled by educated northern Italian women. Most Italian feminists have a peasant background as close as a grandmother; Sicilian women even now remain near to the values of a peasant culture.

Antonio Gramsci, perhaps the major theorist of Italian communism, pointed to the significance of the "southern question"—the different social and economic experience of southern Italians, yet the necessity, in a successful cultural and political revolution, of a coalition of southern peasants with northern industrial workers.[3] With postwar migration from the South, the southern question may refer to all of contemporary Italy (as Leonardo Sciascia has suggested);[4] today's northern industrial workers (and their wives) are largely from the South. For feminists the point is important since Italy's twelve million housewives (many of whom are employed in the *lavoro nero* of cottage industry) share with peasants the experience of marginality. Sociologists of the seventies placed housewives and peasants outside the technostructure; politicians have (until recently) subordinated women's issues and the problems of the South to larger party strategy.

The metaphor is important also because the southern question for Italy brings up the variable of racism. Gramsci pointed out that in the early decades of the twentieth century northerners regarded the South as a "lead weight which impedes a more rapid civil development of Italy."[5] Southern Italians were considered "biologically inferior beings, semi-barbarians or complete barbarians by natural destiny" with negative inherited characteristics: "lazy, incapable, criminal, barbarous."[6] This "bourgeois ideology among the northern proletariat" was given the authority of science in the early twentieth century.[7] Italian feminist understanding of the similar sources of racism and sexism is shown in their identification after 1968 of women with marginal others.

The metaphor of Sicilian women also suggests what has been called the "religious ground bass" of Italy.[8] For Robert N. Bellah, a sociologist of religion, the South of Italy stands not only for a geographical place but for "a region in the Italian soul."[9] Bellah describes the southern undertone (similar to the continuous drone of Sicilian folk music) of Italian beliefs as "emotional and intense in contrast to the ascetic rationalism of high Italian culture."[10] Touching beliefs that preceded judeo-christianity, this low-pitched undertone differs from what Bellah refers to as "the universalism of high Italian thought," pointing instead to a genuine pluralism: a large diversity of peoples and a multiplicity of beliefs "presided over by a woman." Bellah describes this pluralism as an "epiphany of the Great Mother of the Mediterranean world, only partially and uncertainly articulated with the Virgin of Nazareth."[11] The "real" religion of Italy, according to Bellah, is this often unverbalized set of beliefs, while the legal religion is catholicism.

As sociologists have pointed out, these subterranean beliefs may be understandable as a defensive reaction of southerners to a long history of governmental and other oppression, yet deep layers of consciousness are involved. The complexity of the matter may be suggested in the paradoxical behavior of Italians subscribing formally to doctrines of the church while acting politically in a manner that seems contradictory. Feminism in Italy is scarcely understandable without reference to this area of belief where, in Bellah's description, "there seems to be something central about the place of the woman."[12]

Contemporary study of the political implications of peasant beliefs by Italian anthropologists and sociologists has emphasized the role of the madonna and her son, the *"cristo rosso."*[13] Contemporary celebrations of May day in southern Italy feature the madonna and *"cristi rossi"* (red christs). The peasant custom of the mother looking for her son during easter week sometimes takes on socialist implications. The madonna who figures in these rituals of a red Christ[14] is a mother figure closer to peasant memory, perhaps, than to the madonna of church doctrine.

In part one of this book I have sketched the large historical context of Italian feminism. Chapter one is concerned with women deities who preceded judeo-christianity, Graeco-Roman goddesses, christian madonnas, saints and godmothers, and the valence of women figures in nineteenth-century peasant folklore beliefs. The contemporary feminist/socialist argument is placed in its modern setting, in the nineteenth-century history of socialism and the place of Italian women therein. Chapter two sketches the formative period of the Italian worker movement in the period before world war I; women's interpretations of marxism are analyzed for this era of revolution. In chapters three and four the period of the "first feminism" is explored in Italian women's tacit resistance to fascism and women partisans' open resistance to nazis and fascists. The Italian women's union is placed in postwar context in chapter five. Chapter six focuses on the cultural context of contemporary Italian feminism— the cultural revolution to which John XXIII pointed in the sixties.

Chapter seven focuses on the revolutionary lineaments of 1968 in Italy—the immediate backdrop of the contemporary eruption of Italian feminism. Chapter eight puts feminist cultural and political successes in the environment of Italian ferment of the seventies. Chapter nine analyzes catholics, believers, and feminists and the perspective of an unedited gospel. Chapter ten examines one case of feminist unedited marxism: the concept of the unpaid labor of housewives. Chapter eleven refers to the cultural and political views of Italian feminists. Women's studies in Italy are the subject of chapter twelve. The several facets of the concept of *other* are viewed in chapter thirteen: catholic matrons, prostitutes, lesbians, nuns, feminists, and men as others. The political and cultural evolution of Italian feminism from 1968 to the present is studied with a close analysis of the women's union in chapter fourteen. Changing to a wider lens, women and the multibranched Italian movements against violence are put into perspective in chapter fifteen. The particulars of Italian unedited feminism are analyzed in chapter sixteen, offering a comparative view of the difference between Italian feminists working in large movements (chapter fifteen) and their sharper intensity when engaged in separate, particular efforts—with the example of anti-nuclear Sicilian women. The main themes of the book—Italian women and the worlds of catholicism and communism—are reflected in chapter thirteen on the changing views of the major catholic women's organization, Centro italiano femminile (Cif) and chapter fourteen on the evolution of the women's union, Unione donne italiane (Udi) from auxiliary of the Pci to autonomous women's network. I have searched for signs of an emerging women's culture in a variety of women's periodicals, novels, plays, radio programs, in graffiti in *case della donna*, in cartoons, and in theoretical papers of the Italian women's university, Centro Virginia Woolf (chapters eleven, twelve, and seventeen).

For the study of the period before 1968, aside from a few path-breaking secondary historical studies,[15] I have looked to sources in archeology, folklore, theology, novels, private journals, and memoirs. For contemporary history after 1968, primary sources employed included interviews (more precisely, mutual interviews) and conversations with many different Italians on trains, in homes, offices, cafes, as well as participation in political and cultural feminist activities over a period of a decade and a half. First-hand understanding has been checked and deepened by close study of catholic, political, and women's periodicals. Analyses of contemporary Italian culture and politics, predominantly written by men, provided a male perspective. Catholic family periodicals have been culled to understand a non-feminist perspective, uncovering by the mid-eighties considerable convergence with the feminist press.

For the latter part of the book (chapters fifteen, sixteen, and seventeen) concerning the role of Italian feminists in movements of peace, ecology, and opposition to violence (fascist terrorism, violent revolution, sexual violence, violence against the environment, the violence of the mafia, and nuclear violence) participation in conferences, meetings, and demonstrations has been checked and balanced by a systematic study of relevant journals, some of them, like *pace e guerra*, crossing movements of women, peace, and ecology and encompassing theology as well as independent left political analysis. Other journals, like *bozze*, that are addressed to the large purview of left catholic belief reach an arc of believers: *comunità di base*, liberation theologians, independent priests in the church, catholic independents of the political left, and secular "believers."

My working definition of feminism—empowerment of women—has been widened by this study. For Sicilian women, feminist autonomy connotes a struggle involving culture, class, and gender: "self-determination against oppression and exploitation of one people over another, one class over another, one sex over another." [16] With the Italian new left, and with Italian feminists, I share a perspective shaped by a multipolar dialectic: gender as well as class, ecology as well as economics, the nuclear threat to the planet, and the global difference between rich nations of the North and poor nations of the South. My theoretical premises are informed by a keen sense that the enterprise of women's history needs to be undertaken with an open mind, imagination, and questions as well as with theoretical construct and analytic argument. Analytic assumptions may be explicit and placed in the foreground or they may be acknowledged and kept implicit, as they are in the selection of themes and of sources in my historical narrative. In areas of complexity, pictorial documentation is often more suggestive than words and creative literature most helpful for conveying, for example, the layered response of Italian women to fascism or the ambivalence most Italian feminists feel on the issue of abortion. To understand what Italian feminists mean by women's "difference" from men, I have sought a variety of sources from graffiti to theology to lullabies.

Feminist ideas in Italy fell on different ground than they have elsewhere. This poses a problem; to find opposing views the historian may need to track the subject to prose muffled in abstraction, to silence, and to omission. This is an attempt to probe the cultures of Italian catholicism and communism to understand what has been described as a "change in the collective consciousness." Yet after a decade and a half of research and thinking, there remains an elusive quality about the subject. Italian feminism, in comparison with other women's movements, appears to have achieved considerable success (e.g., an average national vote of 70 percent in 1981 sustained the law for legal abortion). Yet Italy remains in the mid-eighties a country where a woman may die of multiple pregnancies and where an advanced bill against sexual violence remains stymied in 1985 not only in parliament but in what seem to be subterranean areas of belief.

Researching and writing this study have left me with many open-ended questions. In the hope that this book will generate more research, I have cited accessible sources and offered a lengthy bibliographical essay.

note

To convey the thinking of Italian feminists, I have let them speak in their own words as much as possible (translation, unless otherwise noted, is mine). I have also adopted their style of removing capital letters from almost everything but proper names, a style Italians consider an extension of democracy to the printed word. This is particularly important in a study concerned with the Italian debate on religious or political integralism; in order not to prejudge either of the two perspectives, words referring to christianity as well as to communism are uncapitalized. In direct quotations (as well as in U.S. titles) other people are left to their own judgments about capitalization. In accordance with Italian style, only the first letters of acronyms and of first words of titles of books, articles, encyclicals, newspapers, and proper names of particular groups are capitalized—unless principals choose no capitalization at all. Consistency may be bent, but the contemporary Italian value of encouraging each person to define her- or himself and to create her or his own initiatives may thereby be suggested.

Lucia Chiavola Birnbaum

acknowledgments

Many Italian women have helped me to understand this movement. They include Simona Mafai, Margherita Repetto, Dacia Maraini, Lidia Menapace, Pia Bruzzichelli, Sara Poli, Giacoma Galante, Vania Chiurlotto, Maria Occhipinti, Letizia Colajanni, Marina Camboni, Anna Vio, Gabriella di Lei, Emanuela Moroli, Matilde Gismondi, Adriana Crosato, Eugenia Bono, Gigliola Lo Cascio, Marisa Ombra, Giovanna Quasimodo, Maria Rosa Cutrufelli, Chiara Ottaviani, Giuliana Saladino, Maria Luisa Moretti, Marisa Galdi, Gabriella Raimondi, Giosi Lippolis, Sofia Del Vecchio, Nilde Carabba, Grazia Borrini, Nadia Ballia, Serena Castaldi, Letitia Argentieri, and many others. Among the Italian women who did not identify themselves as feminists, I would like to acknowledge in particular Carmela Giurato, Anna Di Pasquale, Laura Barone, Graziella Fontanini and Cecilia Ross and Laura Stortoni, who now live in the United States. Ana Noon and Karina Bouchet, who participated in the early Italian movement, shared their insights. My debt to a catholic nun I came to know in Italy is especially deep: Sister Rosalinda Ramirez—then of the Cudip peace office at Comiso, now director of Theology of the Americas—clarified liberation theology in postconciliar catholicism.

Women of the Center for the Study, Education and Advancement of Women at the University of California at Berkeley provided aid and assistance when the manuscript had reached an impasse—in particular Gleoria Bradley Sapp, Margaret Wilkerson, and Ida Dunson. Women of the Feminist Institute and its affiliated study group on women's work have helped me realize that women's research goes forward not only by intellectual criticism but by women sustaining each other. I thank in particular Joan Levinson, Clare Fischer, Marge Lasky, Rachel Kahn-Hut, Maresi Nerad, Sydney Carson, Eileen Boris, Alison Lingo and Nona Glazer; others who were helpful include Rena Vassar, Barbara Davidson, and Jean Harris. Jeannette Hopkins, director of Wesleyan University Press, and Cynthia Wells, editor, encouraged me to write a better book, Nina Loewenstein brought imagination to the book's assemblage of illustrations.

Salvatore and Giorgio Chiavola opened the windows of my Italian heritage; Louis Chiavola showed me the meaning of franciscan morality. Padre Gregorio A. Lantieri took me to archeological ruins and offered franciscan insights. Marcello Vigli helped me to understand contemporary *comunità di base*. Federico D'Agostino's knowledge of Italian theology and sociology sharpened my questions, and Luigi Giurato showed me the human beings behind the categories of twentieth-century Italian history. Claudio Fontanini's wit and acuity led me through the brambles of Italian politics. Henry Farnham May taught me the importance of beliefs in history and William Appleman Williams the significance of heresies. Gerard McCauley offered critical early support. Among the males who have inspired (and encouraged) this study of feminism are three sons—Naury, Marc, and Stefan; and three grandsons—Joshua, Matthew, and Nicolas.

Not least, this book is indebted to Wally, who in Italy carries my research books and in Berkeley takes time from his multiple activities to help me to untangle paragraphs, punctuation, and the word processor. He is a fine example of the truth of the graffito in the *casa della donna* in Rome: "to change everything we must include everyone, men too. (signed) superfeminist."

Errors or misperceptions are mine alone.

part one   her story

1

la gran madre mediterranea,
madrine, e socialiste

the great Mediterranean
earth mother,
godmothers, and socialists

Italy is an ancient land, until the last part of the nineteenth century
a collection of independent principalities, a nation whose contemporary demeanor is that of a country still in creation. Italians live
amidst the ruins of civilizations that arose long before the christian
era.* Ligurians, Latins, Sabines, Sicels, and other indigenous peoples
of the peninsula and islands were invaded by Etruscans, Celts, Sam-
nites, Phoenicians, Greeks, Romans, Germanic tribes, Arabs, Normans, Swabians, Angevins, Spanish and Austrian Bourbons, and oth-

* See Preface for explanation of the style of capitalization used in this work.

3

ers. Traces of all these cultures remain, not only in museum artifacts but in the memories of Italians.

earth mothers and other goddesses

One memory is that of the earth mother. In various forms she was worshipped all over the Mediterranean littoral. Later her dowry was divided by the Greeks and Romans and distributed to a galaxy of goddesses. All these female deities preceded the male god of judeo-christianity. Late in the twentieth century the earth mother and goddesses were rediscovered and celebrated by feminists. In Italy, where the primordial mother may be too near, the celebration was dashed with ambivalence.[1]

In the second century after Jesus, the Roman philosopher Apuleius called her the "natural mother of all things" and listed the diverse people for whom she was mother goddess and her many different names. Phrygians called her the "Mother of the gods of Pessinus," Athenians described her as "Cecropian Minerva," Cyprians named her "Paphian Venus." Cretans described her as "Dictynian Diana" and Sicilians, who held a major center of Demeter worship on the island, referred to her daughter as the "infernal Proserpine." The Eleusinians called her Ceres, others invoked Juno or Bellona or Hecate or Ramnusie.[2] The Roman goddess, Diana of Ephesus (precursor of a later virgin mother), was a virgin nurturant mother with many breasts. She had many consorts but, notably, her son-lover was Adonis (or Osiris or Dionysius), remembered as "the dying and reborn god who dwells with one aspect of the goddess in life and with the other in death."[3]

Among her negative images was Medusa of the snake hair, whose look could turn a person to stone, and Kali, "the wicked mother" of India. In abstracted form, she was the "eye goddess" around the Mediterranean and also in Britain and Ireland. Eyes and spirals, from prehistoric time, have symbolized the mother goddess. For Lawrence Di Stasi, an Italian American interpreter, these opposing spirals "must represent the spiral of generation moving outwards to yield birth, the other, the spiral of decay moving inwards to yield death; the one creating, the other consuming."[4]

The subject of goddesses and an earth-mother deity who were replaced by the male god of judeo-christianity engenders religious, political, and personal arguments among contemporary feminists and antifeminists. Women deities evoke matriarchy—rather than patriarchy—, a subject weighted with contemporary issues of power. Sarah B. Pomeroy, a classical scholar who has carefully evaluated the sources on the subject of matriarchy, has reached reasoned conclusions.[5] In the nineteenth century, J. J. Bachofen examined classical legends and concluded that matriarchy and matrilineal descent were characteristic of ancient societies. Herodotus' description of non-Greek societies corroborated customs Bachofen found in Greek legends of the late Bronze Age. Acknowledging that parts of Bachofen's thesis have been superseded, Pomeroy finds that his evidence "has not been invalidated." The "tremendous wealth of ancient material indicating the high status of Bronze Age queens, the success of Amazon societies, and the freedom enjoyed by some barbarian women in antiquity cannot fail to impress a modern feminist."[6]

Contemporary archeological findings also substantiate a good deal of the history recorded in epic poems. Yet, states Pomeroy, "there is absolutely no evidence, even in realms where queens were powerful, that women were the dominant class throughout the society." Pomeroy puts the issue in analogy: Were women dominant in sixteenth-century England because Elizabeth I was queen? She concludes that the status of some royal women in Homeric epics was "remarkably high" and that feminist scholars can legitimately point to the myopia of male historians (from ancient times to the present) who have diminished the importance of these women.[7]

Were Amazons (who lived at the edge of the Greek world) members of a society in which men were entirely absent? For Pomeroy "it is possible, though of course, not provable, that such a society did exist."[8] Psychoanalytic explanation may be helpful for understanding why the subject holds negative implications for some: "The idea of Amazons can be interpreted as a mythical fantasy, possibly expressing the repressed male notion of female ferocity, and providing a rationalization for the male's urge to subdue women."[9] Although mother goddesses were major deities in ancient times, this did not, according to Pomeroy, improve the "low political, legal, and social status" of women in the classical age.[10]

The adoption of Sicilian women as a metaphor for Italian women is fruitful in this instance because the island has many archeological traces of the primordial mother. A statue of Hybla, round earth mother of the Sicels who suckles two babies, can be found in the Museo Archeologico at Syracuse. The excavations at Megara Hyblaea are rich with evidence of the continued importance of Hybla in the period when Sicily was known as Greater Greece. The mountains named to this day after the Sicel earth mother are thought to have the honeycombs with the sweetest honey in the world. The museums at Gela and Agrigento have an abundance of goddess and other women figures for the period of Greek ascendancy when the temples of Sicily were built. Artifacts of the prehistoric and the Graeco-Roman periods can be found in the ruins at Camarina on the Mediterranean, as well as in the museum at Ragusa. Prehistoric depictions of women can be seen in the Addauro caves on Mount Pellegrino at Palermo.[11] Artifacts of earth-mother goddesses and other women are often in a good state of preservation due to the dry climate of the island.

In Sicily, island crossroad of Europe, the Middle East, and Africa, Phoenicians left evidence of a love goddess at Erice and Egyptians left traces of their goddess, Isis, at Catania. Statues of Greek and Roman goddesses are everywhere. One October day at Palazzolo Acreide in southwestern Sicily, a franciscan monk showed me twelve statues of Greek and Roman goddesses in a field of thistles, boarded up to preserve them from vandals. Depictions of Roman women may be seen in the mosaics at Piazza Armerina (a fourth-century Roman hunting lodge) where they disport themselves, scantily clad, in scenes startlingly contemporary.

Characteristics of different representations of the earth mother and other goddesses varied; they form a legacy that resembles, in Vincent Cronin's metaphor, a honeycomb.[12] Cybele, ancient Mediterranean earth mother, was described as a wild and passionate female who was thought to dwell in a black meteorite and to ride in a chariot drawn by beasts. The Greeks gave the earth mother's endowment to three goddesses: Hera, goddess of marriage; Aphrodite, goddess of love; and Athena, militant maiden goddess of wisdom. Romans renamed these goddesses Juno, Venus, and Minerva (in the 1980s Italian feminists are least ambivalent about Minerva, for whom they have named a feminist journal). Earth mother figures are juxtaposed with Greek and Roman goddesses in Sicilian history and sometimes domesticated; for instance, the ancient name of the town of Ragusa—Hybla Heraia—joins the Sicel earth mother, Hybla, with the Greek goddess of marriage, Hera.[13] Characteristics of the ancient earth mother were later transmuted into the virgin mother of Nazareth. In Italy ancient pagan goddesses coexist with christian saints. Or goddesses became saints, for example, the saint named for Venus, Santa Venere. Only once in a while do all these contradictions cause a commotion.

The Lago di Pergusa, at Enna, in the center of Sicily, was the site of the Roman mother-daughter legend of Demetra and Proserpina (Demeter and Persephone), a story of rape and abduction, winter and springtime. One day when Proserpina was gathering flowers, she was abducted by Hades, the king of the underworld. Her mother, Demetra, the Roman earth-mother goddess of fecundity, darkened the earth with her grief while she searched for her daughter. When she was united with Proserpina, the mother was dismayed to learn that the daughter while in the underworld had eaten six seeds of a pomegranate: for this reason the daughter has to spend autumn and winter as queen of the underworld. When the daughter is with her mother, there is spring and summer, flowers bloom and grain grows. A feminist collective in Sicily today is named Demetra; these women, whose relation with the earth-mother goddess of fecundity is self-conscious, resist the Nato nuclear missile base at Comiso nonviolently, preserving spring and summer against nuclear winter.[14]

madonnas, saints, and godmothers

For feminist history, Enna holds another significance. In this Sicel center of worship of Demeter a slave uprising mounted by Euno confronted the Romans in 135 B.C. With the coming of christianity, the story of Demeter and Persephone was changed from a legend of a mother looking for her daughter to that of a mother looking for her son in the week before easter. In a pre-easter Sicilian custom still practiced, the statue of the madonna (carried by peasants) searches everywhere in town for her son. Closer to the mother than to the church, peasants who carry the statue of the madonna cause it to waver before entering the church, because peasant men and women are not certain the madonna will find her son inside.

The madonna inherited characteristics of her pre-christian antecedents. In Palermo churches seventeenth-century sculptures by Serpotta evoke pre-christian love goddesses—the madonna as a sensual woman. The viewer is stimulated to think about the dualism regarding women bequeathed by history (and by church doctrine), a dualism expressed in the traditional Italian male view of woman as madonna/wife, virgin/prostitute, companion/pupil—and violently conveyed in the terrible curse of some Sicilian males, "puttana la madonna" (whore mother of God).[15]

On Sicily's northern shore at Tindari the pilgrimage site of a black madonna invites jostling insights. Jungian scholars have speculated on the meaning of the archetype of the black madonna whose representations can be found in Russia, Poland, Spain, France, and Mexico as well as Italy, countries where earth-mother artifacts have been found.[16] Gilles Quispel, the Jungian scholar, has suggested that the familiar madonna with blue cloak ("my lady") dates back to the High Middle Ages. Black madonnas are ancient and a genuine archetype: when blackened features of a representation are "restored" to a lighter shade, people often insist on returning the madonna to her original color. Some representations of the black madonna are dated 30,000 years before Christ, linking her with the primordial earth mother.

About 2000 B.C. Indo-Europeans are thought to have suppressed the worship of the great mother, but traces remain, vividly seen in the fifteen megaliths erected to her at Malta, and in many other Mediterranean places as well. According to Quispel, the Greek goddesses were rooted in the black earth mother. Demetra (meaning "mother earth") was also called "the black woman." Rituals of the Eleusinian mysteries at Athens were based on worship of the black mother goddess. Quispel believes that the holy ghost of christian doctrine is a trace of the black madonna.

The perseveration of a subterranean religious tradition may be discerned in the christian era, particularly in peasant traditions of the south of Italy, where *Padre Eterno* was rarely mentioned and the figure of the mother was often more imposing than that of her son. In peasant legends, the madonna was familiarly described as a Sicilian mother who cooked *manicaretti* for the family, yet she was a powerful figure who could successfully intervene with her son. Perpetuating the pluralism of the period before christianity was established, each locality in today's Sicily (as elsewhere in Italy) has its own madonna. Regarded as the sainted mother of God (S. Maria di Gesù), a major saint whose many manifestations trace the history of the island (for instance, S. Maria dei Greci), her helpful role is suggested in her many names (S. Maria di Aiuto, among others). Legends about the many madonnas are a source for the ultimate beliefs of Sicilians; for example, those about the madonna of Chiaramonte Gulfi reveal Sicilian diffidence to northern European ideas brought in by invaders. One legend about this madonna, still recounted in the twentieth century, describes the Normans in Sicily (after the eleventh century) as very taken with the "culto di Salvatore," the cult of the son saviour.[17]

The many madonnas of Italy preside over towns whose legends are full of her messages or interventions during natural and human disasters (for example, la madonnina of Messina). Artists were stimulated to paint her in many ways. One that arrests attention is the madonna depicted by Antonello da Messina. In this fifteenth-century painting of the madonna as peasant girl, the painter suggests pre-christian themes, premillennial peasant theology as well as contemporary feminist utopianism—the peasant girl madonna is holding not the infant but the book that announces the coming birth of the child. A commemorative exhibit in the early eighties of Antonello's work was celebrated throughout Italy with this painting of the madonna as peasant girl.

We have descriptions of peasant homes in which the ordinal placement of statues and pictures suggests the theology of Sicilian peasants: first the mother, then the child Jesus, and then the saints.[18] Immacolata and Gesù Bambino are followed by a variety of saints who embody peasant values: San Giuseppe, father of Jesus and patron saint of workmen, who is celebrated today at festivals of the Italian communist party; Santa Lucia, early christian martyr under Diocletian's persecutions and the saint who protects vision; Santa Rosalia, who protects against famine, earthquakes, fire, and war. Peasant stories rendered the saints in familiar context: San Giuseppe took the child Jesus to an orchard to pick figs for a sick woman, Santa Locanda aided pregnant women, Sant'Antonio protected domestic animals. In the decentralized theology of Sicilians, saints were given almost the same valence as God; children were taught to "Fear God and the saints."[19]

Commencing with the fifteenth century, the modern phase of Sicilian women's history may be described as the godmother period, when Spanish Bourbon rule commenced the deterioration of peasant life. The metaphor of Sicilian women here suggests the history of other Italian women whose lives were molded by conservative church doctrine, a hierarchical class structure, and a feudal economy evolving into modern conditions, with concomitant poverty and humiliation.

In the modern Sicilian political economy of agricultural towns built on a feudal base, a hierarchical class structure pressed peasants into deepening *miseria*. The English word *misery* only partially connotes the powerlessness, numb hunger, and barely suppressed rage of most peasants—rage not only at economic but moral exploitation. Barons kept peasants overworked and hungry and arrogated sexual access to peasant women as a master's prerogative. Feudal custom (alive in some places of Sicily until the last quarter of the nineteenth century) permitted the lord privileges of the "first night" at weddings of his peasant tenants. Powerless elsewhere, peasant men exerted patriarchal control, sometimes streaked with violence, over wives and daughters. Imitating the nobility, they sometimes took peasant women by force. The custom evolved of escaping dishonor by marrying one's rapist, a cultural canon that remained unbroken until the sixth decade of the twentieth century, when a Sicilian woman sent her rapist to jail instead of marrying him.[20]

A cultural dichotomy of good and bad women arose in the godmother period, visible in Sicilian literature of the late nineteenth century. In his widely read collection of children's stories, *C'era una volta* (Once upon a time), Luigi Capuana depicted the good Sicilian mother as a moral guide for her children who taught them obedience to mores that sustained the hierarchical class structure. Giovanni Verga probed the dichotomy, in *Nedda* depicting the selfless, long-suffering Sicilian woman seduced and left with a child to sustain. In *La lupa*, Verga limned an unforgettable female figure whose power derives, perhaps, from tapping unconscious male fears of the primordial earth mother—Verga calls her the "she-wolf." *La lupa* combines nurturance for her child with overwhelming sensual passion.[21] Contemporary Italian feminists are ambivalent about the Mediterranean earth mother, but they have kept one of her characteristics. They define the "terrain" of women as that of passion, extending the meaning of passion beyond sensuality to connote many kinds of love.[22]

Folklore is indispensable for women's history because women (at least in Italy) were the main carriers of this oral tradition. Sicily is a useful reference point because there was great interest in recording its folklore in the late nineteenth century; contemporary Italian scholars, motivated since the papacy of John XXIII to study the religious beliefs of the people, are indebted to a remarkable collection of legends, parables, customs, songs, riddles, games, lullabies, descriptions of spectacles and festivals, popular medical lore, tales of family life, stories of saints, and the like, gathered by a Palermitan physician, Giuseppe Pitré, in twenty-five volumes. Other late nineteenth-century folklorists supplemented the Pitré collection, notably Serafino Amabile Guastella and Salvatore Salomone-Marino.[23]

The Sicilian peasant woman who emerges from folklore and other sources is a figure who understood the meaning of *miseria*. Her daily life was a round of going to the well with a large vase on her head, to the mill with a heavy sack on her shoulders. Whether sick, pregnant, or famished, she mended the family's clothing, cared for the children, swept out the rats. With her husband's small earnings she purchased grain, ground it, kneaded loaves, and sold them, leaving only one for the family. She took her children to the countryside to gather edible greens; in the courtyard, often in company with other women, she prepared lupin and fava beans, carob and figs. She sewed in the home and helped in the fields at harvest time, sometimes earning more than her husband. She understood a hierarchical class structure personally because she was often wet nurse to infants of the local nobility.

These godmothers sustained an unequal society, submitted to a patriarchal system, and taught daughters to guard their virginity and to be faithful wives. Often the church was the only refuge of peace for a peasant woman. The poverty of her life was leavened by a communalism she shared with other women. Peasant godmothers extended the boundaries of the family to women bound to one another by children and mutual concerns, prefiguring contemporary feminist networks. Because men's work often took them away for protracted periods, women, although theoretically subordinate to husbands, made family decisions. Sicilian women sometimes exerted so much family power that Leonardo Sciascia, a writer of the independent political left, said in the 1970s that he could not imagine what Sicilian feminists could want, since they had always been a matriarchate.[24] In their daily activities—doing laundry at the public wash trough or baking bread at the communal oven—, Sicilian peasant women, like peasant women elsewhere, exercised considerable indirect social power, arranging marriages, assigning reputations, helping one another to give birth and, when necessary, to abort.

The Sicilian peasant godmother combined christian and pre-christian beliefs. When her husband was brought home with malaria, she would light a candle to her personal saint, promise her earrings to the madonna, vow to San Giovanni to celebrate a mass for souls in purgatory, then call in Zia Sara, the village healer, who would prescribe a broth of a hen and a pigeon. If illness persisted, she would summon La Stefanu, an old woman with occult powers, who might diagnose the evil eye (*mal occhio*) and exorcise it with salt and water, incantations, and prayer. Lawrence Di Stasi, a contemporary scholar of this ritual, has traced its meaning to the prehistoric earth mother.[25]

The ultimate beliefs of a Sicilian peasant woman can be found in the legends and parables she told her children. The implicit theology of this peasant oral tradition differed from church doctrine: the mother of Jesus was central, universal grace embraced all humanity, morality was grounded on realism. One legend recounted the reluctance of Jesus to extend universal grace to all—until his mother delivered an ultimatum. Either Jesus would allow all souls to enter heaven or she would leave paradise and, as queen of heaven, take her entire dowry with her: all the angels, patriarchs, apostles, martyrs, and saints. Whereupon Jesus, paling before this depopulation of heaven, conceded universal grace.[26]

In Sicilian interpretation, the golden rule was given a realistic bend of meaning: "Quello che non vuoi fatto a te, ad altri non fare" (What you do not want done to you, do not do to others). The decalogue was interpreted in the light of class realities: stealing is a sin, but there are gradations of sin—stealing from the poor is the worst sin. In the late nineteenth century, established doctrine was modified by anarchist beliefs. St. Christopher offered a lamp to poor people dealing in contraband, because stealing from the government was not a sin: in the language of peasants, "the property of the government is the property of the people." (A few years ago a pope unsainted Christopher for this antiestablishment activity, but Christopher remains beloved by Italians.)[27]

peasant women socialists

The inherent radicalism in the peasant translation of catholicism is documented in parables (many of them in Guastella's *Le parità morali*) that affirm that the legitimate proprietor of the earth is not the absentee owner but the person who cultivates it. Sicilian peasant women took this belief into the socialist agitation of the 1890s; other southern Italian women, with similar folklore beliefs, occupied unused lands after each of the two world wars.[28]

The church and the culture counseled "pazienza" for peasants who lived in conditions of *miseria*. Sicilian peasant men thirsting for *giustizia* (justice) have historically risen up in rebellion (against the French in 1168 and 1282, the Spanish in 1516 and 1674, and the Bourbons in 1848 and 1860) but *miseria* can sometimes turn hopelessness into passivity.[29] Women who see children crying from hunger, however, may be catapulted out of passive hopelessness. Sicilian peasant women in the socialist *fasci* of the 1890s declared: "There should no longer be either rich or poor. All should have bread for themselves and for their children. We should all be equal."[30]

Women carried placards in socialist demonstrations of the 1890s that resemble those peasants carry today in Central and South America: "Jesus was a true socialist and he wanted precisely what the *fasci* are asking for, but the priests do not represent him well."[31] Popes, both in the 1890s and in the 1980s, have condemned this interpretation of the gospel, today called liberation theology.

other Italian women

The lives of the majority of Italian women in the nineteenth century were similar to those of Sicilian women. The Napoleonic code, which became the model for most European legislation, fixed a condition of inferiority for women and a double standard of sexuality for men and women. Women were under the guardianship of men— first fathers, then husbands. The husband commanded, the wife assured his descendants. Motherhood was woman's prescribed destination in life. The son was heir and succeeded the father; the daughter guarded her virginity and femininity (defined as subservience to males) as her dowry for marriage.

After the unification of the country was completed in 1870, the new government hoped to extend centralized administration to all of Italy. The highest levels of government were staffed by the men of the Piedmont, who operated a patronage system, a process that eventually brought men from the South into the governmental bureaucracy. Signal characteristics of the new government were an established Roman catholicism, a titular king, a bicameral legislature, and a restricted electorate. The property qualification empowered about 80,000 men of a total population of 4,200,000 to elect the lower house. Women would not secure the vote until 1945.

In spite of a high overall level of economic development until the seventeenth century, subsequent to that time, according to Carlo Cipolla, Italy became "economically backward and depressed; its industrial structure had almost collapsed, its population was too high for its resources, its economy had become primarily agricultural."[32] A North-South economic polarity became evident in the last quarter of the nineteenth century as southern poverty stimulated socialist demonstrations—firmly quashed by the government—and the North commercialized its agriculture and industrialized. Modernity in Italy, according to historians, declined "as a function of distance from Milan."[33] In Sicily and Sardinia (which presented the most contrast to the mainland) there were, at the end of the nineteenth century, unpaved roads, little literacy, little trade, much poverty. In the late nineteenth century, large migrations began from the South to northern Europe and to the new world of North and South America.

Italian industrialization meant not only cottage industry and small-scale enterprises but also woolen and cotton factories, a clothing industry, and metal and machine industries in Piedmont, Lombardy, and Naples. Venice produced silk and Sicily had sulphur mines. For Italian women's history the salient fact is the migration of women from depressed areas to northern textile mills or to service positions. In the late nineteenth century the nobility was replaced by a new middle class. One thinks of the women in Tomasi di Lampedusa's *Il gattopardo* (The leopard), among them the wife of the Prince of Salina who crossed herself and invoked the holy mother and Jesus when her husband insisted on conjugal rights. The prince, who had never seen his wife's bare body, sought women of the lower class for his pleasures. The story of Don Calogero's daughter documents a class reshuffling wherein lower-class fathers used nubile daughters for upward social ascendance.

The catholic church settled into a defensive conservative role after unification. With the loss of the temporal domain of the church, the pope forbade communicants to take part in national politics. Hostile to the secular state, as well as to emerging socialist and labor movements, he forbade clerics to participate in politics and underlined, even as the society rapidly changed, his view that women's role was confined to the home. As part of the secular thrust of the risorgimento, the right of divorce was proposed in 1870. But papal authority on the matter of divorce prevailed for a hundred years; divorce would not be legalized until 1970 in Italy. Continuing to consider itself as guardian and definer of the status of women, the church after 1870 created many new women's religious orders dedicated to education of youth, care of the sick in the home, aid to poor young women, and assistance to the indigent and the elderly.

Women in historic catholic religious communities may be viewed as having refused social assignments and attempted to carve out a separate, somewhat autonomous, area where the patriarchal hierarchical church never attained complete control. Although protestantism is associated with modern advances, the protestant reformation, in removing this option, may be interpreted as a setback for women. As we shall see, Italian feminists after 1968 were inspired by the separatist tradition of catholic women's religious communities.[34] In the late nineteenth and early twentieth centuries, however, convents were staffed by women not only escaping marriage but poverty, and the women in religious orders tended to be passive and conformist to the hierarchy. This would not change until after 1968.

Organizations of catholic women were encouraged by the church in the late nineteenth century to defend the faith, to do good social works, and to oppose socialism. In catholic doctrine, as in secular law, woman's role was subordination to her husband; her circle of activity was the family. Upper-class women could do good works in hospitals and orphanages, and they could give charity to the poor, but they were not to aim to change society. Poor women had the option of emigration elsewhere with their families. Those who remained in Italy faced grim conditions.

However slowly, industrialization changed Italy in the latter part of the nineteenth century and changed the lives of people coming from the land to the cities. The textile industry employed women and girls; children of five and six were put to work as an act of beneficence by padroni. In cotton, linen, hemp, and woolen factories children worked fifteen to sixteen hours a day, earning twenty-four centesimi. Women dressed in rags worked with their babies at their side.[35] The clothing industry became the large source of employment for women as seamstresses, embroiderers, designers, and pressers. Daughters of families in decline or in ascent went to work as typists, secretaries, or bookkeepers. Thousands of women worked in rice, hemp, and tobacco fields as well.

In *Rerum novarum*, the 1891 encyclical, the pope enunciated a social catholicism apparently designed to meet the political unrest of the end of the century. The encyclical enjoined women not to work outside the home; women were to work in domestic tasks appropriate to their condition as the "weaker sex"; their duty was to educate the children—although children, paradoxically, were described as an "extension of the father's personality." The encyclical was promulgated just as poverty was pushing women out of the home to become breadwinners and as women were taking unprecedented direct action. The socialist demonstrations of women in Sicily are but one example. Other Italian women rioted for bread in front of local city halls and engaged in protests against sending sons and husbands to the war in Abyssinia.

Teresa Noce: textile worker to socialist

In her autobiographical novel, *Gioventù senza sole*, Teresa Noce described the evolution of a northern Italian woman from textile worker to socialist.[36] Later Noce became a communist, a partisan in the fight against fascism, and a member of the Pci central committee. Born in Turin in 1900, as that city was becoming a hub of Italian industrialization and worker militancy, Noce had begun to work in the textile industry when she was six years old. The family needed the few cents she brought home, and her mother needed a place to keep the child while she worked. Teresa, called Maddalena in the novel, at first had gone for lunch to a convent, but soon expressed her dislike of the nuns' severe discipline.

In Noce's story, the father had abandoned the mother and three children, an absence the mother and children regarded as respite from his violence when drunk. Maddalena, put to work early, observed the injustices of working-class life in Torino. "It is not fair," she thought, that she and her brother had to work ten and a half hours a day, that she could not buy a book to read, that her mother had to humiliate herself to postpone paying the landlord's rent and to secure credit for bread. Ashamed at school that her shoes were broken, she soon left and went to work in a dressmaking workshop.[37]

The padrona, the girl noted, "did not work." She only commanded from behind her desk, and she took the money. Although Maddalena's mother called socialists "assassins and robbers," the girl, listening to women dressmakers on strike shout, "Eviva lo sciopero!" (Long live the strike!) began to think about the words of revolutionary songs: "We love equality," "We do not want bosses." Equality, for the girl, meant that everyone should have good shoes, warm soup, and a lit stove on coming home in the winter and that a girl should be able to read without feeling guilty for having spent a few cents for a book.

Maddalena secretly began to read the socialist newspaper, Avanti!. Her brother worked in a metallurgy shop in the emerging automobile industry. Pierino told his sister that workers felt they had common interests. When workers in his factory went on strike, his mother told him to break the strike, but he would not. The mother shouted that both of her children, in becoming socialists, had "sold their souls to the devil."[38]

In Torinese elections the mother liked candidates who defended "order, the family, religion"; socialists wanted divorce and abolition of bosses—who would provide work? "There have always been the rich, in all epochs, and there will always be." Socialists were unpatriotic—they had opposed the Abyssinian war, a "holy war against pagans, against the blacks who kill our missionaries." To his mother, who invoked the values of the patriarchal family, Pierino pointed out that the father had abandoned them, would it not have been better if she had divorced him? It was true that socialists did not want bosses, because "we want to work for ourselves, not for them." When the mother said that there have always been and there will always be rich people, she was repeating, said the son, what rich people and priests said. The mother began to pray in church for her children. The daughter wondered what God had to do with all this, or Jesus. She liked the ritual and the church music but did not believe what the priests said about the rich. When she read the story of Jesus, it seemed to her that "Christ had been the first socialist of the world."[39]

When world war erupted, Maddalena hoped aloud that Italy would remain neutral, she and her brother agreed that socialists who supported the war betrayed proletarian interests. To women who told her it was not woman's place to be in antiwar demonstrations, Maddalena responded, better to join a demonstration today than to go to the funeral of a son tomorrow. Still, when she wanted to accompany Pierino to a meeting of the *Circolo socialista*, her brother said she was too young. "But I am older than you!" she protested. He responded, "Women like you should stay at home."[40]

marxists and women

Pierino's response to his sister was characteristic of many socialist party men of this period—women could be supporters of socialism and pupils of the theory, but they would have to wait for full equality. The standard nineteenth-century response of European socialists to women was a shift to the future tense: in the future socialist society women would have full personal, political, social, economic, and legal equality.

The writings of Marx and Engels indicate that they understood the woman question. In studies written by both theorists there is passionate condemnation of the degradation of women in modern conditions. Engels, in the *Origin of the Family*, said that the "overthrow of mother-right was the world historical defeat of the female sex. The man took command in the home also; the woman was degraded and reduced to servitude, she became the slave of his lust and a mere instrument for the production of children."[41] He pointed to the double standard in the Napoleonic code which enabled the husband to indulge in marital infidelity, restricting monogamy, in effect, to women only.[42] In the *German Ideology*, written by Marx and Engels in 1845–46, there is the sentence, "The first division of labor is that between man and woman for the propagation of children."[43] Engels said (in the *Origin of the Family*) that "within the family [the man] is the bourgeois and the wife represents the proletariat."[44] Yet for Engels as well as Marx the solution to the woman question was that women should become equal with men as part of the proletariat. Marx concentrated on the degradation of the family under capitalism: men, women, and children were forced to work for starvation wages, with women often being reduced to prostitution. Eliding over the specifics of power, and the specific oppression of women, Marx and Engels said that the future socialist society would remove all oppression, including that of women.

Some contemporary feminist critics of traditional marxists think that the historic socialist movement internalized the patriarchal division of roles in refusing to see the specific oppression of women. There was also a difference between equalitarian theory and practice; Italian feminists of the 1970s analyzed the disparities between what Marx, the theorist, said about women and what Marx, the man, did; they also pointed to the difference between what contemporary communists said about women and what they did.[45]

Traditional marxists of the nineteenth and twentieth centuries declared that since class would always divide people, feminist efforts for the vote, civil and legal rights, and equal pay for equal work were "bourgeois." From this perspective, the only legitimate role for women was to work alongside men for the achievement of socialism, without deflecting energy into "personal aims."[46]

Anna Maria Mozzoni: feminist socialist foremother

In the period of the risorgimento, Anna Maria Mozzoni, perhaps the major feminist socialist foremother of Italian women, threw the firebrand of the woman question into male circles of socialists. Influenced by Charles Fourier, a utopian socialist, she looked to a future when the oppressive family and state, as well as private property, would be gone. Present goals included transformation of the family from monarchy to equality and of the authoritarian state to democracy and the replacement of capitalism with emancipation of workers, both men and women.

In 1864 Mozzoni drew a parallel between the movement for national independence and the emancipation of women. She advocated the right of divorce. Bringing a woman's perspective to the matter, Mozzoni stated that the woman question was not fundamentally economic. Although she helped to create it, Mozzoni did not enter the socialist party when it was founded in 1892. Mozzoni's organization, Lega promotrice degli interessi femminili (an independent association founded at Milan in 1881 to stimulate women's consciousness of their rights) prefigured the Unione donne italiane, founded in 1944. Mozzoni's significance in the history of Italian feminism is that she pulled the veil away from the idealistic middle-class view of the Italian family in which woman was an angel and the husband a priest and protested the tendency among male socialists to bring a similar ideology to politics. As a feminist historian has put it, Mozzoni said, "Basta!" to idealizations of fatherhood and motherhood "imposed by those who dominated to block the energies of the dominated."[47] For Mozzoni, the authenticity of a revolutionary movement was demonstrated in whether or not liberty and equality were upheld—for both sexes.

Mozzoni, for whom today's women's center of Unione donne italiane at Rome is named, said that if women let themselves be lulled "by this old nursery rhyme" that women do not need special women's rights, they are as stupid as tuna who repeat the same voyage daily, letting themselves be snared. Men socialists who expressed surprise that women could demand the vote, said Mozzoni, wanted women to remain "happy Vestal Virgins, forever at the stove with cooking stains on their white robes." Women's civil, political, and social rights were not "secondary" as some socialists said, but "the supreme, the most important and the most decisive of all social issues."

In a sardonic style similar to that of Italian feminists after 1968, Mozzoni asked how men who conspired for freedom, suffered in Austrian dungeons, and defied the gallows in order to be citizens, not subjects, could not imagine that women also would not be subjects. Divine right, said Mozzoni, had been defeated in theocracy and monarchy, but it remained in male privilege. The "right of force" may have been defeated in the law of "all civilized peoples" but it remained in man's treatment of woman and in male assumptions of "domestic monarchy."

Male socialists who urged women to work for the cause without digression into "personal aims" resembled, she said, those southern slaveholders who armed slaves against northern abolitionists. Assailing the double standard, Mozzoni said that men admired the courage of conviction, passion in battle, and perseverance in their own gender, but flew into a rage when they were confronted with these same characteristics in women.

In statements treasured by contemporary Italian feminists, Mozzoni said: "Forget the idea that men out of their love for logic and zeal for justice will bring you what you deserve when their victory has been achieved." And: "You will not have any freedom that you have not defended every day and in every moment."[48]

2

donne, guerra, e rivoluzione

women, world war I, and revolution

The history of Italy from the 1890s to 1920 may be regarded as acceleration toward a revolution (one that failed) or as backdrop for the first fascist regime of Europe. Syndicalism—which aimed to bring industry and government under control of labor unions by direct action, particularly the general strike—had gained importance in the Italian labor movement after 1900. As anarcho-syndicalism, this was a doctrine of rejection of governmental structures, with the aim of self-government—a strategy of abolishing the state in order to let workers rule.

What may have been the first successful general strike in the world was initiated in 1904 by workers in Milan who protested the suppression (and killings) of striking workers and peasants in the South and in Sardinia. From that time until the 1920s workers struck for political as well as for economic gains. Agricultural workers—at this time the largest sector of Italian labor—also unionized and adopted the strike.

Was the prewar Italian worker movement violent? Louise Tilly concludes that Italian levels of participation in the "collective violence" of workers from 1830 to 1930 resembled those of France and Spain; they were somewhat higher than those of England and Germany.[1] What conservatives called "labor violence" was brutally suppressed after 1919 by fascists who adopted violence as an instrument of the state to suppress labor activism.

One salient fact about the prewar period is that the pattern of Italian worker activism was national. In 1893 as the activity of socialist *fasci* spread through Sicily, street demonstrations and riots took place in Genoa, Naples, and Rome against "exploiters." In 1898 a second burst of labor activism occurred in Sicily and on the mainland at Ancona, Bari, Naples, and Florence. In the northern industrial area, organized workers and peasants demonstrated for better wages and for the right to form unions and to strike. Geographically, demonstrations appear to have started in the South and to have moved to central Italy and then to the North.

Women were often involved. In February 1898 at Troina in the province of Catania, Sicily, a crowd of three hundred men, women, and children, some carrying banners and some with weapons, gathered before the city hall to ask for aid for the unemployed. They were dispersed; in the melee several were wounded, four were killed. This demonstration was not connected with socialist groups.

At Ancona in 1898 hundreds of men, women, and children demonstrated for lower bread prices and an end to the tax on flour. There was street fighting among cries of "Viva la anarchia!" and "Viva la rivoluzione sociale!" In May 1898 at Milan workers protested for the release of men jailed for distributing socialist leaflets. The use of troops and gunfire was followed by a strike. Agricultural and urban strikes in Liguria, Lombardy, Emilia, and Sicily were led by peasants and workers and supported by a band of the middle class.

Worker activism merged into opposition to war. Early antiwar actions were undertaken by women in the 1890s when some opposed Italy's invasion of Abyssinia. At Milan in 1896 when news of the massacre of Italian youth at Adowa was received, a group of women invaded the railroad station to prevent departure of a troop train.

Similar demonstrations took place at Ancona, Brescia, Alessandria, and Rome. After the general strike of 1904, sympathy strikes in 1906 and 1907, and agricultural strikes in 1908, militance shifted to opposition to militarism and to the Libyan war. In 1911 there were antiwar demonstrations; in June 1914, following the killing of an antiwar demonstrator, strikers initiated a wave of take-overs of city governments in what was called a "red week."[2] On May 19, 1915, Turin workers proclaimed a strike against entry into the war, hoping all of Italy would join. The strike was put down by the authorities. In Sicily some women paraded with the cross and placards that declared, "We do not want our sons to leave for war." Others took signs to the piazza which said, "Down with the war!"[3]

pane e pace

Although strikes were forbidden after Italy entered the war, workers in Turin arose again in 1917, in a strike initiated by women for bread and peace. Bread was scarce, women had stood in long lines only to be told that there was no more. When, on August 23, there was no bread for anyone, women protested by staying home from factory jobs. The protest became a general strike of all city workers. A group of women marched toward the city hall; another sacked stores for flour, bread, and food; others wrote "pane e pace" (bread and peace) on walls.[4] This was an autonomous women's action, since the Italian socialist party in 1917 was riven by internal conflict over entry into the war and many had been arrested and jailed.

In Sicily women in demonstrations against the war sometimes carried the white banner of the church and sometimes the red banner of the left. Issues, like their banners, were often combined: "We want peace and we are hungry." In 1917 a number of Sicilian women demonstrated against the war and against prowar propaganda in the schools. Precursors of later feminists, Sicilian women in first world war peace parades protested against the *cappelli*, the prominent men in hats who held power.[5]

In the background was the March revolution of the Russian people who had removed the czar and demanded that Russia and other countries stop the war. Barricades were thrown up in Turin. Women invited soldiers to put down their guns. The uprising was suppressed with tanks: men, women, and children were killed. Hatred of the war deepened, a woman socialist later remembered, into a "desire to create a new and better world, where war is forever abolished."[6]

At the end, many Italian soldiers returned in a mood to take control of factories and to occupy the land; many believed in the "possibility of a radical change of the society."[7] In every region of Italy strikes broke out. Some women in Sicily carried the *bandiera rossa* and demanded *pane*. At Piana dei Greci, Sicily, women shouted "Viva il socialismo e abbasso il militarismo!" Men and women occupied unused lands. A few women joined striking sulfur miners. The mafia killed many peasant and socialist leaders.[8]

The Italian communist party, born at the Livorno congress in January 1921 and led by Antonio Gramsci, broke away from the paralyzed socialist party and encouraged factory occupations. Textile establishments in Biellese, Canavesano, Valle di Lanzo, Turino Pont Canavese, Torre Pellice, Pralafera, and Favria were occupied by groups of women. Women workers were killed or wounded at Bologna, Sarzana, Modena, Ferrara, Turin, Molinella, and elsewhere.[9]

a women's marxist tradition:
Rosa Luxemburg, Clara Zetkin, Alexandra Kollontai

After 1968 Italian feminists searching the history of marxism studied two women in the German movement—Rosa Luxemburg and Clara Zetkin. The career of the only woman in Lenin's first cabinet in Soviet Russia, Alexandra Kollontai, also secured their attention. Rosa Luxemburg, a member of the German socialist party, opposed the war and was imprisoned until war's end for inciting soldier disobedience. The third international was created from the spartacist group formed by Luxemburg and Karl Liebknecht. In revolutionary upheavals, German workers were heavily defeated, and in January 1919 thousands, including Luxemburg, were killed.

Luxemburg was deprecated by male revolutionaries as "aggressive" and "quarrelsome." As a theorist she analyzed the expansion of capitalism into imperialism; as an activist she opposed the German socialist party's unanimous decision to support the fatherland in war. Her socialist vision was that of a humane society where all would be equal and all free to exercise individual talent, not a mass governed from the top, but autonomous human beings determining their own destinies.

Such Luxemburg themes are in affinity with those of Italian feminists. Perhaps the closest similarity is deep ambivalence about political power, in Luxemburg's case aversion to the bureaucratic power of the German socialist party and to the power exercised by bolsheviks.[10] Yet Luxemburg did not identify with the feminists of her time. She disliked their emphasis on equality, which she felt emphasized sameness. She would have been more at home with contemporary Italian feminists who want an equalitarian society leavened by differences. Although they are similar, most Italian feminists do not claim her as a foremother, because Luxemburg accepted the standard marxist premise that the class struggle is uppermost and all oppressed groups, including women, must wait for socialism to be free. What gives Luxemberg significance for feminists is her treatment by male marxists. German socialists derided her ideas. When she died, Lenin criticized her interpretations of marxism as "childish" and "ridiculous." He enumerated her "errors" and denigrated her as a "utopian radical."[11]

Clara Zetkin is remembered by Italian feminists for a conversation with Lenin in 1920 that underlines for them the inability of many male revolutionaries to understand a woman's perspective. Lenin stated that without the women of Russia, "very probably we would not have won,"[12] but noted that he had heard that in women's gatherings, "you occupy yourselves above all with matters pertaining to sex and marriage." Lenin asked about the rumor he had heard that a booklet by a Viennese communist woman on the sexual question was in large circulation. Sexual theories, said Lenin, may sound as if they have subversive, or revolutionary potential, but they are, in the end, "purely bourgeois"; these matters are "personal."[13] In the 1970s most Italian feminists would declare that "the personal is political."

In their challenge to the Pci after 1968, many feminists criticized the ties between the Italian party and the soviets, playing a strategic role in the 1981 separation of the Italian party from the USSR. They found evidence for their worry about the soviets in the life of Alexandra Kollontai. Bolshevik agitator, propagandist, theoretician, and commissar of social welfare in Lenin's first cabinet, Kollontai was a constant critic. Lenin considered her troublesome and exiled her, in effect, by appointing her to isolated diplomatic posts.[14] Soviet laws aimed to ameliorate women's condition but stopped short of equality in two critical areas. Soviet leaders dismissed women's theoretical ability and invoked a double standard of sexual morality, casting aspersions on women's sexual activities when their ideas were inconvenient.

Kollontai criticized socialists who supported world war I and separated herself from Lenin's concept of "managed" revolution. As commissar of social welfare, Kollontai evaluated bolshevik legislation regarding women: equal civil, political, and legal rights; the vote; establishment of the principle of equal pay for equal work; a divorce law; legalization of abortion; availability of contraceptive information; an end to discrimination between legitimate and illegitimate children. More, Kollontai felt, was needed: she proposed free maternity hospitals, state-guaranteed child care centers, communal kitchens and dining rooms, children's living groups, central laundries, and other facilities to help women in their double tasks. In writings after she was isolated from power, she indicated that feminist legislation by itself will not change women's condition of subordination if men's traditional attitudes toward women are not altered.

Kollontai criticized the double standard of male bolsheviks on sex and was accused of advocating "free love." This was untrue; for Kollontai, sexual relations based on physical desire alone, with no moral obligation, were worse than prostitution. She wanted "a new society in which larger social and economic changes would ensure that all human beings would be free to love," free from economic dependency in love relationships. The "new woman" for Kollontai would not only be "strong-willed, politically active, and economically independent, but also possessed of a fierce and pure revolutionary intensity." "Spiritually," as well as economically, the new woman would be independent.[15]

Kollontai's ideas coincide with many held by contemporary Italian feminists. They also regard her treatment by male communists as instructional. When her criticism of the regime became too pointed, the men did not engage her in intellectual dialogue, but ridiculed her as a woman and to invalidate her critique spread rumors about her sexual promiscuity. Bolshevik men said that her writings "reeked of pornography and the gutter."[16]

Kollontai is a precursor of contemporary feminists in insisting that women's perspectives are indispensable to a humane socialism. She articulated a libertarian, self-managed socialism that was threatening to early soviet leaders: "There can be no self-activity without freedom of thought." Class relations, for Kollontai, would not be changed until workers were given the power to control the economy. Workers had to be given the freedom to experiment, to develop new creative capacities, and to discover new forms of production.[17]

In her 1921 article "The Workers' Opposition in Russia" she acknowledged the difficulties faced by bolshevik leaders in a country where the economy was in collapse and foreign forces threatened the revolution. Yet entrusting the management of the economy to specialists seemed to her to contradict marxist principles, by imposing a socialism managed from above staffed by a bureaucratic system inherited from the past. For Kollontai there was a clear choice: bureaucracy or autonomous action of the workers. To eliminate the bureaucracy, she recommended election of all managers, so that they would remain accountable. In the party, she advocated greater public debate, wider discussion of all problems by the rank and file, open meetings of the executive organs of the party, freedom of opinion, and publication of the documents of various factions within the party.[18] By the early eighties Italian feminist criticism of the Pci pushed the party in many of the directions outlined by Kollontai. The experiences of Luxemburg, Zetkin, and Kollontai helped Italian feminists to understand the necessity of a women's movement autonomous of the parties.

Antonio Gramsci: Italian marxist

In the short time before the Italian communist party became clandestine under fascism, there was an attempt to grapple with women's role, even though it was the doctrine of the third international that there was no specific woman question. The Pci newspaper, *l'Ordine nuovo*, edited by Antonio Gramsci, launched a companion woman's journal, *Tribuna delle donne*, edited by Camilla Ravera. The *Tribuna* criticized women's economic dependence on men and stressed women's right to productive work as well as women's social obligation to reconcile motherhood with the right to economic independence—with social facilities provided by the state.[19] The journal was renamed *Compagna* in July 1922.

On October 28, 1922, the king consigned the government of Italy to Mussolini and his fascist troops. In November 1926 Mussolini, in the face of sporadic but persistent antifascist activity, abolished all constitutional guarantees. Communist deputies in parliament were arrested and five thousand antifascists were jailed. Nonfascist political parties and associations were dissolved, nonfascist newspapers were suppressed. A special tribunal was set up to try dissidents. The Pci went underground, as did its newspaper and woman's journal (although a Pci newspaper, *Risaia*, was circulated during the large strikes of women rice workers in 1927 and 1931). Camilla Ravera, jailed from 1930 to 1943, concluded two decades later that it was impossible to create an autonomous Italian woman's movement addressed to specific women's concerns after 1921. Most of the women who were concerned to do so were underground, in exile, or in jail.

Among the few male marxists to whom contemporary Italian feminists refer, although critically, is Antonio Gramsci. Feminists are indebted to Gramsci's emphasis on cultural revolution, the revolution as a dialectical process, the importance of regional differences (particularly the cultural and economic difference of the South), the significance of self-confidence in socialist self-management, and careful strategy in periods of backlash.[20]

Feminists in Italy have placed prime importance on the first theme of cultural revolution. Every revolution, wrote Gramsci, is preceded by cultural penetration, the permeation of ideas among people who are at first unwilling to accept them.[21] Gramsci also stressed the importance of cultural heritage to encourage the self-confidence that people long passive require to express themselves. Feminist interpretation of this idea has encouraged the creation, or rediscovery, of women's culture.

Only through "practical political activity," said Gramsci, could people develop their own authentic ideas. This was demonstrated in the occupation of Italian factories in 1920 involving 400,000 workers and nearly every region of Italy. There Italians learned worker self-management in factories. This worker council movement failed, but it remained in the legacy of the Italian left and was revived after 1968.[22] The principle of self-management (*autogestione*) has been adopted by feminists.

Gramsci's strategy of a "war of position" has been of signal importance to the Pci and is persuasive to feminists in periods of backlash (*riflusso*). Writing in jail after a failed revolution, it seemed to Gramsci that the transition to a new society was going to be a long process of patient, careful moves, as in a chess game, where one advances step by step to victory. For the Pci after 1945 this has meant cautious parliamentary moves that simultaneously advance toward democracy as well as toward socialism. Members of the Pci who recall the fascist regime worry lest precipitous moves provoke the right and another fascist coup. This careful, cautious quality of the Pci exasperated the young left in the late sixties, and women thereafter. Men of the Pci were inclined to worry that the issues of divorce and abortion would upset the party's strategy of compromise with catholics of the Dc. The importance of women's autonomy has been underlined for feminists by this wary attitude of the Pci.

Perhaps Gramsci's most enduring legacy was his emphasis on workplace democracy, embodied in factory and farm councils. The emphasis on workplace democracy held implications for feminists who stressed women's unpaid work in their traditional workplace, the home, as well as women's subordinate status to men in the factory.

Gramsci has been elevated to first rank by the Pci and is admired by the new left because of his stress on cultural revolution. He is evaluated with diffidence by those who point out he never repudiated leninism. Still, Italian feminists find him hard to dismiss. Feminist plays of the seventies criticized male chauvinist assumptions of all marxist theorists, including those held by Gramsci, but Italian women who identify with marginal others are drawn to the courage of the small Sardinian with a deformed body, whose mind was so threatening to fascism that Mussolini kept him imprisoned until just before he died. Italian feminists, who combine realism with utopian vision, understand Gramsci's counsel to the left: pessimism of the mind, optimism of the will.[23]

3

donne sotto fascismo

women under fascism

The prewar backdrop for fascism presents a mottled picture. The liberal policy of the Giolitti government brought together northern industrialists and industrial workers. A program of accepting unions was counterbalanced by increased government centralization and a literacy qualification for the vote, policies that, according to a recent definitive study, ensured "continued domination of the North over the South."[1] Since 1904 the papacy had permitted catholics to vote in elections where their votes could help defeat socialists.[2] As labor became more militant, industrial and agrarian employers retaliated with violence: a Parma employer association, for instance, sent armed squads against strikers. Industrial employers founded a national confederation in 1910; farm owners, a confederation in 1911. Reformist groups organized a national confederation of labor in 1906, representing 700 local unions and 250,000 members. The socialist party and labor movement split into reformist and revolutionary branches.

Anarchists were members of the directorate of a syndicalist federation which differentiated itself from reformist labor unions. Another division in the worker movement became evident in the debate over entry into the war.

In wartime the economy was concentrated to supply war materiel. At the end of the war weapons contracts were cancelled, and unemployment, inflation, and demobilization of the armed forces threw Italian society into volatile condition. Socialist party membership (and parliamentary representation) surged; thousands of Italian communes were socialist in 1920.[3] The Popular Party, often considered a precursor of the Dc, was formed by a Sicilian priest, Luigi Sturzo, whose populist premises were in conflict with conservative views of the party's other catholic constituents. Veterans returned from war with demands that ranged from land to control of factories; some returned with a profound aversion to nationalist wars, others, smarting under patronizing treatment of Italy by the Great Powers, dreamed of national greatness.

Fascists, at first one among many postwar groups, included veterans, ex-socialists, and ex-revolutionary syndicalists.[4] Benito Mussolini brought a background of revolutionary socialism and interventionism to his ambiguous program of patriotism and populist rhetoric. Fascist rhetoric was supplemented by violence against what was called "unpatriotic, internationalist socialism." In 1919 fascists assaulted anarchist-socialist demonstrators who were protesting repression and sacked the socialist newspaper *Avanti!*, which Mussolini had once headed. The national government implicitly accepted fascist violence to suppress the left.

Postwar strikes for an eight-hour day (most of them successful) were accompanied by occupations of land from Rome south to Apulia, Calabria, and Sicily, occupations that were resisted violently by public authorities and landlords. Food protests became strikes and sometimes developed into pillage of bakeries and grocery stores.[5] Food protests and land occupations in 1919 were followed in 1920 by the largest strike wave of Italian history. Strikers often used the tactic of factory occupation, or sit-down strike, and formed factory councils, embodying the principle of self-managed socialism by workers. Owners, reenforced by police, royal guards, and *carabinieri*, struck back—meeting strikes with violence, and with lockouts.

Farmworkers struck peacefully, but soldiers bound for Albania mutinied and joined socialist workers in streetfighting in Ancona.[6] Fascists, together with nationalist patriots and veterans armed in paramilitary units, came to the aid of industrialists and landowners and successfully used patriotic themes to attack socialist and working class groups. Black-shirted fascists assaulted peasant leagues, worker groups, cooperatives, mutual aid societies, and municipal socialist governments. Fascists met at the end of 1921 and defined themselves as a force acting in place of the state. After the king transferred power to Mussolini's troops, fascist violence was supplemented by governmental arrests of socialists and communists. By 1925 fascist violence was legitimated sufficiently that Mussolini could publicly acknowledge the fascist murder of Giacomo Matteotti, a critic of Mussolini, in parliament.[7] Fascists labeled organized workers "dangerous and bolshevik" enemies of the nation and invoked patriotism and law and order to attack workers and peasants. Speaking for the left, Gramsci said that fascist violence was "terrorism ... gone from the private to the public sector."[8]

After the Matteotti murder, Mussolini consolidated fascist power, instituting a repression that weighed most heavily on workers, peasants, and those who supported them. Fascists allowed industry, the military, the church, even the universities to a large degree, to manage their own affairs,[9] but freedom of belief and press were outlawed and the government was permitted to suspend publications deemed to have preached "class hatred or disrespect" for the monarchy, the catholic church, or the state. After 1926 political opposition was outlawed, although a few liberal legislators were permitted to exist. Worker unions that were not already destroyed were suppressed in 1926 and the clandestine operation of the Pci was periodically crippled by police. Except for the destruction of a free press, fascists maintained most existing social institutions, controlling people by intimidation.[10]

Only industrial workers and the radicalized peasantry felt the full brunt of fascism, other classes were allowed to help build corporate Italy. With the onset of the depression in the thirties, some hoped that fascism offered a universal answer to bolshevism and a mission to what was regarded as decadent Europe.[11] Mussolini's government embarked on imperial ventures in Ethiopia, support of fascists in the

Spanish civil war, and overtures toward nazis culminating in the axis pact. After 1938 an Italian campaign against the Jews began, differing from the nazi version but nonetheless clamping terror on thousands of Italian Jews.

The significant lineament of fascism was violence. The glorification of war became the main theme of fascist ideology in the 1930s, as expressed in the slogan "War is to man what motherhood is to woman"—a slogan feminists would remember after 1968. Racism, another component of fascist ideology, was used to justify imperial war, although Luigi Preti, among other historians, has found that the Italian people "were not particularly receptive to racist arguments." [12]

After world war I women obtained the vote in England, Germany, Austria, Sweden, Czechoslovakia, Hungary, Holland, and the United States. Before Italian women secured the vote in 1945, more than two decades of fascist rule, an era of resistance, and another world war were to intervene. In the contemporary recovery of their history, Italian feminists have addressed themselves to the role of women in the fascist era and to the problematic connections between women, catholicism, and fascism. [13]

catholic doctrine and women

Catholic education has been the one constant in the history of Italian women. Catholic premises can be modified by peasant folklore, absorbed into radical social theories, even consciously dismissed, but the world-view fixed by catholic nuns and priests in childhood has reverberated, for Italian men as well as women, and has continued to exert a complex influence on contemporary individual and social morality.

Well into the twentieth century, catholic education was largely the uncritical teaching of the theology of Augustine and Aquinas. Eve, formed from a rib of Adam, was auxiliary to Adam for purposes of procreation. Eve had let herself be tempted by the desire to know good and evil and had caused the fall of Adam. Insofar as Eve was auxiliary, she was subordinate. Man is in the image of God. Woman, auxiliary to man (and fulfilled through her bodily functions), is not in the image of God. Within a couple, the woman represents the "inferior element." In traditional church doctrine, woman's cupidity and sensuality must be dominated by the masculine element, defined as spirit and reason. A woman lives her auxiliary function in the procreation of children.

The relationship between man and woman is hierarchical; Augustine stated that wives should consider their husbands masters. Although christianity abolished the polygamy of the old testament, church doctrine held that the polygamy of the biblical patriarchs conformed to the order of creation insofar as it safeguarded the state of subordination of women. In the new testament, men were to be dominant over women in consonance with laws of "sincere love."[14] Thomas Aquinas reaffirmed that woman is auxiliary and subordinate to man. Woman's subordination is part of the order of creation; this subordination is in conformity with natural law as well as with the nature of woman. Women are different from and inferior to men. The female body, according to Aquinas, is less perfect than the male's.[15]

For both Augustine and Aquinas, the subordination of women corresponded to the order of creation. Church fathers fixed dualisms between body and spirit and between sex and love that determined three stages of life for women: Virginity was regarded as the perfect state, widowhood was next in purity, in third place was matrimony—treated as a compromise with sin. Procreation excused the sin of concupiscence.[16]

This catholic doctrine was reaffirmed by Pius X in 1909. Although women were companions and associates of men, they must be under male authority; women were not equal to men, although they were of equal value. A woman's duty was to form a family, have children, work in the home, and educate the children. A woman was not to look to her own needs but rather to be concerned for the well-being of others and to preserve tradition.

When, after world war I, the church formed many catholic women's associations, these groups were enjoined by Pope Benedict XV to work in dioceses, in the family, and in the schools to restore the power and the authority of the church and to enhance the catholic religion. Women's right to vote was irrelevant because women's place was in the home. A postwar papal statement held that a woman was to be "an angel of love," drying tears and comforting husband and children. Camilla Ravera, a founder of the Pci who respected christian beliefs, thought these papal words were fine for women of the bourgeoisie and the upper classes, but empty phrases for "millions of women who suffer hunger and cold."[17] For the pope and the many catholic women's associations of the postwar era, women's proper struggle was that of affirming the authority of the church by countering socialism.

fascists and women

In the matter of insisting on women's traditional role, the church was to receive after 1922 the support of fascists—whose philosophy of violence, inequality, and the totalitarian state was seemingly incompatible with catholicism. The hostility of Italian fascists to women was not at first apparent. In 1925 fascists presented a bill allowing women to vote for certain city and provincial administrators, but the vote was limited to those women that fascists wanted to reward (for example, mothers or widows of men killed in battle); literacy provisions excluded the majority of women. Shortly after this proposal was made, fascists abolished administrative elections altogether.[18] A fascist policy of restricting women to tasks of the home was implemented; a great number of women were dismissed from professional and school employment, since work outside the home, in the fascist view, was thought to stimulate independent ideas in women and to discourage them from bearing children.

Ferdinando Loffredo, a fascist theoretician, said it was necessary to supplement laws that removed women from employment with propaganda censuring women who left the home to work outside. Loffreddo wanted the "abolition" of women's emancipation. Female subordination to males, said Loffredo, meant "spiritual, cultural, and economic inferiority." To fix this inferiority, it was necessary to make appropriate changes in educational materials in the schools, to discourage women's occupation outside the home, and to impose severe sanctions on women prostitutes who affronted "social morality."[19]

fascism, catholicism, and women

In 1930, a year after Mussolini signed the concordat of reconciliation with the papacy, the encyclical *Casti connubi* was issued by Pius XI; it described women's work outside the home as a corruption of the role of wife and mother and a "perversion" of the family. Middle-class women's groups and women intellectuals did not oppose these restrictive views. A national conference of Italian women in 1923 chose for its theme "the restoration of the family and family education for the greater good of the nation." Catholic women's groups narrowed their activities to restoration of the power and authority of the church and the spread of the catholic religion. Fascists were left unopposed in their campaign to restrict women's role to "maximum fecundity for the reinvigoration and increase of the race."[20] *L'Osservatore Romano* noted on July 10, 1928, that the network of women's catholic groups gathered together a half million women.

In this atmosphere social concerns were remanded to the sense of christian justice of the padroni in which charity is a christian duty and the poor are to reconcile themselves to the lot given by God. The aim of fascist women's groups was the promotion of women's activities (such as handicrafts) that were compatible with women's familial duties. Women in fascist groups were for the most part wives of men in the fascist hierarchy.[21]

As Denis Mack Smith has pointed out, bishops not only supported fascism in its fight against liberalism and socialism, but "strongly sympathised with Mussolini's attitude towards women and the family." Catholic bishops may not have shared the fascist dictator's belief that women were "incorrigibly frivolous, uncreative, and unintellectual," but they considered fascism "sound on birth control."[22]

In his anticlerical and socialist youth, Mussolini had been a supporter of birth control, but in 1924 he introduced penal sanctions for anyone who advocated such measures. Abortion was defined as a crime, with severe penalties. Mussolini specified twelve children as the ideal number for a family: only in this way could Italians provide soldiers necessary for war, he avowed, and stand up to "ninety million Germans and two hundred million Slavs." In 1927 Mussolini set a twenty-five-year goal of increasing the Italian population from forty to sixty million.[23] He imposed a tax on "unjustified celibacy" and proposed another on childless marriages. He ordered the civil service and private firms to discriminate against women in favor of employing family men. Penalties for adultery were prescribed, harshly enforced for women, ignored for men. The authority of the husband as head of the family was enlarged; husbands had the duty of "correcting" the behavior of their wives.[24]

Italian women—conformity or resistance to fascism?

In the late seventies as heated arguments circled around the abortion issue, Maria Antonietta Macciocchi, in her controversial *La donna nera*, said that Italian women had not resisted fascism, that they had not risen up against fascists until bombs fell on them during world war II. Victoria De Grazia undertook a study of how fascists engineered cultural consent; in later work she has utilized Freudian and Reichian theory in analyses suggesting the sexual attraction of Italian women to fascist male charismatic figures.[25] Jole Calapso, a Sicilian woman historian, responding to the argument that Italian women by and large accepted fascism, noted that fascists were adroit organizers, but her research on Sicilian women indicates that some women responded to fascism with a considerable degree of resistance.[26]

Resistance to a totalitarian society may have to be measured in subtle ways. Mussolini said the test of his fascist regime would be the increase of population for the military purposes of the state. On this test, Italian women answered the fascist dictator in an effective manner: the Italian birth rate, far from doubling, fell during Mussolini's regime and has continued to fall to this day.[27] The answer of Italian women to papal interdiction of birth control and abortion, as well as to fascist laws that made both of these a crime, can be seen not only in the decreasing number of Italian births, but in an interesting datum cited by Denis Mack Smith: "In 1929 abortions were thought to be running as high as 30 per cent of all conceptions."[28] Of course many variables are involved in the lowering of the birth rate, but it is clear that Italian women did not respond positively to the dictator's demand for more births.

In Sicily, as elsewhere after 1922, communists and *"sovversivi"* were arrested, labor halls and socialist circles dissolved, files destroyed. But Sicilian agitation and strikes, although diminished, continued in the fascist era, according to Calapso's findings, and women courted punishment in seditious appraisals of fascists. In 1924 the murder of Giacomo Matteotti in parliament aroused committees of protest and public outcry by many women, particularly in Palermo. In 1925 a strike of tram conductors was joined by wives and children shouting, "Vogliamo pane" (We want bread).[29] Clandestine Sicilian antifascist groups began to organize in 1929. Women's protests, often for bread and work, characteristically took the form of verbal violence, throwing pebbles at city halls and the like. When activities of Sicilian subversives became too precarious, some emigrated to Tunisia.[30]

The 1931 encyclical *Quadragesimo anno* reaffirmed that women's work was properly inside the home. This encyclical and the previous one, *Casti connubi*, could be cited to justify fascist dismissal of thousands of women, especially teachers. Fascist ideas about women were incorporated into the new penal code of 1930. It institutionalized the "crime of honor," which had particular import for Sicilian women: men who caught wives or daughters in *delicto flagrante* could, in effect, kill them with impunity.

Although fascist legislation was hostile to women, the 1935 incident of Mussolini asking Italian women for their wedding rings for his war expenses has been interpreted as evidence women consented to fascism. The widely reproduced photograph of women throwing their wedding rings into fascist coffers is freighted with symbolic implication. The incident has invited many interpretations. Emiliana Noether has pointed out that women who threw their wedding rings into Mussolini's coffers immediately purchased new ones.[31] For many, the incident seems to be evidence of acceptance of fascism by Italian women.

For Sicilian women, the fascist era evoked an old object of peasant hostility, *i sbirri*, authority figures who ranged from tax collectors to the police. In Mussolini's era *i sbirri* were identified with fascist authorities. Sicilian police records studied by Calapso contain abundant references to women who "pronounced offensive words" against the duce and his representatives. Angela, a farmworker, uttered "offensive phrases toward the head of the government." Natalina, a housewife, was jailed for five years for "activity hostile to the duce and against national order." Carmela, a peasant woman concerned about her son who was serving in the army, made verbal threats against Mussolini. An unnamed prostitute at Palermo was arrested for using "vulgar phrases" about the head of government. Giovanna was put in prison for "unfavorably appraising" the politics of the regime. Gertrude and Clara were interned for having "shown antifascist sentiments." Lucia of Siracusa was jailed for protesting inadequate food distribution. Alessandra, Giuseppa, and Amalia were sequestered for denouncing the head of state. Another Carmela, a farmwoman, called Mussolini and his authorities *lazzaroni* (bums), and was punished. At Catania, Giovanna was jailed for a year for expressing disaffection toward a priest who assisted fascist authorities.[32]

Literature may be helpful in understanding the complex subject of Italian women and fascism. In Elio Vittorini's parable about a woman in Sicily in the fascist period, a son goes to visit his mother on her birthday, a reversal of the theme of the mother searching for her son. He is concerned about her because she has been left alone by a husband who has gone off with another woman.

Concezione tells the son that he has not understood. The father had gone off with another woman because he was a "coward." When he would beat her, he would cry afterward and ask her forgiveness. He was nothing like her own father, a "great socialist" who would ride his horse on the feast of San Giuseppe. The son asked how could a socialist ride in the procession of St. Joseph? "How stupid you are!" said the mother. "He was a great man. He could believe in St. Joseph and yet be a Socialist. He had brains enough to do a thousand things at once." And the priests? The mother responded, "D'you think he cared about the priests?"[33]

Now that she had no wedding ring, Concezione could eat what she wanted—herring in winter, roast capsicums in summer. She could do what she wanted. With her midwife's bag, Concezione made the rounds of the town giving injections, offering advice to the sick. When a tired wayfarer came by on his way to work in the sulfur mines, she would give him food and take him into her bed.

The meanings of Vittorini's parable are left to the reader to decipher. For this reader, the story suggests the deterioration of relationships between women and men during the fascist era because women did not respect male resort to violence; men under fascism seemed "cowards" in contrast to the wholeness of socialist men. Concezione, a figure who evokes the historic resistance of women peasants to church and state, does not let church doctrine control her sexuality, nor fascist law determine her vocation. Vittorini names her Concezione, suggesting not the immaculate conception of the madonna but perhaps an earlier mother, whose nurturance exceeded conventional boundaries.[34]

4

resistenza

resistance

Italian historians refer to the welling up of resistance to fascism as a second risorgimento. Some women after 1968 called women's resistance to fascism in the second world war "the first feminism." Whatever it is called, this is a movement that involved many women, of all classes. It includes the seditious behavior in the twenties and thirties of Sicilian and other women outlined in the previous chapter. Iris Origo's Italian war diary of 1943–44 is a source for understanding the wide tacit Italian resistance to fascism that preceded, and accompanied, overt armed resistance.

Writing against a background of fascist rule, civil war, and foreign invasion, Origo describes how Mussolini's beneficial achievements (land drainage, reforestation, road building) and her family's "barrier of privilege" had earlier cut off her awareness of fascist cruelties against workers, peasants, Jews, and others. When she began the diary, Mussolini had lost most of his African empire, Allied armies were advancing from Africa toward Italy, the Italian dictator had ceded direction of the Italian war effort to the nazis in Berlin, and the Origos had taken in twenty children who were under bombardment in Genoa.

the tacit resistance

The area of Tuscany where the Origos lived became a beacon for a stream of refugees and a network of Italian help to fleeing soldiers, partisans, and others. "Every day the need for deciding between them would arise: the request for a lodging of a p.o.w. would have to be weighed against the danger to the farm which sheltered him, the dressing of a partisan's wound against the risk to the nurse and to the other patients in her charge, the pleas of the starving townsfolk who, in the last weeks before the liberation of Rome, came all the way from the city to beg for food, against the needs of the children and partisans whom we must go on feeding here." [1]

What was the motive for this Italian help, often given at the risk of being killed, to fleeing soldiers, partisans, and Jews? Origo describes antifascist sentiments, especially among peasants whose sons were in the army involuntarily. An English officer who stayed with the Origos said the phenomenon was the "peasants' native sympathy with the underdog and the outcast." He attributed this to a "simple Christianity" that impelled them to "befriend those complete strangers, feed them, clothe them, and to help them on their way." The officer said this "simple dignity of humble people" helping others could be found "all over Italy." [2] The Origo diary indicates that this behavior was not confined to Italian peasants. Peasants themselves did not consider the characteristic particularly Italian, citing (perhaps somewhat too generously) similar actions by Russian peasants as Italian soldiers fled the bloodshed, similar understanding by German soldiers who drank with Italian peasants to an end to war and to an end to authorities who directed the lives of others.

A book *Noi Donne* gave to its subscribers in the seventies describes the resistance through the eyes of a peasant woman; there is little discussion of simple people, simple christianity, simple dignity of humble people, and so forth. In Renata Vigano's *L'Agnese va a morire* (Turin, 1949, reprinted 1967, 1972, 1976) Agnese had never left her home and garden, but when the nazis killed her husband she undertook dangerous partisan errands on her bicycle until the nazis killed her.

The Origo diary depicts the many kinds of people involved in the tacit resistance and also the range of individuals in the Italian underground who were committed to the overthrow of nazis and Italian fascists; feminists of the seventies would find this an instructive example of the many kinds of people who resist. "The members of the clandestine opposition in Rome, passing from one secret meeting to another, attempting to find common ground in the points of view of parties as widely at variance as the Communist and the Liberal, the Republican and the Monarchist" included "parish priests and Communist workers, ladies of the Princess' entourage and university professors, Army officers and students." Meeting secretly in their houses or in obscure cafes, "hiding their papers behind picture frames, in books, in the soles of their shoes, there is in their doings a certain flavour of Mazzinian conspiracy. But the risks they are taking are real." [3]

It may be impossible to measure with any precision either Italian conformity or resistance to fascism. Outward conformity in the twenties and thirties, as James D. Wilkinson has pointed out, was often accompanied by "internal emigration." [4] The number of men in fascist forces is not a good measure of fascist support. Origo described an incident of five peasants "invited" to "volunteer." They were promised safety, frequent leave, assignment to their own province—and all but one refused. Those who would not "volunteer" were called "Bolsheviks, anti-Italian" and were abused and threatened with deportation to Germany. [5] From Origo's perspective, the only clear fascists during the war were "industrial magnates, financiers, politicians, diplomats" and the "smart young women" who frequented the Hotel Excelsior. [6]

During the war Italian resistance was demonstrated in refusal to obey orders to report to the nazis: "They propose instead to hide in the woods and (since the actual numbers of the Germans here are very small, and the Carabinieri will certainly not be over-zealous in carrying out their orders) I think they will probably get away with it." [7] Doing so required courage not only for fleeing soldiers, but for people who helped them: Germans imposed the "death penalty for possession of firearms, for sabotage, or for sheltering or in any way assisting members of enemy forces." The fascist government also issued a proclamation of the death penalty to those who gave help to prisoners of war.[8]

Fascism at the end of its rope rewrote the words of the catholic credo and left a clue that nostalgia for consolidation of catholic church and state, and transposition of religious symbols to the state and its leader motivated some Italians to support the totalitarian regime. Origo recorded that the broadcasts of the "Fascist Republican Party (from Munich) now begin, after the strains of *Giovinezza* with the following remarkable statement: 'I believe in God, Lord of Heaven and earth. I believe in justice and truth. I believe in the resurrection of Fascist Italy. I believe in Mussolini and the final Italian victory.' "[9]

In the last year of the war in Italy the effective governments were those of the Allies in the South and of the Germans in the North. Everywhere Italians worked out modes of self-government, "fairly successfully," according to Origo, because there was a "truce to party politics and a general feeling of unity in confronting the general misfortune."[10] At the end, the hunting down of Jews by nazis became fierce: "Last night they searched even the convents." Jews were declared enemy aliens, their property confiscated, and they were deported in sealed vans to German concentration camps. Origo noted that "every Italian I have met, irrespective of political opinion is horrified and disgusted by this brutality."[11]

At the end, recruits who did not report within a fortnight were shot.[12] In May 1944 Germans dropped leaflets where the Origos lived: "Whoever knows the place where a band of rebels is in hiding, and does not immediately inform the German Army, will be shot. Whoever gives food or shelter to a band or to individual rebels will be shot. Every house in which rebels are found, or in which a rebel has stayed will be blown up."[13] Nazis hanged the corpse of a partisan on a lamppost on a main street of the town near the Origo farm.[14]

Holocaust historians have concentrated on northern Europe, documenting the heroic efforts of Denmark and Holland in saving their Jewish nationals. As Ivo Herzer suggested recently, the case of Italian resistance to (and subversion of) fascist decrees concerning Jews was demonstrated not only in the efforts of thousands of individual Italians to aid Jews but also in the connivance of the Italian army and bureaucracy in the effort to save Yugoslavian Jews.[15] Italians saved eighty-five percent of the Jews of their country in a story not yet definitively written. The number of European Jews who fled into the Italian resistance during the war and chose to remain in Italy after the war is uncounted.[16]

The Italian writer Primo Levi, in his recent documented story of Jews as European partisans, has suggested some of the lineaments of the complex story of Italian Jews. A European partisan in Levi's story said of Italians, "They helped us not in spite of the fact we're Jews, but *because* of it. They also helped their own Jews; when the Germans occupied Italy, they made every effort they could to capture the Italian Jews, but they caught and killed only a fifth. All the others found refuge in Christians' houses, and not only the Italian Jews, but many foreign Jews who had sought refuge in Italy."[17]

Levi's comments about Italian beliefs are perceptive. In his story someone suggested that the reason Italians risked their lives to help Jews and others was because Italians were "good christians." Chaim responded, "That may be, too ... but I'm not sure of it. Even as Christians, the Italians are odd. They go to Mass, but they curse. They ask favors of the Madonna and the saints, but they don't seem to believe much in God. They know the Ten Commandments by heart, but at most they observe two or three. I believe they help those in need because they're good people, who have suffered a lot, and who know that those who suffer should be helped."

Regarding the number of Jews who chose to live in Italy after the war, one of the characters in Levi's novel points out that there had never been a pogrom in Italy, that Italian Jews are as "odd" as are Italian catholics. Indeed, Jews cannot be differentiated from the catholics of Italy. Levi describes Italy as a "country of good people, who don't much like war, who like confusing issues."[18]

Italian feminists after 1968 in identifying themselves with marginal others consciously recognized that the largest group of marginal others in their country, as well as in all of Europe, were the Jews. Italian Jewish women are visible in the contemporary feminist movement.

women partisans

Most of the women described in Origo's diary belonged to the "tacit resistance." In the 1970s as Italian feminists recovered their history, they claimed as feminist foremothers the women of this silent resistance, as well as those who fought overtly. The line between the two kinds of resistance can not be sharply defined; what is clear is that many kinds of women were involved—not only exceptional women but thousands of uncelebrated persons engaged in day-to-day activities who left papers signed "Rosa" or "Maria," who were identified only as "una contadina" or "una impiegata" (a farmwoman or a clerk). Open efforts to bring down nazis and fascists sometimes began with a small act—hiding a fleeing soldier who might have been a son, a husband, a brother. Women took supplies to partisans in the mountains, blocked streets to impede nazis and fascists, became couriers, nurses, spies, partisan soldiers.

In November 1943 at Milan a few formed a women's network of groups who were committed to fighting concurrently for liberation from nazis and fascists and for women's emancipation. Predominantly made up of communists, these groups were "open to all women—of every social class, of every political and religious faith—who want to participate in the work of liberation of the country and to fight for their own emancipation."[19] Their double purpose was "the defense of women" and "assistance to combatants for liberty"; their task was to organize for resistance in factories, offices, and schools. Resistance activities included sabotage of war production and refusal of forced work, night work, or work under harmful conditions. Women were to demand equal pay for equal work and assistance to mothers. Strikes, work shutdowns, and mass demonstrations were to be initiated to obtain adequate food, housing, clothing, and schools.

The strikes of 1944 marked women's participation on a large scale. Women in demonstrations demanded provisions, an end to deportations to Germany, a stop to fascist and nazi massacres. Women were killed, the movement became larger. Sometimes, as at Turin, women simply laid siege to warehouses that contained coal or wood. Less openly, women sent food and clothing to partisans in hiding and planned among themselves as to how they could assist a partisan effort.[20]

Some women joined brothers or husbands in a partisan band; others became partisans when their house or their town was burned down. Many nursed wounded men, made soup, mended trousers, washed shirts. Others carried messages, waited hours on an icy night for a train to take a package to partisans. All kinds of women joined—peasants, schoolteachers, factory workers, intellectuals—communists, socialists, christian democrats. Many were captured and raped, tortured, or killed.[21] Among the counted partisan groups were twenty-four in the factories of Milan and an equal number at Turin and at Genoa. The provinces of Emilia, Tuscany, The Marches, and the Veneto were strongholds.

Elsewhere, groups of farmwomen, intellectuals, teachers, housewives were loosely connected with the national liberation effort. Military women's brigades engaged in sabotage, broke lines of communication, organized food demonstrations, took supply depots, distributed provisions, impeded deportations to Germany.[22] Some women, when they became partisans, made a *scelta* (commitment) that would last the rest of their lives; many of them were later visible in the feminist movement of the seventies and eighties.

Partisan efforts ranged from traditional women's activities (for example, denouncing women who went with the Germans) to a new one—building democratic institutions. As soon as Germans left a town, women often occupied recreation centers and city halls to install democratic organizations. Sometimes a partisan simply stayed at a telephone, advising where nazis were located. After a town was liberated, women who had undertaken dangerous missions (with arms, documents, clandestine radio) nursed the wounded and fed the hungry. Women in the liberation struggle showed the traditional nurturant attitudes of mothers and wives as well as a self-confidence that was a break, for some, from previous attitudes of passivity and subservience.[23] In the Emilia, women expropriated depositories of supplies slated for nazis and distributed them. In the Bologna area, women directed hospitals, organized cooperatives, coordinated distribution of supplies. Women rice workers created dozens of discomforts for padroni.

Official information indicates that there were 70,000 women affiliated with *Gruppi di difesa della donna e per l'assistenza ai combattenti della libertà:* 35,000 of them were partisans; 512 were military officers; 4,563 were arrested, many of these tortured; 623 were shot and killed; 2,750 of these women were deported to Germany.

formation of Unione donne italiane

Unione donne italiane (Udi) was founded in September 1944, a few months after the liberation of Rome. Coordination between women of the South and partisan women of the North was almost nonexistent until this final insurrection. There had been informal communication, mainly through the Pci, between northern and southern women, but genuine coordination did not come until the war was over. This is an important point, Margherita Repetto (Alaia) has argued, because Udi was already a formed organization when the union with the partisan group of women was effected at war's end in 1945. "This is very important to explain the political blend of Udi," she explains, because the women's union was made up of southern women who were not in the open resistance (since the South was early occupied by the Allies) as well as partisan women of the North.[24] Repetto's point suggests the national composition of the formation of the women's union, a point that sometimes became blurred in the seventies when the "first feminism" tended to be identified only with partisan women of the North.

Women's day, March 8, 1945, was celebrated in the area north of Rome (still occupied by nazis) as "a day of wide mobilization" by Udi women and parties of the left.[25] Udi was simultaneously fighting fascism and working for specific women's concerns, including salary equality, protective legislation, and maternity benefits for women workers. The 1945 congress of Udi at Florence announced the postwar aim: "the emancipation of the masses of women." Among their immediate objectives were laws assuring women's right to work outside the home, political rights, and larger participation of women in social life.

At war's end, the unity of women fighting a common enemy was split. Udi organized communist, catholic, and socialist women for the postwar work of women's emancipation, but many catholic women joined the Dc, forming Centro italiano femminile (Cif), a catholic women's organization whose primary focus was anticommunism. Women of Udi and catholic women worked together, however, for women's vote, obtained on January 30, 1945.[26]

Togliatti on women

The leader of the postwar Italian communist party had given thought to the role of women. Palmiro Togliatti decried Italy's historic subordination of women. Rather than repeating the soviet formula that women's employment outside the home would solve the woman question, he called for women's full political and economic equality. In his analysis of an Italian way to socialism, he envisioned a "new historic bloc" that included women with full autonomy.

In an address in June 1945, Togliatti said that women in the resistance had demonstrated that when women's energy enters the lifestream of a people, there is the dawn of a great renewal. Women, he said, were in the lead in the creation of a democratic society in Italy. In the eighties women of Udi would remember that Togliatti's vision was of a movement of women outside the confines of party.[27] Considering how Italians could "create a democratic regime of a new type," a democracy that "overcomes the limits and fundamental defects of prefascist democracy" and is "open to profound transformations in the socialist sense," Togliatti concluded that autonomous women were pivotal in creating a "democratic-socialist transformation."[28]

women and conventional histories of the resistance

Togliatti was ahead of most of the men of his party. Roberto Battaglia, a partisan division commander and later a professor of history, wrote an exhaustive study of the resistance in 1953. Masculine myopia is apparent: the book contains only one fleeting reference to a woman partisan—Clorinda Menguzzato, who was raped by nazi soldiers, tortured, attacked by wild dogs, and killed without revealing the whereabouts of her companions.[29]

Before the mid-seventies, histories of the Italian resistance usually left out the indispensable activities of the thousands of women who quietly resisted. An even more serious omission was that of women partisans, some of whom were awarded the gold medal of honor by the postwar Italian government—Irma Bandiera: captured, tortured by nazi troops, blinded, murdered, her body left in the street. Gina Borellini: captured, wounded, her leg amputated. Lidia Bianchi: caught with companions, refused a pardon to die with them. Bruna

Davoli: tortured, condemned to death, saved by companions. Gabriella Degli Esposti: tortured, killed. Anna Maria Enriquez: captured, killed. Tina Lorenzoni: spy, captured and shot. Ancilla Marighetto: captured, tortured, killed. Rita Rosani: surrounded by fascist troops, fought until shot down. Modesta Ross: arrested, tortured, shot with an infant in her arms. Cecilia Deganutti: caught, tortured, killed. Irma Marchiani: captured, escaped, captured again, killed. Norma Parenti: captured, killed. Vera Vassale: surprised by SS troops while transmitting radio messages, fled with secret documents, returned to intelligence work behind enemy lines. Paola Del Din: parachuted into enemy area and, despite a broken ankle and spinal injury, successfully completed mission.[30]

5

dopoguerra
e l'Unione donne italiane

the postwar era
and the Italian women's union, 1945–1968

The Italian partisan movement, the largest in western Europe, provided for 200,000 women and men, one historian has noted, an experience that people can be united by trust rather than discipline.[1]
There was a surge at war's end to the chief party of the resistance,
the Pci.

the postwar intellectual atmosphere

Despite the popularity of the Pci, divisions occurred in the early
postwar period that prefigured some of the discontents of 1968 and
thereafter. Intellectuals who enrolled in the Pci as the party most

closely reflecting the hopes and needs of Italians soon encountered problems. The Pci was less demanding of ideological conformity than were the postwar French and German communist parties, but it did not accept the principle that party members were completely at liberty in their "search for truth." Palmiro Togliatti, who had been a member of the cominform, chastised Elio Vittorini, the novelist who also edited a communist newspaper, for "superficiality." Implicitly Togliatti was imposing the primacy of politics over culture, or the primacy of the party over individual conscience. Vittorini refused to give up his moral autonomy.[2]

Along with misgivings about the communist party, some writers of the postwar era restated ancient peasant distrust of the state. Carlo Levi said the country was in the hands of *luigini* (bureaucrats and professionals) and *contadini* (peasants); he preferred the *contadini*. In *Christ Stopped at Eboli*, Levi described the peasant attitude of resignation and distrust of the state. For Levi this was an attractive attribute since he felt it made peasants "morally invulnerable to the appeal of Fascism, just as they had resisted so many other would-be conquerors in the past."[3] Levi's book touches themes that are necessary for understanding Italian feminism after 1968.

In the first edition of his book in 1945, he said that he was writing about a "diverse civilization"—that of the peasants of the *mezzogiorno* (the land of the midday sun that stretches south of Rome) who had been "outside of history" and outside of the values of "progressive reason," embodying instead peasant "antichissima sapienza e paziente dolore" (very ancient wisdom and patient suffering).[4] Levi's perception of the peasant mind confirms the sense one has when reading Italian peasant folklore of the late nineteenth century. In the world of the peasant, said Levi, there is no room for religion "precisely because everything participates in divinity, everything is, really and not symbolically, divine—the sky, the animals, Christ, and the goat." Even the ceremonies of the church become, said Levi, "pagan rites," of the "infinite number of earth gods of the village."[5] The madonna of these peasants was the "black madonna among the grain and the animals," not the "pietosa Madri di Dio, ma una divinità sotteranea, nera delle ombre del grembo della terra, una Persefone contadina, una dea infernale delle messi" (not the merciful Mother of God, but a subterranean divinity, black in the womb of the earth, a Persephone peasant girl, an infernal goddess among the crops).[6] For peasants, this black madonna was neither good nor bad. She withered the harvests but she also nourished and protected and "è bisogna adorarla" (it was necessary to adore her).[7] Levi's title taps the pre-millennial beliefs of peasants of the South.

Levi preferred peasants to bureaucrats. The theme of distrust of organized politics (or of parties) was also sounded in the *dopoguerra* by Ignazio Silone. Silone helped to found the Italian communist party in 1921, overcoming his native Abruzzese "distrust, diffidence, and skepticism" of the state. After the war his doubts surfaced; the communist party when it demanded obedience, said Silone, resembled its fascist enemies.[8] Enlisting with the socialists, he hoped to encourage the development of a socialism uncorrupted by stalinist rigidity, inspired by the idealism of Joseph Proudhon and Giuseppe Mazzini and informed by the federalism of Carlo Cattaneo. Cutting through the bush of ideology, Silone said that "socialism is the aspiration of the poor toward social justice and equality, with the suppression of economic and political privileges."[9] As opposed to the primacy of political parties, he advocated an ideal of self-governing small communities. Themes sounded by Silone, of decentralization and socialist self-management bypassing political parties, would be taken up by feminists in the seventies and eighties.

In the postwar era many intellectuals of the left admired the USSR, which had fought valiantly against the nazis; they also felt a wave of hope from the United States. The United States was respected not only because it had helped to liberate Italy but also because Italian adherents of postwar neorealism liked the literature of Sinclair Lewis, Ernest Hemingway, and William Faulkner.

Italians uneasily watched the postwar scramble for world power between the USSR and the United States, a scramble that had become lethal with the nuclear bomb and repugnant with the recrudescence of anticommunism in Italy. Women obtained the vote, Italians voted for a republic and wrote an advanced republican constitution, but the hopes of the left were dashed as Italian politics settled into a cold-war equilibrium of a dominant anticommunist party and a large communist party kept from participating in the government. The division linked the anticommunist Dc to the United States and the communist Pci to the USSR. Women's issues, in this precarious equilibrium, were subordinated to the Pci strategy of not alienating the Dc—until after 1968.

Udi as women's auxiliary to the Pci

A Udi activist who has written a history of the organization noted in 1984 that the contemporary militance of the women's organization is a legacy of the resistance. Also from the war and postwar period of Udi derives the legacy of women fighting for the advancement of all people, rather than for women in particular.[10] Almost immediately after the war, the antifascist front that had sustained the resistance broke up. Udi, originally formed of women of the political and the catholic left, now became a controversial organization. Catholics disassociated themselves from communists and formed women's organizations dedicated to fighting communism. With Udi's leadership, women petitioned for the vote in 1944 and obtained it in 1945. In the first election in which Italian women participated in 1946, 81 percent voted. Immediately after the war Udi was involved in mass demonstrations, feeding starving children, pressuring to place women in political offices, encouraging cooperatives, distributing the weekly *Noi Donne,* and founding local chapters.[11]

Camilla Ravera has remarked that the postwar Italian nation whose constitution defines it as a republic founded on the value of work was changed by cold war anticommunism into a republic that excluded the parties of the workers—the Pci and Psi. The election of 1948 marked the beginning of the hegemony of the anticommunist party of political catholicism, the Dc, which obtained the votes of 48.5 percent of the electorate. A united left of the Pci and Psi secured 31 percent of the vote, but was excluded after 1947 from participation in government.[12]

The Pci attitude toward women of Udi in the postwar period was never monolithic, maintains Margherita Repetto Alaia. Attitudes of men ranged from considering Udi a "transmission belt" for party policy to conceiving of Udi as an autonomous women's organization. Women confronting the party would quote Togliatti's statements on women as part of a "new historic bloc."[13] In the first postwar period of Udi, the organization was hierarchically structured, a pattern that kept Udi leaders in close contact with the Pci. Men of the Pci were diverse: partisans, men connected with the international cominform, and men concerned to create a "new party" fusing democracy and socialism.[14] As cold war anticommunist feeling deepened and the two major left parties were forced out of the government, Udi women agreed in 1948 to become an *alleanza femminile*, a women's alliance in the popular front of the Pci and Psi.

Udi's focus on women's everyday needs

Although auxiliary to the Pci, Udi was implicitly powerful: by 1949 it enrolled a million members. Its weekly, *Noi Donne*, distributed 200,000 copies throughout Italy. Yet women's representation on governing boards of the labor confederation, Cgil (which allied communist trade unions with the Pci) was, Miriam Mafai remembers, "laughable."[15] It was left to Udi to see to improving the working lives of women.

In 1948–49 Udi supported strikes of farmworkers, among others. One group on strike was the jasmine workers of Milazzo, Sicily. Women and children worked when the flower bloomed, from one until eight o'clock in the morning, from July to September. In 1948 women earned 150 lire for each kilogram of flowers gathered; it took 13,500 flowers to make one kilogram. Farmowners lowered this rate to 50 lire per kilogram in 1948. In 1949 the women struck and reached a compromise of 90 lire per kilogram. In the postwar period other southern farmworkers struck, including women who harvested olives and almonds. At Naples and elsewhere there were hunger marches of women with babies.[16] Early Udi efforts were directed toward protective legislation—for women working in factories in 1950, for farm women in 1953, for domestic workers later. In the mid-fifties Udi opened a debate on birth control with a slogan that was to be taken up in the seventies: "As women we determine how many children we want, and when we want them."[17]

In the early sixties Udi campaigned against dismissal of women from employment on account of marriage and for the law guaranteeing women's right to enter all careers and all public offices (including the magistracy). Although in this period there were strong bonds between the Italian communist party and the USSR, the uneasiness of younger Udi women with the soviets was evident in 1963 when a Udi delegation to a Moscow conference left in protest against "unacceptable" themes of the conference; Udi refused to participate in peace conferences controlled by the soviets.[18] By 1963 Udi was supporting the right of divorce and women's rights within the family. In 1965 Udi women presented a popular initiative for nursery schools to the senate. By 1968 a generational split was evident in the women's organization with many younger members siding with what older Udi women called *neofemminismo*.[19]

A distinctive characteristic of the Udi generation of the *dopoguerra* was a keen sense of the importance of women's everyday needs. Although the resistance had operated primarily in the North and the center (the South was early under allied control), every Italian city, south as well as north, had experienced bombing, fear, and hunger. Even before the war, women of all classes experienced the privation incurred by Mussolini's war in Ethiopia. Some women were increasingly angry at the fascist legislation that remained in the statutes allowing men the right to "correct" the behavior of their wives.

Some conservatives would later accuse feminists of having weakened the family, but the family was in shambles in postwar Italy. Women who lived through the *dopoguerra* never forgot that economic conditions have a great deal to do with well-being, that women (as well as men), out of a need to survive and to feed their children, can be reduced to stealing, dealing on the black market, and prostitution. American troops were welcomed as liberators at first, but as prostitution became a mass phenomenon, there was recognition that Americans had become padroni. "At Naples young girls prostituted themselves out of hunger, young women of the middle class prostituted themselves for money."[20]

Women of Udi turned after the war to the traditional tasks women have always performed—feeding the hungry, putting the children in school, and looking after the homeless. Udi also directed its attention to women working in factories. Women textile workers of Naples, like women workers elsewhere, arose at night to prepare food for the family and to do the family laundry before taking the train and arriving at a factory at dawn. Women worked in factories where men, to whom they were subordinate, sometimes arrogated privileges: "Every morning the *padrone* took a walk through the factory and selected the women he wanted. Then he sent for them." If a woman refused, she lost her job. In airless jute factories women in rags worked barefoot.[21]

Udi style: *Noi Donne*

A Udi style was developed in the *dopoguerra*, characterized by absence of rhetoric and attention to concrete tasks, often in separate women's commissions of the party. Some feminists of the seventies criticized postwar women's commissions of the Pci for having perpetuated a subordinate role for women in the party. Yet discussion of the importance of feminist separatism in the late seventies made the question of these separate women's commissions moot. Women working with women in postwar separate commissions felt they could accomplish more, just as did separatist feminists of the seventies and eighties.

The unpretentious nature of its periodical, *Noi Donne*, reflected Udi style. This journal, which in its lifetime has reached a very large number of Italian women, claims a lineage older than Udi. The first edition was published by Italian women partisans in Paris (where they had fled Mussolini's fascism) in 1937. During the resistance several clandestine editions appeared in northern Italy during the nazi occupation. The first legal edition appeared in July 1944 at Naples, as the Allies fought their way up the Italian peninsula.[22] *Noi Donne* was always able to reach a broad swath of women—the analogous U.S. periodical may be *Woman's Day*. Indeed there was considerable similarity of content in the *dopoguerra* between this communist women's periodical and *Woman's Day:* both periodicals addressed themselves to home, children, and husbands.[23]

Yet *Noi Donne* was a women's communist journal that reflected party influence. A 1980 *noi donne* analysis of early editions concluded that there was little discussion of personal feelings, little reflection on the relationship of men and women; in retrospect, it seemed a political periodical for women, with edifying stories that hewed embarrassingly close to the Pci party line.[24] The sphere of the private was shown in letters asking for a recipe or a pattern to make children's garments. There was some discussion of the difficulties of adjusting to normal married life after years of war separation, some reference to family violence, betrayal, indifference. But most of the stories were about women making a living in factories and shops, about protective legislation for working mothers, and about salary equality. In 1961 the first discussion appeared of a taboo subject—abortion.

Men of the Pci, intent on good relations with the catholic Dc, frowned on women's interest in the issue. This attitude of men of the Pci on abortion would not be changed until women showed their electoral power and Udi defied them in the middle seventies.

equality

Efforts of women partisans and Udi women came to fruition in 1948 with the promulgation of the new republican constitution and the election, for the first time in the history of Italy, of women to the Italian parliament. There were twenty-one women deputies, of whom eleven were leaders of Udi, nine were communists, and two were socialists. The other ten were women members of the Dc. Udi gave to each of these women a rose and a card that restated the principles of the 1948 republican constitution that advanced women's status:

Legal equality with men in every field.
Recognition of the right to work; access to all schools, professions, careers.
Right to protective legislation that "permits a woman to fulfill her task as a mother."
Equal treatment and equal compensation for work.[25]

peasant land occupations in the South

Italian women were to indicate by the end of the sixties that they wanted more than these constitutional rights. This was apparent early in the postwar period when women of the South occupied unused lands. In these direct actions, women carried the *bandiera rossa*, the Italian tricolor, and babies. There was singing by women in throngs of peasants, artisans, students. "Women were always at the beginning of the demonstrations."[26]

A recent study of southern peasant agitation at the end of the war has described how peasant men and women of the South occupied lands that had at one time been common land (interesting evidence of collective memory). Land occupations after 1945 exceeded similar actions after the first world war. In the period when the Pci was part of the national government (prior to 1947), land occupations and demonstrations were usually planned in local Pci offices on a Sunday. "Early on a Monday morning, the men on foot or bicycles or mules, carrying with them their work tools and red and tricolour flags, would move into the countryside to occupy the land. Sometimes the women would go with them, or else they would come later, bringing their children and carrying on their heads large cooking pots. Sometimes too the whole procession would be preceded by the village band and led by the local left-wing mayor. Both men and women would set to work on the land." If the land were already under cultivation, there was immediate trouble from *carabinieri*. In these confrontations, a recent analyst describes how peasant women defused tension, "talking to the *carabinieri* individually to try and convince them of the justice of the peasant cause, surrounding their menfolk in a large circle if it looked as if the police were about to charge, and if all else failed, pretending to faint or to have a hysterical fit in order to distract the *carabinieri* and allow the men to escape unharmed."[27]

One source of southern distrust of the Pci derived from this postwar era, because Pci support for land occupations was moderated by an overall party strategy of averting a radicalization that would jeopardize an alliance with the Dc—a Pci pattern that resembled its perspective on women's concerns and that in effect became subordination of peasant and feminist concerns to party strategy.

The greatest wave of peasant agitation occurred in 1949–50, after the Dc had won its watershed victory in the 1948 election and the left was forced out of the government. Dc agrarian reform legislation of 1950 deflected peasant agitation. A recent appraisal concludes that the Dc reform divided the peasantry and defused the movement for land occupations.[28] Migration of southern peasants to the North continued.

Udi and postwar politics

Anticommunism in Italian politics, a defensive party strategy of men of the Pci, and what seemed to be insuperable problems besetting Udi women stymied any possibility of Udi's becoming an autonomous women's organization after 1945, although a recent history of Udi indicates that many women before 1968 strove to be independent of the party.[29] In the 1948 election the Dc campaigned with slogans to the effect it was a "sin" to vote for left parties; posters

painted the Pci (and Udi) as a threat to the Italian family. In 1949
the pope excommunicated communists—although the Pci accepted
the lateran pacts which gave to the catholic church a privileged position in Italy. The pope, according to a church historian, was responding to communist persecution of the church in Russia, China,
and the countries of eastern Europe and was anxious to ward off the
possibility of communists coming to power in Italy, France, or Greece.
In the papal edict of July 1949 catholics were forbidden to join or to
support the communist party, to publish or distribute, read or write
communist literature. Communism was adjudged to be antichristian
and catholics who professed, defended, or propagated communism
were subject to excommunication. Communists were not allowed to
be witnesses at catholic marriages or to act as godparents of catholic
children.[30]

For Udi women the negative papal attitude presented a large problem, given the preponderance of catholics in the Italian population.
At the grassroots, in spite of imprecations against them by the pope
and the Dc, women of Udi tried to work with women of all parties,
but there were obvious tensions between Udi and the women of
Cif—catholic women who simultaneously worked for women's concerns and engaged in anticommunist publicity. Even more effective
were the anticommunist efforts of women's commissions of l'Azione
cattolica, who were governed by the papal hierarchy. These catholic
women's organizations were organized by age, class, school, and rec-
reational activity, an impressive women's network that was to sustain
the Dc until the religious and political reverberations of the sixties,
seventies, and eighties.

After 1945 Italian capitalism found that its traditional ally, the
liberal party (Pli), had been weakened during the fascist regime; it
turned to Democrazia cristiana (Dc), a catholic political party whose
early origins had been populist and antifascist and whose stated purposes after 1945 remained antifascist as well as anticommunist. Yet
the Dc supported conservative papal doctrine regarding women and
openly indicated it was not interested in helping women who sought
employment outside the home (one widely reported statement of
the Dc was that women who looked for outside jobs wanted to buy
"silk stockings"). The Dc took as its objective to isolate the left, particularly the Pci. Politically the Dc represented dominant economic
classes, although it was supported by a broad interclass spectrum of

Italians from peasants to small shop-keepers, who supported conservative positions of the papacy, including papal views of women.

In this unpromising environment for women's concerns, many Udi women threw themselves into the peace movement, an activity clearly consonant with Article 70 of Italy's new constitution: "Italy repudiates war as an instrument of offense against the liberty of other peoples and as a means of resolving international controversies." A group of Udi women organized a conference of women of the resistance right after the war. Six thousand delegates attended and chose "defense of the peace" as their major task. In November 1947 in a *settimana* of peace activities Udi launched a referendum for peace, bringing three million signatures to the president of the republic in March 1948. During this period of international cooperation of women for peace, Udi women were invited by soviet women to Russia where, Camilla Ravera recalled later, Italians were greeted as representatives "from the country most advanced on the path to women's emancipation."[31]

Some Udi women who had been in the resistance when the soviets were regarded as courageous allies reciprocated the admiration. In 1953 Ravera praised the socialism of the Soviet Union, where "women work in all fields with equal rights to those of men." She listed women's employment in soviet factories, offices, collectives, laboratories, hospitals, and cultural institutions and noted that soviet legislation facilitated women's tasks as mothers and wives. Women's equality could also be seen, she said, in other countries following a socialist path—China, Poland, Czechoslovakia, Bulgaria, Romania and Hungary.[32] Ravera did not add that equality in these countries was accompanied by loss of freedoms. The fifties and early sixties are regarded today by Udi women as a bleak period. A sole sustaining beam was Togliatti's view that it was not possible to attain a renewed democracy without emancipation of women, in all aspects, "economic, political, social and moral."

Italy advanced rapidly into modernization. Over four million southerners migrated to northern Italian cities, other European countries, and elsewhere between 1945 and 1975. Rapid industrialization created a belief that there had been an "economic miracle," yet when Italy entered the European Economic Community in 1957 it did so with the lowest wage rate of any Eec country. From 1950 to 1963 Italy's gross national product rose at an annual rate of 7 percent (compared to the European average of 4.5 percent), but benefits were spread unevenly.[33] The North-South disparity deepened; when women demonstrated in 1954 for water at Mussomeli, Sicily, they were assaulted by police and three women were killed.

Udi, despite adverse conditions, worked for women's advancement. In 1955 the women's union proposed salaries for housewives; in 1956 parliament approved the principle of salary equality for women. In response to Udi criticism, the law providing benefits to the State from legalized prostitution was abolished in 1958. In 1959 Udi supported women's strikes for salary equality in the clothing industry; in 1960 the clothing industry accepted the principle of salary equality. These efforts were accompanied by work for peace, an assignment men of the Pci felt appropriate to women.[34]

Called "godless" by the pope, by the Dc, and by catholic women and treated as auxiliary by Pci men who subordinated women's issues to party policy, Udi still made impressive efforts to help women in the postwar era. In the sixties, as the untenability of their auxiliary status became more vivid, Udi helped to secure laws that prohibited firing women on account of marriage, guaranteed women's access to all professions, and posited equality of women's work in agrarian contracts.

Udi and Pci in ferment

All communist parties were thrown into crisis after the revelations of Stalin's barbarities at the twentieth congress of the communist party of the Soviet Union in 1956. The Italian communist party concentrated after 1956 on devising an Italian way to socialism grounded on the thought of Gramsci and Togliatti, looking toward a "new type of democracy and socialism" with autonomy for significant social sectors, primarily the labor unions.[35]

In the early sixties socialists left their partner in the postwar united front of the left and entered a governing coalition with the anticommunist Dc; the Psi asked socialist women to leave Udi. Udi became an organization of communist women affiliated with a Pci that was riddled with tension. When the woman question was brought before the central committee of the party in the sixties, more than half of the men left the meeting. Togliatti wrote a letter to the committee, pointing out to communist men the gravity of this behavior that indicated disrespect for the genuine equality of women.[36]

In 1967 the European left, whether social democratic or communist, was in crisis, an instability prompted by continuing aftereffects of the 1956 soviet denunciation of Stalin, soviet suppression of the Hungarian rebellion, and realization that the international communist bloc was fracturing. Instability, as we shall see, was deepened by a new attitude toward the left encouraged by John XXIII, by the sino-soviet split, and by impatience on the part of the young left as European social democratic administrations subsided into managing mixed economies. The Pci, respected as the largest communist party of Europe, was internally divided. A left branch of the party was uncomfortable with Pci justification of soviet interference in cultural and artistic life. Closer to home, the expulsion from the Pci in 1950 of Pier Paolo Pasolini on account of homosexuality continued to rankle. The case of Pasolini, widely respected poet and dramatist of the urban subproletariat, stimulated criticism of Pci intolerance toward different ideas, different life styles.[37]

In his study of the Pci in the sixties, Grant Amyot concludes that mainstream thinking in the Italian communist party wanted to break with the leninist view of revolution as an assault on the winter palace with seizure of state power by a politicized vanguard. Social transformation, it was hoped, could be achieved by way of an alliance with the middle classes, a strategy considered appropriate to conditions of advanced capitalism.[38] In Togliatti's thinking, Pci alliance with the middle class was essential to ward off fascist danger. Worrying about the right, the emphasis of the Pci was on moderation, avoiding aggravation of a crisis that might lead to another fascist coup. The emphasis on a mass party encompassing the middle class was an unavowed separation of the Pci from Lenin's concept of a vanguard.[39] There were other unavowed departures from leninist principles. Pci support of the concordat with the pope after the war, was, in effect, part of an Italian road to socialism, a perspective that had been denounced by the cominform in 1948 when Yugoslavs suggested there could be "different" roads to socialism.[40]

After 1956 the Pci implicitly rejected the concept of a dictatorship of the proletariat. Italy's advanced constitution, the party hoped, would make possible a parliamentary transition to socialism grounded on the support of workers, peasants, and the middle class.

In the transition period the state would neither be bourgeois nor yet socialist. Monopolies, including electrical energy, public services, credit institutions, chemical, steel and other basic industries were to be nationalized. Along with a universal social security system, the advanced provisions of the 1948 constitution were to be implemented. In the interim period, as well as in the new society, constitutional rights of freedom of speech, press, and religion were to be guaranteed.[41]

This thinking on an Italian road to socialism was influenced by Togliatti, who emphasized the importance of problems of "underdevelopment of the south, the continued existence of 'semi-feudal' relations of production in agriculture, such as sharecropping and large estates, and the oppression of women."[42] In 1964 Togliatti outlined an "alternative model of development" wherein worker struggles would be more than economic, emphasizing qualitative changes in investments and production, and focusing on the development of the South and of social services. Togliatti's reasoning was that to prevent stalinism in Italy it was necessary to decentralize power by creating a network of centers of local power and direct democracy.[43] Some of this thinking influenced feminist thinking in the next decade, particularly that of women in Udi.

In the sixties, as socialists formed a coalition government with the Dc, a new sector of the population in Italy (and elsewhere) was coming to the fore—youth. Italian youth gravitated to the left but were impatient with the fruitless results of the Psi coalition with the Dc and also impatient with the Pci and its two-stage strategy of democracy and socialism. Some in the young people's organization of the Pci, the Fgci, emphasized the proletariat as agent of social revolution. Others were critical of the democratic centralism that aligned the party with labor unions, a strategy that was likened to Lenin's view of revolution as seizure of power by a small disciplined vanguard. Some of the young left envisioned institutions of direct democracy: assemblies elected on a territorial basis, factory councils, and decentralized, democratically based communities.[44] Perspectives referring to direct democracy were to be taken up after 1968 by the new left, by left catholics, and by feminists.

Traditional Calabrian woman (ca. 1960)
Photograph by Russell Lee, by courtesy of Russell Lee

Courtesy of siamo in tante . . . , © 1975

Women's roles: baking bread, carrying firewood

Courtesy of noi donne *(Feb. 1979)*

Courtesy of noi donne *(Feb. 1977)*

Courtesy of noidonne *(April 1983)*

Women serving in the church and in a Tuscan home

Two women of Molise, Campobasso
Courtesy of noi donne *(Feb. 1979)*

Le donne d'Italia e la lotta partigiana

"Italian women and the partisan struggle":
Headline from *Noi Donne*, July 1944

Partisan woman
Courtesy of siamo in tante ..., © 1975

Women as breeders of Fascist
soldiers (KKK = Kinder, Küche,
Kirche)
*Caricature by Lydia Sansoni, by courtesy
of effe (April–May 1974)*

Pane, lavoro e pace

Headline from *Noi Donne*, June 1945:
"Bread, work, and peace"

"Recognition or exploitation?" The man is
paid more than the woman for an 8 hour
workday. Then he rests, while she begins a
second 8 hours of household work.
By permission from Noi Donne, *1944–1945*
© *1978 editrice cooperativa libera stampa*

COSTITUIAMO L'UNIONE DELLE DONNE ITALIANE

"We are the Union of Italian Women":
Headline from *Noi Donne*,
October 1944

Udi poster, October 20–30, 1945

"Peace—Liberty—Work: To live not in anguish but in joy—unite with us!": Udi poster, 1949

6

liberazione della donna e degli altri:
segni dei tempi

liberation of women and of others:
signs of the times

The papacy found a ledge of stability in its postwar position of anticommunism, but inside the church there was stirring. Right after the war some worker-priests in France took manual labor jobs, joined communist trade unions, and participated in communist activities in the belief that the place of the church was not with dominant classes but with proletarian workers. The church hierarchy intervened; by 1959 worker-priests were under wraps, but they had attracted world attention. Other currents washed against the rock; protestant theological reform stimulated interest in catholic doctrine. Rudolf Bultmann, the German theologian, encouraged biblical criticism that looked closely at the world in which the new testament was written.

Among some catholics there was anxiety produced by books and plays exposing papal looking-away while nazis killed millions of Jews.

In 1958 Angelo Roncalli became Pope John XXIII and proposed large reforms—an *aggiornamento*—to make the catholic church relevant to the twentieth century. After a few months in office he announced an ecumenical council, the third since the sixteenth century. When vatican council II opened in October 1962, progressives were in the majority; for a brief while, concurrent with the hope aroused by John F. Kennedy, and before a rollback by subsequent popes, the venerable church of catholicism became a beacon of hope to the world. After John XXIII, frightened men in the church hierarchy dampened the implications of John's papacy, but his teaching continued to inspire others and to influence the history of Italian feminism.

John XXIII and women

John advised his bishops that they were to be concerned with all the anxieties that afflict human beings, especially the "most humble, the poorest, the weakest," those in hunger, poverty, and ignorance.[1] The contemporary movements of workers, colonial efforts for independence, and the advancement of women were described by John as "signs of the times."[2] With similar papal iconoclasm, he said that every person, whether believer or nonbeliever, catholic or marxist, is a human being first.[3]

The anomaly of John XXIII in the early sixties is highlighted when his teachings are considered in the context of postwar papal condemnation of communism, and in the context of a church that one catholic historian noted "inveighed against nude arms of women in church while not saying one word in protest against naked Jews forced by nazis to dig their own graves."[4] In a prayer of penance written shortly before he died on June 3, 1963, John XXIII asked forgiveness for not recognizing the "features of our first-born brother" and said that the mark of Cain was "on our forehead" for spilling the blood of "our brother Abel."[5] John encouraged the liberal catholic biblical criticism that refutes two thousand years of christian antisemitism by describing Jesus as a Jewish reformer who never intended to create a new church. Since John's papacy, some catholic theologians have been "dismantling" traditional theology (according to

Thomas Sheehan, who shares this perspective) and have put scriptural scholarship "at the service of a radical thinking of their faith."[6] In contemporary catholic seminaries, for example, "it is now common teaching that Jesus of Nazareth did not assert any of the divine or messianic claims the Gospels attribute to him and that he died without believing he was Christ or the Son of God, not to mention the founder of a new religion."[7]

For women, the great implication of liberal catholic biblical criticism is that it has superseded the theology of the biblical commission of the early twentieth century that "obliged Catholic scholars to hold to the literal and historical truth of the Biblical stories that Eve had been formed from Adam, that the human race had descended from one couple, that ... the devil had tempted the first woman in the form of a snake."[8] Fading in importance, within the theology emerging from liberal biblical criticism, are dogmas regarding the trinity, the founding of the catholic church by Jesus, the infallibility of the pope, and the virgin mother.[9]

After the papacy of John XXIII there continued to be discrimination against women, but the official doctrine of the church, enunciated in the encyclical *Gaudium et spes* of vatican council II, is that discrimination against women is contrary to the design of God. In 1970 the church named two saints, Teresa of Avila and Catherine of Siena, as the first women doctors of theology of the church, but in that same year the papacy objected to the presence in the vatican of a woman lawyer attached to the German embassy.[10]

For John, the advancement of women, the workers' movement, and colonial struggles for independence were all signs of the times because they were alike grounded on awareness of "the same dignity of all human creatures." The advancement of women, according to the 1958 encyclical *Pacem in terris*, was as appropriate in the home as in public life. A French theologian has argued that this encyclical implied the rejection of the patriarchal conception of the family.[11]

For the history of catholicism, John's emphasis on conscience, rather than church doctrine, is significant. In his handwritten copy of the statement, there is a phrase that everyone has the right to worship God according to *coscienza* (conscience). The church cleric who edited the statement changed the wording to "instructed conscience" (reinstating the traditional role of the church in defining correct doctrine).[12] But John's original statement conveys a principle that has historically been associated with religious liberty, with the protestant reformation, and with an antinomian spirit associated with women dissenters. The spirit of freedom of conscience was visible in Italy in the rebellions of 1968, in the emergence of the new left, in left catholicism, and in the Italian feminist movement.

After John, controversial theologians who were teachers of conciliar thought came to the fore: Marie Dominique Chenu, Yves Congar, Edward Schillebeeckx, Hans Küng et al. Theology as the unique prerogative of the church was in a sense taken away from the hierarchy; John said it was the turn of "ordinary christians" to help the church emerge from the corner into which doctrine had placed it.[13] Italian and other feminists were to take up this theological task.

liberation theology and 1968

The revolutionary implications of John's message for some Italians can be seen in the theology of Giulio Girardi, the most widely read liberation theologian in Italy. Girardi's theology was aligned with the movement of christianity from the base (*comunità di base*) in the seventies and eighties that converged with, and supported, feminist issues.[14] From Girardi's point of view, marxist theory was not a critique of God, but a critique of man who calls himself "religious."[15] The message of John and vatican council II, said Girardi, was a central intuition of the gospel: "One does not show faith in heaven except by faith on earth." Conversely, faith in man does not imply refutation of God. Believers and nonbelievers can work toward a civilization that is neither religious nor atheist but "simply human."[16] In a chapter entitled, "philosophy of revolution," Girardi spoke of the "future city" that people of good will aim to construct. Political and economic democracy are the aims of the revolution, yet they are not sufficient, said the liberation theologian, unless these ends are considered within "a system of values in which each man, every man, is considered an end and men together are called to assume initiative for history."

Feminists did not care for Girardi's masculinist pronouns, but they shared his new left belief regarding the insufficiency of a revolution for political and economic democracy unless it is part of a new set of values wherein each and every human being—women as well as men—is called to assume "initiative for history."[17]

Most Italian feminists also shared Girardi's philosophy that movement toward democracy is advancement toward liberation; women widened the meaning of democracy and tested it in personal relationships as well as in political forms. Feminists also agreed with the view of history articulated in Girardi's liberation theology. Evolution toward a future city can be characterized by moments of rupture, "qualitative jumps." The golden age is not in the past, but in the future. Progress does not mean returning to primeval origins, but inheres in a perspective that hopes for "that which has never been" and looks at established truths in an "unedited" manner.[18]

Girardi's stress on an "unedited" interpretation of established truths held protestant overtones of the priesthood of all believers— for catholicism. The unedited perspective also held implications— for the Pci—of an encouragement of different interpretations of marxism. The phrase *inedito* became commonplace in Italy in the seventies and connoted a rejection of intermediaries in religion and politics. For feminists the term connoted a rejection of male definitions of women's concerns and the necessity for each woman to make her own decisions about personal matters like abortion and sexuality as well as other important issues. For most Italians the term *inedito* implied direct democracy, an unwillingness to let anybody else speak for one's self.

Writing in 1968, Girardi said that the dialogue encouraged by John XXIII between catholics and marxists had been fruitful, yet christians saw in socialist countries a rigid antireligious polemic and severe limitations of liberty and marxists considered catholics wedded to social conservatism. In Italy the two camps shared an aversion to the *integrismo* of the other.[19] Christian integralism holds that all values are relative to religious values, that there is no convergence in the profane sphere except in a convergence of religious values. Marxist integralism considers all values essentially relative to socio-economics, and, more precisely, to revolutionary action conducted by the proletarian class and the communist party.[20] In christian as well as marxist integralism, there is the implication of unity imposed from above—overriding the differences, or pluralism, of a free society. The Italian emphasis on "unedited" interpretations of marxism and of the gospel are particularly important for feminists, and for the libertarian, self-managed socialism they envision.

In the book he wrote in 1968 as the Soviets were invading Czechoslovakia to suppress an experiment in Czech socialism, as the U.S. war in Vietnam was reaching a crescendo, and as young men and women were demonstrating all over Italy, Girardi said that liberty is conditioned by economic freedom, but it can not be reduced to this. Economic liberation, although facilitating the solution of other problems of humanity, will not resolve them automatically. There will remain, above all, "the problem of the sense of life and of death, of suffering and of solitude."[21]

In the perspective of Italian liberation theology in 1968, capitalism was regarded as an unjust and violent political economy; there was simultaneous revulsion against soviet action in Czechoslovakia and awareness that "even graver alienation" was engendered by "existing socialist states." The key to a good society, for Italian believers of this genre, was a synthesis of socialism and democracy.[22] By 1969 when the book was published, with Italy's work force locked into massive strikes, Girardi said that matters had gone beyond dialogue. For christians, the choice was reform or revolution. For the left, said the theologian, the choice was monolithic or pluralistic socialism, authoritarian or democratic values.[23] Over the next decade and a half, feminists were to help make these choices.

social and economic signs of the times

The environment into which these ideas fell was a country undergoing rapid change. Italy in 1968 was an advanced industrial society, but one that differed from other nations of the west. As several analysts have noted, the "differences are so sharp that the resemblance between the Italian system and that of the principal European countries becomes problematic."[24] In the sixties Italy experienced "intense yet unbalanced modernization" while politicians worked to secure equilibrium: by the end of the decade, revolutionary upheaval, not equilibrium, was at hand.

The center-right, from peasants to middle-class employees, constituted the support for the Dc, a party that represented the interests of large business and the managerial class of Italy's numerous public and semipublic enterprises. The left was comprised of the organized working class (in the unions) and large sectors of the middle class, white-collar workers, and intellectuals. In the sixties, the Pci was in opposition to the majority party, the Dc, while the Psi, the socialist party, attempted to work for planning and a more equitable distribution of income in a center-left coalition with the Dc. By 1968 the young left considered this coalition a failure.

Contradictions of the Italian system were highlighted in the sixties by the changing nature of the "southern problem" as hundreds of thousands migrated from the impoverished South to the industrialized cities of the North. From 1951 to 1968 the per capita income of Italians expanded two and a half times, but in the South the per capita income was lower than the national average. As to economic inequality, Italy in the sixties maintained a level of inequality similar to that of the United States.[25] Economic development in Italy favored the middle classes. Mobility was characterized by large waves of migration from the country to the towns, from the South to the North, and from Italy to other countries of Europe. Improvement in highways, postal services, and media enhanced the environment of a highly mobile society. In the two decades after 1950 there was an increase in the school population and a sharp increase in political participation.

Anthropologists studying the transformation of the traditional society of the South (as well as of old centers of the agrarian economy and earlier pockets of northern industrial capitalism) found cultural residues in these more traditional regions which they considered understandable as forms of economic and cultural marginality "or as methods of self-defense in a substantially modernized context."[26] The path of modernization in Italy began in the northwest in the 1880s, spread to the northeast and the center after the second world war, and formed the basis for the advanced industrial economy of the North. This advanced society, with large private and public bureaucracies, contrasted with traditional societies of the South (and pockets of the North) where farm workers still battled with landowners for traditional agricultural contracts.[27] Advanced classes were represented by high-level managers (in private as well as public enterprises). The intellectual class had evolved from the clergy to teachers, professors, journalists, writers, and artists. The role of politicians grew as Italy, under the center-left coalition of the sixties, became a welfare state.

Italy edged toward crisis at the end of the sixties as the difference between North and South grew, a difference expressed in the dichotomies of development/underdevelopment, advanced/backward, tradition/modernity. Yet this picture of a divided Italy, North and South, requires an overlay showing the migration of the middle class of the South to the North to staff bureaucracies, and (as had happened throughout modern Italian history) the journey of exceptional southerners—Antonio Gramsci, Enrico Berlinguer, Aldo Moro—to the North to become major leaders.

A partial explanation of the anomalous nature of contemporary Italy lies in this combination of development and underdevelopment, of modern and traditional values, a society that is at once agricultural, industrial, and postindustrial. While the South was for a long time after unification almost a colonial dependency of the North (supplying the underdeveloped region with industrial products to consume in exchange for southern labor),[28] it was the infiltration of southerners into the North that may have contributed one of the volatile factors of the period after 1968.

By 1972 farming accounted for only 10 percent of the Italian gross national product and "backwardness, unemployment, illiteracy, a high infant mortality rate" remained characteristic of the South.[29] More people lived in towns than could find employment. Women and youth had particularly high unemployment rates. In terms of class structure, some sociologists saw the emergence of a significant lumpenproletariat in the cities, referring especially to people in or from the South who found employment only intermittently.

Analysts of Italian class structure tentatively agreed in the seventies on a schema wherein an upper stratum was comprised of landowners, financiers, industrial managers, professionals, heads of governmental bureaucracies, leading scientists, intellectuals, and political leaders and an upper middle stratum composed of the less affluent bourgeoisie and office workers. The lower middle stratum was made up of industrial and agricultural workers. The lowest stratum consisted of the lumpenproletariat who were outside the bounds of Italy's capitalist technostructure and who often held southern (or other regional peasant) traditional attitudes. Some sociologists in the sixties and seventies placed housewives in the lumpenproletariat. Others with only spasmodic employment who were also consigned to this nether region of traditional marxist analysis were jobless students and old people, groups whose shared characteristic was that they were economically marginal.

According to Sabino Acquaviva, a highly regarded Italian sociologist, the "social bombshell" of 1968 and thereafter "exploded in the midst of university students and intellectuals." Shock waves spread to younger students and to workers, and then affected other groups and social strata, extending, according to Acquaviva, "to the *lumpen-proletarian* element and to women, embracing them in the militant feminist movements." [30]

Pasolini and the new urban marginal class

The life and writings of Pier Paolo Pasolini illuminate some of the meaning of the new marginal classes whom sociologists called the lumpenproletariat, as well as the empathy of many Italians toward these marginal people. A northerner with a Jewish great-grandmother, Pasolini arrived at antifascism by way of a fascist father and a mother who loved her son inordinately, a love the son passionately reciprocated. The father was confronted with a wife and son whose ideas opposed established views—a pattern that may be said to characterize Italy after 1968. When a daughter is added to this pattern, one can glimpse some of the psychodynamics of the feminist upheaval.

As a young writer, Pasolini described the Friulian peasantry of his childhood as a world of uncorrupted christianity and innocence. [31] Hidden meanings in peasant dialect intrigued him. His biographer, Enzo Siciliano, sees in Pasolini's early writings a precursor of Italian neorealism, which in the novels and film of the *dopoguerra* focused on the marginal people of Italy.

Pasolini was attracted to the catholic beliefs of simple people—beliefs, he felt, that had "nothing to do with Rome or the glory of the Church"—beliefs that could be found in peasant pockets of Italy. Not only in Sicily, Sardinia, and the *mezzogiorno* (the land of the noonday sun, south of Rome), Pasolini pointed out, but in the North as well these beliefs could be found; for example, they could be seen in "the entire lower Po valley." [32]

Pasolini had joined the Italian resistance, which he described as "pure light" and "the hope for justice," and enrolled in the Pci during the war. [33] An atypical marxist for his time, he believed that reason could not be separated from feeling. His marxist beliefs, he said, presupposed "some idealism, some Catholicism, some anarchy, some humanitarianism, but also life and the will for renewal." [34] Pasolini knew his ideas to be "different," he felt himself, as a homosexual, to be "different," and he sensed a kinship with peasants who dreamed of social regeneration, yet hid the dream as if it were something "shameful." [35] In 1950 Pasolini was tried and acquitted of the charge of corrupting minors but was convicted of "lewd acts." He was absolved for insufficient evidence, but regional and local units of the Pci expelled him from the party for "deviationism" derived from reading "bourgeois and decadent" writers. He responded: "I am and will remain a Communist."

Cast out of the party, he considered himself in exile, living in the "land of others." [36] He went to live in Rome and began to write about the street boys, or *ragazzi di vita*, of Trastevere, whose hustle for survival included selling their bodies. For Pasolini the hope of revolution lay in the despised, the marginal, like these *ragazzi di vita*, perhaps in carrying Saint Francis' kiss on the lips of lepers to an embrace of the despised. [37] As a critic, Pasolini simultaneously looked for a new literature and a renewal of marxist ideology. He wrote a poem entitled "The Ashes of Gramsci," in which his biographer finds a demand for a new individual morality grounded on criticism ("as a christian and a catholic") of "a dramatic deficiency within the ideology of the left." [38] For the film *La dolce vita*, Pasolini showed the film's director, Fellini, the underside of Roman life, the territory of the "periphery." In *Il bell'Antonio*, a film of southern life, Pasolini conveyed "the heartbreak resulting from the absence of love." [39] He collaborated as a writer for the film *Accattone*, which depicted the people whom sociologists called the lumpenproletariat in a manner that evoked intense empathy in the audience. This film has been called protest that is simultaneously political, religious, and existential: "The world of the Roman shantytowns, the world of the subproletarian poor, is now that of the *finis historiae*, an apocalypse of the spirit." For Pasolini, the destiny of the southern Italian subproletariat was the same as that of peasants of the third world in Africa, Asia, and Latin America. [40]

While writing the scenario for his film *The Gospel According to Saint Matthew*, Pasolini called himself an anticlerical "defender of two thousand years of Christianity," but at the film presentation he described himself as an "atheist," prompting Mario Soldati, in his review of the film, to point out Pasolini's contradictions. According to Pasolini's biographer, Enzo Siciliano, it is impossible to "understand the motivations, not only individual but objective, that led to the realization of a film, like the 'Gospel ... ' without the environment created by Pope John XXIII and Vatican Council II."[41]

It may also be impossible to understand some of the contradictions of Italian feminists without understanding the impact of Pasolini on a generation of Italians. He was murdered in 1975.[42]

part two an Italian
feminist movement

7

sessantotto

1968

revolutionary contours

Contemporary Italian feminists emerged in the new left explosion of 1968. With the attraction of the young to the Chinese cultural revolution and the stimulation of the Frankfurt school of sociology (particularly Herbert Marcuse's critique of one-dimensional man), watchwords of the new spirit were spontaneity, direct democracy, quality of life, and identification with peoples of the third world.

The democratic centralist structure of the Pci was a major target of the new left. Although it was regarded by the party as a framework for circulating opinion from the base to the central committee and back again, critics saw hypocrisy in what in effect turned out to be undemocratic discouragement of dissenting views. Women, for the most part, were not consulted at all. The new left also criticized what they considered an "economistic" interpretation of marxist theory, a focus that for left catholics and the young new left excluded significant concerns in the passionate environment of 1968.

The new left across the world in 1968 considered formal democracy a façade, with its primary exponent, the United States, napalming Vietnamese peasants to carry out a democratic policy of containing communism. The soviet system was seen for what it was—a large socialist country invading a small one to suppress a Czech attempt to create its own socialism. The Pci, still aligned with the soviets, was vulnerable. Although the Pci disassociated itself from the aggression of the USSR in Czechoslovakia—calling the invasion contrary to the principle of autonomy of every communist party and of every socialist state—a dissenting group within the party issued a manifesto criticizing the "contradictions" and "reformism" of the Pci.

When the dissenters formed a group called Utopia and promulgated a critique of soviet and East European socialism, the Pci "radiated" them out of the party (radiating was a step short of expulsion, allowing the possibility of reentry later). This new left group founded the periodical (later the newspaper) *il manifesto*. Identifying with new left extraparliamentary groups, dissenters subsequently formed an autonomous communist party, Partito di unità proletaria per il comunismo (Pdup), generating, a few years later, a splinter democratic proletarian party, Democrazia proletaria (Dp).[1] These independent communist parties were important as friendly critics and supporters of feminists in the seventies and eighties.

feminist manifestos, 1968–72

Italian feminism incubated in the environment of *sessantotto* and the emergence of an Italian new left. Like feminists elsewhere, many women participated in student and worker demonstrations but felt marginal. In the large strikes (involving five million workers) of the "hot autumn" of 1969, women participated, but men made the strike decisions. Extraparliamentary new left worker groups (potere operaia, lotta continua et al.) split away from the large labor confederations, but most feminists felt these extraparliamentary groups were as male-dominated as the traditional left and were identified, furthermore, with an implicit violent strategy of revolution.

Another front in the rebellion became evident after 1968 when hundreds of women began to celebrate international women's day, March 8, with banners declaring: "Non c'è rivoluzione senza liberazione della donna. Non c'è liberazione della donna senza rivoluzione." (There is no revolution without liberation of women. There is no liberation of women without revolution.) The cultural dimension of women's rebellion was suggested in another banner: "Tremate! tremate! Le streghe son tornate!" (Tremble! tremble! The witches have returned!). The slogan provoked laughter, but there were serious theological and political implications in feminists identifying with women who had been persecuted, often burned, by church and state for holding convictions contrary to accepted religious and political doctrine.[2]

After 1968 women's collectives formed, at first in the North, by 1972 in the South. These institutions of participatory democracy were called groups for *l'autocoscienza* (self-knowledge). Called consciousness-raising groups elsewhere, in Italy these were nonmediated gatherings of women who explored female identity and the roots of women's subordination. Themes of the collectives varied. In Milan feminists advocated separatism, other groups coalesced around wages for housewives. Le nemesiache (named after Nemesis, goddess of retributive justice) of Naples concentrated on feminist creativity. The Roman collective Pompeo magno (feminists often named groups after their neighborhoods) developed revolutionary social theory. All tried to reconcile the problem of *doppia militanza*, the double militancy required in reconciling politics (immediately branded as "masculine") and feminism. Some women left the parties, others joined, in a maelstrom of activism that stirred tumult within the parties and inspired the founding of a feminist theater and feminist bookstores, periodicals, publishing houses, and radio stations.

The only clear message of feminist manifestos, slogans, and shouting of the early seventies was that some women were enraged. Anna Riva has sorted through boxes of feminist leaflets and banners to find the main themes of feminist rage. A banner carried in many feminist demonstrations declared:

Siamo donne (We are women)
siamo tante (we are many)
siamo stufe (we have had it)
tutte quante (all of us)[3]

In the early period, 1968 to 1972, feminists numbered maybe a few thousand in each major Italian city. They felt they were speaking for all women; more precisely they were speaking for urban women closer to the "world of communism" than to the "world of catholicism." The history of the next decade and a half may be regarded as the expansion and evolution of these feminist demonstrations into a women's movement.

Riva noticed phrases feminists used repetitively: "opposition," "demystification of authority," "autonomy of women." The word *liberation*, she found, held many meanings, most often it held the connotation of freedom from "patriarchal and bourgeois ideology" in which women were considered sexual objects and objects of consumption of material items. The word *culture* was employed in rejection of patriarchal, bourgeois, and masculinist culture and in affirmation of a "new way to make culture with self-determination and self-management of women."[4]

Most of the themes involved rejecting authority, including the delegated authority of representative democracy. Delegated representation in masculinist institutions was interpreted as "subordination." The topic of abortion caused rage to boil over: "If men gave birth, abortion would be a sacrament." With a style that shocked bystanders, feminists adopted the directness and pungency of peasant women: "L'utero è mio e me lo gestisco io" (It is my uterus and I will manage it).[5]

Dario Fo's 1970 play, *Accidental Death of an Anarchist*, captures the environment of early feminist manifestos, with Italy become a theatre in which the line between reality and the imagination is blurred. Fo's play refers to a 1969 bombing in Milan (later found to be perpetrated by right-wing terrorists) followed by a roundup of leftists and the suspicious death (a fall from a window) during the police investigation of an anarchist accused of involvement in the bombings. Fo's play suggests not only the madness of people in power, but the complicity in madness of everyone.[6]

Feminist outbursts had the quality of a subterranean eruption, stunning some women into incomprehension at first. To some women in the Pci and Udi, some of the manifestos seemed anticommunist. Lidia Menapace, a new left dissenter herself, was at first confounded and concerned that feminists of the United States had influenced Italian feminists toward what she considered an unhealthy preoccupation solely with personal emancipation. It would take older women of the left a while to recognize that feminists were expressing left-wing rage: "Le donne proletarie escono dalle cucine/ fascisti, padroni, per voi sarà la fine" ("Proletarian women are coming out of the kitchen/ fascists, bosses, this will be your end.")[7]

It was a rage on the left that assaulted established left doctrine: "Mettiamo in discussione il socialismo e la dittatura del proletariato" ("We are opening a discussion of socialism and challenging the concept of the dictatorship of the proletariat" [Carla Lonzi, *Sputiamo su Hegel. La donna clitoridea e la donna vaginale e altri scritti, di Rivolta femminile* (Milan, 1974), p. 17]). Subsequent citations in parentheses are to this work. These writings were circulated in the streets of Milan and Rome in mimeographed form in 1970). Feminists challenged the dogmatism, rationalism, and the *integrismo* of the left: "*Rispetto del diverso e poi eliminazione del concetto di diverso: tutti sono diversi*" (Respect for difference and then elimination of the concept of difference: everybody is different). (P. 17.)

Early feminists suggested an epistemology to replace marxist rationalism. "Coinvolgimento dell'altro"—involvement in others—was not a matter of reason, but of emotion, of caring.[8] Some Italian communist philosophers in the eighties would give up the traditional marxist philosophic pose of rationalist objectivity and state that "one knows anything only by participating in the phenomenon."[9]

Early Italian feminist manifestos are better understood when placed in the context of women (with husbands, lovers, and sons in communist and socialist parties and in the labor unions to which the parties were affiliated) watching men seem to push toward a revolution for which women had not been consulted, provoking right-wing violence that killed bystanders. Neither in the parties nor in the labor unions did women hold decision-making power over tactics or strategy for the massive strikes and demonstrations of 1969–70 that were punctuated with violence. The violence was initiated by the right in the bombing in Milan in 1969 and by the left (in this early period) in confrontations with the police.

Were early feminist manifestos heard? Reasoned responses to early feminist charges are difficult to find, but it should be noted that a divorce law that had weltered for one hundred years was passed in a midnight parliamentary session in 1970, that a nursery school law, a repeal of a prohibition on birth control information, and a protective law for working mothers were passed shortly thereafter.[10]

In effect, early feminists formed their own contingents in the revolutionary melee. Early slogans made it apparent that their revolution held cultural implications: "Marriage is an institution that subordinates women to male destiny" (p. 12). Feminists said they were "against marriage" because they had "too much respect for life" (p. 13) and they were "tired of rearing sons who will become bad lovers" (p. 13). In their view, joint political action, like marriage, subordinated women to male policies. Men in the unions and in the party were working for a "hypothetical revolution" (p. 16) because equality of wages was an inadequate goal for women, who have, in addition to work outside, domestic work in the home (p. 15). Polemical feminists did not want to be associated with male strategies because "war has always been the specific activity of men and their model of virile behavior" (p. 15). Men and women have different views of culture, said feminists; men derive their strength identifying with culture; "our strength is in refuting culture" (p. 17). "We spit on Hegel" (p. 17). The major cultural institution in Italy was the church, whose doctrines, said feminists, "identified women with sex" (p. 16) and whose presiding pope in 1968, Paul VI, in condemning contraception seemed to be reversing conciliar advances for women.

As in all war zones, there was more confusion than clarity. Feminist manifestos sent messages to men, to sisters on the outside, and to themselves. Sisters outside the war zone were advised "there is no liberation of women without revolution." What was the revolution Italian feminists wanted? For early (and later) Italian feminists it was "obvious" that a necessary revolution was the one "against capital." A signal difference from other feminist movements is the dislike of capitalism: "We detest mechanisms of competition and the hegemony of the cult of efficiency" (p. 15). In messages to themselves, feminists said, "Almost the totality of Italian feminists gives more credit to the class struggle than to their own oppression" (p. 8). Subordinating women's concerns to the class struggle meant in effect subordinating women's issues to male purposes: "No human being and no group can be defined by another" (p. 22).

Women's strategy had to be devised by women, early manifestos declared, because women's problems were not solved by equality nor by revolution, although these were proximate steps. The central point was that women viewed the world differently than did men. Italian feminists early enunciated a utopian vision: a world in which "terrorists throw away arms and abuse gives way to respect for the variety and multiplicity of life" (p. 21).

Equality, said early feminists, was a juridical principle. Difference refers to the existential fact that women have for millennia been excluded from history. Let us profit by this difference: "The world of equality is a uni-dimensional world" (p. 21). Turning toward church doctrine regarding marriage, feminists said that "the myth of complementarity has been used by men to justify their own power" (p. 12). Traditional church virtues for women were analyzed: "Virginity, chastity, fidelity are not virtues, but chains to maintain the family" (p. 12). Addressing conventional marxists, feminists charged that "in contemporary communist countries, the socialization of the means of production has not changed the traditional family, indeed it has re-enforced it" (p. 32). As for the main adversary—the men of the Dc who invoked the family to sustain anticommunism and pejorative views of women—feminists declared: "The family is the capstone of the patriarchal system, founded not only on economic interest but also on the psychological needs of men, who in each epoch have held women as an object of domination and as a footstool" (p. 33). Abolition of the family "does not mean communality of women, but the liberation of one part of humanity" (p. 33).

Patriarchalism, feminists felt, was not only characteristic of past and present culture but also implicit in the future society projected by marxist-leninist revolutionary ideology. From this feminist perspective, when women emphasized the class struggle more than their own oppression (i.e., letting men of the Pci, men in the labor unions, and men in the extraparliamentary left make revolutionary decisions) women could be hastening the coming of a new society that would perpetuate women's oppression. Women's consciousness groups, they felt, could ensure that women's efforts for liberation would not be self-defeating. In these small women's groups, major marxist-leninist premises were placed into question, including the concept of vanguard leadership of the party aligned with industrial workers as the way to socialism, violence as a revolutionary tactic, the dictatorship of the proletariat, and the nature of power.

The ideological quarrel was with *marxismo-leninismo*. "Woman is oppressed as woman at all social levels: not at the level of class, but of sex" (p. 24). Woman's exploitation has been hidden in her unpaid work inside the family. By assigning the revolutionary future to industrial workers, "marxism has ignored woman as oppressed and as carrier of the future; it has expressed a revolutionary theory in the matrix of a patriarchal culture" (p. 24). The hope lay in women who refused the patriarchal family and in young men who refused to go to war (p. 28). For Italian feminists, the leninist concept of the dictatorship of the proletariat had been shown to be invalid for changing values insofar as it was violent, and in countries of "existing socialism" it perpetuated the traditional patriarchal form of the family (p. 32). A necessary revolution, said feminists, included a change in the relationships of the sexes, a revolution considerably more thoroughgoing than that projected by Lenin, who said women would be liberated when freed from "unproductive" domestic work so that they could engage in "productive" work outside the home. In the next decade and a half Italian feminists refuted this leninist interpretation of women's work by demanding wages for housewives.[11]

Implicit in feminist writings of this early period is a quarrel with the fathers, not with the sons and daughters. With the young there was an unavowed alliance and something of an Italian mother's reprimanding a son for wrongheadedness, and wrongdoing. A new social morality was suggested: "Man as a species expresses himself killing, women as a species expresses herself working and protecting life" (p. 51). In the family morality of feminists, "we do not give our children to anyone, neither to man nor to the state. We give them to themselves and restore us to ourselves" (p. 52).

Feminists spoke of the dialectic of gender differences generating momentum; this was more than thesis-antithesis-synthesis. A familiar Italian feminist phrase referred to "putting the men into crisis" by adopting tactics of separatism, an Italian version of female/male contestation. Most feminists believed in "jumps" in history. In the early period of the movement, they spoke of the necessity "to move the struggle to a higher level" (p. 54).

Most women on the sidelines gathered that behind feminist shouting was not condemnation but a compassionate view of a tangled situation. Corruption in democracy could be seen, said feminists, in capitalist and communist forms and would continue until women, and others, exercised self-management. "Men are involved in themselves, in their past, in their culture; "reality seems exhausted for them: the voyages into space are proof of this" (p. 57). Women's vision was different: we are willing to look at "the dark past of the world" in order to "affirm that life must yet begin on our small planet" (p. 57). "We are the dark past of the world, we realize the present" (p. 61).

In the dark past of Italian women was the large number of dangerous, clandestine abortions. In 1971 between one and three million abortions were performed, in the face of a law that defined abortion as a crime. Abortion was to become the major issue of Italian feminists in the next decade. A referendum to repeal the punitive abortion law was launched in 1971 by Movimento di liberazione della donna (Mld), an umbrella organization of Roman feminists.

The nuances of the abortion issue were soon to be lost in political agitation, but its complexity was suggested in early feminist writings. Feminists wanted to make their own decisions about sexuality and motherhood. Women abort because they become pregnant. How do they become pregnant? "For whose pleasure am I aborting?" Early feminists put the abortion issue in a long perspective. Let us think, said Carla Lonzi, about "a civilization in which freedom of sexuality is not apotheosized in free abortion. In this civilization it would be clear that abortion is not a solution for the free woman, but for the woman colonized in the patriarchal system" (p. 75).

Early (and later) Italian feminists did not take the easy path of blaming all on men. Women, they felt, had to find their own way, at first by searching for resonance in other women. This was a path women had to take alone with other women—"not because men are to be excluded"—but in recognition that men have their own problems, notably their inability to see women in other than the traditional patriarchal context (p. 147).[12]

8

femminismo e rivoluzione

feminist cultural and political revolution

Italian feminists proposed from the beginning to work for a revolution that was both cultural and political. Implicit in the term *cultural* was the role of women in catholicism and in left political parties, particularly the Pci. The word was also used to refer to the values women hoped to discover in themselves in groups of *autocoscienza* and, after 1975, by recovering their history.

Feminist issues, particularly divorce and abortion, collided directly with doctrinal catholicism and upset the strategic priorities of the left, yet the years after 1968 are a halcyon period for feminist successes. Why this happened is a tangled story of women asserting their autonomy after 1968 in Italy's pluralist political environment, throwing their manifestos into the maelstrom of an ongoing cultural revolution. This cultural revolution is analyzed in subsequent chapters on feminists and left catholicism, unedited marxism, and peace consciousness. A significant aspect of the feminist cultural revolution was adoption of the metaphor of *other* and the theme of differences, a metaphor and a theme that reached many women and that changed feminists themselves. In this chapter the concentration is on the environment of the seventies, the interplay of politics and feminist issues, an attempt to measure the feminist phenomenon, and an effort to understand the women who were feminist communists.

the environment of feminist successes

Italy's ambience following the confrontations of 1968 and the subsequent season of five million workers on strike was disturbing to some but exhilarating to others. In the seventies, Italy ranked seventh among the world's industrial powers. The country also held the highest strike record of Europe, a very high wage level, and very strong labor unions protected by a 1970 statute of workers' rights. Worker political activism was encouraged by the statute that forbade companies from maintaining employee records of political affiliation and guaranteed freedom of assembly and speech on the shop floor. In the seventies Italian unions negotiated workplace wage agreements that included social goals: education of workers in "150-hour classes," health care, rent control, housing, and pensions.[1]

Feminist political successes in the decade and a half following 1968 included:

repeal of punitive law against unfaithful wives (1968)
divorce law (1970)
nursery schools legislation (1971)
repeal of law forbidding birth control information (1971)
protective legislation for working mothers (1971)
referendum campaign to repeal punitive abortion law (1971)
protective legislation for women in cottage industry (1973)
defeat of referendum to repeal divorce law (1974)
court decision declaring constitutionality of therapeutic abortions
    (1975)
law for family health clinics with provision for birth control counseling (1975)
maternity and infant legislation (1975)
law clarifying equal family rights (1975)

house approval of bill on abortion (1977)

law clarifying equal pay and equal treatment of male and female workers (1977)

law legalizing abortion (1978)

referendum campaign for law against sexual violence (1979)

300,000 referendum signatures for law against sexual violence presented to parliament (1980)

defeat of referendum to repeal the abortion law (1981)[2]

Feminists achieved legislative and other victories by adopting cultural as well as political tactics and strategies. The chief periodical of feminism in the early seventies, *effe* (the letter *f*, for *femminista*), secured attention by breaking conventional cultural canons with bold graphics and discussion of previously taboo subjects. Feminist political conferences became festivals: the 1971 *festa della mamma per una maternità libera* (mother's festival for "free motherhood") emphasized women's choice to become mothers—or not. In conferences such as the 1972 meeting at Padua on wages for housewives, cultural and political issues were combined in revising marxist theory. Udi successfully used its political skills in support of laws for divorce, nursery schools, and family rights. Subsequently Udi worked for legal abortion and a referendum and law against sexual violence—earlier considered cultural, not political, issues. Using parliamentary means and direct action, Udi negotiated politically while mounting large demonstrations; *Noi Donne* was turned toward publicity and education for feminist concerns. Udi (and the Pci) initiated annual festivals for women, *feste della donna*, that combined entertainment, serious politics, displays of women's cultural interests, and play areas for children. If *effe*, the cultural feminist periodical subsidized by Psi, caught people's attention with its boldness, *feste della donna*, sponsored by Pci, invited people to a celebration—where women presented their issues, men of the party did the cooking, and others were invited to dance. If the constituencies of political parties were thereby enlarged, so was the audience for feminists.

Cultural feminists outside the parties took the lead in promoting feminist issues and a network of women's *collettivi* throughout Italy sustained the theme of women's autonomy. Demonstrations splashed women's issues into the newspapers and feminists persuasively explained issues in a variety of ways. Only a minority of Italy's twenty-seven million women walked in feminist demonstrations, but they drew the attention of a wide audience. According to figures in the journal of feminist communists, *donne e politica*, there were fifty thousand women in the 1975 demonstration for the equal family rights law, twenty thousand in that of 1975 for legal abortion, five thousand in the 1976 protest against the insistence of Dc and Msi (Italy's small fascist party) that abortion was a crime. In 1976 simultaneous demonstrations throughout Italy with the theme "Let's take back the night" involved an unestimated number of women. (This phrase had several layers of meaning. One was opposition to sexual violence. Another suggested the strategy portrayed in the ancient Greek play *Lysistrata*—women withholding sex as a lever of persuasion.) Fifty thousand demonstrated at Rome in 1977 for the legal abortion law, as did an equal number at Rome in 1981 for its retention, with countless similar demonstrations throughout Italy. Fifty thousand women in front of parliament protested Dc mutilation of the sexual violence bill in 1983. The numbers of women in scores of other feminist protests and manifestations, notably the one against terrorism in 1978, remain unestimated.

Organizing for demonstrations and legislation was early propelled by the Mld, the feminist network of a myriad of "autonomous" feminist collectives, and by Udi, the women's union associated with the Pci. *Piccoli gruppi* (little groups) who called themselves *femminista-comunista* pointed to a problem of priorities that the Italian women's movement was continually to confront in the seventies and to try to resolve in the eighties. Groups wrote position papers identifying themselves by locality ("collettivo femminista milanese," "collettivo femminista di Torino," "gruppo femminista gelese," "collettivo femminista bolognese" et al.). Early on, city collectives decentralized into neighborhood groups ("collettivo femminista milanese via Cherubini, 8"). Others coalesced by priority ("movimento per la liberazione della donna autonomo") or by cultural identification ("nucleo romano di collegamento fra le donne su 'questione femminile, questione cattolica'"), or by special concern ("gruppo femminista 'per una medicina della donna'"). Then there were women's groups inside the political parties, notably Udi in the Pci, but also women's units in Pr, Pdup, Psi, and Dc and women's sectors in extraparliamentary

formations such as lotta continua and avanguardia operaia. Important feminist groups of the seventies addressed themselves specifically to abortion and to women's health clinics (like Crac [centro
romano contraccezione aborto]). In addition there were women's
networks in the labor unions, women in catholic organizations who
were listening intently, and an uncalculated number of women
throughout the country who organized in schools, neighborhoods,
and at the workplace.

Women's militance was important but the political environment in
which women acted was critical to feminist successes. Italy's pluralist
competition of many parties, the pivotal significance of a libertarian
party (Pr) that early espoused feminist issues, lay parties that stressed
individual rights, the soft center of women inside the dominant
party—the Dc, and the entry into the Pci after 1968 of many
women and young people helped to put the women's legislation that
has been called the most advanced of Europe into the Italian code.[3]

political parties and feminist issues

Of the parties that are significant for feminist issues, farthest right
is the neofascist Msi whose attitudes toward women echo those of
the fascist era. *Missini* are opposed to anything that disturbs their
conception of the traditional family and traditional Italy. They are
for the church, the army, law and order, and a strong centralized
state; they are opposed to divorce, abortion, laws against sexual violence, "permissiveness," and the behavior of the young.

Msi patriarchal attitudes toward women are probably shared by
more Italians than the 9 percent of the electorate whose votes the
neofascist party secures. There is a reluctance to admit publicly to
fascist ideas, or to acknowledge today that one had been fascist. One
man I interviewed said he had become a fascist when, as a returning
soldier after the first world war, he had been spat upon by socialists.
This former colonel in Mussolini's army does not vote for the Msi
today, his party is the Pri—the small republican party representing
industry, planning, internationalism, and secular attitudes. In a
milder form, some of this man's behavior recalls his earlier affiliation;
walking with him in the park I watched him oust a young couple from
a bench where they were kissing. At home he is paternalistic toward

his wife; in my interviews with her, she said she had been a socialist for fifty years. When one of her husband's cronies telephoned for the "colonel," she responded with the sabotage she has practiced for half a century: "There is no colonel here."

Women in the neofascist Msi were invited by Pci women to the *festa della donna* at Palermo in 1979. Msi women I interviewed at this festival wanted to discuss a newspaper article in which I had suggested there was a continuum from the nurturant characteristics of earth mothers to bonds between godmothers of traditional Italian culture to concerns of contemporary Italian feminists. Women of the Msi waved to me and my feminist companions at the Udi-Pci event.

The arch adversary of most Italian feminists is the center party of political catholicism, the Dc. In the seventies this party enjoyed "a longer period of unbroken political dominance than any other democratic party in the world."[4] From 1948 to 1970 it had won electoral pluralities, provided all but three prime ministers, controlled the appointments to the civil service, state industries, banks, and public bodies; the party entered the decade, as a recent U. S. analyst concludes, "a great popular political success."[5] This success, according to Frederic Spotts, can be attributed to effective use of the fear of communism and to the Dc's relationships with the United States and with the papacy; bolstered by the support of the former, Dc success was facilitated by the network of church associations of the latter. Since 1948 the Dc had opposed women's issues with campaign slogans claiming that the party protected *la famiglia cristiana* against "communist" ideas on divorce, abortion, and prohibition of sexual violence. Dc campaigns relied on symbols—for example, a poster attacking the divorce law featured a snapshot of a family being ripped apart by the law. On feminist issues the Dc was often close to the neofascist Msi; both defined abortion in 1976 (as had fascist legislation) as a "crime," both worked in the eighties to cripple the sexual violence bill in parliament. One advantage to Italian feminists in the seventies and eighties was remembrance of the fascist era—when women's subordination, as was analyzed in chapter 3, was made very clear.

Dc hegemony was threatened for the first time since 1945 when its 1974 referendum to repeal the divorce law was defeated. Thereafter the Dc continued to oppose feminist concerns but it became implicit party policy not to speak about feminist issues publicly, letting the vatican and the antiabortion "right to life" movement take the brunt of feminist criticism.

In the late seventies the Dc was preoccupied with a cat's paw game it played with the Pci. By 1976 the Pci had gained electorally (largely due to the vote of women and youth) to the point the Dc could not govern without communist support; in the election of that year, the two parties took 75 percent of the parliamentary seats. In spite of the party's public rhetoric of anticommunism, the Dc acknowledged privately that the Pci was not a leninist organization and that it was independent of Moscow.[6] Aldo Moro, who had brought the Dc and the Psi together in coalition in the early sixties, strove in the seventies for a working alliance of the Dc and Pci. Giulio Andreotti, a leader of the Dc, engineered two governments after 1976 based on an accord with the Pci. According to a contemporary analyst of the "historic compromise," the working arrangement between the two parties "was a bravura performance"; the christian democrats used the communist party "simultaneously as a bogeyman to frighten voters and as a partner to guarantee the country's governability."[7] In 1979 the Pci, responding in part to the hostility of the new left and of many feminists to this equivocal arrangement, broke off the accord with the Dc.

The electoral strength of feminist issues was evident to women, if not to men, in the 1974 defeat of the referendum to repeal the divorce law and in 1975 when the Dc lost control of most municipal and regional governments. Subsequently there were other blows to Dc hegemony, notably the kidnapping and murder of Aldo Moro by left terrorists on the day in 1978 he was to establish a government supported by communists. Later there was the P2 scandal implicating the Dc (and all parties but the Pci) in an ambiguous network of conspiracy and corruption. Another, largely unacknowledged, wound was the resistance, or secession, of the women of this party which claims the highest number of female constituents. The thinking of women in the Dc (in its women's auxiliary, Cif) is closely examined in chapter 13. Women in the Dc whom I have interviewed were eager not to seem antifeminist and offered examples of their up-to-date thinking. Sticking points before 1981 and 1982 (when these criticisms were met by changes in the Pci and in Udi), were the soviet connection of the Pci and the auxiliary relationship of Udi to the Pci. Dc women emphasize the moral implications of the abortion issue (as do most Italian women) but the Dc women I interviewed were uncomfortable about criminalizing abortion, thereby forcing a desperate woman to have a life-threatening illegal abortion.

Political analyses based on the truism that Italian women like the party of the church have not given sufficient valence to the changing nature of catholic beliefs after John XXIII. The modification of catholic beliefs is shown in the erosion of Dc support in strategically located catholic organizations: Fuci (university graduates movement), Acli (the catholic workers association), Cisl (the catholic trade union), and Cif (catholic women's organization). Acli began loosening its ties to the Dc in the fifties; in 1970, on the issue of divorce, it broke with the christian democrats. Cisl took an independent stance from the vatican after 1969. The secure base of the Dc remained the confederation of small farmers, but this organization was weakened with migration from farm to city. A new group of the seventies, Comunione a liberazione, hoped to renew the Dc by moving it closer to vatican policies, but this attempt was not successful in augmenting Dc support. By the end of the seventies, membership in institutions of the catholic subculture had diminished and many had veered away from the Dc, thereby removing central support from the party's electoral strength.[8]

By 1983 the Dc reached an all-time low electoral figure of 33 percent. In the eighties, to Enrico Berlinguer, Pci party secretary (if not to all men in the party), it was evident that women had caused "one government after another" to fall on women's issues. Women claimed credit for their central role in the decline of the Dc.[9] Perhaps the answer to the critical question—whether or not the Pci would overtake the Dc in the eighties—lay with the large middle population of women and men and whether or not they believed the Pci genuinely aimed for a socialism reached by parliamentary means, a new society grounded on Italian cultural values and one that joined democracy and socialism. As we shall see in subsequent chapters, women have played a significant role in this area of belief.

After 1968 the Pci was outflanked by a new left and thereafter beleaguered by a critical feminist movement. Its closest ally, the unions, had been shaken by autonomous actions of the rank and file in strikes and factory councils—an implicit repudiation of the ability of the Pci allied with unions to mount a challenge to Italy's system of welfare capitalism. Yet, in a process that has not yet been satisfactorily analyzed, the Pci gained strength in the seventies. It is clear that many young people joined the party after 1968 and that many women joined the party to help defeat the antidivorce referendum in 1974. Regional decentralization after 1970 helped the Pci capture a succession of local and regional governments. Triumphalism was put aside as the Pci watched a democratically elected left government in Chile be quashed and its leader killed. Pci strategy in the seventies did not aim for communist control of the national government (which would leave the party vulnerable to outside attack) but for a governing coalition with the Dc, the *compromesso storico* embodied in the Andreotti government of 1976 formed with indirect Pci parliamentary support and in another Dc government formed with Pci parliamentary support in 1978 on the day Moro (the symbolic leader of the Dc) was kidnapped by the red brigades. The Pci (and all parties but Pr) refused to negotiate with terrorists for release of Moro and led a law and order sweep against violent revolutionaries. The response of Italians (particularly of Italian women) to politics which put abstraction above a human life was shown in the 1979 elections, in which the Pci lost 4 percent from its 1976 level.[10] Yet by the eighties, according to an evaluation by a historian with several years experience in the U. S. embassy in Rome, Pci "loyalty to the constitutional system was by now all but universally acknowledged and its legitimacy beyond question."[11]

A central critical question was the relationship of the Pci to the USSR. Since 1956 the Pci had emphasized an Italian way to socialism. In 1968 the Pci criticized soviet suppression of Czech socialism; in world conferences of the 1970s Berlinguer asserted there was no single model of socialism. In what came to be known as Eurocommunism there was a short-lived attempt at collaboration of the several communist parties of Europe, a coalition for socialism based on parliamentary democracy and individual freedoms. In 1977 there was an attempt to find agreement among the Italian, French, and Spanish parties, but the French party was essentially unwilling to leave the soviet orbit. The Pci tilted toward the Atlantic—accepting NATO, condemning the soviet-backed invasion of Cambodia by the Vietnamese in 1979, criticizing soviet deployment of SS-20 missiles in Europe, while not opposing European NATO missiles (before 1983).

In 1980 the Pci condemned the soviet invasion of Afghanistan and in 1981 openly broke with the soviets. Criticizing the imposition of martial law in Poland (which Berlinguer believed was instigated by the USSR), the Pci secretary condemned not only soviet interference in Poland but the soviet system as well. Censuring soviet repression in satellite nations, Berlinguer said that the "completely new forms" that were necessary for socialism and democracy would come from the Western European left, not from the soviet model. *Pravda* replied in tones that recalled secessions of Yugoslavia and China from the soviet fold, accusing the Pci of aiding imperialism and of a "truly sacrilegious" attitude.[12]

If the soviet connection of the Pci was no longer an issue for Italian politics by 1981, Pci democratic centralism continued to be criticized. Although the Italian communist party has institutionalized a system of meetings with the grass roots (notably in neighborhood festivals where party officials speak and anybody in the audience can "intervene" for as long as she or he wants), in effect, Pci authority had been vested in a central committee and a seven-member secretariat headed by the party secretary. Although this centralization of authority was no greater than that in other Italian parties, scrutiny of the Pci for fealty to democracy is intense and criticism continued.[13] At the 1983 Pci party congress, democratic structural changes were made that demonstrated to earlier critics that the party had "changed."[14]

The changes wrought by feminists in the Pci are explored in subsequent chapters. They ranged from public prodding of the men by women of the party (picketing Pci men in front of parliament on the issue of abortion, for example) to "accelerating the maturity" of Pci men by insuring the autonomy of the women's union, to breaking the traditional party code of discipline wherein disagreements among communists were regarded as matters to be kept within the family by pushing the party by open criticism, or by feminist separatist strategies that "put the men in crisis" to push the men where the women wanted.

Feminist efforts were significant, but Italy's political pluralism also prodded the Pci in a democratic direction. People in the Psi taunted the Pci, particularly at the crest of left terrorism in 1978, as to

whether the party was on the side of democratic socialism or marx-
ist-leninism. In the revision of Pci party statutes in 1979 there was a
statement that the thought of Marx and Engels was given "an impe-
tus of historic importance" by Lenin. Writings of Gramsci, Togliatti,
and Antonio Labriola (a nineteenth-century socialist) were recommended not as dogma, but as "sources of orientation."[15] Since the
early eighties the Pci hope of revolution has been aligned with peaceful social movements (antiviolence, women, ecology). In local and
regional governments where it holds power in Italy the Pci acts in a
moderate, pragmatic manner in coalition with a variety of political
forces.

In Turin, which may be Italy's critical city because of industrialization and migration that has made this city of the North Italy's
third largest "southern" city, the Pci has given a glimpse of what it
means by socialism with a human face. Diego Novelli, Pci mayor of
the city after 1980, worked with a left coalition to govern the city.
He provided 21 day care centers, 121 nursery schools, additional
public transportation, free bus travel for older people, restoration of
old parts of the city, a public sports club, new libraries, meeting places
for young people, swimming lessons for children, and public concerts
and art exhibitions.[16]

One singular characteristic of the Pci may be its identification
with traditional Italian culture while it works for "social transformation." Unique among the documents of world communist parties,
the 1979 party theses state that party members are not obliged to
subscribe to marxist beliefs and that they may be practicing catholics.[17] Pci membership (ca. 1,750,000) places it as the largest communist party of Western Europe and the third largest communist
party in the world (after those of China and the Soviet Union).
Women contribute 23 percent of its membership, a percentage that
should be considered in the context that many women who vote for
Pci programs do not choose to be enrolled in the party. Communists
claim that the Pci has the "largest women's consensus" of any party,
referring to the support the party has given (sometimes only after
prodding) to feminist issues.[18]

Among the main organizations who support the Pci are the large
labor union confederation (Cgil) and the National League of Cooperatives. The other major source of Pci support, the women's union,
in declaring its independence in 1982 has shown that women's sup-

port is contingent on Pci adoption of women's issues and the ability of the party to persuade not a few women leaders, but millions of individual women. The Pci has, of all the parties, the largest communications network: *l'Unità*, *Rinascità*, *Critica marxista*, *Politica ed economia*, *Studi storici*, and its publishing houses, all of which were pivotal in broadcasting Pci support for feminist issues. A woman editor-in-chief, Lina Tamburrino, headed *Rinascità*, the chief ideological organ of the Pci, in 1984.

Pci electoral totals grew from 19 percent in 1946 to 34 percent in 1976 and have hovered around one-third of the electorate ever since. In the first regional elections of 1970 the Pci secured the provinces of the "red belt" (the partisan strongholds of Umbria, Emilia, and Tuscany). In 1975 Liguria, Lazio, and Piedmont became "red" provinces. In 1975 the Pci governed in Rome, Naples, Florence, Genoa, Turin, Milan, Bologna, and Venice, often in coalition with socialists. The striking trend since the late seventies has been the growth of support for the Pci in the South. By 1978 half of all Italian provinces had left administrations and 50 percent of Italians lived in cities whose administrations were predominantly communist. In the political scandals of the seventies and eighties, there was large acceptance of the Pci as an uncorrupted party with *"mani pulite"* (clean hands).

The catholic factor continues to be critical for the Pci. In 1948 catholics carried placards reading "either Christ or communism." Influenced by John XXIII and the growth of a catholic left, attitudes had changed sufficiently by 1976 that the Pci invited catholic laymen to run on Pci lists; six were elected. The following year, in his correspondence with Luigi Bettazzi, the bishop of Ivrea, Berlinguer reiterated the Pci principle that catholic belief is compatible with Pci membership, but bishops in conference rejected this overture. More successful in reaching individual catholics than in persuading the catholic hierarchy, the Pci has been aided by the preference of liberation theologians, feminists, and left catholics for the term *credente* (believer). The growing tendency in Italy to identify oneself as a *credente* (instead of catholic, protestant, Jew, christian, marxist, atheist, or other) leaves the content of belief to individual conscience and removes the polarity from catholic/communist, christian/marxist, believer/nonbeliever for Italians who believe that the new society will be brought into being by everyone.

Italy's second largest left party, the Psi, attains small electoral totals (ca. 12%) but sits, since the 1960s, in government coalitions with the Dc. The secular principles of the Psi, as well as competition with the Pci, propel the party to support feminist issues—the Psi wrote the divorce law and subsidized the early feminist journal *effe*—but support for feminist issues was moderated by its governing coalition with the Dc. In 1983 Bettino Craxi became the first socialist prime minister in Italian history.

The history of the Psi since the war has been marked by continuing decline in electoral totals as those of the Pci have risen, a continuing movement toward the center, and the loss of young socialists to the Pci, of feminists to Pr, and of other socialists to an independent position since the late seventies, particularly on the issue of peace. Distinguished by self-criticism and a desire to stand on its own socialist turf autonomous of the Pci, the Psi oscillates but usually supports progressive measures. Until the ascendancy of the Pr in the seventies, it was the main defender of minority and liberal rights. During the period of the center-left coalition of the 1960s, the Psi drafted the divorce law, encouraged regional decentralization, worked for the statute of workers' rights, and pushed the Dc toward acceptance of the welfare state.[19] By 1984 it strengthened its criticism of Pci structure by implementing democracy itself in the form of a party national assembly that is a cross section of Italian expertise and public life. Perhaps the most significant function of the Psi in Italian politics is its ability to taunt the Pci, successfully, as to which is the more democratic party. It has replaced the symbolic hammer and sickle with a red carnation in its pragmatic, gradualist, and reformist version of socialism. In 1979 a socialist defense minister accepted NATO plans for cruise missiles at Comiso, Sicily; subsequently it has been helped on the right and hurt on the left by its alignment with U.S. defense policy. In 1984 the Psi renewed the concordat with the papacy, with the significant amendment that religious education in Italy is now voluntary. In its 10 to 13 percent of the electorate, the Psi has the support of some intellectuals, some feminists, and some labor unionists—those who do not want to be identified with the Pci—as well as those who work with the Pci but prefer a Psi political identification.

The parties of the liberal middle class—republicans (Pri), liberals (Pli), and social democrats (Psdi)—secure together about 10 percent of the vote; as mentioned earlier, these parties have been sources of feminist support because of their secular orientation and stress on individual rights. Called "lay parties," because they are in the secular tradition of the risorgimento, these small parties stress individual rights and internationalism. Frederic Spotts in his synthesis concludes: "Perhaps the greatest single irony of postwar politics is that ✓ contemporary Italy is far more in the image and likeness of the internationalist, non-ideological, modernizing, northern European, Atlanticist and secularist ideals of the lay parties than in that of either of the two major parties."[20]

The small radical party, Pr, was critically important for early support of feminist issues. Formed in 1955 as an offshoot of the Pli, it shares with other lay parties a liberal, secular, and Europeanist outlook. Unlike other small parties, it has a great deal of cultural importance. Marco Pannella, its ascetic and charismatic leader, undertakes fasts to publicize issues like world hunger. In the seventies Pr defined itself apart from Italy's major ideologies, differentiating its views from catholicism and from communism, taking principled stands for direct democracy, civil liberties, and world justice. The principled libertarianism of Pr propelled it to defend the civil rights of violent revolutionaries in the late seventies. It was also the first party to espouse legal abortion. Pr support of abortion on demand in its 1981 referendum was grounded on its belief in civil liberties and the primacy of conscience; this view of abortion lost to a more moderate version identified with women of Udi. In its stress on civil liberties, Pr defends homosexuality, emphasizes rights of conscience, and, as a party of principle, is an annoying gadfly when larger parties make opportunistic moves. Pr in the seventies appealed to communists and socialists who wanted to be autonomous of their parties on issues of feminism, world peace, and ecology. Innovative in party forms, Pr offered a "dual system" for people who wanted to join the party on one issue (e.g., abortion) while remaining in the socialist or communist parties. The dual system of Pr tended to make the party a way station (or a structure for exercising leverage) for feminists in the Psi and a register of opposition for independents inside the Pci on a variety of issues ranging from feminism and Pci action in the Moro affair to antinuclear concern and ecology.

The Italian new left in the early seventies divided into extraparliamentary groups (some hardening into violent revolutionaries) and an electoral sector that did poorly at the polls. Although without electoral significance after 1976, the autonomous new left party for communism, Pdup, inserted new left and feminist premises into the Italian political and cultural dialogue and has exerted important cultural and political leverage for feminist gains.

Feminist criticism was largely directed against "conventional marxists" of the Pci who "ignored women's oppression" and deprecated the importance of women as "carriers of the future." Yet feminist priorities for divorce, equal family rights, and abortion impelled many women into the party in the early seventies. As will be discussed, younger women who swelled the ranks of the Pci to secure feminist legislation entered the party with feminist and new left attitudes. In part because of the electoral strength of these younger women, the Pci moved, by the eighties, in their direction of feminist and new left premises.

The middle generation of Pci women in Udi was simultaneously criticized by younger women and unsettled by the knowledge that they shared similar criticism of the Pci. Privately and publicly these middle-generation women criticized Pci men while remaining in the party. These women and their counterparts in Psi were described by younger feminists as belonging to "historic left parties." In a gesture of autonomy some of these women publicly cancelled membership in the Pci after 1976. Party women continued to criticize the Pci for its focus on industrial workers, a doctrine which elevated men of the party allied with male workers to the vanguard. Male workers might be revolutionary in confrontation with capitalism, said feminists, but they remained patriarchal in the family.[21] Cultural feminists argued with political women of Udi, insisting that "genuine equality comes with changing the culture." The tension between different groups of women proved to be productive for achieving feminist goals. By the end of the decade cultural and political feminists had influenced one another.

The meaning of the term "feminism" began to blur as middle-generation women insisted that younger women were "neofeminists," that partisan women of world war II were the genuine first feminists. Cultural feminists tended to appropriate the term, but this became ambiguous as political feminists worked for legislation directed to concerns of cultural feminists—notably the 1978 abortion law and the referendum campaign launched in 1979 against sexual violence.

divorce, equal family rights, and legal abortion laws

The right of divorce, which the Pci had earlier considered too dis-ruptive to party strategy of working with the Dc, was accepted in the confrontational atmosphere of 1968. The divorce bill, written by so-cialists and encouraged by the spectrum of secular parties—radicals, socialists, liberals, republicans—as well as by feminists, passed in par-liament in 1970. When the Dc immediately mobilized to repeal the law, the women's organizations, Mld and Udi, and left parties orga-nized to defeat the antidivorce referendum in 1974.

The right of divorce, gained much earlier in protestant countries, marked a momentous change in Italy. Traditional church teaching held marriage as sacred and indissoluble. The divorce law of 1970 permits dissolution without requiring that a reason be stated; this "no blame" provision is counterbalanced by a provision requiring a minimum legal separation of five years (seven, if the other party ob-jects). In the mid-eighties groups from the center left to the left have introduced bills to remove the waiting period. Divorce, as many have pointed out, need not be a feminist issue. It became a feminist issue in Italy during the campaign of the church and the Dc to repeal the divorce law.[22]

In 1974 the antidivorce referendum lost, with 60 percent of the electorate voting to sustain the divorce law. In a pattern that came to prevail, 90 percent of the voters participated in this election on a feminist issue. This has been called an "earthquake" vote for Italy. The 1974 vote indicated that feminist issues could swell the ranks of the Pci and defeat the Dc. In 1976, largely because of the vote of women and the young, the Pci attained its highest historical tally, 34.4 percent. Feminists noted that men of the Pci did not publicly credit women with party gains. This feeling of being taken for granted, as well as disaffection for the Pci strategy of historic com-promise with the Dc (the party opposed to women's concerns) stim-ulated many feminists after 1976 to espouse a stance of rejection of politics.

The 1974 vote put a spotlight on fissures within the church, re-vealing that catholics did not reflexively obey papal authority. The largest swing after the papacy of John XXIII and the confrontations of 1968 was from a catholic posture of anticommunism to commit-ment to the belief of liberation theology that the gospel is compatible with marxism. After 1968 catholics ranged in political affiliation from the Dc to the Pci, and from the new left to the independent political left. For some catholic organizations the referendum on divorce precipitated a crisis with the church—a sign of the emergence of an "other" church of catholic groups and base communities who reserve the right of conscience for matters on which they differ with the vatican.[23]

After 1974 Udi promoted national discussion of a new family rights law, and in April 1975, supported by all parties but the neofascist Msi, the law passed. Equal rights were spelled out for husbands and wives in choice of domicile, control over family finances, and education of children. Children born outside of marriage were assured their rights.[24] The provision protecting *illegittimi* was the controversial point in the legislation, because it threatened Italian cultural beliefs sanctifying marriage.[25] The 1975 equal family rights law points to a new Italian family; replacing the patriarchal structure is a family governed by both father and mother with legal protection for all children.

The feminist theme that came to be the most important in the 1970s was "the right of a woman to her own body is the capstone of her liberation." Women were forced to seek illegal and dangerous abortions, declared an early manifesto, as the consequence of a sexual act "directed to male pleasure." An essay circulated in mimeographed form in large cities in 1970 was entitled *La donna clitoridea e la donna vaginale* and compared women's clitoral versus vaginal orientations.[26] The effectiveness of simultaneous work by political and cultural feminists—the use of traditional politics, direct action, and creative as well as informational agitation—was evident in the abortion campaign. Cultural feminists broadcasted the issue in graphics and language that shocked people. Political feminists gathered the testimony of thirty thousand women on maternity, sexuality, and abortion and published the accounts.[27] Small groups and assemblies of women discussed the issue. Neighborhood, workplace and school collectives formed around the controversial topic.

New political forms emerged. Mld simply arranged safe abortions for women, organizing trips for women in need of abortions to legal clinics in Britain and to an illegal center in Florence. The weekly chartered flights and the direct practice of abortion helped several hundred women each month.[28] The Pci was moved on the issue of

abortion by women in the party; the spectacle of Udi women picketing Pci men in front of parliament was followed by a wave of "ac-
celerated maturity" on the part of Pci men as the party carried the
abortion law through parliament in 1978.

The abortion law of 1978 is an advanced one, providing abortions
paid by the national government within the first ninety days of pregnancy for any woman over eighteen years of age. Reasons for the
abortion can be "health related, economic, social, or familial."[29] Doctors or recognized health facilities can issue a permission for an abortion after discussing alternatives with the woman. Feminists wanted
authorization by women's health clinics, not by doctors. Their anxieties proved to be well-founded; implementing the law has run into
obstacles. The Pci had insisted on a freedom of conscience rider (ap-
plicable to doctors) to the law; after the law was passed, two-thirds
of the doctors in state institutions and entire staffs of catholic hospitals declared themselves conscientious objectors and refused to
perform abortions. Feminists pointed out that some of the doctors
who claimed objection of conscience continued to perform clandestine abortions for high fees. Other doctors indicated their hostility
to the abortion law with brusque treatment of women, a treatment
that feminists have called "violence in white shirt."[30]

cultural feminism

The bold, innovative features of cultural feminism were apparent
in the periodical *effe*, whose aim was "facciamoci sentire!" (let's make
them hear us!). Striking cartoons and daring articles did succeed in
making people listen.[31] Amusing and direct, an article on the economy was accompanied by a cartoon depicting a naked Eve looking at
a stack of highly priced apples presided over by a snake. Eve, bare-
bosomed, avows: "E chi le tocca!" (With double entendre, Eve is saying, Who wants to touch the expensive apples!) Articles in *effe*
opened a new continent of topics for women, ranging from women's
knowledge of their bodies to orgasm. Those considered antifeminists
(from Henry Kissinger to Italian professors who lumped women with
the lumpenproletariat) were satirized in ribald cartoons. *Effe* pio-
neered the feminist practice of toppling capital letters from everything, including the names of their own publications.

After 1974 the abortion issue dominated the pages of *effe*. One cartoon depicted a pregnant woman whose swollen body was stamped, "Monopoly of the Italian state." The fight was carried to the source in 1976 when an entire issue of *effe* charged the catholic church with the responsibility for perpetuating ideas that disparaged women.[32] Regarding itself as the center of an Italian feminist network, *effe* attempted to keep track of feminist collectives. The bright young women and middle-aged matrons who looked up from the laundry to agree with feminists were winningly illustrated on *effe* covers. As the abortion issue evoked more intense emotions, *effe* graphics grew bolder: a naked woman with children issuing from all the openings of her body, a great lady bird so full of eggs she could barely walk.[33]

This periodical of cultural feminists was always ambivalent about whether traditionally conceived politics could solve women's concerns, insisting that feminist politics must derive from women's experience. As political machinations around the abortion issue became convoluted, there were more doubts that genuine change can be brought about by legislation, more articles about the "insufficiency of marxism," and anxiety about mounting sexual violence.[34]

The creativity of cultural feminists was shown in the newly founded Italian feminist theater at Rome. At Teatro Maddalena feminist plays shocked the right, the center, and the left. One play featured a dialogue of a prostitute and her client on stage. The male client is unclothed; he is also a member of the Pci. Changing the gender of the traditional object of sexism, the play is a telling critique of party men who rhetorically acknowledged women's equality, but treated some of them as objects.

The theme of most of the women's collectives was "the personal is political." In one Italian definition of the phrase, "a politics without internal transformation of the participant is manipulation on the part of an elite."[35] This concept reflects a dimension that was widespread on the Italian left by the eighties—changing the culture and the political system must include changing yourself. Sources for this concept may be closer to ultimate beliefs than to social analysis: individual conversion must precede social transformation.[36]

The unity of the period 1968 to 1976 began to be broken by mid decade with some collectives emphasizing the personal and others concentrating on the political. Some women hoped to resolve this contradiction by "double militancy," participating in small feminist groups while working in the party, the union, the school. But tensions continued.

feminist communists, communist feminists, or autonomous women?

The internal feminist argument after 1968 largely found younger feminists on one side and men of the Pci and the middle generation of Udi women on the other. Younger feminists charged that middle-generation Udi women were not autonomous because of their auxiliary status in the Pci. Feminists did not quarrel with older Pci women; women of the partisan generation were regarded as foremothers and were often consulted for advice.

Camilla Ravera, a Pci founder who had worked with Gramsci and been jailed by fascists, was appointed senator-for-life in Italy's parliament in 1982. Ravera encouraged younger women to be independent, affirming, as a founder of Udi, that the women's union was intended to be a mass organization "autonomous of the parties." Although she was regarded as the grand old woman of the Pci, Ravera indicated that her ultimate beliefs were her own. She advised feminists that communism was not her life perspective, it was her "historical perspective."[37]

Teresa Noce, another communist foremother, told young feminists that she had never had any trouble with the party, "only with men of the party." Married to Luigi Longo, the Pci party secretary in the 1960s, Noce publicly announced that her husband held the patriarchal attitudes of the Piedmont peasantry. She described herself as a "proletarian" and "housewife" and commended the "second feminism" for shaking up the Pci.

The Pci, said Noce, had always maintained a good perspective on women's issues but always "from the point of view of males." She herself had never felt deterred in what she wanted to do because she had the security of being a "proletarian" when many male party leaders were of "bourgeois" origin. Although her life was a heroic one of struggle and internment by the nazis, she did not want to be a national monument. She was content that she had never taken orders from anyone: "Se non mi va, non lo faccio" (If I don't agree, I don't do it).[38]

Young feminists who entered the Pci after 1968 exhibited a variety of motivations and points of view that loosened Pci doctrine from traditional moorings and infiltrated feminist thinking into the party that had, before 1968, held that there was no specific woman question.

Angela Migliasso, the daughter of farm workers, enrolled in the Pci in 1968. Her mother had taught her to be independent, saying that a woman ought not depend on anyone else for her livelihood. Migliasso chose the Pci because she felt the party corresponded to her beliefs in liberty and justice; she became a party worker. Simultaneously a feminist and a communist, Migliasso joined a women's group that helped organize one of the first feminist demonstrations. Asserting women's right to emancipation from oppressive institutions, as well as from "oppressive men and lovers," Migliasso worked in Udi in the pattern of "double militancy," as a feminist and a communist. Violence, for Migliasso, is "abortion without assistance, being molested in the street, working in inhuman factory conditions, being constricted to be a housewife, being forced to do anything arbitrarily."[39]

Grazia Zuffa was drawn to Udi after 1968 as the organization closest to her beliefs. On her scale of priorities as a feminist and a communist, she ranked feminism as most important to her life. In the seventies she found a "disequilibrium and tension between the women's movement and the politics of the party." "Everyone is aware that women are a volcano in eruption," she said, and "within the party they are regarded with some unease."[40]

Fiamma Nirenstein stated that the party changed because of confrontation with women. The Pci has "discarded a narrow economism for a broader appreciation of cultural issues." Nirenstein summed up her feminism: "I want to live in a country where women have work; where they can, if they need one, have an abortion; where they are not violated and regarded with disdain. I want guarantees for me, for my friends, and for the thousands of women that feminism has not yet touched."[41]

Daniela Bacacci was affected by the Vietnam war, which gave her a sense of solidarity with all oppressed peoples. Reading studies of Marcuse, Reich, and Adorno deepened her understanding of authoritarianism and the unequal roles of women and men. Catalyzed by experiences of 1968, she entered the Pci in 1972 when the abortion issue was beginning to expose, she said, the "contradictions" within

the party. Bacacci felt the "disequilibrium" of simultaneously wanting socialism and wanting to work solely with women. This, she said,
was the schizophrenia of the double militancy. She was awed by the
vastness of the women's movement in Italy—old groups, new ones,
and "spontaneous aggregations who never call themselves feminist"
who were nonetheless drawn to feminist concerns.[42]

Anna Casella, a southern Italian feminist who was convent-bred,
did not become politically aware until 1969. Enrolled in a marxist
group, she found it "rigid and bureaucratic" and was thereafter in
"terror of hierarchy, of authority" and unwilling to enroll in the Pci.
She did enter the party in 1974 at the time of the campaign against
the referendum to repeal the divorce law. Casella was impressed by
bonds she observed within the party between older and younger
women. She found that "women of the Pci have been greatly influenced by feminism."[43]

Angela Francese said that her belief in equality derived from the
poverty of her childhood. In 1968 she participated in worker demonstrations. She observed that southern Italian women in northern
factories were uninterested in a class analysis of their condition, but
they were ready to strike. She worked in Udi: "I am simply a communist woman. The fact that I am a woman enables me to work with
women." Feminist autonomy for this southern Italian woman is less
acute a concern than is self-determination for her region.[44]

Giovanna Filippini was born in the North. Her parents had always
voted Pci; she had always been a catholic activist. In 1968 she read
Bertrand Russell, Che Guevara, and all the marxist studies she could
find. Active in the student movement, she enrolled in the youth section of the Pci, the Fgci. In Rome in 1975 when feminists were demonstrating, she "began to think of the contradictions of my life as a
woman. To be a woman communist means that you want women to
count for more, that you want to carry the battle for emancipation
and liberation not only within the society, but within the party."
Filippini does not accept the "hegemony" of any group—not "of
the catholics, of the feminists, of the radicals, nor of the orthodox
communists. I do not accept impositions or stereotypes from any
quarter."

Filippini identifies with the partisan generation of women. She
often speaks about feminism to her grandmother, who had been a
partisan. When they discussed a modern feminist slogan, "Make love

without fantasy," Giovanna saw that her grandmother smiled ironically. The older woman said she could understand her granddaughter's feminism; she had shared her life, she said, with a man who was buried wrapped in the *bandiera rossa*, but he had not been a "good communist" at home.[45]

Maria Grazia Gianmarinaro became a communist after 1968. Her feminist consciousness is rooted in her Sicilian background. Women need to join the struggle, she stated, but "we want to find a different society when we get there, with a different role, not subordinate, for women."[46]

Livia Turco was born into a worker family who held the characteristic secularism of the wartime generation of communists. Turco, who grew up in the fervent atmosphere of John XXIII and vatican council II, was strongly catholic. She entered convent school and enrolled in the youth section of the Pci simultaneously. Reading christian marxist theologians helped her to resolve philosophical problems. Berlinguer's proposal of a historic compromise with catholics helped remove any remaining doubts: "I understood the Historic Compromise as a union of catholics and communists, politically and culturally." Neither did she have any problems resolving communism and feminism: "I have found no dilemmas in being a member of the Pci and a feminist."[47]

Some of the contradictions of Italian feminism of the seventies are suggested in the 1977 laws for equality of treatment (*legge di parità*) which promote the hiring of women and forbid discrimination based on sex in access to jobs and promotion. The laws also equalize pensions, family allowances, and retirement benefits. Child care leave is extended to fathers. This law was important to women who worked in factories, but some feminists criticized it because the law did not provide mechanisms for retraining women in new skills and therefore reenforced existing roles in the job market. The positive effect of the law could be seen in Fiat's policy of hiring more women after 1978.[48]

The ability of a younger generation of Italian women to identify themselves as simultaneously catholic and communist was a pattern increasingly apparent in the Italy of the 1970s and 1980s. Balancing communism and feminism was sometimes more difficult. Italian feminists, as we shall see, did so in a variety of individual, unedited ways.

9

cattoliche, credenti, e femministe

catholics, believers, and feminists

feminists and postconciliar catholicism

Italian feminists after 1968 were simultaneously engaged in confronting traditional catholic church doctrine that they believed denigrated women and contributing to an emerging feminist theology grounded on an unedited (in the sense of unmediated) reading of the gospel. The feminist critique focused on the historical role of the church in perpetuating patriarchalism, sexism, and a subordinate role for women—all epitomized, feminists believed, in postconciliar papal condemnations of contraception, divorce, abortion, women in the priesthood, and liberation theologies.

In the ensuing debate some Italian feminists identified themselves as "dissenting" or "left" catholics. As issues became engaged, feminists (along with other dissenting catholics) preferred to be known simply as *credenti* (believers).[1] The term *credente* bypassed religious in-

termediaries and left the content of beliefs to the privacy of conscience. In the wake of John XXIII and vatican council II, the feminist
perspective was encouraged by left catholics—those who lived in
comunità di base, liberation theologians, priests and nuns in and out
of the church, and a large body of *credenti*.

The first stage of the battle concerned the divorce law of 1970.
When the pope and the Dc immediately launched a campaign to
repeal the law, it was inevitable that the church would become a
target of feminist criticism.[2] During the first skirmishes with the
church there were brash articles in *effe* and cartoons that would have
been unthinkable a decade earlier. *Noi donne*, in part because the Pci
was concerned to effect the "historic compromise" with catholics,
was more circumspect. In campaigns for divorce and legal abortion,
some Italian feminists chained themselves to posts at St. Peter's or
demonstrated at the *duomo* in Milan. Others studied the history of
the church and explored feminist theology.

Italian feminists named a bookstore, a center, and a theater *la
Maddalena*. This was also the name of a neighborhood in Rome identified with feminist activities. There was more to the association with
the "fallen woman" of the bible than first appeared. Mary Magdalen,
not a disciple of Jesus in the bible written by men, has a significant
role in the gnostic gospels and in contemporary feminist thinking.
Mary Magdalen challenged those who followed Peter. She was the
first to see Jesus after his death—it was she who brought the good
news to the others. Because she was a woman the other disciples did
not believe her, but during the first centuries after the death of Jesus
Magdalen held apostolic authority in some christian communities.
Other women in this period of early christianity held prophetic,
priestly, and episcopal functions in the many different christian communities that existed before the faith was standardized with male
norms in the fourth century.[3]

The 1965 encyclical of vatican council II, *Gaudium et spes*, described the family as a community of equivalent persons, but postconciliar documents reenforced the traditional roles of the sexes.
The 1968 encyclical *Humanae vitae* condemned contraceptives. In
1976 the church responded negatively to the question of women in
the priesthood, restating early church doctrine that the priesthood
is an office exclusively male: man, not woman, is in the image of God
and the male sex is the norm in social life. The papacy of John Paul

II has vigorously restated condemnation of contraception, abortion, premarital sex, homosexuality, women in the priesthood, and liberation theologies.[4]

feminism at the cittadella christiana

Perhaps the most significant dimension of Italian left catholicism of the sixties and seventies was identification with the radical implications of Italy's patron saint, Francis, the "poor man of Assisi" who confronted a changing society at the dawn of the modern era. By the eighties the era from the contestations of the late sixties to the changed culture of the eighties was called franciscan, and *il poverello* was called *Francisco un "pazzo" da slegare** His madness was the utopian hope for peace in all of its meanings (see discussion of Umberto Eco's *The Name of the Rose* in chapter 14). The arc of left catholicism and feminism in the 1970s and 1980s may be followed in the career of Pia Bruzzichelli. In the seventies she was a director of the cittadella christiana in Assisi, the city of St. Francis; in the eighties she was elected chair of the management board of the cooperative that publishes *noidonne*, now considered the major women's journal of Italy. For a decade and a half she brought feminist perspectives to organizations of catholic women, advising them that feminism is christian; in the eighties her left catholic beliefs inform her feminist activities.

Given the papal opposition to most feminist ideas, it was daring in 1975 for the cittadella christiana to call the first conference on feminism to be held in a major catholic center. Speaking for cultural feminists at the conference, Dacia Maraini summarized the experiences of feminist groups of *autocoscienza*.[5] Whether factory workers, students, teachers, nuns, rich or poor housewives, all Italian women, said Maraini, held in common a catholic education. Educated in a convent herself, Maraini said that the significant legacy of a catholic education for women was absence of information about their own bodies and negative attitudes about sexuality. As mothers traditional catholic women perpetuated patriarchal ideology: teaching their children that sex, for women, is a sin; motherhood is a woman's sole

* (Francisco: A "madman" to untie) A book by this name was published by the *cittadella* at Assisi in 1983. The English counterpart of this notion is "God's fool."

social expression; and that a good mother sacrifices all for her children.

Observing the rebellious example of sons and daughters in the seventies, said Maraini, women had begun to think about their own lives. Women, she said, have great power; men and women procreate together, but only a woman can bring the seed to maturity, only she can bring a child into the world. This women's power, venerated in ancient times, has been appropriated by fathers—of church and society—who placed a set of taboos on woman, took away her autonomy, and "made her a slave to repressive rules and laws."[6] Women live alienated from their own bodies in the society of the fathers, a patriarchy that maintains a social equilibrium based on women's exploitation: all societies, said Maraini, are grounded on the unpaid labor of housewives.[7] Pointing to the double standard reenforced by catholic education, Maraini said that sexual freedom for women is condemned while sexual liberty of men is considered a sign of virility and of independence. For Maraini, the morality and laws imposed by the fathers protected masculine sexual interests as well as their ruling class prerogatives.[8]

Women are similar, said Maraini, to some Blacks in the United States who internalize attitudes of self-denigration: "The fact is that the oppressed take on the values of their oppressors."[9] Because men want women to be fragile, dependent, masochistic, voluble, and incapable eternal wards, that is what women become, repressing their creativity, their desire to be autonomous, and their intellectual independence. Having internalized these values, women disparage other women because they deprecate themselves.[10]

Among the women at the Assisi conference were two who were to turn to feminist theology: Adriana Zarri, a nun and theologian, who described "pseudo-spirituality" as an instrument of oppression, and Roberta Fossati, who developed a theology that was simultaneously feminist, franciscan, and aligned with liberation theology.[11]

Roberta Fossati, feminist theologian

Roberta Fossati's 1977 study, *E Dio creò la donna*, adopted marxist philosophy as an analytic instrument for studying the political, economic, ideological, and religious power of the church.[12] (Page references that follow are to Fossati's study). Explicitly directing her work against religious alienation, Fossati charged that alienation was deepened by the stance of the church opposing divorce and abortion. Women, in Fossati's theology, were described as a marginalized and discriminated-against stratum of the working class (p. 11).

Differentiating between church doctrine and religious belief, Fossati found an "almost complete estrangement" from the preaching of Christ in the official daily practice of the church (p. 12). As a *credente* Fossati felt it necessary to separate faith from institutionalized religion, to return to the gospel as it existed before Constantine connected faith and the state, to remove bourgeois cultural content from church teaching, and to welcome the actual pluralism of catholicism (p. 14).

Fossati posed probing questions: What is the connection between the safety valve of religion and the social control of women? What is the significance of the opposition of the church to women as priests? What is the connection between the notion of women as impure/men as pure and the sexist attitudes of the church? The feminist theologian called for a rereading of the old and new testaments from the standpoint of women and for a feminist rereading of church history. Religious celebration of marriage by the church was not institutionalized, said Fossati, until the council of Trent in 1563 when the sacrament of matrimony was proclaimed. The *famiglia cristiana* upheld by the Dc and conservative parts of Italian society, said the feminist theologian, was a "gross distortion of gospel accounts" (pp. 47–48). Fossati found a "red thread" in the bible, a *bibbia dei poveri* (bible of the poor) that expressed the anxiety of the disinherited. She saw idolatry in the "cult of Christ" and a justification of hierarchy in the description of Christ as king (p. 132). Because the bible was written by male celibates, women needed an unedited gospel (p. 133). Feminist theology, Fossati believed, coincided with a franciscan interpretation of christianity and beliefs of the liberation theology associated with the peasant struggle of Latin America. Feminist, franciscan, and liberation theologies converged in looking at the bible, history, and the world from the standpoint of the poor and oppressed (p. 134).

The significance of support of feminist issues from the franciscan center of Italy can probably not be overestimated. The *cittadella* periodical, *rocca*, has a large readership that brings liberation theology and feminist views of religion to a thousand schools. Conferences at

Assisi bring together teachers, students, theologians, academic experts, and lay people to discuss issues of church, belief, and society. Feminist issues ventilated in this catholic center strengthened the tendency in Italy to transfer authority from the papacy to private conscience for issues like legalized abortion.

liberation theology

Along with a continuing series on reading the bible for contemporary relevance, *rocca* has published pieces on popular religious beliefs—describing Jesus Christ as a revolutionary workman and his mother, Mary, as a woman of the people. Topics of books published by the *cittadella christiana* outline the topography of Italian liberation theology: antifeminism and christianity, the human class struggle, believers and unbelievers for a new world, Marx and the bible, and the morality of love and sexuality.

Giulio Girardi (discussed in chapter 6) is probably the most influential Italian liberation theologian. His 1969 study, *credenti e non credenti per un mondo nuovo*, was in a third edition in 1976. His *marxismo e cristianesimo* was in its eighth edition in 1977; at a conference of *comunità di base* in the late seventies, I was told by several people that this book on the compatibility of marxism and christianity had changed their lives. Liberation theology in Italy has a franciscan imprimatur; all of Girardi's books were published by the cittadella christiana at Assisi.

The left catholic periodical, *rocca*, of the *cittadella* also made the work of other liberation theologians available in Italy. A book given to new subscribers to *rocca* suggests the contours of the liberation theology read in Italy in the seventies and eighties. Alfredo Fierro's *Introduction to Political Theology* expressed indebtedness to Marx, to the Frankfurt school of sociology, to Rudolf Bultmann ("One can speak of God only by speaking of us" [p. 14], and to Helmut Gollwitzer ("There does not exist a christian politics, just as there does not exist a christian medicine—there exist christians in politics" [p. 69]). According to Fierro, this theology was founded by vatican council II in the 1960s.

Affirming the declamation of Marx that philosophers have interpreted the world but the point is to change it and intent on "defatalizing" society and "demythologizing" beliefs, liberation theologians like Fierro renounce theology of the past as having served as an instrument of social accommodation whose effect has been to erase social conscience. Marxist philosophy, for these theologians, is an instrument of analysis helpful for "desacralizing" the existing political order (p. 29).

The history of catholicism since Constantine is criticized not only for sacralizing the state but for erecting a "christolatry" as blasphemous, they believe, as the idolatry of socialism. Socialism is considered a process of liberation; neither fanaticism nor dogmatism is considered appropriate in working for a just society that recognizes the importance of a genuine pluralism of beliefs in a free society (p. 54). Some Italians who share the beliefs of liberation theologians stay in the church while criticizing it; others prefer to be called christians rather than catholics; many feminists and other Italians consider the term *credente* most appropriate, wherein the believer alone knows whether she or he is a christian, a catholic, a Jew, a protestant, a pagan, a marxist, a troubled believer, a nonbeliever, or other.[13]

Lidia Menapace, new left theorist and feminist theologian

An Italian feminist who carries the left catholic perspective to a severe conclusion is Lidia Menapace, a major new left spokeswoman for Italian feminists. A professor during the confrontations of the late sixties, Menapace's radical views were involved in her dismissal from the Catholic University of Milan. Radical in politics as well as religion, she charged in 1969 (along with other left catholic dissenters) that the Pci was reformist and listed the "contradictions" of the party. When other dissenters were "radiated" out of the Pci (she was not) she helped to found the new left party Pdup.

For Menapace Italy has attained a "historical maturity" that removes the "atheistic prejudice" from those who work for socialism; she reconciles any contradictions with *silenzio consapevole* (knowing silence), citing the way many Italian workers put religion aside for political activism. If the faith is not alienating at its source, states Menapace, it will rise again. If religion is an alienation, to be liberated from it will be a liberation for everyone.[14] Echoing earlier mystics, Menapace refers to the experience of faith profoundly lived in a particular historical epoch as *notte oscura*. In our time we may have to live through this dark night in the "absence of God" in "knowing silence." This may characterize our age as "atheist," but the person who fears this, for Menapace, is a "person of little faith." She considers this "christian atheism" more radical than the atheism of Marx.[15]

For Menapace there is maturity, hope, prophecy, and precariousness in contemporary Italy. She finds a small opening in the dark from which faith can perhaps enter—in the tin tambourine and whistle of workers' demonstrations and in the laughing fury of feminists shrieking, "Tremble, tremble, the witches have returned!" There is no easy way, she acknowledges, to sew all the hopeful movements of Italy together with red thread and with faith. The issue of abortion, for example, is difficult to reconcile with christianity. Yet, "one must help the cause and be silent."[16]

For Menapace and other *credenti*, living the faith is more demanding than being baptized, confirmed, married, and buried in the church, since one can perform all these rituals and remain an unbeliever. Living the faith means accepting moral tension and avoiding easy solutions. The political implication of this perspective, for Menapace, is that the "necessary revolution" is not a simple substitution of parties, nor of classes, nor of property, nor of the means of production. It is all of these, accompanied by a simultaneous change in the way one thinks and acts. Otherwise, traditional roles of men and women will not be changed. Her revolutionary activism is lined with religious purpose: "If one leaves one's self submerged in the dust of reformist tasks, religious alienation will continue."[17] Several years before the December 1981 Pci repudiation of the soviet model, Menapace said that socialists had no models to imitate, no mother countries, no socialist solutions appropriate for every country.[18]

the "other half of the church"

Menapace wrote the introduction to what may have been the most widely read book of the seventies on women and the church. Feminist theology, said this new left theorist, is based on the belief that the message of the gospel has been "betrayed by the ecclesiastic hierarchy" who demand obedience, docility, conformity and compromise with prevailing political and economic power, identify sin with sexuality, permit the "absurd" identification of women with sin, and impose their own values (for example, church referenda on divorce and abortion) on society.[19]

In this volume entitled "the other half of the church" feminist theology is written by two women influenced by the teaching of John XXIII that the church is the people of God in history: Franca Long, a waldensian protestant, and Rita Pierro, a catholic believer; both identify with Jewish women and with nonbelievers as well as believers. All women, said Long and Pierro, want to be liberated from violence and taboos and to make decisions in the first person without delegating to anyone the control of their own destinies. Like other liberation theologies, this feminist redaction of the bible looks to the first centuries after Jesus, when christianity was a religion of slaves and of women, and before the church institutionalized an antithesis of spirit/sexuality that feminist theologians consider "absent in the word of Jesus." For Long and Pierro feminism is "an essential integral part of a cultural revolution, capable of liberating all the energies that can upturn an order based on egoism and inequality" inserting in public and private space values of "'love' and 'equality'."[20] The initial premise of feminist theology, for these women, is the "connection between sexism, classism, and racism."[21] Italian feminist theology in this widely read volume included men: "Men are also victims of masculinism and the project of feminist liberation includes men's liberation."[22]

Rossana Rossanda, new left theorist and dialectical theologian

Italian feminist theology was part of the new left current, but it was not identical with it. Rossana Rossanda, Menapace's colleague on the new left newspaper *il manifesto* is an example of an itinerary from catholic dissent to dialectical negation. In the early seventies as a new left activist and a catholic dissenter, Rossanda might vow to do something in the name of the madonna, but her preoccupation was political. A skilled dialectician, she later said she was "not" a *credente.* Early on she said she was "not" a feminist because she could not feel sisterly toward Susanna Agnelli, whose family owns Fiat; Rossanda said she identified instead with overworked male operatives on Fiat assembly lines. Rossanda's thinking about feminism evolved over a decade and a half. In feminist/marxist arguments of the seventies,

she tended to side with marxism; in the mid-eighties she found herself in the feminist camp of the argument[23] (see chapter 17).

Deeply held beliefs tend to catapult Rossanda to the radical edge,
no matter what subject is at hand. In a *rocca* symposium on "Which
socialism?" she said that the only socialism that interested her was
the end of exploitation and alienation and the end of the state: that
is, as she saw it, communism.[24] The word *socialism* she held, was
obfuscating, particularly in light of extant models. She preferred
"communism," which she described as "a dream truer than reality."
In the season of left uncertainty at the end of the seventies, Rossanda declared that the fault lay not in marxist hypotheses but in
the "insufficient radicalism of revolutions to date." Alienation will
continue even if the means of production are owned by the state. A
genuine revolution is a process of liberation of work: a liberated
workplace is indispensable for a free society. In her widely translated
book on Italian feminism, *Le altre*, Rossanda concluded that the major aim of feminists is to construct a political dimension that does
not destroy the diversity of persons. The political task of feminism
is a difficult endeavor because it entails a tactic of criticism and a
strategy of coalition with all alienated groups—including men.[25]

comunità di base

A major source of support for feminist issues in Italian society was
the set of beliefs identified with liberation theology and its institutional analogue, *comunità di base* (cdb). People in these communities
of men and women that emerged in Italy in the late 1960s and early
1970s try to bring the beliefs of liberation theology into their lives.
In cdb, where the gospel is studied for contemporary relevance, wom-
en's concerns are immediately understood by men as well as women,
and supported.

In the seventies *credenti* spoke of a church in "diaspora" or of
monolithic catholicism in "inexorable disaggregation."[26] Politically
this was expressed in a movement from the Dc to left parties, as
people formerly in catholic action groups now preferred to be considered *credenti* and voted for parties of the left or became left mili-
tants.[27] Many *credenti* considered themselves marxists. This stance
was not without tension, given the postconciliar papal intransigence
toward marxism. *Comunità di base* became places where people could

work in a marxist movement "without abandoning their spiritual-ity."[28] People who joined cdb initially for spiritual reasons often moved left politically. Some of them disagree with Menapace regard-ing a "dark night without God," maintaining that a christian "is called today to contribute to the change of this society, without hav-ing to renounce his faith."[29] Faith for these *credenti* is not a palliative that tranquilizes conscience but a process of "continual confronta-tion between the Word and the world," working with believers and nonbelievers for a world of justice and peace.[30]

One cdb that I have visited is the comunità cristiana di base di Piazza del Luogo Pio at Livorno. It meets in the neighborhood called Venezia, whose canals and ancient buildings adjoin the large seaport. Founded in 1969 when two franciscan friars decided to combine their religious and political commitments, it was joined by a seceding group from one of the local parishes, pane e vino. In 1974 a group of young people called ricerca cristiana (christian research) asso-ciated themselves with the cdb.[31]

A central premise of people in Italian base communities is that the church is pluralist and that diversity enriches everyone; they con-sider themselves not a parish but a "community which feels itself convoked by Christ." They hope to realize in the community "a com-plete experience of the christian faith." This, they feel, is "being church." They say, "Siamo chiesa"—we are church.[32] For people in cdb the church is made up of plural and diverse groups, all of whom *are* the church. They believe they are working against religious alien-ation (against the alienation produced, for example, when the pope excommunicated communists in 1949). Taking a stance against the church aligned with power, cdb identify instead with the church of the poor and oppressed everywhere. Being a church means seeing a problem and doing something about it—bringing water to a parched area, building roads, caring for the afflicted. Bypassing the official church, they also interpret the sacraments and liturgy for themselves; the eucharist, for the cdb at Livorno, means "hearing the Word," par-ticularly the word in Exodus, Matthew, and Acts. Hearing the word may take the place of other sacraments (of baptism and marriage, for example). The sacrament of the priesthood is reinterpreted with the aim of giving up privilege. Many ex-priests are members of cdb; those who remain priests wear lay clothes. Obviously a challenge to the church hierarchy, people in cdb think they prefigure the church of tomorrow—"small communities, poor, disarmed, leavening the bread of the world, humble witnesses of the Gospel." The birth of these small communities is considered an "instrument of revolution" and an act "of genuine conversion."[33]

Their influence wider than their numbers indicate the cdb movement has supporters inside the church.[34] For Luigi Bettazzi, the bishop of Ivrea, the church is vitalized by such "dissenting, contesting" groups who are critical of the church.[35] Pointing to the communal and ideological pluralism of early christianity (when women held considerable religious power), cdb point out that uniformity of belief and practice was a later development.[36] "While today the unity of the church is founded on hierarchy and on canon law, in early times, the unity of the church was guaranteed by one God."[37] In the early church, Bettazzi points out there was a fruitful dialectic between Jewish christians, hellenistic, and pagan christians. "Il popolo, non i vescovi, fa la Chiesa," states Bettazzi, (the people, not the bishops, make the church).[38]

Regarding themselves as autonomous of the church and of society, cdb people hope to be the salt that will act as leavening in both as they engage in encounter and dialogue, affirming love, refuting injustice, and sharing "with the least." *Comunità di base* hope and work for an equalitarian and just society that acknowledges differences of beliefs, building, as one ex-cleric said, "communism from the base."[39]

idoc, com-nuovi tempi, il focolare

Among the journals of men and women believers whose views are in consonance with those of feminists is *idoc*, established on the eve of vatican council II. The founders of *idoc* rejected "religious ideology" but gave space to church organizations and to "non-official" groups like the Italian movement of christians for socialism. One of the aims of *idoc* is the recovery of the religious beliefs of the people through the study of dialects and folklore and the study of women's history. In an *idoc* article entitled "The challenge of feminist theology," G. Gianna Sciclone said: "A rebellion of women, who are still the means the hierarchy uses to maintain cultural power over the family, could cause the explosion of many contradictions and open the way to a profound reform of the church."[40]

Com-nuovi tempi is the journal of men and women *credenti*: catholics, protestants, Jews, and others. Waldensians, the major denomination of Italian protestantism, are significant not only on the *cut* staff, but they are, like Jews, a leavening in Italian catholic society.[41] Catholic critics of *credenti* sometimes charge that catholics who now call themselves *credenti* have become protestants. There are some similarities: cartoons in *com-nuovi tempi* have a lively anti-clerical irreverence. A poster depicts a reader of *com-nuovi tempi* asking the pope, "Excuse me, am I disturbing you?" He answers, "Yes, very much!"

Liberation theology enunciated by left catholics and *credenti*, and combined with a marginal protestantism and a marginal Judaism, offers the possibility of genuine innovation. The creative potential of pluralism is evident in a leaflet written by women on the *cut* staff at the height of the campaign promoted by institutionalized catholicism to repeal the 1978 law that removed criminal penalties from interruption of pregnancy. The widely distributed *cut* leaflet endorsing a *no* vote on the referendum to repeal the abortion law contains the premises of an emerging set of moral beliefs. Difficult ethical questions are not evaded: for example, the leaflet acknowledges the conflict between the potentiality of life (the fetus) and an actual adult life (that of the mother). This morality rejects abstractions: refusing to help a desperate woman in the name of a "higher principle" is not considered moral. Significant for politics as well as theology is the emphasis on the "right to express our own convictions as citizens and as believers." Especially significant for catholicism and for authoritarian politics is the admonition of the leaflet not to obey external authority blindly.[42]

Documenting the argument with biblical citation, the *com-nuovi tempi* leaflet affirmed that life is a gift of God. To be "for life" is to be able to live. To be for life means working for a society that permits everyone, including the weakest, to have the conditions of living in dignity, for a new society where there will not be hatred, fear, unjust death, a society in which the dilemma of abortion need not exist. The birth of a child can not be imposed on anyone; in the bible, children are a benediction, not an imposition. Abortion is not an act of liberty but a tragic recourse in the case of extreme difficulty.

The feminist writers of this leaflet emphasize the right of conscience. Their position is not a justification of abortion, but one of understanding and solidarity with women forced to make the poignant choice. The leaflet urged No to clandestine abortion, Yes to self-determination of women and Yes to a commitment to transform social conditions so that "no woman need suffer the violence of abortion, so that women and men can make a genuinely free, and joyful, choice of parenthood."[43]

The feminist issue of abortion made visible a catholic church in rapid transition. Change was most vividly apparent in Italy in *comunità di base*, but also evident in regional church publications. *Il focolare* is a Sicilian church publication dedicated to the family. It is published by franciscans, *cappucini minori*. The 1981 vote in Sicily to sustain the abortion law reached large pluralities: 68 percent in the city of Palermo. In January 1982 *il focolare* saluted the "decade of women": "We can not reappropriate the patriarchal structure of the family." What we must do, said the writer, is to "emphasize values that are central to the family." This catholic writer did not mention opposition to divorce nor to abortion—the central value stressed was "respect for the elderly." Feminist influence on the catholic mainstream is apparent: "We can not ask the family to proliferate by chance; we must evangelize responsible parenthood." A major feminist point had been accepted by the catholic spokesperson: "We cannot base the family on the subjection of women."[44]

The influence of the pope Italians call *Papa Giovanni* is evident; the cover of each issue of *il focolare* carries his testament: "Figlioli miei amatevi tra voi; cercate più quella che unische che cio che divide" (My children, love one another; look for that which unites rather than that which divides"). For most Italians the continuing legacy of their patron saint, Francis—whom they call *"il poverello"*—is concern for the weak, the poor, "the least." Most left catholics consider the franciscan legacy consonant with looking at the gospel from the standpoint of the poor and the marginal, the least (*"gli ultimi"*). The epigraph for the section of *rocca* which contains letters and appeals from readers is a statement of the gospel: "Ogni volta che avete fatto qualcosa a una dei più piccoli di questi miei fratelli, lo avete fatto a me" (Matt. 15: 40) (Whenever you do something to one of the least of my brothers you have done so to me). The affinity of the franciscan legacy for the Italian left is vivid the first week in October at Assisi when the saint's birth is celebrated. Folk music and dancing mingle with communist political posters in celebration of the saint whose life is considered closest to that of Jesus. A catholic periodical with world-wide circulation, *messenger of St. Anthony*, devoted its issue of October 1979 to the world poor and to St. Francis. The left catholic journal *bozze* is a good source of Italian liberation theology, as are *rocca, idoc,* and *com-nuovi tempi.*

"the other church" in Italy

For some Italian sociologists, an "other" church was emerging in the Italy of the seventies. The chapter headings in a book entitled *L'altra chiesa in Italia* (the other church in Italy), edited by Arnaldo Nesti of *idoc*, are revealing: "the 'catholic world' ends, the church is reborn"; "the crashing of the temple, and the reconstruction of the community"; "from sacred ghetto to commitment in the world"; "from clerical monopoly to a participatory church." Chapter four analyzes "the situation of women in the Italian church."[45]

The significance of postconciliar currents for women in Italy was that the ferment crossed religious boundaries of catholicism, protestantism, and Judaism, belief and nonbelief. The new spirit recovered "popular religion" not as folklore but as "faith" and examined church taboos on sex, birth control, and abortion in a new light. For the mainstream catholic periodical *La famiglia cristiana* the ferment was a frightening whirlpool in which the traditional family represented stability in a troubling time; for conservative catholics the anxiety evoked by rapid change was translated into a need to hang onto the rock of the traditional patriarchal family—or everything would sink.

Yet strong currents impelled what *credenti* called the "irreversible disaggregation" of monolithic structures—not only the messages of John XXIII and the continuing vitality of Italy's franciscan legacy but individual work and silence. Oliviereo Ferrari, an ex-priest, in a 1984 *cnt* article emerged from fifteen years of silence, of work and solidarity with *gli ultimi.* He did not care to talk about his faith because he believes there are many paths to God—from buddhism to mohammedanism, hinduism to anarchism. Jesus, in his view, is suffering, famished, persecuted, homeless, black, without work, sick, always poor, at times even a thief (one of the unattractive characteristics, said Ferrari, of people who are poor). When, a few years ago, his bishop criticized him again, Ferrari answered that for "poor devils" like himself the example of Jesus, the gospel, and the beatitudes were enough. The ex-cleric evaluated his vocation: Why should he preach to people who may have more faith than he had, an anarchist, for example, who gave him one of his two shirts?[46]

A church without priests? asked a cdb booklet in 1981.[47] Papal condemnation of liberation theology has fixed on clerics of South and Central America who work with the poor. Italians know that the papacy faces this problem in its own bailiwick. The pages of Italian left political newspapers in the mid-eighties, as well as Italian religious journals, are full of critical discussion of the pope's condemnations, notably the censure of liberation theology.[48]

Adriana Zarri, feminist nun

The volatile implications of feminism for catholicism are evident in the writings of Adriana Zarri, a catholic nun who writes a column for *rocca*. A cloistered nun, Zarri came out of solitude and silence in the early seventies when Marco Pannella, of Pr, asked her to sign the referendum to repeal the prohibitive law on abortion. The racism of the fascist law on abortion had assaulted Zarri—fascists had placed prohibition against abortion in the context of protecting the "purity of the race." In the abortion campaign Zarri worked with another nun, Marisa Galli. Galli, attached to a congregation, actively supported legalized abortion; she was ousted. Zarri felt her own responsibility deepened: as a cloistered nun, she was not beholden to a congregation.

Zarri wanted to rip away the veil of politeness that hid, she said, the "ignorance of the bible, history, theology" shown by clerical defenders of prohibition of abortion.[49] She thought it ironic that she, who was called a "subversive," helped many doubters to remain in the church. She took upon herself the responsibility of speaking as a catholic nun for alienated catholics.[50]

The nun's views were close to those of Italian feminists. She approved of feminist removal of capital letters: absolute regimes, said Zarri, admire capital letters; under fascism the word *duce* was printed entirely in upper case—DUCE.[51] Analyzing official catholic rhetoric, the nun said that the reality behind idealizations of a woman as "queen" of the household and "angel of the hearth" was women as instruments of male pleasure, women as reproducers for the state, and women as passive instruments of society. The pious and devoted woman whose life was circumscribed by church and home, the woman conservatives positively described as "tutta casa e chiesa" (all home and church) was, in reality, said Zarri, a woman in constant terror of the consequences of sexual acts demanded by her husband.[52]

A few years ago, Zarri noted, abortion had not been a problem; women just aborted in life-threatening, illegal ways and often died. Then women tired of dying to sustain the beliefs of others. Women had reappropriated their own bodies which had traditionally belonged to fathers, husbands, children—to everyone but to women themselves. By repossessing their own bodies women have discovered the values of personal responsibility and of conscience. Women have found the strength to say, I belong to myself, I shall answer for myself. Zarri put the major maxim of Italian feminism, "Io sono mia" (I am my own person), into theological context: "For a believer, every human being belongs to God, but after God, each person belongs to herself or himself."[53]

Zarri worked in support of divorce and of legal abortion as part of her hope to change the church into the one she felt was promised by vatican council II: "poor, disarmed, respectful," a church that does not induce by force ("and law is force"), "a church that gives space to individual choice of conscience."[54] Opposed to the renewal of the concordat between the vatican and the Italian state (it was renewed in 1984) Zarri described the promised church as one without diplomacy and without secular support, "a church that takes Christ and Paul seriously and chooses "people over the sabbath."[55]

The problem, in Zarri's view, was at the top of the church, in the papal presumption of deciding who is "in," and who is "out" of the church, who is faithful and who is not. Yet she called the catholic church "my church" while penning this indictment. To be "in" the church, said this feminist nun, is to support making abortion punishable by jail incarceration, to support a prohibition on birth control, to support maintaining women in inferior status. To be "in" the church is to deny women the pulpit, to allow them some entry into the professions but to regard those who stay at home as better; to be "in" the church is to support the "blasphemy" of a "catholic" political party, an "infallible" pope, little pluralism, no criticism, dependence not on the gospel but on legislation, condemnation of worker priests (who "give a hand to the communists") and intransigence toward eastern countries. To be "in" the church, the nun continued, means closing one's eyes to dictatorships of the right and accepting theology without moral tension.[56]

In an evaluation of five years of the papacy of John Paul II, Zarri said that these years had not been positive for anyone but those who want a "blasphemous" consolidation of church and state. She found his abstract principles a refusal to recognize multiplicity in history and diversity in human situations. The nun ascribed the antifeminist positions of John Paul II to "massiccio virilismo" (gross male chauvinism).[57]

Zarri's feminist theology, articulated in *rocca* and elsewhere, sought to eradicate traditional catholic dualism wherein the body is a prison, the world a vale of tears, and women's sensuality is negatively tied to the earth. For Zarri, "the material order is the place where the spirit becomes visible."[58] In her work of demystification, the nun described prayer as "a mode of being, a life." The feminist aspect of this theology was apparent in Zarri's description of traditional catholic prayers as "masculinizing" and destructive of the spirit. For Zarri, the natural state of prayer is a condition of acceptance, like that of Saint Teresa of Avila. Why Teresa has become almost the patron saint of Italian feminists is suggested in Zarri's comment that the saint's mysticism was "frankly sensual."[59]

Zarri believes the contemporary Italian enterprise of recovering the religion of the people, as well as the tendency to look to an unedited gospel (unmediated by church doctrine) will bring to light religious beliefs "more passionate, more lyrical, more emotional, less rigid, more visceral and chaotic, more audacious in confrontations with God." The religion of the people may be "more superstitious and more pagan," but there is in it a richness, declared Zarri, that the church for all its splendors cannot attain.[60]

Teresa, feminist saint

Italian feminists call her *la gran Teresa* because she was highly controversial, defied the church, and in spite of opposition, carried out necessary reforms. They also like her theology of mysticism—which is inaccessible to spiritual directors—and her plain prose: in one passage Teresa described men in a crisis as apt to crumble like dried parsley.[61] The 1984 curriculum for Centro Virginia Woolf, the feminist university at Rome, included a course on Teresa di Gesù, the name the saint preferred to Teresa of Avila. The course was taught by Lidia Menapace, the new left theorist and feminist theologian, and Teresa Rossi, biographer of Saint Teresa.

The sixteenth-century catholic saint was born into a Jewish family who had been forcibly converted to christianity in the period of the inquisition. Teresa was named for her Jewish grandmother; before Teresa's time the name had not existed in the martyrology of the church. Her grandfather had been brought before the inquisition for the "crime" of returning to the faith of his people despite his forced conversion to christianity. Teresa's life was one of subtle defiance of the church hierarchy and celebration of the "interior life." She was in constant fear, her biographer states, of being condemned by the inquisition.[62]

In the first convent Teresa entered, some nuns had brought with them their status of wealth and honor, even in their new life committed to spirituality. Teresa decided to found a new order of convents dedicated to absolute enclosure and rigorous silence, an order based on the primitive rule of the convent at Mt. Carmel in Israel. Teresa and her discalced carmelites came under suspicion by the authorities, not only because they insisted on a rule of poverty but because they occupied a building to form their convent (as feminists would do in Rome in the twentieth century). Teresa and her carmelite nuns rejected subsidy from the learned theologians of the church and devoted themselves to a life of contemplation and communal work. The only personal possessions of a carmelite nun were her own thinking and her love of God. Carmelite nuns are inspired by Clare, companion of Francis of Assisi. Teresa liked Clare, but considered Mary Magdalen special—the ardor of her love enabled her to know God. Women, said Teresa, are different from men in their relationship to God.

Teresa's stress on the interior life and "mental prayer" was controversial; her *Libro della vita* was denounced as heresy before the inquisition. Heretics who were persecuted at this time in Spain shared a desire for a personal relationship with God: all valued "mental prayer." Among these persecuted heretics, many were converted Jews and many were women.[63] [64] Although persecuted, Teresa was not officially tried by the inquisition.

Bernini's masterpiece of the saint in ecstasy in the church of Santa

Maria della Vittoria at Rome is a sign in marble of the riddle of Teresa. For contemporary feminist theologians who regard the "Jesus movement as a renewal movement within Judaism"[65] there is theological implication in the life of this Jewish woman who was canonized a christian saint and who in 1970 was named one of the two women theologians of catholicism (the other is Saint Catherine of Siena). Teresa evokes themes of contemporary feminist theology: the *"ekklesia* of women" instead of the patriarchy of the church and "women as paradigms of true discipleship."[66]

the advanced—and ancient—feminists of Italy

For many social analysts, feminist laws of the seventies and eighties—particularly legalized abortion—are evidence of the growing secularism of Italian society. Perhaps the abortion law is evidence not of secularism, but of an advanced stage of morality. In a roundtable discussion promoted by *donne e politica* there was agreement across party lines, from the Pci to the Dc, that the important work before women was to see to it that birth control information reached everyone, so that there need not be a resort to abortion. This was a change, women agreed, from morality imposed by the church or by punitive laws of society to morality adjudicated by individual conscience.[67]

Of Italian feminists it is sometimes said that for them there is nothing too advanced nor too ancient. Their view of morality, grounded not on church doctrine nor on prohibitive law, is very advanced. Yet Italian women are also drawn to ancient wisdom. A seminar at Centro Virginia Woolf in the eighties studied the gnostic gospels. Gnostic emphasis on equal access to truth by means of direct experience—equalizing the clergy and the laity—is in affinity with contemporary left catholicism and with feminism. In the gnostic gospels there is also criticism of beliefs in the virgin birth, the resurrection, and the monolithic church, offering considerable evidence that there were many kinds of believers before the church was institutionalized and bound to the state in the fourth century.

A poem in the gnostic gospels has a view of women that is simultaneously ancient and advanced. A close student of the gnostic gospels has concluded that the poem is spoken in the voice of a "feminine divine power":

For I am the first and the last.
I am the honored one and the scorned one.
I am the whore and the holy one.
I am the wife and the virgin. . . .
I am the barren one,
    and many are her sons. . . .
I am the silence that is incomprehensible . . .
I am the utterance of my name.[68]

10

casalinga

Italian feminists and unedited marxist theory: unpaid work of the housewife as a lever of social subversion

Mariarosa Dalla Costa and traditional marxists

The theory of the unpaid work of the housewife illustrates the unedited use of marxist theory by Italian feminists. The career of the issue of wages for housewives in Italian politics seems enveloped in a dialectical process; the issue was taken up, with differing aims, by diverse groups, yet agitation successfully publicized and legitimated feminist demands.

Mariarosa Dalla Costa's analysis of women's power and social subversion, *potere femminile e sovversione sociale con "il posto della donna" di Selma James* (Padua, 1972), has been clouded by a confusion of her argument with the reformist campaign for wages for housewives. English translations lose the humane wit that Dalla Costa (and most Italian feminists) brought to their analyses. Many Italian women understood, as rationalistic interpreters did not, that wages for housewives is an excellent stratagem to promote controversy, and action, on feminist demands.[1]

Traditional marxists had pointed out that housewives are a reserve army of labor, available when capital needs them and expendable when they are not needed. The family serves capitalism, also, as a center of consumption. Dalla Costa took the argument farther. Above all, she stated, the family is a center of production. Countering traditional marxists (she referred to them as "so-called marxists") Dalla Costa declared that women are the ultimate producers, because "women produce the workers" (p. 8). (Page references in parentheses refer to Dalla Costa, *potere femminile*.)

In spite of protective legislation, the condition of women had continued to deteriorate in Italy, said Dalla Costa, because there more than elsewhere, women were secluded in the home. More than in other industrialized countries, Italian capitalism had "liberated" man from household work in order to "render him more exploitable in the factory" (p. 9). The orthodox Italian left continued to see male factory workers as the central protagonists of the social struggle. Speaking for Italian feminists, Dalla Costa declared that it is the house, and therefore the woman, who is "the central figure of social subversion" (p. 10).

The housewife, contended Dalla Costa, is central simply because women who work outside the home continue to do housework. Women in factories are exploited, but housewives married to factory workers are also indispensable to capitalist production, and it is these housewives who "determine the position of all other women" (p. 13). The oppression of women did not begin with capitalism but capitalism destroyed the previous family group and community, and commenced "the most intense exploitation of women, as women" (p. 16). Under capitalism, first the men are excluded from the home, then the children, who are sent to school. The precapitalist form of community, in which the home was a productive and educational center, has been destroyed. Dalla Costa scored capitalism for worsening relations between men and women. For this theorist (and almost all Italian feminists), women's liberation is necessary for the liberation of men also: "Se non si conosce quanto le donne sono sfruttate non si conosce realmente quanto gli uomini lo sono" (If one does not recognize how women are exploited one cannot really understand men's exploitation) (p. 30). Recognizing the subversive potential of the world gay movement, Dalla Costa said that capitalism had elevated heterosexuality to a religion while denying tenderness (p. 27).

Women's autonomy, in Dalla Costa's thinking, means that the autonomy women want for themselves should be extended to all excluded people, beginning with the elderly, children, and the handicapped. In this respect Dalla Costa was close to catholic thinking that in the 1970s amplified women's role in the family beyond the traditional duties of caring for husband and children to include caring for the elderly and the handicapped. Yet Dalla Costa was a feminist: she encouraged a critical look at church doctrine that imposed premarital chastity and confined women's sexuality within marriage to procreation.

Not, said Dalla Costa, wages for the unpaid work of housewives, because wages may sedate women in the house, but emphasis on the unpaid labor of the housewife as a lever for a "higher degree of subversion" in the women's movement (p. 31). Stressing the issue of the unpaid labor of the housewife could, she believed, promote women's solidarity in demanding their due and put women's perspectives in the light of class interests. For example, "To make love and to refuse night work in order to have the possibility of making love is a class interest" (p. 34).

The traditional socialist notion of "socializing" all the functions of the family was not appealing. We do want communal facilities and child-care centers, said Dalla Costa, "but we also want to eat with our own, and to have time to stay with children and with older people, and with the sick when we want, and to have the means to work less. To have time to stay more with men means that they, too, must work less" (p. 35). Women do not want "child-care garages" nor "warehouse space for the old" (p. 36).

In the women's ambience in which Dalla Costa was writing, the issue in 1971 was larger than divorce and abortion. In a leaflet distributed by Lotta Femminile di Padova in June 1971 ("Maternità e aborto," included in the Dalla Costa volume) the main premise of feminists was "to have the possibility of becoming mothers all the times we want to become mothers" (p. 86) and "to make love all the times that we want, to make children all the times that we want in a comfortable, warm, and beautiful environment" (p. 87).

For Dalla Costa, women could use their unpaid household labor as a lever to demand good housing—because their household labor had paid for it. The point was to use women's solidarity to secure a better life. Under prevailing capitalist conditions the work men do mutilates them. Women isolated in the home are also maimed: "The people with whom we have sexual relations are our bosses and they are also mutilated by their work" (pp. 38–39). Dalla Costa cited Frantz Fanon as saying that when the colonized do not organize against the oppressor, they turn on one another (p. 43). In advanced capitalism, the house can be regarded as a "colony governed by the metropolis via the local hierarchy" (p. 43).

versions of the theory of unpaid housework

The concept of women's unpaid household labor, perhaps because it tapped traditional as well as contemporary values, became accepted wisdom in the Italian feminist movement and familiar among the banners of international women's day demonstrations of the seventies. By 1975 there was a reformist version of the theory. In Padua a collective formed around international wages for housework. To overcome the injustice of the *doppio lavoro* (double work) done by women throughout the world, the collective advocated an international strategy of wages for housework.[2]

Women of Great Britain secured family allowances in 1973. Feminists in Germany have produced a considerable body of theory on the issue of unpaid household work.[3] Welfare mothers of the United States in the sixties had taken up the issue, but the cultural climate of U.S. feminism is perhaps gauged by the inability of proponents of the issue of unpaid household work to secure much enthusiasm among feminists. U.S. feminism tended to emphasize strategies for improving the lot of women in the prevailing system; in this context there was little interest in the agitational potential of the issue for a radical subversion of society, as there was in Italy.

In Italy the issue proved to have considerable potential for prodding people to think for themselves. In 1974 Berlinguer said at a European conference of communists that the Pci was opposed to the reformist concept of wages for housewives, whereupon some feminist collectives challenged the prerogative of the communist party to interpret marxist philosophy. The demand for wages for housework was, for these collectives, the "most revolutionary" of all issues because it touched all classes.[4]

The wide appeal of the theme of unpaid household labor was indicated when Cif, the large catholic women's organization, supported the issue. Catholic rendition of the theme stressed the importance of extending the work of the housewife to assist the sick, old people, children, and the church in an "open family" that would alleviate the isolation of women in the home.[5]

Feminist arguments on the issue contended that only in the context of unpaid labor could women's demands for legal abortion, nursery schools, women's clinics, and women's cultural centers be considered seriously. The point was a marxist one: looking to the "material conditions of our lives." As Dalla Costa had pointed out, the issue could be used to push for more radical change. Men were disposed to concede a few nursery schools to women so that women could go out to work, but never enough nursery schools, because legislators counted on the unpaid child care of grandmothers, aunts, and others.

Wage strategists held that only if paid for household work would women have the force to determine the conditions of their external work and the quality of social services. Wages for domestic work would also equalize the household environment and provide a healthier context for decisions on procreation and sexuality. This issue was the only one that could demystify the canard that men worked and women were "parasites" and that could make possible a united movement of women for social change.

"Up to now," declared wage strategists, "we have been the support of men in the struggle for a better society, now we become the protagonists." The issue was important because "it has been the lack of our own money that has always constrained women to sell themselves in the 'market' of marriage, that constricts us to stay in a marriage when we no longer want it." The issue went to the roots, many Italian feminists felt, because women were exploited by those who themselves were exploited by capitalism. Wage strategists maintained that emphasizing women's unpaid household work was the only way women could put their struggle for autonomy on a material basis.[6] Faced with the demand for wages, said women in the campaign, the state was more likely to distribute free dishwashers and laundry machines than to pay women for ninety hours of household work per week, and would be more likely to provide child-care centers immediately rather than to pay for each hour each mother spends taking care of her children.

The campaign engendered a women's nonviolent version of syndicalist strategy: women proposed a general strike for a thirty-six-hour work week for women and men alike. This would be the first genuine general strike, because it would include "all workers." The general strike would mark the end of the assumption that women worked voluntarily in the home; it would also, some said, mark the beginning of the end of the forced labor of men, too.[7] A wages for housework campaign could become a fulcrum for demanding free houses, green spaces, urban planning, as well as free birth control, and accessible and safe abortions.

Some wage strategists stressed that this campaign could improve deteriorating relationships between men and women, which they attributed to women's economic dependence on men. Most important was the potential of this issue for embracing the entire spectrum of women: teenage mothers, prostitutes, wives of soldiers, wives of prisoners, divorced women, separated women, nuns, old women kept unwillingly in the family home or thrust into nursing homes, wives of unemployed men, wives who want, or do not want, to stay with their husbands, women with work outside the home which they cannot abide et al.[8]

The issue of the unpaid household work of women held more resonance in Italy than in other countries because the matter was clearly in consonance with the Italian constitution, viz. Article 1: "Italy is a democratic republic based on work" and Article 3: "All citizens are equal." Italian feminists argued that there was violation of the constitution if bosses were "class A" citizens, "men commanded by the bosses to work" were "class B" citizens, and women, commanded both by bosses and by male heads of family, were "class C" citizens.

In answer to those cultural feminists who criticized the wages campaign as an "economist" measure, its supporters responded, "under capitalism, everything is political. It is a mystification of the bosses to separate the economic, the psychological, the political." The central theme that the unpaid household labor idea touched—"being commanded to work by others who exploit our labor"—tapped a major new left theme: a liberated workplace.[9]

commanded to work by others who exploit our labor"—tapped a major new left theme: a liberated workplace.[9]

the issue—from the left to the center to the right

The proposition of the unpaid work of housewives was accepted as common wisdom in Italy by the mid-eighties, not only by feminists but by others. Mainstream catholic associations of Italian women have addressed themselves to improving the lives of housewives and have implicitly accepted the thesis of unpaid work in advocating wages for housewives. The movimento diritti lavoro casalingo (move- ᵥ/ ment for rights of household work), with an office in Florence, has campaigned for recognition of housework and the people who do it, male or female, as well as for an amplified definition to include the work of taking care of those who live in the house. Wages are to be paid, in their plan, by the state, with a tax on the manufacture of cigars, cigarettes, and spirits.[10] Other Italian women's organizations have campaigned for public aid to the family, to minors, to the old and the handicapped—not as "welfare" but as redistribution of income on the basis of social justice.

In 1979 the Dc presented a bill in Parliament addressed to the "crisis in the family." The bill praised the role of women in the family as the "first and unsubstitutable educator of the next generation." Woman's role as housewife was exalted in the proposal to give allowances to the housewife-mother. After their defeats on the issues of divorce (1974) and legal abortion (1978), the Dc hurried to point out they had supported the vote for women in 1945. The Dc now held that family income should be adequate enough to maintain the family, to enable women to give up outside work, and to encourage motherhood. The Dc proposal for family allowances for women was predicated on women abstaining from outside work; allowances were to be increased for each child (up to the third). Allowances were designated only for children born to married couples, not for other unions.[11] Some of the Dc proposals called up memories of early papal encyclicals and of fascist measures to keep women excluded from the outside work force and confined to their primary task of reproducing children for the state. In the seventies Dc measures did not sound like a return to Mussolini in the context of feminist successes, particularly the abortion law of 1978. Yet the Dc measure for wages for housewives was motivated, in part, by anxiety about preserving the traditional patriarchal family.

Apparently, so was the papal encylical *Laborem exercens* (1981), which underlined the "unsubstitutable" role of women in the family.[12] From the papal perspective, men need remuneration adequate enough to sustain their role in maintaining the family. The pope recommended that a family allowance be given to the male head of the family to induce women to leave work outside the home and to return to the family. This encyclical was consistent with earlier papal statements that the place of women is in the home, but it is noteworthy that women were now to be indirectly influenced to return to the home by a higher wage to the male head of the family. Papal statements did not take into account the large number of women heads of family, in Italy and elsewhere.

The concept of the unpaid work of the housewife has received support in Italy implicitly from the pope, as well as from the far right Msi, the center Dc, and the left-libertarian Pr. The right-wing associations of the issue put the wage campaign in a dim light for many women on the left. Women in the Pci claimed that catholic support for wages was manipulative: "The Cif women knew very well that this demand would never get any real response on the side of the government."[13] Women on the left believed that parties of the right seized the issue in order to refute the Pci emphasis on women's right to work outside the home. To some women on the left the wage campaign seemed to be a return to the fascist policy of meager family allowances for women and children paid to the male *capofamiglia*. The rhetoric of some men on the right who supported wages for housewives did seem to connote returning women to the role of angel of the hearth.[14]

What has not been acknowledged by some Italian feminists (nor by many feminists elsewhere) is that the issue of wages for housewives can produce a broad band of women's solidarity, and did so in Italy, where it has been a major pivot of discussion of women's condition in groups not otherwise open to other feminist issues. Although some feminists were not pleased by what they saw as a campaign to return women to the home, other women welcomed the proposal for family allowances and the left libertarian Pr endorsed the Dc proposal for a L350,000 *(about $200) monthly family stipend. Other people on the left regarded the matter as a cynical game:

* 1985

the center and the right proposing family allowances that cannot be funded by the Italian budget. The Pci, by 1983 visibly instructed by feminists, stated that "economics" is not the nexus of the problem of the family. The party described the Dc family allowance proposal as manipulative; under the benign guise of rewarding women for household work, the family allowance would keep women in a subordinate role in the family and society.

In Italy, as elsewhere, the subject of the family and the home is in flux. Some feminists in the United States hold, for example, that having men share household work is a way of bringing men back to the household from which they were ousted by industrialization. Everywhere the subject has been made more complex by the advances of computer technology. Some Italian feminists have suggested that computers may mean the return to the home of men as well as women, but the immediate consequence will be even more isolation of the family from the rest of society. Some recommend an alliance of technicians, small and medium-sized business, and women to see to it that the new technology is used for democratization.[15]

In another direction, some feminists in Italy have been working for humanization of conditions inside factories where women work—flexible hours, child care, and women's health clinics inside factories. To encourage more women to participate in public life, Italian feminists recommend close-by child care facilities for women legislators and administrators. One proposal (not implemented as of the mid-eighties) called for a child care facility in Italy's parliament building; this would not only be a convenience for women legislators, it would enable children, said feminists, to visit the nation's solons during discussion of critical bills (for example, legislation about nuclear missile bases) that implicated the lives of the younger generation.

Agitation around the issue of the unpaid work of housewives was a significant factor in the successful fight of Italian feminists for legislation on divorce, equal family rights, child care facilities, and legal abortion. The conflict between feminists who wanted to use the concept as a lever of social subversion and feminists who simply wanted wages for unpaid work kept the matter in ferment. Udi (perhaps in deference to party policy) did not advocate wages for housewives, but did emphasize the centrality of *casalinghità* (the condition of being a housewife) for women.[16] The theme fell into a receptive en-

vironment not only because the Italian constitution, and contem- /
porary polls, indicate that work is the uppermost value of most Italians; the pervasive awareness of marxist principles enables most
Italians to feel the injustice in the case of the unpaid work of housewives.

In the early 1980s women in the Pci acknowledged the significance of the wage campaign in having helped feminist issues be
understood by twelve million housewives.[17] (The number of Italian
housewives had declined from thirteen million in the previous decade.) In 1984 the concept of wages for housewives continued to
demonstrate its agitational possibilities. A new Italian women's party,
formed around the primary issue of nuclear disarmament, recommends wages to housewives, with monies to be secured from funds ˅
now used for military appropriations.[18]

from unpaid housework to lavoro nero
to the exploited work of the third world

Dalla Costa, who is among the most influential theorists to have
emerged from the movement, surveyed the several directions the
feminist movement was taking in 1976. She noted that relations between men and women were becoming tenser and that "reformist"
tendencies were dominant in the concerns of contemporary feminists. Convinced that patchwork measures would not improve wom-
en's lot, she said that the point was not reform but social subversion.

Dalla Costa documented the progress of women in the lowering of
birth statistics: "The decline in births is a decline in the production
of forced labor."[19] She theorized that the decline in births had precipitated a crisis in capitalism: insofar as women have refused to procreate forced labor, capitalism is now exploiting them with part-time
and seasonal work, and cottage industry, particularly evident in the
lavoro nero (literally "black work"—illegal work performed without
benefit of protective industrial legislation). In Dalla Costa's view, exploitation was put into the Italian canon in 1976 when a woman
minister of labor (Dc) removed the restriction on child labor and
abolished the prohibition on night work for women.

Dalla Costa located the sources of future energy for the Italian
women's movement not in the industrialized North, where educated
women had taken the lead, but in the underdeveloped South, where

most women were still caught in the thrall of the patriarchal family. Migration from the countryside to the city produced deracination, but one merit was that it sometimes gave a southern woman more control over the family salary and more power to spend money on her children's education. Women who remained in the South after their husbands emigrated north to find work found themselves free to look to the conditions of their lives. Their children (the post-1968 youth generation) were often radicalized; a new type of family emerged in the seventies in the South, of mothers and children who were radical.[20] To Dalla Costa, the migration of southern men contained another radical implication: "They become a class of international workers."[21] They and the wives they took with them suffered, in addition to other indignities, the oppression of being regarded as negatively *other* in cities of northern Italy as well as northern Europe.[22]

The perceived connection between unpaid domestic work and the exploited work of people of the third world concerns contemporary theorists, notably German feminists like Claudia von Werlhof, who argue that if the nature of housework is understood, we have understood the political economy. In this unedited view of marxist theory, the proletarian is disappearing, the sources of capitalist accumulation are the exploited work of peoples of the third world and of unpaid housewives everywhere.[23]

In Italy's contemporary economic crisis women who had earlier been able to find jobs outside the home are now unemployed. There is also an increase in the marginal work of *lavoro nero*. Women engaged in *lavoro nero* in the home while continuing to have the responsibility for housework readily understand the feminist concept of *doppio lavoro*, or double work—the unpaid housework plus outside work that most of the world's women do.[24]

11

casa della donna

"this house belongs
to all women in struggle"

Evaluating Italy in the mid 1970s, a United States political scientist, Giuseppe Di Palma, said that since 1969 the country had sustained the most prolonged period of "social conflict, turmoil, and even violence in its postwar history."[1] In the seventies not only factory workers went on strike but also professionals and scavengers, civil servants and teachers, gravediggers and hotel employees. Some of these strikes were promoted by the large labor syndicates, but others were undertaken by autonomous factory, school, and other committees—an autonomy that might eventually reflect one individual's decision: on an *autostrada* we came across a toll taker who put out his own *sciopero* (on strike) sign and waved motorists through.

Student confrontation of the late sixties developed into what was called "permanent agitation," the extraparliamentary perspective sometimes disintegrated into little groups consciously or unconsciously involved in violence. Bombings—beginning with the right-wing incident in Milan in 1969—were attributed thereafter to the left as well as to the right. Ransom kidnappings, bank robberies, inflation and economic recession, worsening conditions in the South, and calls for law and order were the backdrop for frequent shifts of government in the center-left coalition of the Dc, Psi, and smaller parties that had governed since the early sixties.

Politics covered an Italian's life, from government-owned radio and television (with different channels for different points of view) to the clientelism that filled all bureaucracies with party appointments. The sector of public-owned corporations (large since the era of fascism) grew. The thirty-first government of Italy since the war came to office in 1973. After the defeat of the referendum to repeal the divorce law in 1974, Italian theorists began to write articles with the word *crisis* in their titles. A major realignment of Italian politics began to be evident in the local elections of June 1975 when communists attained 33 percent of the votes and the Dc fell to approximately 35 percent, their lowest percentage since 1946. If votes for the Pci were added to votes for socialists and new left parties, an unprecedented 46 to 47 percent of the Italian electorate was on the left by mid decade.[2]

High unemployment, and what conservatives regarded as a rending of the social fabric, followed the election of 1976. Both strikers of 1977 and autonomous bands of young people became violent. Kneecappings and kidnappings by the red brigades took newspaper headlines, culminating in the 1978 kidnap and murder of Aldo Moro. Italians call the last part of the seventies "years of lead" because of the number of shootings.

Inflation in Italy was the highest in Europe (real wages rose by 72 percent between 1969 and 1978) and unemployment, mostly of youth under thirty, increased. To curb inflation, unions in 1978 accepted wage restraint in return for economic development, particularly of the South. Terrorism was countered by antiterrorist legislation that included provisions for preventive detention.

Non-Italian social scientists surveying the Italy of the seventies found familiar theoretical models inapplicable. For some scholars Italy embodied "the crisis of the West"—an organic crisis for the left, a crisis of governability for the right.[3] Others said that the Italian crisis "cannot be reduced to a single dimension, however profound, and consists precisely in the multiplicity of crises—economic, political, social and international—in which the country finds itself."[4] And yet others believed that Italy was in transition, "confusing, contradictory, absurd or dangerous—but a transition nonetheless, toward a new synthesis of democracy, capitalism and social equality."[5] The synthesis, in the hope of the Italian left, would join democracy, socialism, and social equality. Feminists, more allusive than explicit, left signs that their efforts tended toward wider democracy, self-managed socialism, and equality with respect for differences.

After 1976 death hovered over the consciousness of Italian feminists. In a feminist demonstration for legal abortion in Rome in May 1977 Giorgiana Masi was killed—in unclear circumstances and it was never known by whom. Women placed a plaque on the spot she died on the Trastevere side of the Garibaldi bridge. Ana Noon has translated the poem on the plaque:

If the October Revolution
    had only been in May.
If you were still alive
    if I weren't powerless in front of your murder
If my pen were a winning weapon
    if my fear could explode in the streets
    courage born of rage strangled in my throat
If having known you could become our strength
If the flowers that we gave
    to your courageous life in our death
    at least had become garlands
    of the struggle of all women
Then . . . it wouldn't be words searching for life
    but life itself without adding anything.

anonymous

On October 2, 1976, an old unused church building on a street off the Corso in Rome was occupied (without the formality of paying rent) by the movimento di liberazione della donna (Mld). This collective, which had taken the lead in raising the abortion issue, founded a *casa della donna* on a street called Governo Vecchio (the old government). The *casa* became a birth-control center, then a child-care place, then an office of concern about violence against women. On May Day 1977 all the women's collectives in Rome joined in the occupation of the building. Despite threats to cut off water and electricity, and other harassment, the women were not ousted. In the first days a telegram was sent to the church authorities who owned the building: "We need a space where we can organize our struggles, where we can develop our creativity, where we can meet one another and grow politically." The women named spaces in the palazzo: "room of the moon," "room of the witches."[6]

The *casa della donna* became the center of agitation for the 1978 abortion law and the organizing hub for the 1981 defeat of the referendum to repeal it. Also from here was launched the signature campaign for a referendum against sexual violence in 1979, precipitating a wide-ranging national discussion of sexual violence, broadly defined to include marital rape. The referendum against sexual violence engendered male anxiety and internal arguments among feminists and, when it became a bill, parliamentary sandbagging; in the mid eighties the bill was still a pivot of feminist protest.[7]

The referendum against sexual violence was presented to parliament by the Mld, Udi, Women's Network, the women's collective Pompeo magno, and the labor syndicate of metal and mechanical workers, Fim. The referendum brought to the surface many differences among women: some did not like putting suggestive acts and carnal violence under the same rubric of punishment (two to ten years); some did not think it possible to make a clear distinction between physical violence and love; antiinstitutional feminists did not like to solve a problem with a law. Discussion around the referendum became subtle: there is "real" rape and there is "symbolic" rape expressed in women's madness, women's fantasies about having been raped, and so forth. Some women worried about unjustly accusing men.[8]

To sustain the activities of the *casa*, women sold handicrafts and used clothing. There was a *collettivo* for alternative food and women's health, a dance group, and a daily newspaper—*quotidiano donna* There were two radio stations, radio donna and radio Lilith (named for the woman in Judaic folklore who was the first wife of Adam, preceding the creation of Eve). Among other groups associated with the *casa* was one that coordinated women's health clinics and a *collettivo* of Alitalia stewardesses. There were yoga classes, student collectives, teacher collectives, and a collective concerned with the "150-hour" law that enabled women factory workers and housewives to take classes in women's studies. The *casa* became the place where la Maddalena planned its street spectacles; where the collective Pompeo magno called a national conference on separatism; where the feminist university, Centro Virginia Woolf, began.

In an instantaneous network, women gathered here in crises (for example, when Giorgiana Masi was killed) or for confrontations between "autonomous" feminists and Udi women over the abortion issue. Some women lived here, arguing continually over space, calling the women who came to meetings at the *casa* the "nomads." All left their traces—people who were curious, women who had been violated, women in need of help. The graffiti women wrote on *casa* walls may be a historian's best source for the cultural and political beliefs of Italian feminists in the last years of the decade of the seventies.

love, woman, fantasy

In 1979 during one of the periodic housekeeping binges it was decided to paint over the walls; this catalyzed some women into a rush to photograph the graffiti on the walls. Somebody counted the most frequently used words: *love, woman,* and *fantasy.* The graffiti presented a women's dialogue. A woman from France: "Vous reproduisez les memes schemas que cette societe de merde e d'interdicts." (You are reproducing the same schemes of this society of excrement and prohibitions). A gentler visitor: "Ciao compagne, sono felice di essere venuta qui anche se non ho trovato nessuna. Grazie" (Hello companions, I am happy to have come here even if I did not find anyone. Thank you.)[9] Dacia Maraini, the feminist playwright and novelist, camped here during the occupation and noted the contradictions among the graffiti. The ambivalent voice: "We are the mountains of the ego," the wispy hope: "I would like to have the liberty of that butterfly," the voice of rage: "imbecilic life," followed by the rational advice, "No power games among women," and the voice of fatigue: "I am tired of waking in the morning I am tired of taking the autobus I am tired of lighting cigarettes I am tired of eating of drinking of sleeping I am tired of giving love I am tired of being tired I would like to disappear softly silently without bothering anybody." "Io sono mia," the maxim of Italian feminists, was repeated over and over: "I am my own person."[10]

There were political and cultural exhortations: "The task of women is to revolutionize the revolution." "Become homosexuals!" "Homosexuals yes, but let live those of us who are heterosexuals." Maraini said the graffiti were characterized by a sardonic rage and yet a tender understanding that she considered "historically feminine" and in sharp contrast to the "exaltation, fanaticism, myopia, and violence" that "are plentifully found in places of masculine revolutionary politics."[11]

Not a comfortable place (most of the time without electricity and water), the *casa della donna* was a last stop for women who needed to abort, for women who sought employment, for women who did not know where they were going to sleep that night, for women looking for legal help, for women who had lost themselves. For this U.S. observer, the place was strange and powerful. The shouting at the meetings, the graffiti I tried to read by candlelight, the contrast of the grandeur of the balustrade and the crumbling walls, the sheer density of this women's movement that gathered here by word of mouth. The lyricism of some of the graffiti caught my eye: "Our desires are memories projected into the future." "One sees only with the heart." "This house belongs to all women in struggle." The urge to life: "voglioviverevogliovivere" (iwanttoliveiwanttolive). The political analysis: "It seems to me mistaken to close ourselves up in this bell jar, because if we need to change everything, it certainly means that we must stand together, but we must include everyone, men, too, because not all of them are as imbecilic as we think. This is my view. (signed) superfeminist." The dominant view, however, was: "Only women can change this society and transmit the love that the men want to destroy." Repeated themes: "Liberate me from the family and I will liberate the world." "Let us put flowers in the cannons of the world." "Madness is life; discipline is death. *Viva* the beneficent chaos of life." "Woman is beautiful, witch is better, lesbian is best." Self-determination was defined to include "my body, my commitment, my joy, my pain, my destiny." Gramsci's dictum—"Optimism of the will, pessimism of the mind"—was given a feminist translation: "In socialism, the harvest of potatoes is tripled—this is optimism of the will." Pessimism of the mind: "What place will there be among the potatoes and the wine and the grey sense of the bureaucrat for our delirium, my anxiety, my thirst for life, our weeping and laughter, the fantasies of our lunar cycles, the contorted roots of our being women?"[12]

This last was the unspoken refrain to all the activities at the *casa della donna*. What place would there be in a socialist society for women's delirium, anxiety, thirst for life, weeping, laughter, and fantasies? In 1976, largely because feminist issues swelled support for the Pci, the communist party received its highest historical percentage of votes and campaigned as a "government" party entering into a working coalition with the Dc; precisely at that point many feminists threatened to withdraw from politics, in some cases disenrolling from the two "historic" left parties, the Pci and the Psi. This was something of a Lysistrata strategy, in consonance with feminist demonstrations that year to "take back the night."

the personal is political; liberty, equality, and "not a single woman's wretchedness is alien to me"

The central knot of Italian politics, noted Rossana Rossanda, is that for centuries women have been thrust out of politics. The irony now was that many women rejected politics. She spoke of the malaise among women by 1979: "Thinking back on it, ours was a bizarre age. We ceased to think, as had our mothers, of sex in an inhibited and puritan manner, but the release of inhibitions did not bring the happiness of the classical world, nor unity among ourselves; we dressed freely and threw ourselves into bikinis in the sun, only to hide how uneasy we were under our skins."[13] At least, said Rossanda, emancipated women knew they were anxious, nonemancipated women knew less.

Rossanda, a founder of the new left Pdup, tried to understand herself and feminists and reflected on her own life. She had been born in the North in 1924; in 1943, as a partisan, she entered the Pci. By 1959 she was a member of the central committee of the largest communist party in the West; in 1969, as a member of the *manifesto* group, she criticized the "reformism" of the Pci and was "radiated" out of the party. As an editor of *il manifesto* and a Pdup spokeswoman she supported all feminist issues but would not call herself a feminist. As a theoretician in the new left party, she conceived of her role as constructive critic of the Pci. She brought the same critical perspective to feminism.[14]

Asked to participate in a radio series with other women, she used the opportunity to find out what feminists actually believed, as well as to clarify her own thinking. The series became the basis of her book *Le altre* (The others), an exploration of what Italian feminists mean by liberty, fraternity, equality, democracy, fascism, resistance, the state, the party, revolution, and feminism. Translated into many languages, the book is an indispensable source for the political thought of Italian feminists.

In the radio dialogues, the women discussed "politics" (the word is of Greek origin and refers to the city and to organized society). For millennia women have been relegated to the family and generally been excluded from deciding matters regarding the city. Politics has been the dominion of men who made the laws and the rules, who created nations with just and unjust wars. "Wars have been initiated by men," said Rossanda, "and then they send women to bury the dead."[15]

In Italy it is no more than a century or so ago that women ventured outside the home to enter politics—only a few women. Rossanda herself had been "invaded" by politics. At seventeen, studying philosophy and history of art, she looked out the window and saw British airplanes dropping bombs on Milan. She felt that her life in the library was a delusion and that communists were the most resolute and rational of the political forces; she put her art studies aside and became a partisan.[16]

Clara Gallini, an anthropologist at the University of Naples, said she was brought up in a well-educated family where she was taught that politics was the business of men and a sordid matter—*una cosa sporca*. In her southern Italian family, the second principle she learned was, "Don't become involved." Involvement meant compromising one's self. She did not realize until later that this message was directed to women; men were obviously "involved" and obviously "compromised" participants in political life. She did not become involved until she was transferred to Sardinia, where the reality of southern Italian life became a catalyst to her political thinking.[17]

Other women discussed how they had become political. It happened to Anna Maria Romolo while working in a labor union, because it seemed to her that the large parties of Italian workers (Pci and Psi) and the unions were identical. The younger women in the dialogue became involved in politics by way of the student movement. Politics for them was a way of interpreting reality and society;

they did not become personally engaged until the seventies when they became participants in women's collectives and felt for the first time as if they were protagonists, not spectators.[18]

Anna Maria Magnani Noya, of the Italian socialist party (Psi), said women in the leadership of contemporary political parties in Italy were "ghettoized" to areas of their "competence"—interpreted as health, welfare, abortion, etc. Other women discussed the econo-mistic bias of men: "The marxism of the parties has been one which sees economics as the pivot of society, and economics of develop-ment as the lever of change." All labor union meetings today begin "Compagne e compagni," said Noya, but she wondered if women's insights had been incorporated into union practices.[19]

Others said "tens of thousands" of women found feminism in Italy in the seventies, "even those who do not become feminists sense it, it is transmitted throughout the culture, becomes culture, arrives even to women who listen silently, and changes them." "Perhaps no other cultural transformation has been, in these years, so pro-found."[20]

Rossanda tried to find the components of a feminist political model in the radio dialogue. In the traditional revolutionary triad of liberty, equality, and fraternity, feminists are closest, she believed, to liberty. Equality, the word used among male workers, "is a communist value." Fraternity, she maintained, is conveyed in salutations among communists. Although women, "atomized in the verticality of the patriarchal family," are unequal, they nonetheless prefer liberty to equality. Men like equality as a value because it seems more attain-able; women like liberty, because it has utopian implications.

Rossanda, herself, preferred equality: liberty, she argued, implies subordination of others, but equality suggests liberating everyone. She recognized that liberty connotes the need of oppressed minori-ties and of the colonized for freedom. A young feminist explained that liberty to her generation meant "libertà di essere diversa,"—liberty to be different, perhaps like Antigone, who wanted the liberty to be "of those who love, not of those who hate." Thinking about this, Rossanda said that the liberty to be different suggested separa-tion from society. She recalled that Gramsci had said that no libera-tion movement is born without a stage of separation and negation, only then can you project outside yourself an affirmation that is no longer fragile.[21]

Fraternity (in feminist translation, sisterhood) was illustrated by Lidia Compagnano: a self-managed women's clinic—a small space of two rooms in a person's house, an environment of "gentleness, grace" in which volunteer workers give frightened newcomers a sense of warmth and friendship without roles, hierarchy, or difference between those who help and those who need help. Instead of "solidarity of women" Italian feminists often say, "not a single woman's wretchedness is alien to me." [22]

The significance of the resistance in the heritage of Italian feminists was discussed in the radio dialogue. Rossanda saw endurance as the feminist value derived from this experience: "the obstinate capacity of holding on, of suffering, of not letting one's self die, of not letting one's self be killed, of resisting." Men win or lose with a great deal of clamor, women resist often in silence. She cited the silent resistance of many Italian women to fascism. Someone added that this was similar to many women who do not call themselves feminists but who daily resist masculinist power silently and effectively. [23]

"Historical feminists" (those allied with traditional left parties, the Pci and Psi) are willing to share the power of the state; newer feminists are not, said Rossanda. She considered this a dilemma that harked back to Antigone: the ancient heroine commemorated in Sophocles' play was not, said Rossanda, a democrat: she did not consult with anyone in making her decision to bury her brother—nothing could stop her but death. This unwillingness to accept the compromise of institutions, said Rossanda, was characteristic of many contemporary feminists. Someone pointed out that this was not so much unwillingness to be compromised as the fact that prevailing institutions were guided by a masculine vision. Women feel that the forms of politics must change to convey the specific dimension of feminist consciousness; governments that bring the world close to catastrophe, destroying resources and risking nuclear holocaust, are scarcely likely to attract feminist participation. Manuela Fraire said that women's proper dominion is society not government; changing that will change the world. [24]

Rossanda insisted that political power can be used constructively as well as destructively. The discussants concluded that women must move simultaneously in two directions, inside and outside institutions. Referring to the Pci, Margherita Repetto Alaia said that women must keep in mind that when they are inside large institutions, women really cannot change anything, because they are in a world ✓ that men dominate.[25]

political parties and women's autonomy

The radio dialogue pinpointed the salient fact that the institution feminists most distrust is the political party. All parties, including those on the left, were accused of being heavy, conservative in structure, and unable to live up to their professed aims. In the parties of the old and new left there were in 1979 few women in leadership positions. Italian feminists cited statistics from the Soviet Union (where women are 70 percent of the population) that indicate that women have practically all the responsibility for the schools—but not the universities—and for health, yet women comprise only 24 percent of the communist party. There are even fewer women in Soviet leadership. The conversation revealed that the situation in Italy was complex; not only is there male resistance to women at the top of the parties, but there is the resistance of women to being identified with the parties. "Women see in the parties a reflection of the structure of the world that they abhor."[26]

Women are estranged from a hierarchical and competitive mode of politics. A woman of the Psi said that nonetheless women in the parties could change them. Adele Faccio pointed out that Pr had created a new form for women who want to be identified with a horizontal and cultural, rather than a vertical and political, dimension. A woman in Pdup said, "There were many women in the explosions of 1968, but there have never been many women in the leadership of the new left."[27] All parties in Italy give some territory to women, but that is not the issue.

Feminists and many others in Italy have focused on political parties as their favorite target of criticism. Yet participants in this radio series regarded the process of many political parties in competition to be the core of Italian democracy: "When no political conflicts exist in a society there is no democracy."[28] Fascism was defined as the destruction of conflicting political ideas.

The contradiction between distrust of political parties and recognition of the importance of many parties in democratic pluralism may perhaps be unknotted by considering the desire of feminists and others to extend democracy beyond political institutions, as well as the widely diffused Italian distrust of political parties. Italians criticize their political parties in the context of a highly politicized society and within a widely held belief which was expressly stated (by women and men) in the radio dialogues: Italy, "in spite of everything," is the "most democratic country in the world."[29]

Italian feminists use membership or nonmembership in political parties as a lever. A good many withdrew after 1976 and feminist institutions like *quotidiano donna* made nonaffiliation with a political party a condition for writing for the newspaper. The decline of the vote for the Pci in the 1979 elections reflected the ability of Italian women to express their will by not voting. Most returned to exercising the vote in 1981 to defeat the antiabortion referendum. Afterward, some stayed in the Pci for "sentimental reasons." Among feminists who return to the parties, pointed out Lidia Menapace, there is a cold, "lay" attitude that what they can accomplish inside the parties is very small. "They stay inside as secret agents of feminism," perhaps conquering a little ground.[30]

Others stay in the party as an acknowledgment of reality. Margherita Repetto Alaia said that first she belonged to Udi then to the Pci; she remained affiliated with the Pci as a feminist because "in the history of our times, we can not measure political reality without the Pci. That is the reason for my being communist." Two years later, Repetto was instrumental in severing Udi from the Pci. In 1979 she stated, "It is very important that a women's movement exist outside the parties. It is not possible to win from inside the party solely. Only from the outside can women have the strength to have a dialectical relation with the party."[31]

What did revolution mean to Italian feminists in 1979? Rossanda pointed out that whenever there have been revolts from below against oppression and for radical change, there have always been women: in the French revolution; in 1848; in the Paris Commune; in the Russian revolution; in the Chinese, Algerian, and Cuban revolutions. Women are revolutionaries today in Latin America. A woman factory worker said revolution for her meant "continual change of situations, of things, also of persons, a process that should never have an end."[32]

Participants in the radio conversation acknowledged what may be a distinguishing characteristic of the Italian movement: "We feminists were born inside, alongside, the left and marxism."[33] There was agreement that a revolution against capital had to happen, "obviously." But women had to confront "our specific revolution" in the relationship between the sexes. Here is the rub, said Rossanda: "We have presupposed the revolution against capitalism and we wanted to go deeper."[34] The problem, she said, is that women have lost contact between these two levels—the revolution against social structure and the personal revolution.[35]

Manuela Fraire was asked what revolution meant to her. She said she had lost the idea that good people are on one side and bad on the other. She also was repelled by the excesses of contemporary socialist societies. "I still believe in the revolution but not as a precise moment when we change everything. I believe the revolution is a process." For Fraire, and most cultural feminists, marxism is not sufficient, nor is it a simple matter of taking power. Fraire agreed with Michel Foucault that power exists in all the connective tissue of society. Rossanda: "How do we start to change it?" Fraire: "One starts with one's self. I am convinced that power is part of the psychological structure of the individual." Who is the vanguard? Fraire: "Not the Fiat worker. In Italy I don't know." Rossanda, "What is communism?" Fraire: "I don't know, even if, for me, this idea continues to evoke the idea of cooperation between individuals who do not all have the same beliefs. Communism is, for me, the possibility of coexisting in a society with a diversity of beliefs, of capacities, without being unequal."[36]

feminism

What did *feminism* mean to the women gathered in that Rome radio station in February 1979? The presiding feminist critic (a role she has held as a lecturer at the Centro Virginia Woolf, as editor of *l'orsaminore*, of *Antigone*, and as participant in many symposia), Rossana Rossanda, said that although the term was born in the last century, it has been transformed in this generation. "It is a movement born under the sign of separatism, jealous of itself, with a tormented itinerary, and still on the road of transformation."[37]

Lidia Compagnano said that *feminism* was a political word that means that women undergo oppression, that subordination is a condition common to all women, that this subordination keeps them enchained and separate from the government of the city (organized society). The chains, in feminist perception, come from the deflection of one of women's possibilities—that of procreation—into predetermined destiny. A destiny defined as natural becomes the social and personal destiny of women. This is the opposite of masculine destiny, which is considered productive and social and entrusted with governing the city. It was pointed out that *feminism* is a political word because it sets before women the necessity of uniting. Women are divided by men into their roles as wives, mothers, housewives, prostitutes—roles that keep them atomized in the social network.

For Margherita Repetto Alaia, Italian feminists tend to emphasize difference from, rather than equality with, men because they hope to give to society that difference in a qualitative transformation: "One does not liberate society from exploitation if one does not address the particular exploitation that "il maschilismo" exercises over women."[38] For Lidia Menapace, the first phase of feminism was a fight for equal rights; this has been widened to include the modification of the relationship between women and men; the end of women's emotional, even intellectual, dependence on men; and an appreciation of the relationships of women with women. Rossanda noted that what seemed new about the feminism of the 1970s was the criticism of formalism, of abstraction, of institutional generalizations—as opposed to direct, immediate expression, with one eye on politics and one eye on a sphere that cannot, said Rossanda, be called political.[39]

what of the men?

The women who organized the radio dialogue at the *casa della donna* invited men to participate. A few young men from the Liceo Mamiani of Rome responded to the invitation, inserting pointed interpolations ("What do you mean by liberty?"). In a discussion of the state, Pietro Ingrao, the Pci statesman who was in 1979 head of the Italian house of deputies, was asked to give his point of view. His good will, and bafflement, were apparent.

Ingrao said he could understand women's desire to have their separate perspectives, but he did not agree that in every instance an institution is "una gabbia" (a cage). Indeed, for women to be able to change the traditional role of women, they needed an institutional strategy. And if women insisted on a counter role, how could an international victory of workers come about? Rossanda explained that feminists regarded politics as "masculine"; hence their diffidence. Ingrao said matters should change, but what good does indifference to politics bring about? "Nothing, absolutely nothing." For women to espouse an attitude of distrust of politics, said Ingrao, meant insuring their subordinate role.

The dialogue illustrated the process of one gender being "atomized" by the dominant gender because Ingrao subsided into silence when women took over the discussion at this point.[40] In the interest of fairness, Rossanda invited him to a subsequent conversation, which was printed as an appendix in *Le altre*. Addressing Ingrao in his capacity as president of the house of deputies, Rossanda said that women in the resistance had indicated that they could determine the future of their country, did Ingrao think that the small number of women in political office in Italy reflected women's ability? Ingrao said he would first concentrate on positive points. He said that the resistance was a first break with the "monopoly of politics" which should not be underestimated. The second positive point was the "acceleration that there has been in the last few years." There was a profound difference before 1974 and afterward for women; Ingrao listed the divorce law, the family rights law, laws for health clinics, equal pay, and legal abortion. In addition to laws favorable to women, their representation in parliament had increased. Rossanda inquired, were not women in parliament assigned to traditional areas of infancy, family, and assistance? Ingrao insisted there had been profound changes for women in recent years, but because women's issues touched "the very foundations of society," changes for women could not be "drastic and immediate." What was needed, said Ingrao, was a qualitative jump in the nature of politics.

In a revealing concluding statement, Ingrao said the woman question was analogous to the southern question. When people from Calabria had come to Rome to demonstrate for jobs, he had told them that the issue must be considered in the context of "all the political problems of Italy in 1978." And this, said the Pci leader, is "even more true for the women's movement."[41]

In the 1979 elections some feminists registered their anger at what seemed to be an inability of Pci men to comprehend a feminist perspective by staying away from the polls. Political estrangement was deepened by tiredness, disillusionment after a decade of militance, and horror at increasing violence, including violence toward women. In 1979 fascists attacked women of the Rome radio station radio città futura. Shortly thereafter two young male terrorists, without apparent reason, shot a woman at work in Turin.[42]

Incomprehension, myopia, or inability to cope with the matter may be demonstrated in the inability of men of the Pci to credit women for post-1974 party successes. The same reasons may account for the omission in most Italian political studies written in the seventies of any reference to the women's movement. A non-Italian woman, Karen Beckwith, has written a valuable external observer's evaluation, "Women and Parliamentary Politics in Italy, 1946–1979." Beckwith argues that Italian women secured the vote in 1945 because they had fought as partisans against fascism. The Dc supported enfranchisement because they expected that catholic women would support their party. The Pci supported enfranchisement in large part because of Togliatti's hope to build an indigenous Italian communism. Both major parties were allied with women's organizations (Cif and Udi) that were formally autonomous but in effect dependent because subsidized by the parties.

In Beckwith's view, the Dc perspective emphasizes woman as wife and mother, with home and family regarded as having precedence over all of women's needs. The Dc does call for equal participation of men and women in public life, but its tie to a conservative catholic constituency requires it to take negative positions on contraception, divorce, and abortion. Feminists have influenced the Pci, in Beckwith's analysis. In the seventies Berlinguer urged communist party members to incorporate women's issues into party work; in 1979 the Pci congress discussed the need to have more representation of women in leadership positions, to strengthen ties with the autonomous feminist movement, and to address attention to issues of male-female relationships. A significant statement was inserted into party theses of the 1979 Pci congress: the woman question is not "automatically resolvable" by overcoming class conflict.[43]

The parties with large support from women, according to Beckwith's analysis, are the Dc, the Pci, and the Pr. The Pci has the best record for electing women deputies. In the elections of 1972, 1976, and 1979 the Pci elected more women to parliament than all other parties combined. In 1979 Leonilde Jotti of the Pci was elected president of the chamber of deputies, the first woman to hold the post.

The confounding quality of Italian politics is suggested in Beck-with's analysis that Italy's fascist party (Msi)—which is explicitly an-tifeminist and without the Dc's posture of concern for women—has placed as many women representatives in parliament as have the so-cialist and the republican parties; furthermore, the Msi record on women's political representation is better than that of the liberal party. Although the Pci sustained a slight loss in elections of 1979, the number of women representatives remained the same.

women's diversities

The season of withdrawal from politics after 1976 was precisely the period when political feminists were left with the work of seeing to the passage of the abortion law in parliament. Because they em-phasized differences, Italian feminists could depend on one another to do what needed to be done, but differences also provoked polem-ics: political feminists declared pointedly to cultural feminists that spontaneity by itself could not produce legislation. As feminist col-lectives began to dissolve by the end of the decade, a placard I no-ticed at a feminist meeting advised: "non c'è liberazione della donna senza organizzazione" (there is no liberation of women without or-ganization).

There were differences between political and cultural feminists and differences within each of the categories. An analysis of the per-spectives of two women leaders of the Pci, Adriana Seroni and Si-mona Mafai, indicates differing responses by two political women of the partisan generation to feminist criticism of the Pci. Seroni was born in Bologna and worked in the North, Mafai was born in Rome and worked in the South. In a 1977 volume Seroni said that "neo-feminist" characterization of the Pci as a "patriarchal structure" with "male" values of work, struggle, discipline and reason was mistaken, these were not solely "male" values. She defined the Pci as the party most committed to women's liberation. "Neofeminists" occupied themselves unduly with culture, she believed, holding concerns closer to those of "intellectuals, women of the middle class, students" than to those of all women.[44] Seroni was also worried about feminist utopianism: "Utopia is not enough if one does not create a bridge between today and a new tomorrow." Women who criticized the un-democratic nature of contemporary Italian institutions forgot, said

Seroni, that in the recent past Italy was fascist, with democracy for nobody, and that the resistance and the last thirty years had constructed democratic institutions in Italy—a "struggle that must continue."[45]

Feminists who do not want to be associated with institutions they consider male-dominated, Seroni maintained, "leave institutions, in the name of feminism, to men only." She pointed out that the number of communist women had continuously increased in parliament, in regional governments, in city councils, and in the decentralized bodies of the Pci. To the feminist charge that the Pci was "puritanical" about sex, Seroni agreed; older women of the Pci were often embarrassed by open discussion of sexuality.[46] Shortly after publication of her response to feminists, Seroni was appointed to the Pci central committee.

Simona Mafai, the communist senator from Sicily who carried the abortion law through parliament for Italian women and for the Pci, combines communist and feminist concerns. A partisan at the age of fifteen, she was given the task after the war of typing Gramsci's prison notebooks; later she sat in the central committee of the Pci, was elected a senator in the Italian parliament, and helped to edit the journal that addresses feminist concerns of communist women, *donne e politica*. In the mid-eighties she is probably the leading communist feminist of southern Italy.[47] Born in 1928 of a Roman father and an Italian Jewish mother who were painters and intellectuals, she—and her sister Miriam (a highly respected feminist journalist in the seventies and eighties)—distributed clandestine literature during the war. Her father, a left liberal, told his daughters that he was bound to the communist party because it was the only organization that offered the possibility to struggle against fascism.[48] Mafai herself always held doubts about the Soviet Union, but this did not impede work for communism in Italy. She is married to Pancrazio Di Pasquale, a Sicilian who has been a Pci organizer, the president of the Sicilian parliament, and a delegate to the Eec.

In the postwar era, Mafai spoke earthily to her constituency of Sicilian women: "First one must have running water in the house, then one can think of higher things." She told peasant women, to great applause, that they need no longer bring gifts to the landlords, "nor clean their floors, nor send our daughters to work for them." In the mid-eighties she is at a center of an enlarging network of aroused

Sicilian women—older matrons, young firebrands, many journalists and teachers.[49]

Mafai has always believed in the necessity of an autonomous women's movement. Crediting Udi for successfully maintaining its independence of the Pci (even before the 1982 separation from the party), she states that feminist criticism has brought women's issues from the margins to the center of the party's concerns. She applauds the spirit of Sicilian feminist communists who often say, "First I am a woman, then I am a member of the Pci." Mafai says this is evidence of the pluralism of the Italian communist party. She rejects as a simplistic strategy the election of more women to office, although that too is important. "One must criticize men, particularly men of the left, men of the trade unions, men of the parties, but it is necessary for women to struggle along with men." This is particularly important in the South of Italy where women have traditionally been segregated.

Whether on the central committee of the Pci, working in the Palermo office of the party, or in the city council of the Sicilian capital, Mafai speaks her own mind: "Women are the carriers of the future." At the 1979 *festa della donna* at Palermo, when the announcement came that the mafia had killed an investigating judge, Simona Mafai and Adriana Seroni led a long cortege of women to the civic center of Palermo. Under a hot sun we listened to Mafai enumerate the crimes of the mafia and urged women to address themselves to the mafia as an example of male chauvinism that had become criminal in its violence. In party meetings Mafai objects to the customary remanding of the woman question to the evolution of democracy, pointing out that Palermo is an example of democratic institutions in deterioration, not progressive evolution, because hidden institutions in the city exercise power, from the mafia to the *lavoro nero* of the economy. "Neofeminism," says Mafai, "has provoked a new sense of solidarity among women. This is a great conquest which I do not believe will be reversed."[50] In Sicily she works with a regional council of women of all parties.

Adopting Sicilian women as a case study for Italian women may be helpful for probing the question, How do very different and individualistic women sustain the solidarity of all women? Gigliola Lo Cascio is a feminist inside the Pci who disproves accepted marxist theory; a striking blonde-haired woman she drives with her young son (Lo Cascio's husband is also in the Pci, a newspaperman) in a large jeep through the chaotic streets of Palermo. She teaches psychology at the University of Palermo where her research has focused on attitudes of Sicilian women. Lo Cascio's book *Occupate e casalinghe* is a comparative analysis of the attitudes of women factory workers and housewives.[51] Although marxist-leninist theory held that the woman question would be resolved when women left housework for work outside the home, Lo Cascio's investigation demonstrated that workers inside and outside the home are both alienated, that there are no genuine differences between attitudes of housewives and women factory workers. Women's liberation, Lo Cascio concluded, is considerably more complex than is implied by the orthodox marxist-leninist concept that a woman would be liberated by simply securing a job outside the home.[52]

Giovanna Quasimodo (a niece of the Sicilian poet Salvatore Quasimodo) is a television reporter in Catania. Quasimodo refuses to be inscribed in the Pci, although she considers herself a communist. Her investigative journalism has taken her to Africa to cover a conference of women judges and to mental asylums to expose the conditions of institutionalized mentally ill women.[53] She took me to visit her godfather, Ignazio Buttita, the Sicilian poet whom the Pci treats as its poet laureate. A portrait of Marx presides over Buttita's study; his books of poetry, written in Sicilian dialect, spill on the floor.

Letizia Colajanni, in her eighties now, has been fighting for social justice since 1919. Jolted by the grief of women who had lost husbands in a Sicilian sulfur mine shaft, she left a comfortable life in a Sicilian governing family for continuing efforts to improve Sicilian conditions of life. After the second world war she joined women's protests for water on the arid island. Although her nephew is party secretary of the Pci in Sicily, in the early seventies Colajanni preferred the more audacious *effe* to the sedate *noi donne*, then closer to the party. When I interviewed her in a busy office in the interior town of Caltanisetta, women were making posters for a street fair whose themes included restoring historical Sicilian sites, restoring the ecological balance of the island, and feminist concerns. Colajanni was working on one that declared, "Old age is not a malady!"[54]

Eugenia Bono is a feminist communist whose husband, a professor and party activist, helps prepare dinner in their apartment in Palermo. I accompanied her while she delivered the traditional confetti from her daughter's wedding party—along with feminist literature—on her rounds in Palermo. A peasant woman gave Eugenia some of the grapes she had just harvested. Stopping by an upper middle-class matron's apartment, we were offered *gelato*. Bono belongs to a variety of women's groups, many of them conservative, to whom she brings feminist issues as a Pci activist.[55]

Maria Rosa Cutrufelli, a Sicilian scholar of aesthetics, has written academic treatises on the sentiments, as well as an essay for an anthology, *Che cosa è un marito?* (What is a husband?).[56] She is an activist promoting cooperatives who agrees with Phyllis Chesler: "Women must not betray the 'wisdom of the heart' and become men. Women must not cease to be tender, compassionate, and preoccupied with the feelings of others. They must begin by being tender and compassionate with themselves and with other women."[57] Cutrufelli writes regularly for *noidonne* and has conducted her own inquiries on a range of topics: prostitution, women of Africa, and women's working conditions in Sicily.[58]

diversity and solidarity

One conundrum posed by Italian feminists is how they can simultaneously express diverse beliefs, life-styles, and strategies, yet come together in solidarity. I watched the very different women who came to the *casa della donna* at Rome to engage in lively discussions; peer pressure, I noticed, was sometimes exercised in the form of one woman criticizing another for *menefreghismo*—in polite translation, this is a censure of someone for not giving a fig for others.

The day in the fall of 1980 when the pope, the Dc, and the Italian right-to-life movement announced they were gathering signatures for a referendum to repeal the 1978 abortion law, I happened to be at the *casa della donna*. At sundown women streamed into the building from all parts of Rome to sit in concentric circles on the floor and express their feelings. When their rage (expressed both in the dialect of Trastevere and the careful diction of women professors) seemed to have reached the ceiling, somebody called for five minutes of silence. The women kept the silence perfectly. This was the pattern: first the rage, then the silence. "Tomorrow," someone said, "we will organize." The next week their large demonstration put the traffic of

Rome in gridlock. Six months later Italian voters threw back the referendum that would have annulled the abortion law.

Italian feminists seem highly individualistic yet it is an individualism within a system of values that takes others into account. Judeochristian concern for others is implicit in the censure of *menefreghismo* discussed earlier. The shared belief "Not a single woman's wretchedness is alien to me" may have been the underlying motivation for the hundreds of thousands of different women with diverse beliefs who voted to sustain legalized abortion in 1981. The morality of Italian feminists keeps harking back to prechristian sources. The original quotation was "Homo sum, et humani nihil a me alienum puto" (I am a man, and nothing pertaining to man is alien to me), attributed to Terence, a Roman said to have been a North African, who wrote plays in the second century before christianity.

LE DONNE ITALIANE HANNO DIRITTO AL VOTO

"Italian women have the right to vote": Headline
from *Noi Donne*, January 1945

"For the emancipation of women. For the future of your children. For peace: Vote
Communist": Pci poster, postwar

"Women of Sicily: for the future of our island, our emancipation, the good of our
families. Vote the Italian Socialist Party": Psi poster, postwar

By permission, from Adriana Sartogo, ed., le donne al muro (Rome) © 1977

"Mothers! Save your children from Bolshevism! Vote Christian Democrat": Dc poster, postwar
le donne al muro

Women of anti-Communist Catholic Action marching under Arch of Constantine, Rome 1948
Year Annual, 1948

"Women: You must vote—your future and your families are at stake. Vote Christian Democrat": Dc poster, ca. 1950

"Vote Christian" (and slay the vipers of divorce and free love): Dc poster, postwar

"You betrayed me, you wanted a divorce, you abandoned me with two children and gave me pennies for food. Vote YES against divorce to save the family": Msi—the fascist party—poster, ca. 1970

le donne al muro

New left poster depicting "marriage" between anti-divorce groups Dc and Msi (il manifesto = Pdup)

"Women say NO" to the annulment of the divorce law: *effe* cover, April–May 1974
le donne al muro

National Conference on Abortion, sponsored by Movement for the Liberation of Women (Mld) and Radical Party (Pr) (Rome, ca. 1975)

A cartoon illustrating the concept of "unedited Marxism." The players follow their choice of paths. A caption reads "Uscite dove volete ma uscite" (Exit where you wish, but exit)
Courtesy of il manifesto, *June 1985*

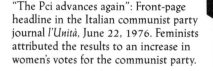

"The Pci advances again": Front-page headline in the Italian communist party journal *l'Unità*, June 22, 1976. Feminists attributed the results to an increase in women's votes for the communist party.

"Fight for your future. Achieve emancipation. Vote Psi": Socialist party poster, ca. 1975

"March 8: Our day of celebration. Women in struggle for the alternative": Psi poster for International Women's Day, ca. 1975
le donne al muro

Militant posters for the Movement for the
Liberation of Women (Mld)
le donne al muro

**MOVIMENTO DI
LIBERAZIONE
DELLA DONNA**

**CONGRESSO NAZIONALE
MILANO 11-12-13 APRILE**

PALAZZINA LIBERTY   CORSO XXII MARZO

12

"spacca la mela"

literature of feminist cultural revolution

Italian feminists like the image of Eve's apple. In 1982 a women's daily newspaper entitled an organizing calendar *Spacca la mela*—"the apple is splitting." [1] Illustrations showed that feminists hoped to share the apple with all women—all of the fruit of the tree of knowledge that enables a person to distinguish between good and evil and to be in full possession of physical and mental powers from sexual awareness to wisdom. *Noidonne* often prints a cartoon of Eve with an irresistible snake.

women's studies in Italy

Interest in women's studies surged after 1976 as more Italian feminists realized that the struggle was cultural as well as political. Women's studies have been widely disseminated throughout Italian society through the 150-hour classes that reach uneducated housewives, through considerable radio and television programming, through the university for women, Centro Virginia Woolf, and, perhaps most strategically, through the diverse feminist press.

The metalworkers' union, as part of its national collective agreement in 1972, secured the "right for a limited number of workers to attend classes of public, free education, for up to 150 hours per year per worker." This provision was soon emulated by other unions and the constituency of students was enlarged. Unemployed people and housewives, as well as factory workers, were entitled to attend the free 150-hour classes. For many, women's studies classes became the first step in governing their own lives.[2] Women professionals taught the courses, often without pay, in a learning/teaching process that crossed class lines.[3] In the beginning most students were clerical workers, later most were blue-collar workers and housewives. The 150-hour classes drew large institutions into supporting women's issues: the classes were sponsored by unions, universities, and regional governments. The content of the classes evolved from study of women in the labor force, family law, and protective legislation to post-1968 themes of women and sexuality, motherhood, and patriarchy.[4]

a feminist radio program: "equal and different"

Women's issues were projected to large audiences through radio and television programs. If women were not given broadcast time, they sometimes occupied radio and television stations. Radio conversations conducted by Chiara Saraceno are a good source for the thinking of Italian women on themes of equality and diversity, as well as helpful for understanding how feminists reached nonfeminists. Saraceno, who had taught 150-hour courses, addressed her radio series to women who did not consider themselves feminists.[5] The theme of her talk program was "women and the family," stressing women as "equal and different."

Daily radio and television programs on women's issues originated in large cities of the North; in the eighties almost every woman, in every part of Italy, was within range of one of these programs.[6] The effectiveness of this feminist programming to large audiences is re-

lated to the persuasive way women's issues were presented. In Saraceno's radio dialogues, the family is discussed as a historical phenomenon, as the place where woman is oppressed but where she has
demonstrated her capacity for resistance, creativity, and solidarity
with other women. Feminism was put in homely terms by discussants
and listeners: contemporary feminist collectives, said a listener, were
recovering the experience of grandmothers who sewed together with
their women friends.[7] In programs on women's history, women listeners were encouraged to remember the lives of their peasant grandmothers; listeners recalled that the work of men and women in peasant culture was similar, but that women's leisure time was more
constricted than that of the men, and a woman's social recognition
tended to be connected to whether or not she had sons. Radio dialogues explored the implications of conservative concepts and
church doctrine. Fascism, said a listener, had emphasized the centrality of the family and the importance of many births. The church,
said another listener, had reduced the meaning of religion for women
to sexual morality and had isolated the value of women to the figure
of the madonna as mediator between man and God. Conversations
explored the catholic family and the tendency to limit a woman to
her functions as wife, mother, sister. A caller from an audience of
catholic women said; "In a sense the cross has become feminine."[8]
Another listener pointed out that christianity had not been authoritarian in the beginning; this led to a conversation on reading the
bible with a feminist perspective.

The unpaid labor of housewives and the ambiguous emancipation
of going out to work were also analyzed. The traditional family
(which upheld the value of respect) and the contemporary family
(with its emphasis on the value of intimacy) were compared. Conversations evoked insights about the ambiguous progress of contemporary women. The attainment of intimacy in marriage had been
realized at a cost: "a loss of self-determined identity, a major dependency."[9] The change in the Italian family from patriarchy to partial
recognition of the work of the housewife was examined by Laura
Balbo, a sociologist who was elected in 1983 to the Italian parliament.

Conversations circled the plural meanings of the word *woman*, the
multiplicity of forms the family has taken in different times and different social classes, and the diverse psychological perspectives that

derive from different states of a woman's life: unmarried, separated, divorced, women who choose not to have children, women who do choose to have children, women who choose to marry ... "What woman is, is unknown, but each one of us creates a meaning every day, a meaning that is related to the culture, to the society, but also to one's personal experience."[10]

The history of women's resistance as it emerged from the radio dialogues was traced to two interconnected themes: a history of continual resistance to the condition of subordination and the necessity of making a decision as to whether or not to have a child.[11]

feminist publications

Feminist teaching and learning were undertaken on a large scale with widely distributed publications, notably *effe* and *noidonne*, discussed earlier, but also the innovative *sottosopra* of Milanese feminists, and the unpunctuated and unedited journal of Roman collectives whose title accented a central Italian feminist theme: *differenze.*

Donne e politica was the periodical of feminist communists. *Rocca, idoc,* and *com-nuovi tempi,* as noted earlier, emphasized feminism as part of a left catholic, or believer, orientation. After 1976 professional feminist journals appeared: *donnawomanfemme; memoria;* and a feminist literary journal, *l'orsaminore;* these journals were addressed to cultural feminists who were also political activists. Italy's wide spectrum of political newspapers covered feminist activities; the new left newspaper *il manifesto* and the new *la repubblica* of the independent left were major sources of feminist news and features. In 1978 feminists in the casa della donna launched a daily newspaper, *quotidiano donna (qd),* that aimed for mass circulation. The successful reach of feminist communication was evident by the early 1980s when keychains were available everywhere in the Italian capitol with the feminist message *Io sono mia.*

In an interview with Emanuela Moroli, the managing editor of *quotidiano donna,* she explained that *qd* has "no one political line. Each of us in the editorial department has a different political position. Italian politics are characterized by diversity of points of view. We do not have political confrontations in the newspaper; each of us has space for our point of view. As editor I guarantee space to points of view different from mine."[12] The only absolute principle upheld is that no person enrolled in a political party can write for *quotidiano donna;* feminists are interested in politics, but not the politics of the parties.[13] We are interested, said Moroli, in the "politics of the movement which aims for cultural revolution."[14] All aspects of women's lives are to be reconsidered. With regard to the central theme of women and work, feminists looked toward alternative women's work spaces, particularly cooperatives.[15]

The newspaper explored the sources of women's culture. Located in the casa della donna, *qd* had emerged from the experience of radio donna, also located there. The women hoped to capture in a newspaper the reciprocal telephone relationship of radio broadcaster and listener. In addition to being an informative newspaper written by women, *qd* hoped to develop a female code of communication with bold photographs, cartoons, and audacious language. One cartoon made fun of the Dc proposal to give salaries to housewives (a fairy godmother asks a woman what she would like to be: "I'd like to be a floor washer, that way I'll be paid better!"). *Qd* printed first-hand accounts of marginal women; prostitutes, politically committed wives of men who had given up left militancy, women of lesbian collectives, and women of color were given primacy in the search to "create a new language for women." When euphoria was the mood (for instance, in 1981 when the abortion law was sustained) the newspaper reflected hopefulness and lived up to its name as a daily newspaper. But most of the time it was without money and publication since 1981 has been erratic.

A newspaper that lived close to the edge, like the women who live in casa della donna, *qd* had a street instinct for organizing. Subscribers were given a calendar entitled *agenda '82* which listed *qd* offices in Milan, Genoa, Turin, Venice, Treviso, Florence, Pistoia, Siena, Naples, Potenza, Reggio Calabria, Taranto, Catania, and Palermo. Evidence that "the apple is splitting" was documented with lists of women's centers not only in Italy (Milan, Brescia, Turin, La Spezia, Venice, Modena, Florence, Rome, Salerno, Bari) but in France, Spain, Germany, Great Britain, Austria, Belgium, Holland, Switzerland, Denmark, the United States, Canada, and Australia. Women's health clinics were listed for Italy (Bari, Bologna, Bolzano, Catania, Ferrara, Fiumefreddo di Sicilia, Giarre, Milan, Rome, Trieste) as well as for

France, England, Switzerland, Germany, Holland, Denmark, and the United States.[16] Qd enumerated important dates in women's history, from the Mozzoni generation of socialists at the turn of the century to the recent history of separatism. Traditional as well as iconoclastic, the women's newspaper included a monthly menstrual chart for the church-approved rhythm method of birth control.

A resource book for organizing, the *agenda* listed women's bookstores, publishing houses, cultural centers, film groups, antidrug collectives, antiviolence centers, work collectives, women's bars, and sports centers. The newspaper rendered feminist theory and the recovery of women's history accessible to every woman. Qd defined separatism as the "refusal of women to be defined by others, the research of a culture, of a practice of life that is the expression of woman's unveiled body, recognized and not repressed, the force to put one's self against every patriarchal mystification. Each woman is a real point of reference and unique from every other woman."[17] The daily newspaper emphasized the importance of women's clinics, which were never adequately funded—although their aim was birth control not abortion. These public places offered free psychological and medical help to women, and served as a center where women could discuss problems with other women and where a gynecologist could issue a certificate for the interruption of pregnancy.[18]

Although it had decades of experience in organizing, *noidonne* emulated *qd*'s calendar in 1982, calling their own *Il diario delle lune* (diary of the moons), turning the traditional franciscan calendar (familiar to all Italian catholic households) in a feminist direction. The calendar marked the saint of the day, noted zodiac information, and explained feminism as the Italian women's union (Udi) understood it. "Peace: has been violated many times by masculine society to affirm power. For us women, peace is the only dimension that renders possible our revolution." "Courage: up to now we have spent it in powerless doses for small things. We are learning to use it more largely to change life. Carry *noidonne* to another woman and give her a gift of courage."[19]

The journal of academic feminists, *donnawomanfemme (dwf)*, reflects a hope for international connectedness of women. It originated in a women's collective interested in undertaking a critical reexamination of culture. With an early publication subsidy from the Pci, its aim has been to promote research, provoke debates, gather together feminist scholarship that is scattered throughout the academic disciplines, and relate research to the feminist movement. *Dwf* is directed simultaneously to feminists in the academy and to feminists in the movement. Udi's center, sala Mozzoni, at Rome is used by *donnawomanfemme* as a feminist research library and publication office. The first issue of *dwf* embarked on a rereading of Marx, Engels, Lévi-Strauss, and Freud; the second examined the role of the schools in perpetuating sexist stereotypes; the third explored women's history; the fourth debated the issue of women and institutions.

Dwf (which resembles *Signs*, the academic feminist publication of the United States) has examined women and literature, maternity, women in film, the ideology of woman's body, women's groups, women and the church, women and science, women writers, and feminist methodology. An analysis of the relationship of the Pci to Italian feminism was written by an editor of *dwf*, Anna Maria Buttafuoco: "It is extremely difficult for a single political party, even the Pci, to incorporate the totality of feminist demands. Still these parties (again including the Pci) are faced with the political reality of having to recognize the vitality of the women's movement and of having to adapt to a feminist critique, without which the social transformation of Italy cannot effectively be accomplished."[20] *Dwf*, like other feminist entities, is intent on autonomy. In 1982 Udi gave up its subsidy from the Pci, shortly thereafter *dwf* did so also. *Dwf* engages in feminist critique while never losing sight of the goal of social transformation. One issue was devoted to the "political economy of liberation for women," examining women's roles as housewives and consumers and the significance of the issue of household work for the women's liberation movement.

A *dwf* essay, written by Margherita Repetto (Alaia) was an historical analysis of socialist feminism.[21] Stimulated by a close reading of Sheila Rowbotham's *Beyond the Fragments*, Repetto praised the British feminist for writing a critique of left political parties that could have been written in Italy. The bond between the women's movement and the movement for socialism, said Repetto, is the shared aim to construct a society without exploitation; the challenge of feminism is the conviction that socialist society can not be separated from the process of its construction.[22] Feminists are concerned to wrest sexuality, maternity, fertility from the historic control of the patriarchy because a woman's autonomy is grounded on the control of her own body. But challenge by itself, said Repetto, is insufficient; women need more historical perspective. Rowbotham did not adequately understand Italian feminism nor the postwar "qualitative leap" represented in the creation of a democratic constitution for Italy and the union of democracy and socialism in the postwar women's movement. Contemporary tasks for feminists, maintained Repetto, include "accelerating the maturity" of men of left parties which subordinate women, reconstructing many aspects of marxism, and ensuring women's cultural and political autonomy.

By 1981 differences in the cultural movement were evident. While *quotidiano donna* aimed for a large audience with some of the features of a tabloid, academic feminists, concerned about standards, narrowed their readership. *Memoria* strove to put Italian women's history in the context of world intellectual history, stating that women's history was "more than a simple story of oppression."[23] This academic periodical dealt with subtle subjects—the Greek concept of female reason as evil, the complex feminist thought of Georg Simmel, an interpretation of melancholy, and the paradoxes involved in use of psychoanalytic theory by feminists.[24] Livelier than *memoria* was the monthly *l'orsaminore*, written by the cultural stars of Italian feminism, for example, Rossana Rossanda and Biancamaria Frabotta. Both periodicals appealed to learned feminists who were engaged in founding women's research facilities and cultural centers. *L'orsaminore* drew some satirical criticism from plainer women of the provinces; meant, in part, to be tongue in cheek, even its name was sardonic: in contrast to bigger bears (in the heavens or in the USSR) the title of the magazine was "little bear." Its board of seven stars, the editorial constellation of *l'orsaminore*, reflected the reality that "the world in which we live is contradictory," the "diversity that we want to affirm is not always, or only, or dominantly, separatist." The periodical affirmed the strategy of cultural revolution, wanted to connect with feminists internationally, and suggested implicit standards for feminist creative work. (There were articles on George Sand, Katherine Mansfield, Gertrude Stein, and Virginia Woolf.) A strained and eventually pessimistic quality crept into the pages of *l'orsaminore*. The grim photographs of Diane Arbus in a 1982 issue suggested an ambivalent response to diffuse charges that learned feminists were inclined to be too pedantic, that they were "americanizing" Italian feminism. The monthly ceased publication in 1983.[25]

Centro culturale Virginia Woolf

The university for women, Centro culturale Virginia Woolf, attempts to bring together all levels of women's culture. Inside the *palazzo* on Governo Vecchio in Rome, a place of political encounter and refuge for women, Italian feminists founded a university with high standards of teaching and curricula that emphasize themes that women share. The 150-hour classes had revealed that perhaps the central concern of Italian women is motherhood; feminists, searching for a locus of study, designed a 1981–82 curriculum around the theme "the ambiguity of motherhood." There were also classes on linguistics, philosophy and semiotics, women and architecture, separation and depression, division of sexual and reproductive labor, aspects-symbols-rituals, pornography, biological sciences and feminine nature, love in western culture, motherhood and death in Venetian renaissance painting, the content of the American feminist press, women's health and the practice of self-help.[26] The masculine interpretation of the earth-mother legacy was examined in courses on the myth of Medusa and bad mothers in seventeenth- and eighteenth-century painting.

Subsequent curricula have taken as themes the "indecent difference" of women from men and women's "excessiveness" (referring to women's tendency to exceed boundaries in fantasy, remembrance, and desire). Seminars offered in 1984 addressed the concept of chastity in Greek and christian belief, Eros and women's writing and desire and loss in women's love relationships. And, as discussed earlier, there was a popular seminar on Saint Teresa and the interior experience; this seminar was tied to the theme of the curriculum, "gift of excess: the lives of female saints and other women." A seminar inspired by the peace movement was concerned with "life and survival," an exploration of the connection between the culture of everyday life and the culture of peace.[27]

The essays in the syllabi of Centro culturale Virginia Woolf are valuable sources of Italian feminist cultural thought. One on "the ambiguity of motherhood" in the 1981–82 syllabus rescued the theme of motherhood from male poets, documenting its analysis of motherhood with statements of women in *autocoscienza* groups. The traditional saintly portrait of motherhood, it appeared, was not quite true. This was exemplified in the statement of a woman in a small group who said, "I am a pacifist, I find violence horrible, I am against the death penalty, against life imprisonment—yet if anyone touched my child . . ." Motherhood, in this essay, is defined as the "territory of passion," the terrain of "rapport with the world." This is not a celebration of the ancient earth mother, because Italian feminists, taking male perceptions into account, consider her legacy to be a mixed one: "How can women break the spell of enchantment that also casts over her bad mother, witch, Pandora, Gorgona?"[28]

The 1984 essay on women's "excessiveness" described women as grounded in everyday reality, yet with a secret, often silent, proclivity for passion.[29] Passion can be invested in any of women's territories: motherhood, religion, politics, work. Sometimes characterized by a need to exceed the self in self-denial, women's passion is often evident in identification with another, in compassion, and in the need to seek refuge in "fantasy, silence, secrecy." Passion (loving, maternal, religious, political) may be defined as a search for fusion with other than one's self. For the authors of this essay, women may be the "carriers of the idea of absolute love" elaborated in western culture from the renaissance to romantic poets, "an idea in which distance, absence, open wounds are always present."

Women's "different forms of loving and dreaming" may be a reaction to their daily role as "administrators of everyday necessity" and may seek that which is extraordinary, free, unbounded by necessity. Women seem to prefer suffering and depression or "lighting a fire that may consume them but also illuminates them" to the absence of emotion. The oppressive aspect of this characteristic can be glimpsed in the lives of women who live solely for others, as well as in the lives of women who live solely for themselves: in a woman's "solitary journey" or in a woman's decision to conceive a child "tardily" or in the "search for pleasure in work."[30]

Women need to find their "own form" which will, said the essayist, express their need for unbounded desires, hopes, memories, and for "projecting life more in the past and in the future than in the present." In interior experience, women have always found a secret and silent and inaccessible place, a place where women can distance themselves "from the bright lights of our excesses while not wanting the lights to be extinguished." [31]

Along with mind-stretching seminars, the university for women offers workshops in woodworking.

anarchist critical literature

Women's studies in Italy, or the study of women's experience, was accompanied by self-criticism. An insightful critique of Italian feminists, as well as an articulation of one dimension of what feminists meant by cultural revolution, was expressed by a Sicilian novelist called the grand old woman of Italian feminist anarchists, Maria Occhipinti. Italian anarchism is by no means limited to Sicily, and Occhipinti, who now lives in Rome, is not unique in suggesting that reality is not seen in the same way by all women. Her postwar novel *Una donna di Ragusa* is the story of a Sicilian woman who did not regard the arrival of the Allies as an unmixed blessing; in the Sicilian world view, one conqueror follows another conqueror in rhythmic beat. [32] Occhipinti has never been comfortable as a member of any movement, although she was put on the cover of *effe* in the seventies. She considers herself close to the Sicilian peasant tradition.

When I interviewed her in November 1981 she said that "the genuine revolution is lived every day, in the way one comports one's self with one's family, one's neighbors, with reactionaries." The revolution can not be made by "one Berlinguer, one Craxi." For proof, she pointed to the "schifo" (disgusting and shameful things) created by the "leaders of soviet communism and of U.S. capitalism." The importance of going beyond "leaderismo" is shown in existing socialist states that "have created an abortion of socialism because the consciousness of the people has not been changed and leaders have dominated." Not a pessimist, Occhipinti said that there have been honest leaders in history—"communist leaders and religious leaders." Occhipinti noted that feminists have paid attention to her, but she prefers to be called a "Sicilian revolutionary woman."

The anarchist writer agreed with feminism insofar as it referred to liberation from the parties and from suppression of all kinds, but feminists "must speak in a manner that all women understand." "A genuine feminism," for Occhipinti, "speaks not only of sexual liberation, but of liberation from all oppression." Furthermore, "women should concentrate on their humanity, not on emulating men." Women should think less of attaining seats of power. Just look, said Occhipinti, at notable women who have attained power, who often behave, "not like women, but like monsters."[33]

Occhipinti sees a wrong and does something about it herself. When she pickets the Italian president's office protesting the exploitation of Sicilian peasants, she often finds that she is all by herself. Sometimes, she said, a few men companions come by to bring her warm milk or rum. "I have always been regarded as different from the others. Because I always say what I think, even when it is critical. So I do not fit into groups very well." She opened a trunk full of picket signs and placards from her many solitary protest demonstrations: "These are my bequest to my grandchildren." The communists, she noted, have never recognized her book, although *noidonne* had published an article on it. "The test of genuine revolutionaries is the way they behave toward other people. Not what they say or write." She feels women must be united to fight "racism," the "racism of the bourgeois woman against the common woman, the attitude of superiority of the intellectual to the 'ignorant.'"[34] In her usage of the word *racism* Occhipinti was referring to the marked cultural difference between northern and southern Italians, a difference that has racial overtones in Italy because the racial strains of southern invaders have produced southerners who are often darker than northerners (yet differences are at hand here, as elsewhere in Italy; there are also blue-eyed, fair Sicilians who are contemporary reminders of fair invaders, notably the Normans). Any reference to race in Italy is paradoxical; Italy, it has been pointed out, is the world's melting pot, since the country has been invaded by almost every world conqueror.

Adele Cambria, another anarchist feminist, has made a significant contribution to the literature of world feminism. Applying the anarchist perception that a person is finally judged by personal behavior, Cambria evaluated Marx, Lenin, and Gramsci. She put her studies in the form of plays that were staged at the feminist theater la Maddalena in Rome. Cambria's play about Marx underlined the fact that Italian feminists may respect marxist theory, but they do so with the dampening knowledge that the patriarch of world socialist theory took advantage of the governess-maid of the household and fathered an unacknowledged child.[35] Cambria's play about Lenin stressed that the other patriarch, Lenin, left a theoretical legacy that made women's liberation dependent on women leaving the home for employment in industry—a premise which has not appreciably changed the lot of women in the USSR. Cambria, "settling accounts" with Lenin for Italian feminists, laid at his door leninist residues that continued to mutilate the Pci: the democratic centralist form of the party and its myopia about women.[36] Lenin was also blamed for the violence that continued "to seduce a few male revolutionaries."[37] Clara Valenziano, in the introduction to the study, agreed with Cambria: "the terrorists have legitimate cultural roots in Lenin." Responding, in the same introduction, to Valenziano, Leonilde Jotti, the highest ranking woman in the Pci, said that some of Lenin's statements certainly conveyed contradictions, but that the Pci lived with contradictions. A contradiction Italian feminists would not live with by the 1980s was the 1921 statement of international communism that "a particular woman's question does not exist."[38]

Sending a riposte to the Pci elevation of Antonio Gramsci to premier status as Italian marxist theorist, Cambria wrote a study of Gramsci whose thesis is that the monumental work of one male revolutionary was paid for by the suffering of three women. In her wounding feminist rejoinder to Gramsci's *Lettere dal carcere* (Letters from prison) Cambria published Gramsci's jail correspondence with his wife and her two sisters.[39] Cambria's argument that Gramsci's revolutionary commitment entailed the subordination of three women was documented by (a) the mental illness of his wife; (b) the acceptance of the feminine role of sacrifice by Giulia, Gramsci's sister-in-law who looked after Gramsci's well-being; and (c) the ambiguous emancipation of Gramsci's other sister-in-law, Eugenia, who was in effect recruited for the purposes of male society.

Questions on the jacket of Cambria's book on Gramsci asked: How does a woman revolutionary love? Is a woman's revolutionary role limited to loving and sacrificing for a male revolutionary? Does a liberated woman liberate a man? Is it possible to love the masses if you have never loved anyone? A young woman in Cambria's play *Nonostante Gramsci* (Gramsci notwithstanding) declares: "I want the revolution of women as one wants a lover. I want the end of the struggle, of fear, of lies. For a single time in my life I would like to dance all alone and nude on a rocky peak under the cypresses without fear of where I put my feet. I am dying tonight suffocated by desperation and the moral weight of this struggle—which is also against those few men I love."[40]

feminist critical literature

Maria Antonietta Macciocchi, a woman journalist in the Pci and editor of *Noi Donne* in the 1950s, personally experienced some of the contradictions of the 1970s. In the polemics aroused by the abortion campaign, Macciocchi charged that Italian women had accepted male domination under fascism, that they had not been roused from their torpor until bombs dropped on them during the war. She was expelled, in unclear circumstances, from the Pci in the late seventies.[41]

Regarded by some people as a political martyr, Macciocchi has written essays highly critical of contemporary feminists. In a hyperbolic description, she said that abortion clinics in Britain and the United States were places where women aborted mass-production style in the inhuman rhythm of Charlie Chaplin's movie, *Modern Times*; is this, she asked, feminism?[42] In the late seventies, as Italians grieved over the death of Aldo Moro (*noi donne* printed the picture of his widow, in sympathy, on its cover), she pointed out that one of Moro's assailants was a woman, the lover of a man of the red brigades. Maybe, said Macciocchi, the last master of women is the marxist-leninist terrorist.[43]

In an essay on marxism and feminism, Macciocchi explored "masculine marxism" exemplified in Marx, Engels, Bebel, Lenin, Mao, and Gramsci.[44] She defined as "feminine marxism" the thinking of Luxemburg, Zetkin, and Kollontai, pointing out that male marxists continue to bar women from the inner circle of marxist theorists.[45] Women in the Pci behaved, she said, like nuns in convents, for the most part silent; if they speak, men of the party depart. "A surgical operation is urgently needed," said Macciocchi, "to remove the cataract that obscures the woman question from marxism."[46]

In an essay written before the Pci severed its connection with the soviets in 1981, Macciocchi said that the Pci had more women in parliament than any other left party of Europe, but as a member of the third international, it subscribed to the dogma that "there is no specific woman's question, nor a specific woman's movement."[47] Are the women inscribed in the Pci, asked Macciocchi, being co-opted?

Or seduced? Her studies of Italian women and fascism fasten a connection between women's sexuality and fascism, using psychoanalytic
concepts to explain the irrational element in women's consent to to-
talitarianism. Adopting premises from the writings of Wilhelm Reich,
she analyzed the link between marxism and the sexual revolution
and posed the problem of not considering the implications of poli-
ticizing sexuality. Perhaps, she advised feminists, it is more important
that women reappropriate their minds than their bodies.[48]

feminist creative literature

A considerable body of Italian feminist literature had been produced by the mid-eighties on themes of rediscovering, or creating,
women's culture based on women's experience. Dacia Maraini, perhaps, the most prominent cultural feminist associated with this endeavor, is not only the founder of la Maddalena (the feminist experimental theater), she is a prize-winning novelist, a poet, a literary
and film critic, a film writer, a historian of the Italian feminist movement, and a political activist. In the seventies she worked to found a
women's cultural center in a poor neighborhood of Rome, campaigned throughout Italy in support of legalized abortion, and joined
in the occupation of the *casa della donna*. In the eighties she has been
engaged in connecting the disarmament movements of other countries (notably, that of Japan) with the Italian effort and understanding feminism in an international context. She has lectured on the
feminist theater in Brazil, Holland, Spain, and the United States; in
1983 her play on Mary Stuart was staged in Spain and the United
States. Her contemporary interest is a series of plays about women
in historic Italian court trials, including one about a prostitute who
was killed to save the reputation of a man.

Aiming to widen the horizons of women's experience, one of Maraini's novels conveys the impact of feminism on a young woman
from the South,[49] another is a collection of unsent love letters from
one woman to another.[50] Maraini adopts diary and epistolary forms
for hitherto undiscussed subjects: a girl's love for her father, the
temptation of incest with the mother, a woman's secret loves.[51] Her
plays, staged at la Maddalena, sometimes shocked the placid, sometimes gave love bouquets to the audience. The play *Dialogo di una
prostituta con un cliente*, is a stinging dart in response to the query of

men (often men of the left) who ask, "What do these women want?" *Suor Juana*, a play about a nun at the time of the counter reformation, reflects Maraini's continuing concern about the role of the catholic church and women. Maraini encourages the recovery of prechristian sources for women's culture: the continuum with the prehistoric earth mother and other women who preceded the christian era (see Maraini's play *The Dreams of Clytemnestra*).[52]

In an interview in November 1981, Maraini said that marxist premises informed Italian feminism from the beginning and have remained in the current of feminism that emphasizes exploitation of women by bosses and husbands. The other current has been the feminist attempt to analyze the roots of cultural and religious discrimination against women. Maraini states, "The two currents, in Italy, have been parallel."[53]

In an essay on the dissolution of feminist *autocoscienza* groups in the late seventies, she said that feminists must take structure into account: "Genuine democracy needs structure and formal lines of authority, so that there is responsibility."[54] Like other feminists who lived through the seventies, Maraini stresses the importance of women taking responsibility for their own lives. The *consultori*, in her view, are very important not only because they are sources of information about birth control and abortion, but because they become women's centers where women can discuss issues that pertain to them. She recalled round tables during the abortion agitation when professionals (doctors, priests, psychoanalysts—all males) discoursed on the subject of abortion.[55]

Maraini stresses that a woman in traditional catholic culture could find autonomy only by choosing the religious life. But autonomy within the church, in Maraini's view, is double-edged: autonomy in a religious order is premised on accepting subordination to the church. Suor Juana, in Maraini's play (based on a true story), chooses to be a nun rather than to marry and risk giving up her mental life. The nun wrote many books, but when her writings edged radicalism, the church intervened. Characteristics inculcated by the church, Maraini believes, are passivity, obedience, and sacrifice: "These are all opposed to autonomy."[56]

There is a strain in Maraini's novels that reminds the reader of Pier Paolo Pasolini. They were close friends and collaborators on the film *Arabian Nights*. Both shared a concern for marginal people. Pasolini looked behind the words of Friulian and Roman dialectic for covert meaning; Maraini, in *Storia di Piera* and other works, listens to women's life stories with psychoanalytic insight and awareness of survivals of prechristian beliefs.[57] The story of Piera is played on a devastated family landscape (the father was an idealistic socialist cruelly tortured by fascists) where the bonding between mother and daughter is very close and the territory of love ambiguous. Using language that aims to "explode" fantasy and reality, Maraini alludes to a young woman's love for a priest concurrent with her desire to be simultaneously male and female.

In Italy one cannot depend on what people call themselves to understand their beliefs. For example, Oriana Fallaci, whom almost everybody associates with Italian feminism, does not call herself a feminist. Fallaci, whose writing as a world journalist reflects the sharpness and clarity of many Italian feminists, differed with them on the issue of abortion. Some feminists find it hard to forgive Fallaci for *Letter to a Child Never Born*, an epistolary document that conveys the deep ambivalence most Italian women, including most Italian feminists, bring to the subject of abortion while insisting that women must make their own decisions about their own bodies.[58]

Fallaci's book is a feminist document. "Yes, I hope you're a woman." But "I'll be just as glad if you're born a man. Maybe more so, since you'll be spared many humiliations, much servitude and abuse. If you're born a man, you won't have to worry about being raped on a dark street. You won't have to make use of a pretty face to be accepted at first glance, of a shapely body to hide your intelligence." "If you're born a man, I hope you'll be the sort of man I've always dreamed of: kind to the weak, fierce to the arrogant, generous to those who love you, ruthless to those who would order you around."[59] In her description of the kind of man she respected, Fallaci said he would be "the enemy of anyone who tells you that the Jesuses are sons of the Father and of the Holy Spirit, not of the women who gave birth to them."

A unique amalgam of rage and tenderness characterizes many Italian feminists. Oriana Fallaci caught it: "the fruits of paternity [are] ladled out to you like a well-prepared soup or placed on the bed like an ironed shirt. You've nothing to do but give it a surname if you're married, not even that if you've succeeded in getting away. The woman has all the responsibility, all the suffering and insult. You call her a whore if she's made love to you. There's no male equivalent in the dictionary. . . . For thousands of years you've been forcing your words on us, your precepts, your oppression. For thousands of years you've been making use of our bodies and giving us nothing back. For thousands of years you've imposed silence on us and consigned to us the job of being mothers. In every woman you look for a mother. Everlasting children, right up to old age you go on being children, needing to be fed, cleaned, served, advised, consoled, protected in your weaknesses and lazy habits. I despise you. And I despise myself for not being able to do without you."[60]

13

femministe e "le altre"

feminists and "others"

the "other" as metaphor

For catholic women after world war II, "others" were Udi women who were called "godless communists" by the pope. For cultural feminists of the 1970s, "others" were political feminists in the Pci and Udi; for political feminists, "others" were cultural feminists who were unenthusiastic about politics. For most feminists of the seventies, reversing the earlier equation, "others" were catholic women who acquiesced in papal condemnation of divorce, contraception, and abortion

Other is a distancing metaphor, yet feminists felt close to the marginal women whom society called *other:* prostitutes and lesbians. Feminists also felt close to nuns, whom they regarded as "others" in the patriarchal church. For a unifying metaphor for their movement, feminists considered the shared roles of unpaid housewives, or of mothers and daughters, or women's common terrain of passion (in motherhood or in religious, political, or professional commitment), as the Centro Virginia Woolf essay had suggested. In the environment of the late seventies, with emotions aroused by the abortion issue, revulsion at terrorist, sexual, environmental, nuclear and other violence, and the psychological battering involved in living through a cultural revolution, feminists themselves felt marginal, dissociated, or "other." The metaphor "le altre"—the others—kept imposing itself as the term that seemed to Italian feminists most expressive of the several dimensions of their movement.

The metaphor "other" has connotations of dissociation, yet it also holds positive implications when used in the sense of "different." Emphasizing difference, the metaphor enables women to exhibit solidarity with all women while reserving the personal right to be different or the individual right of conscience. The psychological effect of adopting the metaphor of "other" becomes a process of seeing other people, and yourself, differently.

catholic matrons

Udi women were acutely aware of the large catholic and anticommunist women's organization Cif, aligned with the Dc. From 1945 until the seventies, the Dc held more women members than any other Italian party. The gains feminists made after 1968 were in large part dependent on the number of catholic women who came over the line from the Dc. Although feminists and catholic women had worked together for the vote in 1945 and for family rights legislation in 1975, they divided over divorce and abortion. Women in the catholic Movimenti per la Vita said they stood for a "culture of life" and identified abortion with the "culture of death." The pope linked terrorism, the arms race, and the destruction of the family with abortion.

Yet feminist ideas reached the significant political bloc of catholic women in the Dc. This was evident in a 1978 Cif conference and even more apparent in a Cif conference of 1981. The regional catholic women's meeting at Palermo of March 1978 coincided with international women's day. In a pattern that may have been unique to Sicily—where some of the clergy often share their parishioners' sense of difference from the mainland, and where in the early eighties many priests joined women and men in opposing the mafia and nuclear missiles at Comiso—the proceedings of this catholic conference contain many references to international women's day. These references suggested that the festival was not the sole possession of the left, but a day for Dc women to celebrate women's values and catholic clergy could bless their efforts.

The archbishop of Palermo, Salvatore Pappalardo, advised "Sicilian sisters" who were gathered to "celebrate the eighth of March, Women's Day" that he wanted to convey the greetings of the churches and of the bishops of the island. A recent church conference, said Pappalardo, had "underlined the importance and the significance of such celebrations" for the women's values which "christianity stimulates and exalts" in the "conquest of equality and of liberty that are new realizations of women's dignity."[1] The archbishop quoted from the encyclical *Gaudium et spes* and commended women's development of their talents and participation in cultural life.

In a world dominated by "egoism, brutal passions, aberrations and material and moral violence," women were called, said the archbishop, to be carriers of the values of Maria, the virgin mother, and of the saints of the first centuries of the church. For Sicily, Pappalardo pointed out, this referred to the patron saints of the island: Agata, Lucia, Silvia, Oliva, Ninfa, and Rosalia. Women, in addition to their specific vocation of being faithful wives, mothers who are responsible for the education of their children, and virgins consecrated to the Lord, said the archbishop, could be committed to activities outside the home. He urged women to consider the celebration of March 8th to be a moment of serene verification of their "human and christian identity" and a sign of renewed commitment to women's tasks.[2]

The archbishop, like other clergy in Sicily that I have interviewed, conveyed to women a sense of encouragement, not prohibition. This was apparent in the address of Monsignor Alfredo Garcia, the bishop of Caltanisetta.[3] Garcia quoted *Pacem in terris:* "The promotion of women is 'a sign of the times.'" He recalled a recent gathering of bishops in which a woman, in a precedent-breaking incident, had spoken to bishops on the "woman question."

Bishop Garcia said that in countries of the third world, the condition of women was still in great part servile, "in short woman is still considered the 'servant of man' and, in certain areas, is still bought and sold." In industrialized countries women's condition is better; she is recognized as of equal dignity with men, has an equal position in the family, and can realize herself (other than in the home as wife and mother) in work and in the professions. He enumerated Italian laws that had advanced women's status: admission to all public offices, including the magistracy (1963), prohibition of dismissal on account of marriage (1963), improvement in the protection of working mothers (1971), the national plan for nursery schools (1971), protection of work in the home (1973), equal rights in the family (1975), equality of wages with men (1977), and dramatic improvement in women's education.

In his listing of feminist legislation, the bishop did not mention the controversial issues of divorce and abortion, but he did censure a double standard of morality and sexual violence. Bishop Garcia addressed himself to the left catholic critique of the church that the church had oppressed women by conditioning them to the sacralization of virginity and of motherhood: "For the church, women have never been considered women but always virgins or mothers— women have been conditioned to obedience, docility, and meekness." The bishop's response to this critique was an affirmation that "Cristo è venuto per liberare l'umanità che è composta di uomini e di donne" (Christ had come to liberate humanity, which is composed of men and women), and he led his audience into a thicket of biblical quotations documenting this view.[4] Catholic women listening to clergymen like Pappalardo and Garcia sensed their good will; the silence of the priests on the issues of divorce and abortion left the feeling that women had to do their own thinking on these matters.

The 1978 Cif conference was attended by a representative of the antiabortion Movimento di Vita Cristiana. Cif organizers had also invited a representative from left catholic base communities, movimento di base per un dialogo politico, as well as a delegate from Acli, the catholic worker organization, which had declared its autonomy of papal doctrine on the issue of divorce. The papal view condemning abortion was represented but so was the view of left catholicism that abortion was best left to a woman's conscience. There were very few references during the conference to the divisive issue of abortion.

A feminist academic psychologist who was asked to address the audience, Carlamaria Del Miglio, spoke in terms persuasive to her catholic audience. She referred to the many facets of woman in images of Maria, and said that the point of the woman question was for everyone to work together not only for women but for *gli altri*. And in this metaphor of the "others" said Del Miglio, she was referring to all the "others," men as well as women.[5]

In his presentation, Ennio Pintacuda, a priest as well as a sociologist, indicated a familiarity with feminist literature and revealed a masculine worry: Pintacuda said that the women's movement "implied a redistribution of power." He indicated his awareness of the unsettling implications of a feminist view of the gospel and the church in his undocumented assertion that "christianity did not discriminate against women." Yet he shared with feminists an unedited view of the gospel in stating that women were, as "carriers of salvation," "equal to men."[6]

Maria Eletta Martini, Dc vice president of the national house of deputies, said she had been opposed to the recently passed abortion law because she was opposed to all violence, including violence to the unborn child, but stressed that responsible parenthood was an equal duty of women and of men. Speaking during the period when the Pci and Dc cooperated in the national government, Martini said she shared with "i marxisti" the belief that women should participate at all levels of social and political life.

The major reason many Dc women could converge with feminists was suggested by Martini's statement that the church historically had some problematic attitudes toward women, but "our times are those of vatican council II." The emphasis on the gospel and on the first centuries after Jesus indicated, said Martini, that women were bearers of the "good news" of the gospel and "first witnesses" of the resurrection.[7] (This statement by a catholic woman of the Dc was closer to feminism than to church doctrine and reveals the erosion of papal catholicism in the seventies).

The motions passed by the women of this 1978 Cif conference stressed the theme of liberation: "In an awareness that the message of Christ" is "liberation" for all humans, women as well as men, the issue was larger than equality. Although legal and political equality is important, said catholic women, the point was to recover genuine values founded on the conception of each human as unique, unrepeatable, with "equality and difference." Women, committed as women, were to work for a "more just and more human society," overcoming all forms of "discrimination and subordination."[8] These statements by catholic women were strikingly similar to the beliefs of women who called themselves feminists.

The spirit of John XXIII may have legitimated feminist ideas in Italy for many catholic women. The themes of the 1981 Cif conference at Palermo called for "more space for women, for a new family, for a more humane society." Some feminists worried about cooptation, but feminism interpreted by catholic women was sometimes widened. Cif women at the 1981 conference declared, "We are convinced that the project of women's liberation can not be seen by itself; it is an essential emerging component in a global project of the liberation of humanity."[9] Word changes made the family, not women, the "agent of change of society." Nonetheless, references to the necessity for overcoming "old stereotypes of hierarchical relations and preconceived division of roles" broke with tradition and were obviously indebted to a decade of feminist agitation.

The Cif view was that women becoming "co-protagonists" of the family meant that society would become more respectful "of the rights and needs of all."[10] One young woman said that the Cif concept of the family as the place of welcome not only for the child but for the old, the sick, the marginal was ambiguous. This concept of the "open family" could, she said, be interpreted as placing more burdens on the shoulders of women. It must be recognized, said Laura Barone, that "the classic catholic family with the husband sultan of the house representing hierarchy" and "the subordinated wife" no longer existed.[11]

A professor of education, M. Teresa Moscato, of the University of Catania, described feminism as a sign of the times and an indication of the maturation of the human conscience. "Marx," she pointed out, as well as the church, had underlined the significance of the relationship of the couple.[12] Bringing the catholic doctrine of complementarity (of the roles of husband and wife) up to date, she said that the contemporary interpretation of this catholic doctrine was "reciprocal complementarity." The "first feminism" had emphasized "identity" of competence, and, therefore, equal rights. Contemporary feminism, on the other hand, theorized that what was specifically feminine was "other." In a discussion that ignored church doctrine on the subject, Moscato said that the division of humanity into two distinct sexes was "contrary to scholarly opinion"—contrary to Jung, for example, who had analyzed components of the feminine in men and components of the masculine in women.[13]

Carlamaria Del Miglio, professor of psychology, in her presentation to the 1981 conference sounded feminist themes more openly than she had at the Cif conference three years earlier. She was also very persuasive. Del Miglio said that the answer to the question "What is a woman?" had seemed self-evident not long ago. Woman was what nature created, what her husband demanded, what the children expected, what society requested, what her mother educated her to be, what culture taught her to be, what God wants. Thus from birth until death, women lived, silently, the way others wanted them to live. In the traditional schema, any approvals or disapprovals surrounding her activities were anchored in the established truth that woman's nature was thus, and that woman's biology determined her psychosocial role.[14]

The feminist movement stressed the influence of the culture in the process of becoming woman, said Del Miglio, and some women no longer wanted to live passively; these women were reevaluating their condition in order to make decisions about their own lives. Knowing can be blinding and some women do not want to know that they are powerless victims, without cultural, political, or economic means for escaping their subordination. It was understandable, said Del Miglio, that some women did not want to recognize themselves in the suffering described by feminists, declaring themselves exceptions who were content with their lives.

Del Miglio explained in psychological terms the partial ways women's traditional role could be refuted or accepted. Partial refutation manifests itself in an anorexic rejection of one's own body. When the refutation is determined only by a woman's superego, refusal of the traditional role becomes sterile competition with men. Even when the traditional role is accepted, this acceptance is often accompanied by unconscious rejection—shown in psychological depressions, and feelings of inadequacy associated with the tasks of wife, mother, and housewife. Women who accept the traditional role without conflict can live in a satisfied manner, although narrowly and within iron limits; these women enjoy being sexual objects or maternal figures who renounce the erotic component of sexuality.[15]

Having left her audience of catholic women wondering into which category they fell, Del Miglio described feminists as women who value being women, who regard differences as a richness that can transform society. Respect, service, pleasure, and joy need no longer be limited to the private daily life of women, but can become dimensions of social living.

Del Miglio focused on three themes of feminism: solidarity, reappropriation of the body, and mother-daughter relations. Solidarity, she said, was based on knowledge, not on friendship; solidarity in the sense of sisterhood does not leave space for differences among women but emphasizes only the differences from the other sex. Contemporary feminists refuse the banality of simply being the other side of the coin and underline the multiplicity of possible forms of being a woman.

How does one live in solidarity among women? By avoiding criticizing the different ways women respond to traditional women's role. By valuing instead the positive attributes of each woman. Solidarity replaces hostility and coldness in women's relationships with interest and sympathy for every other woman—of whatever age, class, degree of education, religious or political affiliation. Feminists, said Del Miglio, are overcoming a history of subordination to men and rivalry among women and are pointing to a future of hope that bypasses fears and anxieties and liberates women's energies. They are constructing their own identities and their own histories. Praising "dialogue, confrontation, and collaboration," Del Miglio said that feminism does not mean rejecting the values of christianity. Feminism means living in a climate of reciprocal respect and constructive pluralism, apart from abstract ideologies and the "power games of men's politics."

When feminists speak of liberation of the body, said Del Miglio, they mean accepting one's own sexuality. She referred to a feminist theologian who said that a religion founded not on fear or placation of God, nor on exorcising evil forces but on feminist values would be a religion of life, death, encounter, love, and pleasure.[16]

To start on this new path, Del Miglio argued, a knowledge of mother-daughter relationships is necessary. Every woman is a daughter and many women are mothers. When they are oppressed by a role imposed by others, women themselves become oppressors in their relationships with their daughters. Instead of empathy and spontaneous emotions, the relation becomes one of incomprehension and coldness. Del Miglio quoted the statement of the U.S. feminist, Adrienne Rich, that the mother who can enlarge the horizons of her daughter's life must widen her own life. Only a mother who does not hold herself in contempt nor humiliate herself in silent passivity can transmit to her daughter love for her own body, fidelity to her own intelligence, courage and perseverance in the path she chooses.[17]

In the business session following the conference presentations, Cif leaders urged members to concern themselves with problems of unemployment, quality of the schools, and the feminist theme, the "double work of women." There were reports on surveys conducted by Cif showing that young people respected women open to innovation, women who carried equality beyond words to life decisions. Small groups at the conference concluded that the family must have reciprocal duties and that self-knowledge was necessary before acceptance of another in marriage. Parents needed to leave the refuge of the past in order to talk to their children. The catholic women praised women's health clinics, although the church was unwilling to relinquish this traditional area of church teaching. Eighty-five percent of Sicilian women responding to a Cif survey felt women should have their own opinions (not those of their husbands) in politics— a finding that upturned traditional Sicilian wisdom. Almost all respondents felt that family authority should be exercised by both spouses. The proposed new family was to be composed of a responsible mother as well as father. Although Cif formally opposed legal abortion, it did (in opposition to church dictum) recommend sex education in the schools and the availability of methods of contraception.[18] "The patriarchal family is today completely gone" was a recurring declaration at the March Cif conference.[19] A few months after the 1981 Cif conference, women and men voted to retain the 1978 abortion law—with a 68 percent plurality in Palermo.

A shift in the attitude of many catholic women toward feminism can be traced over the period 1978 to 1985. Laura Barone, a Cif activist, writes a column for the Sicilian catholic periodical dedicated to the family, *il focolare*. In the fall of 1981, when I interviewed her in Ragusa, she agreed with feminism in almost everything but the issue of abortion but differentiated herself from "feminists." In an article entitled "8 marzo" in March 1984, Barone said that international women's day had entered Italian customs, but there remained women who still did not want to discuss feminism, saying it was a "false problem" or that the problem "does not exist" or that ("in most cases") the issue does not exist for them and that they are not interested. This attitude, said Barone, was analogous to rising satiated from the dinner table and saying there is no hunger in the world.[20]

prostitutes

Traditional Italian culture divided women into good-chaste-obedient and bad-sensual-insubordinate. In the last category were placed the women who defied church, state, and social morality, from witches to women like Verga's passionate *la lupa* to prostitutes. In the seventies and eighties views about prostitutes changed. Women who had earlier been described as "fallen" in church doctrine, as "offending against social morality" by fascists, and who had been cast out of respectable society by Italian culture were now regarded differently. In the vibrant environment of Italy in the seventies, the catalytic combination of an unedited gospel and an unedited marxism produced a new image: "le ultime" (the last, in feminine gender)—a theme that could be found in the gospel and in marxist philosophy.

Feminist theology referred to the apostolic authority of Mary Magdalen and the feminist campaign for unpaid domestic work touched on the theme of prostitution, but it was not until 1982 that a committee for the civil rights of prostitutes was formed in Italy to remove from the legal code discriminatory legislation referring to prostitutes. Prostitutes of Pordenone spoke out and the movement grew rapidly.[21]

Feminists recognized in prostitutes a poignant example of women whose bodies were not their own. Women prostitutes early defined the problem as one that included men prostitutes. In the pages of *lucciola*, the periodical of the committee for the civil rights of prostitutes, dialogues and letters from readers held flickering insights (*lucciola* means firefly, referring to women who come out to glitter in the evening).

A round-table discussion of six women, four of them prostitutes, was reported by Roberta Tatafiore in the October 1983 issue. The women discussed husbands and clients. One remarked that she could never say no to a husband because he brought the money home, now that "I am on the street I choose my clients."[22] The client is nearly always somebody else's husband. Italian men, more than Italian women, the panelists agreed, insist on dividing women into wives and whores. Yet a woman, whether she is a wife or a prostitute, can be treated like a commodity. The root of the problem, the panelists believed, was the inability to express emotion. Men are afraid of emotions because they are a sign of weakness in the dominant culture. Prostitutes learn to live with the fact that for men they are interchangeable: "The problem is when, having finished your hours, you are free. Then you reconcile accounts with yourself and with your true securities or insecurities."[23]

Who were these women who sold their bodies? The testimonies of prostitutes revealed that many come from the economic and intellectual poverty of the South, from a culture of subordination. Often they are women who are separated from husbands, or awaiting divorce, or women who are divorced. They are housewives who have been left with nothing after years of unpaid household work. Usually they have children to support. For a person with no work experience except that of being a housewife, jobs are difficult to find. Prostitution often becomes the only way to survive.[24] For Italian feminists prostitution was a two-way mirror of "others."

lesbians

Lesbians were "others" and the strength of the sash of solidarity among Italian women was tested most critically, perhaps, over this particular difference. *Quotidiano donna* was the first Italian feminist periodical that included lesbians in its audience. *Effe* embraced the issue in March 1981 with an article titled "*Mamma, amo una donna*" (Momma, I love a woman). *Noidonne* followed, in a July 1981 article, "*Lei ama lei*" (She loves her).

The issues of homosexuality and lesbianism had ancient echoes in Italy; In the Greek and Roman ages, sexuality was regarded differently than it was by early church fathers who associated sexuality with sin. When, in October 1981, two young women were arrested for kissing one another in Agrigento, Sicily—the city renowned for its valley of ancient Greek temples—a spontaneous women's protest arose at Rome in front of the Pantheon, the Roman monument to honor the Greek gods. Lesbians began organizing. A network was created, collegamento fra le lesbiche italiane; a newsletter, *bolettino del cli*, began publication in 1981. In December 1981 the first national meeting of lesbians was held in Rome, somewhat later than in other feminist movements. Discussion continued; another conference on "sexuality, love among women, rapport between heterosexuals and lesbians in the women's movement" was convened in September 1983 at Udi's women's center in Rome.

The July 1981 issue of *noidonne* brought letters to the editor. To a few readers, it seemed that *noidonne* had become "too feminist" and "too separatist"—and that it wrote "too much about lesbians." Discussion settled into whether lesbianism was a choice, a political act, or a private matter; whether lesbians were oppressed or not; whether the subject related only to a small minority.[25]

By 1982 abstractions were put aside for testimonies, life stories, and appeals for support. It became apparent that lesbianism was not confined to a small minority of sophisticated women in large cities, but was, rather, a widespread ancient and contemporary phenomenon. One reader of *noidonne* said that feminism had made it possible to talk about lesbians openly. "If women exist with sexual and emotional needs different from ours, why don't we open a dialogue with them, so that they will not feel isolated and dramatically unhappy, as many letters indicate? Let us take courage let us demonstrate that we are truly sisters."[26]

As in the campaigns for divorce and abortion, personal statements from women became the persuasive pivots in turning mainstream feminists toward sisters on the edge. Women knew what it was to feel different; letters from lesbian women resonated: "My manner of living has been a continual concealment of my manner of being and of feeling, in order to conform as completely as possible to the lives of others, the 'normal' people."[27] What was normal and what was "other" had become for Italian feminists by the early eighties a room with many mirrors reflecting different images of the self.

At the September 1983 conference, lesbianism was discussed as an issue that pertained to all women: "the first step, for all of us, is to accept ourselves."[28] When she had understood that it was possible to love another woman, said Marina Camboni, a *dwf* editor, all of her internal barriers had fallen regarding lesbians. There is no fixed and immutable line between lesbianism and heterosexuality, maintained Rina Macrelli of Udi. "That which divides women, in reality, is the patriarchate."[29] What should be avoided, said Roberta Tatafiore, feminist activist, was the separation of lesbians from heterosexual women, a separation that "had happened, for example, in the United States."[30] Like other women, lesbians had differences among themselves; some considered lesbianism a political act and some did not, some considered themselves separatists and some did not. The conference concluded with an affirmation of the importance of differences: "We must look at differences among women without distrust and without fear."[31]

One Italian feminist commenting on lesbianism has remarked that up to a few decades ago in the North and still true today in the South, "a woman may only go out with another woman; a girl can go for a walk or to the cinema or stay overnight only with female friends."[32] Paola Zaccaria continues, "Up to the age of fifteen I went around hand in hand with my girl friends. I slept with them, and we often kissed. I was completely ignorant of the word 'lesbianism'; otherwise most probably I would have lived through the experience without the sunny radiant innocence of my years." "The passage to male-oriented sexuality," said Zaccaria, "put an end to a "natural— although exacerbated by the social mores—preference."[33]

She made an elliptical statement about lesbianism and catholicism: "In this land of virgin martyrs, it is very likely that lesbianism has been allowed, or even, ironically, promulgated precisely by those who condemn it." The deflection of the issue into somewhat abstract debate on "separatism," said Zaccaria, has smothered the real issue, since few women practice separatism."[34]

The many dimensions of Italian women were suggested by Zaccaria: "Stubbornly we go, I go, women go—through the world and against it—not only to rediscover ancient truths, but also to discover their own time 'seen with their own eyes, spoken in their own language, thought with their own minds'—and the visions they discover and invent are *womanist*, fresh and true."

Zaccaria teaches languages at the University of Bari and lives with her husband (whose field is ecological energy) in a relationship "continuously under discussion." In a statement that may have summarized Italian women's history from the time of the earth mother to the modern age of Freud, Zaccaria said that she was "shamelessly continuously in love" with her four-year-old son, Daniele.[35]

nuns

One different group of women in Italy are catholic nuns. In 1970 there were 165,902 convents in Italy in contrast to 27,415 male monasteries. In a sense, choosing to live as a nun has always been a deep rebellion, liberating women from cultural assignments, since the vocation bypasses matrimony. Mysticism—or, as Teresa described it, interior experience—also bypasses male priests as intermediaries. In catholic countries women were excluded from the priesthood, but in the choice to become a nun, a woman could refuse the subordinate, often exploited, role she would otherwise endure in society—although, as Dacia Maraini pointed out, the autonomy women found in religious orders was purchased by subordination to the church.

Some nuns (but more priests) left their orders in the atmosphere of vatican council II in the late 1960s. John XXIII's definition of the church as the "people of God in history" destabilized all catholic institutions. Nuns in Italy who remained in convents were characterized by a deepening unease, visible in the recourse to psychiatry, a practice that has become commonplace.[36]

For nuns who did not leave orders, the feminist critique could be uncomfortably close. Division of labor within catholic ecclesiastical institutions traditionally allocated to priests the intellectual work of theology and preaching, while nuns taught approved doctrine. A feminist study of Italian nuns entitled *La casalinga di Cristo* (The housewife of Christ) points to the housewifely tasks (preparing the host, embroidering altar cloths) nuns were assigned while priests presided in the church.[37]

This study also finds the role of mother (usually a severe mother) visible in the nuns' function as teachers of catechism for the young.[38] Passivity, subordination and obedience to superiors are inculcated early, the authors conclude, and determine the lives of most Italian nuns thereafter. Nuns take vows to Christ, a consecration seen as a kind of matrimony. The vow of poverty is realized in not being paid for their work. When nuns do rebel, they do so dramatically, as in the case of Adriana Zarri. But not many in Italy did so. In the middle of the decade of the seventies the unease of nuns was evident for the most part in statistics. Their number was diminishing, as more left than entered orders. Almost one-half were over fifty-six years of age. Until very recently, the vote of the sisters was securely fastened in the pockets of christian democrats. Women therapists for nuns point out that "nuns, like women in general, are taught to be subordinate." In the case of nuns, they are not only subordinate to male priests, these same men are their spiritual counselors.[39]

Italian feminists feel a particular sisterliness for nuns; a favorite feminist place for lunch in Rome is a restaurant where nuns wait on table and lead diners in singing "Ave Maria." Aside from a few highly outspoken women, nuns were not part of the Italian feminist movement. It was not until the crisis over nuclear missiles in Italy became intense after 1979 that more nuns started taking public stands.

feminists

In discussions I have had with Italian feminists regarding the significance of the concept of difference for a new society, they have pointed out to me that this is not utilitarian individualism nor right-wing stress on superior individuals, but a truth of the gospel: "Do not do to others what you would not have done to you."[40] This is a slight rewording of the golden rule; as in the version of Sicilian peasants, the rewording changes the meaning. For Italians who have, since 1968, rejected the *integrismo* of monolithic catholicism as well as the *integrismo* of monolithic socialism, the traditional version of the golden rule—"Do unto others what you would have done to you"—is equivocal in meaning: others might have beliefs different from yours.

For feminists, the implication of this is not only that women have perspectives different from those of men, but also that no particular group of women has privileged insights into the nature of what it is to be a woman. The continuum of Italian women is rippled with differences: catholics-marxists-believers-nonbelievers-matrons-prostitutes-nuns-lesbians-feminists-others. For feminists, women find their identity by looking into conscience—and by looking at others.[41]

men as "others"

Following the metaphor of the "other" can be a women's journey
leading eventually to men. Earlier regarded as unfeeling exploitative
patrons of prostitutes, by the end of the seventies men were included
in the ambit of "other." In her study of prostitution, Maria Rosa Cutrufelli said, "If women's sexuality is still an undiscovered continent,
male sexuality is an iceberg about which nothing is known but what
appears publicly. . . . If women do not receive satisfaction, neither
does the man." [42]

Deepening her inquiries, Cutrufelli asked, "Why do men seek prostitutes?" At the end of her interviews with men who sought prostitutes, she found herself anguished: "If one in three Italian men ha-
bitually pays in order to make love, then the problem is not a small
one." It is a problem that refers not only to the client and to the
prostitute, but also to the wife, lover, fiancee, because "it is from
these relationships that the man is fleeing." The metaphor of "other"
engendered concern for the other: "Every woman should have the
right to her autonomy without selling herself, every man should be
able to attain sexual satisfaction without purchasing it." [43]

14

unione donne italiane

the Italian women's union, 1968–1984.
other people and other unions

women as protagonists
in the transition to socialism

In 1968, the year contemporary feminism emerged in Italy, a generational split within unione donne italiane was evident. Younger Udi
women shared the view of other dissenters (who became the Italian
new left) that the Pci was doing nothing in a situation that seemed
to have revolutionary implication. They were also in agreement with
new left criticism of democratic centralism, party procedure that had
the effect of discouraging dissenting opinions. Udi women disliked
the leninist concept of the vanguard (the party in alliance with large
labor syndicates) because this strategy subordinated women's concerns to larger party policy. Yet in the confused polemics of the early
period, Udi women did not see eye to eye with those they called

"neofeminists." From 1968 to 1973, spontaneous feminist groups took the limelight, assailing Udi women for being connected to a "pyramidal, male-dominated" party.[1]

By 1973 it was apparent that what the Udi called the "second feminism" had influenced the women's union. The Udi conference of that year stressed that subordination of women derived from the division of roles in a "masculinist" society. While "autonomous" feminists launched a referendum campaign to repeal the punitive aspects of the fascist law criminalizing abortion, Udi affirmed Togliatti's premise that women were "protagonists" in the process of democratic transition to socialism[2] and concentrated on helping to defeat the antidivorce referendum in 1974, on spearheading the effort to secure equal family rights legislation in 1975, and on working for social services: child care centers, full-time schooling, and housing. "Autonomous" feminists challenged Udi women in confrontations at the *casa della donna*. Charges were hurled back and forth. The upshot was that Udi women were thrust into leadership in the campaign for the abortion law. By picketing the men of their party in front of parliament, Udi exerted the leverage that produced the abortion law of 1978. Udi women remember this as an action that removed women's concerns from the control of the patriarchy. Udi women also worked for *consultori* (women's health clinics) and for the sexual violence referendum—issues associated with "neofeminism."[3]

the women's movement as more important than participation in left parties

By the late 1970s, Udi women agreed with feminists who stressed their independence of parties by calling themselves "extraparliamentary." To achieve women's liberation, a women's movement was more important than participating in parties in which women did not have genuine equality. This was a strategy bypassing not only the Pci but other parties (e.g., Psi) who gave their verbal support while equivocating on women's issues. The strategy also offered an invitation to women of the Dc, whose party was opposed to divorce, legal abortion, and the bill prohibiting sexual violence. Affirming the "necessity of women's liberation," Udi defined itself as a "movement of autonomous and organized women" stressing "consciousness, dependence on experience, criticism of prevailing forms of politics,"[4] phrases which indicated that Udi had absorbed the themes of the "second feminism" and of the new left.[5] The 1978 Udi congress criticized "pyramidal structures," including the national orientation of Udi itself.[6] Another declaration called for the "autonomy of Udi," a declaration that was to be actualized in the Udi congress of 1982.

spontaneity and organization

The May 8, 1981, issue of *noi donne* offered a glimpse of how Udi women mobilized to sustain the legal abortion law: they canvassed neighborhoods, arranged small-group discussions, and distributed information about women's clinics. Udi women distributed questionnaires on abortion to find areas of women's concern that would become discussion topics for small groups. Street spectacles dramatized what would happen if the abortion law lost. Udi women met with antiabortion groups, stressing Udi's difference from the referendum of Pr which proposed abortion on demand: Udi's position was support for women's health clinics (for dissemination of birth control information) with legal abortion as a last resort—leaving the decision to the conscience of the woman. In the 1981 vote sustaining legal abortion, the Pr measure failed, the Udi position was upheld: birth control, woman's conscience, and legal abortion as a last resort.

Udi, a self-determined organized movement, May 1982

In its congress of May 20–23, 1982, Udi dissolved its organizational structure and "refounded" the women's organization on the basis of "self-determination."[7] Udi rejected Pci subsidy, the national secretariat resigned, the right to vote was given to conference delegates who were not members of the union, and abstractions were dismissed for "specific, personal concerns of women." A horizontal, rather than vertical, structure was implemented, leaving the actual power of Udi to local chapters and ultimately to the conscience of each woman; leadership in the new structure lay in the initiatives of all parts of the organization. The Pci subsidy had in the past paid the salaries of a few full-time professionals; by rejecting the subsidy, the organization eliminated the central office, in an affirmation of democracy from the base.[8]

As evidence of sincere commitment to "autonomy and collective responsibility of women," *noi donne*, at this congress, was reorganized into a weekly "bulletin of the movement" with notices of local, regional, and national women's activities. The journal was renamed *noidonne*—the joined words connoting women's solidarity. A monthly *noidonne* magazine supplemented the weekly with thoughtful articles.[9] A cooperative since 1969, the journal was financed by membership campaigns. Echoing spontaneous feminist collectives, Udi said that the aim of the women's union was to be open to the initiatives of all women. A note of realism was inserted with the proposal of the congress to elect a committee to "guarantee the financial continuity of the association."[10]

"women's task is to change the culture"

A 1981 interview with Margherita Repetto (Alaia) revealed how the first and second waves of Italian feminism had converged by the 1980s, lifting the movement, activists hoped, to a new level. Pci women who were called "politicos" in the early seventies took the lead in 1982 in moving Udi toward cultural concerns of neofeminists and the political aims of the new left—to "democracy wider than political forms."[11]

Implicitly the aim was to enlarge the feminist movement to include women who were in agreement on issues but who did not want connection with the Pci: women of the Dc, but also socialist and new left women and independent catholics. Udi strategy also offered a place for those extraparliamentary feminists who had been left isolated and anxious when some extraparliamentary youth went off to groups intent on violent revolution. Another implicit aim was to "accelerate the maturity" of men of the left. For Udi women, simultaneously suffering the slings and arrows of cultural feminists while contending with men in the Pci, the last straw may have been the Pci amendment of the bill against sexual violence (rendering it acceptable to the general electorate, rather than to women).

The "rights phase" of the Italian women's movement, said Repetto, was "now exhausted." The point was to move, in concert beyond demands: "women's task is to change the culture. . . . If our society is masculinist, it is because we allow it to be."[12] Udi, said Repetto, was to be a women's organization "not determined by the strategy of the Pci, nor the needs of the worker movement." Did this development mean that Udi had embraced separatism? "Udi has never been sepa-ratist, but we must now recognize that separatism is implicit in the recognition that women's struggle must be carried on by women." Separatism, from Repetto's perspective, meant: "We do not want to destroy our counterpart, the male. Only his power. And we have scarcely begun."[13]

This historic turn of Udi reflected an awareness that "there are many points of view" among Italian feminists, as well as "many re-gional differences in Italy, notably the difference between northern and southern Italy." Udi was attempting to renew itself at a moment of crisis for women, not only in Italy, but across the world. What did this renewal of Udi mean? "Out of the feminist experience of recent years, remains the wisdom that liberation signifies conflict with the male, with the masculine in our society, our culture, our institu-tions—conflict with masculinist forms of organization."[14] What was the role of women in social change? "We have many battles to un-dertake." Above all, "women should be the eyes of society." What is the relation of the Udi to catholic women? "There have always been catholic women in Udi, even among its founders." The abortion issue had created a fracture, if not with individual catholic women, with "organized catholic women."[15]

The new direction of Udi would make it possible for women who differed ideologically—as to communism and catholicism—to work together on women's issues at the local level.

evolution of *Noi Donne* to *noi donne* to *noidonne*

The evolution of Udi after 1968 can be documented in the pages of its journal. *Noi Donne*, the journal of Udi as women's auxiliary of the Pci, evolved after 1968 into *noi donne*, a Udi journal with feminist concerns in a critical relationship to the Pci, and then in 1982 to *noidonne*, a journal associated with an autonomous women's move-ment, its title connoting the solidarity of all women. As other femi-nist journals ceased publication in the early eighties, *noidonne* recap-tured the role it had before the seventies as Italy's foremost women's journal.[16]

The abortion issue was probably the turning point for *noi donne*. In 1977 a special issue on abortion appeared, entitled "From Herod to Pilate," implying that women were being crucified by masculine hypocrisy. Udi's articles at the height of the abortion agitation stressed not abortion but the importance of women's clinics, because these meeting places enabled women to discuss maternity, sexuality, and contraception as well as the last option, abortion. The clinics also focused on infant care and health education.[17] By the end of the seventies, as feminist collectives dissolved and as Cif absorbed many Udi themes, Udi emerged as the strongest women's organization of Italy. Some early neofeminists, tired and somewhat disillusioned in the mid-eighties, said to me in interviews that the feminist movement had been "co-opted"; it was unclear by whom.

A clear watershed date in the evolution of Udi's journal was 1969. While neofeminists were making their charges against men of the Pci, a series was initiated in the Udi journal that developed into a direct polemic of party women against party men of the Pci. The diatribe is better understood when kept in the context of the fact that the men being criticized were often husbands or lovers. Pci men were described as "supporters of women's liberation in words but conservatives, bourgeois, and opportunists in the facts."[18] Thereafter letters to the Udi journal and articles pursued the argument, but it was not until 1973 that *noi donne* began using words that connoted male chauvinism.[19]

The method of gathering testimonial stories to support legislation became characteristic of the journal. The tactic was first used for support of the divorce law, then for women's rights in the family, then for the abortion law and for the referendum against sexual violence. Paying attention to regional differences among Italian women, the covers of Udi's journal featured women of each province.

Sexuality, early treated openly in the pages of *effe*, was at first discussed indirectly in *noi donne*; some subjects were originally taboo, including women's sexual dissatisfaction and the obstacles to self-determination for women in the traditional family. In a significant 1975 departure, *noi donne* printed inquiries into sexuality, motherhood, and abortion based on the testimony of 30,000 women. Hitherto undiscussable subjects were brought into print: conjugal sex regarded by wives as an imposition, women's terror of unwanted pregnancy, the bizarre sicknesses to which women resort to avoid pregnancy. Most striking was the discovery that Italian women practiced life-endangering clandestine abortion on a large scale. Old women publicly discussed birth-restricting methods that had always been used during the great peasant famines, methods that included infanticide.[20]

By the late seventies *noi donne* was printing articles on sexual violence and graphic discussions of sexuality and abortion. A 1977 issue discussed "housewife prostitutes" who worked to supplement the family income with the caption: "wife-prostitute two faces of the same coin." Articles on lesbianism appeared in 1981.

Women turned to the pages of *noi donne* for help. A young woman wrote, "Please help me escape. My father will beat me if he sees me speak to a young man. I don't want to end up like my mother, like my sisters, who married very young: always shut up in the house; if they complain they are beaten." An editor investigated the condition of peasant women and wrote an exposé entitled, "Bread and beatings." In 1975 *noi donne* published a letter from Franca Canfora, a worker in a mushroom factory where women worked eighteen hours a day in conditions that produced involuntary abortions. This story brought responses from many women about the conditions of their work lives. By 1978 the magazine had become such a resource for Italian women that they sent in their diaries for publication. Marcellina Masiero, a rice worker in the Piedmont, now gravely ill, wrote that she had wanted to write about her life as long as she could remember. Masiero, a grandmother, suggested that the feminist movement may be new, but feminist insights are ancient.[21]

differences among Udi women

An older generation of Udi woman has been perceptively described by David Kertzer in "The Liberation of Evelina Zaghi: The Life of an Italian Communist."[22] Zaghi lives today in a working-class neighborhood of Bologna where everyone is a supporter of the Pci. She had joined the Pci and Udi simultaneously; Udi meant to her that "women should have the same rights as men" and that she "could do what [she had] to do." In the early 1970s she organized demonstrations for day care, for schools, and for women's issues. "We always organize for March 8, international women's day. We have little girls going to every door with flowers and leaflets talking about women's problems." Zaghi indicated the organizational significance of *noi donne*: "The way we keep the women here united is through the magazine, the calendar, membership and leafletting. It's a magazine that many women find difficult to read, because it's a feminist magazine without any comics. It deals with serious problems women face, like the cottage industry and women working in the factories." When a new person moves into her neighborhood, Zaghi visits and invites the woman to join, saying that "Udi is a feminist organization which is democratic and which defends the rights of women."

Engaged in what Udi calls *doppio lavoro*, Zaghi is simultaneously a Udi activist and a traditional woman; she cooks for the family and helps her daughter with the children. This generation of Udi women has one signal difference from other traditional women: they are communists and, like many of their generation, have an indifferent attitude toward religion. In this respect, Zaghi differs also from young communist feminists, many of whom are simultaneusly feminist and *credenti*. Although men of the Pci rarely go to church, said Zaghi, "women have always gone to church." Pci membership does not inhibit their religious activities; in any event, "it's true that a lot of communists send their children to catechism." She herself is not a *credente*, but when she talks with one, "I leave her to her own ideas. Women here don't discriminate. They are friendly with catholic and communist alike."

Of the widespread employment of women in cottage industry in their own homes, Zaghi said that this is a way of keeping women closed up, away from outside contacts. Going to work outside the home may give a woman some "new ideas." Employing women in their own homes is also advantageous for the "bosses" who do not have to worry about employers' tax and employee health insurance; bosses do not even have to provide machinery, because women have their own sewing machines. Women are willing to work in *lavoro nero*, said Zaghi, primarily because it keeps them close to their children. Candid about the "male domination of the Pci," she thought this was caused in part by women's preoccupation with their homes—women were "just too tired to do more." The influence of women in the Pci is limited, said Zaghi, but "greater" than in any other Italian party.[23]

An article in the December 1982 *noidonne* described the various ways women have interpreted Udi's reorganization of May 1982. Most are still enrolled in the Pci. The implications of emancipation may be illuminated by statistics; whatever their relationship with men, Italian women, more often than men, live alone (the statistics include widows, and wives whose husbands have gone elsewhere for work, as well as women who choose to live alone). The last census indicated a sharp drop in the Italian birth rate; the average Italian family of this generation has one child.[24] It is a season of doubt for some Udi women. For years they worried about reaching the others; in interviews they indicated that they feel now that *they* are the others; there is more concern now with being "authentic" than in being "credible." There is an acute sense of the differences among women.

The challenge of a restructured Udi is to see if there can be a different way of people governing themselves than the prevailing model of delegated, or representative, democracy. One alternative to representative democracy is direct democracy in assemblies. This model, Udi women agree, is beautiful, but after a while it does not function. Udi women who voted to restructure Udi at the May 1982 congress wanted to convert what they saw as the passive militancy of most women to activism by leaving decision-making power to local chapters. They were also aware, as the most important women's political organization in Italy, of their responsibility. Spontaneity, they believed, was very important, but organization was too.[25] Some veteran *udine* do not consider the 1981 restructuring a drastic change. They remember that the 1978 Udi congress was attended by two thousand delegates, most of whom insisted on the connection between the private and the political. With a dart at somewhat hypocritical Pci men who did not care for the neofeminist maxim that the personal is political, Vania Chiurlotto, the former editor of *noi donne*, said the 1982 Udi departure was refreshing in a country that politicized everything—including the celebration of Saint Joseph's day (whom Pci men like as patron saint of workmen).[26]

the Pci and an autonomous Udi

Men of the traditional left are somewhat perplexed by Udi's radical decentralization and insistence on autonomy. Pci women understand decentralization better: "the women's movement differs from others in that it wishes to cherish its diversity yet remain organized." Udi women denied that they were being anarchic in dissolving the national secretariat; they saw decentralization as important for democratic implication as well as an earnest of the willingness of functionaries to step down.[27] Some Pci women expressed uneasiness in discussions of the new Udi. Lalla Trupia said that both spontaneity and organization were important, but that spontaneity is often accompanied by division and weakness. Italian women need a strong organization because "we have a responsibility not to forget that this is a country whose overall vote to sustain the abortion law was 70 percent—but this is also a country where a woman "can die" while giving birth to "her eighteenth child."[28]

Criticism of the new direction of Udi was published in *noidonne*. Mina, an older member of Udi from La Spezia, did not like the new decentralized structure. She wrote that she has been an activist all her adult life; people now ask her in the street, Is it true that the Udi office is now closed, that you no longer do anything? Decentralization has more appeal for younger women, as well as for women in marginal regions. Gisella lives in Sicily, is married, a student of psychology, and a member of the Psi and Udi. Her husband is a militant communist: activism in Udi and the socialist party gives her, she feels, her own space.[29]

Discussion of the restructured Udi also generated pride: "Italy has probably the most advanced women's legislation in all of Europe, and probably the world." There was agreement that the Pci was an advanced communist party; not unrelated to this was the fact that the Pci held the "largest women's consensus of any Italian party." In contrast to other feminist movements of the world, said Italian women, their movement had "changed the collective consciousness" on women's issues.[30]

A specific women's consciousness was earliest apparent in the Pr; by the mid-eighties it was pervasive in the Pci. It was also apparent in the Psi among women who wanted to differentiate themselves from the communist party. Early in the 1970s the socialist party's equivocations on feminist issues propelled women socialists into working with Pr for women's concerns, while remaining members of the Psi. The Pci tended to secure the credit for defeating the 1981 referendum that would have annulled the abortion law. Some women, in a gesture of affirmation of feminist autonomy, preferred membership in the other Italian "historic" left party—the Psi. Elena Marinucci of the Psi said that women's presence in the socialist party was due to the feminist movement. Feminism in Italy, in "contrast to the United States," had "changed the collective consciousness." She cited the 1981 vote to sustain the abortion law as proof of this.[31]

Separatism, like other Italian feminist principles, held a variety of interpretations, as a conference on separatism in the fall of 1983 at Rome indicated. For Udi, separatism was reflected in more *noidonne* articles on lesbianism, on a woman's right to define her own sexuality, and on the new prostitutes' union. The impact of this on women of the communist party can be seen in the 1983 summer issue of *donne e politica* in an article on the prostitutes' union and its periodical, *lucciola*.[32]

The implications of self-determination became evident after the Udi congress. Without the money customarily received from the Pci, everybody had to learn to take responsibility, not to delegate less gratifying tasks to others. Most women activists in the national secretariat were relieved to transfer responsibility to the base, speaking of the "costs" of militancy for one's personal life. For some women, self-determination meant founding women's cooperatives. There are Udi coops that manage hotels, some that operate restaurants; at Forlì a women's coop restaurant has beome a women's center. At Turin, women planned a tea room with regional cooking and music; at Genoa, Udi is planning a weaving coop; at Brescia, there are plans for a Udi consumers' coop. In other places Udi women give classes, sometimes in conjunction with a labor union. Sometimes local institutions help Udi financially,[33] but the aim is to achieve financial as well as other forms of autonomy; service coops, particularly for women's health clinics, are a goal.

Politics for Udi women has lost its monolithic character: " I don't know if I feel myself first of all a woman or a communist." "I'll tell you the truth. At the beginning I was perplexed, then I felt liberated; there is no longer a national office that decides for me. What a beauty—I'll do with Udi what I want." Some Udi women speak of a "postpolitical" era. Does this mean they are disenchanted? A woman who has thought about this a good deal said that it does not mean disenchantment; it does mean that women's politics begin in women's experience.[34]

How did women activists in the Pci regard this development in Udi? Electoral totals for the party had jumped with the insertion of feminist issues into the elections of 1975 and 1976, declined with women's withdrawal from politics in 1979, jumped again after the success of the 1981 vote on abortion. In the 1983 election, a record 93 percent of young people went to the polls and enlarged the vote for the Pci. An article in *donne e politica* noted that there was division as to whether Udi's autonomy was weakening or strengthening the party. Decentralizing Udi did lead to women choosing the commitment that seemed to them most important: some choose to work in the disarmament movement, others to help in women's health centers, others concentrate on cultural work. For politically minded feminists, the solution seemed "fragile" and insufficient if the goals of decentralization were interpreted solely as widening communications among women and elevating individual conscience. Even if they agreed with decentralizing Udi, they regarded it as important that women continue to work toward changing basic conditions of life while radically renewing the goals and means of politics. Some political feminists applaud the development within feminism that has brought everything into question: values, the economy, social organization, politics. Yet consciously or unconsciously there has been a refrain of worry among Italian feminists that the restructured Udi will lose its obvious political strength: it is this "political function of the women of our country that renders it different from other feminist movements in Europe and the United States." [35]

A graffito on the walls of the *casa della donna* at Rome declared: "I want to have the liberty of that butterfly." The logo the contemporary *noidonne* uses for its coupon to find all the women's groups in Italy (health groups, cultural groups, groups involved in political projects et al.) is a cherub riding a butterfly. The logo is an appropriate one for any attempt to coordinate the flight of different women, all intent on self-determination.

To feminists, a butterfly connotes liberty. The radical decentralization of the Italian women's union may be a unique attempt to encourage a network of autonomous women, fostering diversity and spontaneity at the base that is an example of "democracy wider than political forms." "Our history has scarcely begun," states Margherita Repetto (Alaia), "The women's movement is part of the creation of a society in which there are no forms of domination and that society can not be separated from the process of its creation." [36]

The Italian feminist itinerary from the old to the new left (and beyond)—and from an identification with the *other* that includes men—was visible in the program of the new editor of *noidonne* in 1985. Mariella Gramaglia, earlier associated with the new left newspaper *il manifesto*, plans a new format for the Udi journal to reach women largely ignored by surveys because they are not inscribed in any political party. There will be a new column on controversial issues—"seen by her/seen by him." [37]

what of men of the left and women?

An important fact about the Italian feminist movement after 1968 is that in spite of large demonstrations, in spite of the upheaval engendered by women in the parties, in spite of their work for pathbreaking legislation, an eerie silence on the movement remained in most of the definitive histories and accounts (still considered under the purview of men) of the 1970s and early 1980s.

This is not to say that men of the left, as well as many men of the center, did not support feminist legislation; electoral tallies would not have reached large majorities without men's support. Men of the Pci who accompanied their wives and daughters to *feste delle donna* may have had private questions, but men of this large communist party supported divorce, equal family rights, child care, legal abortion, and the bill against sexual violence.

To probe men's silence about women, one might examine two significant writers who wrote first-hand chronicles of the 1970s and 1980s: Alberto Ronchey and Umberto Eco. Alberto Ronchey, an essayist for the independent left newspaper *la Repubblica*, gathered his columns from 1981 to 1983 in an anthology. [38] In its lengthy index, there are references to a few foreign women (Simone de Beauvoir, the czarina Catherine II, Mary McCarthy, Marguerite Yourcenar) but there is not one reference to Italian women. The issues of the early eighties that preoccupied Ronchey were the Pci's separation from the soviets, Ronald Reagan's European policy, the possibility that communists and socialists could form a governing coalition, the oil crisis, and the nuclear threat. The one reference to the imposing 1981 vote sustaining legal abortion is contained in an essay discussing the "cattolici anomali, comunisti anomali" of Italy.

Ronchey talked with a French benedictine monk who had visited the *comunità di base* in the Rome neighborhood of San Paolo Fuori le Mura; the monk said that he could not understand Italian catholicism. Ronchey and the monk considered Italy's "anomalous catholics"; no other catholic nation with so many baptized and christened communicants had produced similar majorities of popular votes sustaining divorce and abortion in the face of appeals of the pope and other clerical representatives.

Italy's "anomalous catholics" were matched by its "anomalous communists." Ronchey and the monk thought about the plank of 1979 party theses which stated that members of the Pci "may be catholics, but they are not held to be, or to declare themselves, marxists."[39] "Anomalous catholics, anomalous communists," concluded Ronchey; in Italy, "anything is possible."[40]

An Italian writer who wrote a world-wide best seller in the early eighties entitled *The Name of the Rose*, offers a glimpse inside the thinking of men of the Pci.[41] Umberto Eco, a highly respected member of the party, was considered friendly to women's concerns; feminists asked him to write an introductory article for a collection of women's political posters.[42] Eco's novel is a story almost entirely about men. *The Name of the Rose* may also be considered a parable for events in Italy from 1977 to 1983; Eco's mind was not on the women's movement. *sette anni di rabbia*

This scholar of semiotics turned novelist set his story in the age immediately following that of Francis of Assisi, the end of medieval history and the beginning of the modern era. The first sentence of the novel refers to a document handed the author in 1968 that "claimed to reproduce faithfully a fourteenth-century manuscript." The writer notes he read the manuscript while "in Prague, waiting for a dear friend." Six days after the writer received the manuscript, Eco pointed out, the soviets "invaded that unhappy city."[43] The book suggests the itinerary of Italian communists from disillusionment with the soviets in 1968 to a declaration of autonomy in 1981.

One target of the new left confrontationalists in 1968, and of feminists thereafter, was the "unidimensional" view of life of soviet communists and their adherents. The path of the Pci from 1968 to 1981, in Eco's parable, not only included a rejection of the soviet model and a repudiation of the violence inherent in leninism, the itinerary led to a deepening understanding that Italian communism has a dimension that reaches beyond rationality. Eco explores these themes of doctrine, heresy, violence, and belief in *The Name of the Rose*.[44]

Reflecting Italian anxiety about terrorism in the Italy of the late seventies, Eco's book (which has been highly praised by the Pci) has among its many facets a condemnation of violence for religious, or revolutionary, beliefs. In a book of essays written at the same time as the novel, Eco says of the age from 1977 to 1983, these were years of "desiderio"—of desire, or longing, seven years marked by the rediscovery of the private, of desire.[45] The four years of terrorism from 1977 to 1981 were religiously inspired by a death wish. (One should keep in mind, said Eco, that some religions require human sacrifices[46]) The second three years, from 1981 to 1984, were marked by the confessions of imprisoned terrorists.

The Name of the Rose symbolically traces the evolution of beliefs from the old to the new left. In Eco's essays, he says of 1968, "all of us were there ... professors as well as students." He chronicles the disillusionments of the 1970s: loss of sentimentality about the Chinese revolution, acknowledgment of the grim realities in countries of "existing socialisms," and exposure of the gulags of the USSR.[47] Eco called the violent revolutionaries of the late seventies (most of them schooled in catholic institutions) unfrocked priests, disillusioned communists who became a generation of vipers. Of the comunists of his generation who sat in judgment on the violent revolutionaries, Eco said that even more dangerous than the disillusioned young are communists who act like unsmiling fascists, *senza sorriso.*[48]

There is an unacknowledged similarity between Eco's views and those of many Italian feminists. While historians and others were documenting the "secularization" of Italian society with the laws for divorce, equal family rights, and abortion, what may have been happening was an internalizing of belief—a process whereby conscience, not papal or party doctrine, has become, for many Italians, the arbiter of moral judgment. This is seen in the pamphlet written by *credenti* supporting legalized abortion (see chapter 9), in the converging Italian movements against violence (see chapter 15), and in Eco's writings, in which rationalist Italian marxism has been invaded by a sense of the void, and of the sacred. Eco, whose rationalism appears to be grounded on a world view encompassing Saint Francis, Karl Marx, and Martin Heidegger, might well be one of the "anomalous catholics" and "anomalous communists" of Italy described by Ronchey. A dialectician as well as novelist, Eco states that he is aware that practicing rhetoric, logic, and dialectic may bring the charge of impiety;[49] his views are not far from those of Italy's liberation theologians, who hold that believers and unbelievers are both necessary in bringing into being a new society.[50]

Although the prevailing pattern was masculine silence about the women's movement, there were a few exceptions. Umberto Cerroni wrote a study of the relationship between men and women in bourgeois culture in 1975.[51] His orientation does not appear to have been shaken by feminist analyses and activism. Concerned as a marxist to address the question on a theoretical level, he placed the man/woman antinomy among other dualisms: spirit/body, culture/work, intellectual/simple, governors/governed. The study does not progress beyond dualist paradox.

Somewhat clearer is Giovanni Cesareo's 1977 study of the "feminine contradiction."[52] A journalist in Palermo, Cesareo wanted to demystify the "false equalitarianism" that envelops everybody in "one totalitarian model," which he described as a masculine model elaborated in a society of bourgeois capitalism. A marxist, Cesareo found revolutionary potential in women's everyday actions and evaluated the cry to "save the family" as an attempt to save the patriarchal family within capitalism. Agreeing with feminists, Cesareo said that the forms of the family had varied throughout history, that the same system that exploited women oppressed the majority of men also, and he adopted a feminist metaphor—patriarchy. At the summit of this pyramid, in Cesareo's analysis, were men of the dominant classes who held privileges of sex as well as class. In the modern age, capitalist production was the source of male privilege and the subordination of women. Less concerned with logical coherence than with moving toward a new society, Cesareo said that contradictions of sex and class were entangled, but he considered women's affirmations of themselves as a promising development in achieving a society with a better relationship between men and women.[53]

By 1982 more men were willing to give women credit. In an article in *donne e politica*, Eugenio Manca said that "everyone knows that if all of Italian society today feels more free, mature, and civil, this is owed to the results that women have produced."[54] Men and women were both more mature and freer, said Manca, because women had taken the field.

what of men and women in the labor unions?

Perhaps a good lens through which to view relationships between men and women from 1968 to the eighties is Italy's large left union confederations. Men in the labor unions generally supported women's issues (at least electorally) as part of their adherence to left parties—or in consonance with beliefs of left catholicism.

In the postwar period the relationship of trade unions, like that of the women's union, to the Pci was one of binding cooperation.[55] As "transmission belts" of party policy, both the large labor unions and the women's union were, in effect, subordinate to the party. As a recent collection of Udi documents indicates, this pattern of "binding cooperation" with the Pci was not always maintained by women of Udi and the women's union officially declared its independence of the party in 1982.[56] Men in Italian trade unions attained considerable autonomy even earlier. After the confrontations of 1968, factory councils were elected by all workers, whether or not they were members of the union. The Italian practice is that of an open shop. In 1980 women made up 26 percent of the labor force (a statistic that does not include *lavoro nero*).[57]

In the postwar era, labor confederations had accepted industrial agreements that contained discriminatory wage differences. Despite the constitutional provision of equal pay for equal work, pay scales for workers in the South were lower than for workers in the North for the same work. Pay scales for women and young people were set at a lower level than for adult males.[58] Italian labor policy was constricted in the postwar era by cold war anticommunism promoted by the papacy, the Dc, and the U. S. government, but the Cgil in the postwar period "agreed to the wage structure which discriminated against women."[59] Yet political principle propelled communist party and union men to sign a first pact, in 1960, abolishing separate wage scales for women. The principle of equal pay for equal work presided over subsequent union pacts, although women remained in the lowest level jobs.

In 1968 the new left criticized the undemocratic structures of the unions as well as the parties. Rank-and-file people in the unions joined the revolt of the young in 1969 in a democratic thrust to abolish regional salary differentials. After 1968 skilled and unskilled workers collaborated for equal fringe benefits for white- and blue-collar workers. Perhaps the lasting significance of post-1968 labor militance in Italy was the insistence on worker control and on direct instead of delegated participation. In factory assemblies, themes of workers' self-management, economic decentralization, and democratic planning were stressed. Joanne Barkan, who has closely studied Italian labor unions, has described the aims of the strikes of the "hot autumn": "They conceived of a new political order that would link workplaces to communities and situate significant power at the grass-roots level."[60]

Just as the feminist movement gathered steam in the early seventies, the workers' movement tapered off, losing earlier innovative qualities as unions regained control over the rank and file. Factory councils became less representative, women became "more severely underrepresented in the councils."[61] In 1972 a federation of the major unions was created, Cgil-Cisl-Uil. In the middle of the seventies, as economic recession overtook the "economic miracle," the worker movement became defensive. Viewed in retrospect, the imaginative qualities of the factory worker movement of 1969 became characteristic of the women's union, Udi, after 1975. While the innovative factory councils of the "hot autumn" subsided into bureaucratic bodies and the Pci retreated to a policy of historic compromise with the Dc and a program of worker austerity, marginal women and youth protested in 1977. Subsequent terrorism of the right and the left disheveled all worker plans and hopes.

Women in the unions were obviously influenced by feminism. In the 150-hour courses they brought up the paternalism of labor organizations. Networks of union women were organized to overcome plant, industry, and union divisions and to give priority to questions affecting women. Like women of Udi, women in the large unions felt they needed their own structures. In worker demonstrations it became characteristic for women's contingents to march separately under their own banners. Women also developed their own ways of striking. At Mirafiori, in protest against inadequate women's dressing rooms, the women marched through the factory and sacked the white-collar workers' lunchroom, taking ham and cheeses, which they then ate in the factory. A specifically feminist strike was another one at Mirafiori when women held a "strike against the strike"—refusing to participate in the union strike until "the men kept their hands to themselves."[62] By 1980 unions in Milan held factory assemblies during working hours to discuss the proposed bill on sexual violence.[63] But women's advances in the unions have not been dramatic. Day-care facilities provided by factories remain inadequate.

The amount of help at home that working wives receive from husbands or lovers remains undocumented.

Women's networks in unions have tried to put women's demands into union platforms, for instance, work-study programs for skill development, combining assembly-line work with other tasks, better safety and health conditions, paid child care leave for women and men, a thirty-five-hour work week, better social services. By 1983 three components of the Italian women's movement converged on the theme of women's work and organized the international conference on women and work at Turin: autonomous feminist groups, Udi, and the *interecategoriale donne* of Cgil-Csil-Uil.

Joanne Barkan's interviews with women and men Fiat workers in the early eighties confirm my own interviews with a random sample of workers in the same period. Marisa from the Veneto said that women factory workers have the same rights as men—but men are promoted more rapidly. A left catholic, she believes there are "more contradictions" in the church than in left parties.[64] A woman in an 150-hour class felt there "has to be a revolution for things to get better," a revolution brought about not by parties nor by unions but by workers organizing themselves "autonomously."[65] Maria, from the South, is a member of the Pci because she considers it "a serious party."[66]

What about the relationship of men and women in the factories? Sondra said there is good will to women on the part of some men workers, "the comrades"; the problem is the "bosses" who "make you feel inferior." A member of the Pci, she defines equality as "women active and politically conscious in society." Men are not far from factory women's analyses: women must work in solidarity with women, states Sondra, otherwise "men won't go forward."[67]

As feminists pointed out in the seventies and eighties, there is some accommodation of men to women workers, but the understanding of the woman question, for many men in the factories, remains at a shallow level. Palmerio, from Sardinia, a member of the Pci, said that previously there was one woman on the factory council, now there were two. He thought that there were so few women on the council "because they do more work at home." In any event, Palmerio regards women as useful ("they participate in the strikes") to advance his goal to remove the bosses. For this male communist, the important issue is that bosses are unnecessary: "We can control production ourselves."⁶⁸ Tommasso's understanding of the woman question is even more superficial: "The women's movement is correct. They should be equal. I've always said we men are the weaker sex. Some men, Southerners, kept their women as slaves, but I'm for the women's movement." Terrorism and industrial pollution are Tommasso's main concerns.⁶⁹

Feminism has become part of the world view of most women factory workers in Italy, but there are regional and other differences. Liliana, from the North, who states that the "women's movement is what really changed my life," thinks the rapport between women and men is bad, even in factory councils, that men are hostile to women raising new issues. "They take the attitude that if women want to work, they'll have to suffer the bad conditions."⁷⁰ Telesca, born in the South, states, "I agree with the feminists. I am a feminist. But I want to be next to men, not under them or over them." She said that she and her husband (they work on opposite shifts) were "comrades, not just husband and wife." Equality, for Telesca, is "something you have to feel inside. But men have to change if women are going to have real equality."⁷¹

One difference between the women's union and other unions may be that the women's union has met, and largely surmounted, the problem of racism, which in Italy is identified with the "southern question." The ties between sexism and racism, as feminists have pointed out, are close. Barkan's conversation with a male Turin taxi-cab driver in the eighties indicates this. The biggest Italian problem, said the driver, "is the South and the Southerners. They're a mixture of races. The South was invaded so many times, and what's come of it is a *razza malfatta* (a badly made race). It's not their fault. It's just the way they are by nature. They're deceitful and crafty and mean. The mafia is all southern." That, said the driver, "is not racism."⁷²

15

violenza e pace

violence and peace

The history of Italian feminism since 1969 has been intertwined with a history of violence and with a deepening peace consciousness. Feminists early spoke of a world where "terrorists of all types" threw away arms and abuse gave way to respect for the beauty and diversity of life—even in an environment of more terrorist violence, from the right and the left (after 1969) than that experienced by any other Western democracy. A close analysis totals 14,000 acts of violence causing the death of 409 persons and injuries to 1,366 others. Yet, as a careful study concluded in 1985, Italian "calm and firm response to the terrorist challenge demonstrated better than anything since 1945 the underlying stability of Italian society and the tenacity of the country's commitment to democracy and a government of laws." [1]

Response to the violence of fascists and to the revolutionary violence of the red brigades, popular opposition to the 1979 parliamentary approval of installation of NATO nuclear missiles at Comiso, and ultimate questioning by many Italians fused into a deepening peace consciousness at the outset of the 1980s.[2] Feminists circulating a national referendum against sexual violence secured 300,000 signatures and presented them to parliament. On October 24, 1981, 250,000 to 500,000 Italians demonstrated against nuclear missiles in Europe. The Pci's declaration of autonomy of the soviets protested violence in Poland.[3] In February 1983, 50,000 women demonstrated in front of parliament against mutilation of the sexual violence bill. Other Italians protested violence against the environment and the violence of the mafia. On October 22, 1983, a national demonstration for peace—in all the meanings of the word—drew 700,000 Italians to Rome.

This deep chord for peace is in the spirit of franciscan christianity, with which Italians from the left to the right identify. A popular anthology of essays in the eighties was entitled *Francesco, un pazzo di slegare* (Francis, a madman to untie). The spirit of Italy's patron saint, who is thought to have embodied the meaning of the life of Christ, was described as a "madness" that if set free could fulfill utopian hopes.[4] Close to this franciscan spirit is the "immense invisible network of groups from the Alps to Sicily" of *comunità di base,* who bring a utopian perspective to democratizing Italy and to "dismantling violence" in everything from human relationships to the world nuclear arms race.[5]

sexual violence

The phrase *"Tremate! tremate! Le streghe son tornate!"* (Tremble! Tremble! The witches have returned!) captioned an account in *rocca* of the feminist parade of February 5, 1983, in front of parliament. Women were incensed that the Dc had changed the feminist definition of rape (crime against a person) to rape as a crime against "social morality." Observers said that the continuing vitality of feminist collectives as well as the energy liberated by the decentralization of Udi was evident in this spontaneous demonstration. Women paraded with placards that rejected abstractions and affirmed the importance of every human being: "person—Marina," "person—Stefania," "person—Anna."[6] The event reminded some feminists of the large spontaneous protest of December 1975 demanding legalized abortion.

The even larger February 1983 feminist protest was noteworthy because conservatives had been hoping feminists had disappeared. Previously feminists had argued about the imperfections of the sexual violence bill; with the bill under attack by the Dc, feminists united in support.[7] A demonstration placard declared: "We defend the law presented by the women's movement with 300,000 signatures; sexual violence is a crime against the person that must be prosecuted even in the case of marital rape."[8]

Christian democrats were reminded on parade signs that the issues of divorce, abortion, and now sexual violence always ended badly for them (referring to the defeats of Dc referenda against divorce and abortion). Different from the past was the wording of feminist banners. Previously, the names of women's groups were prominent; in 1983, the movement identified itself by city and by workplace. This was a careful decision; women wanted it known that they had gone into the street "as women and not as members of this or that party, of this or that organization."[9]

On October 18, 1984 the house of deputies approved the sexual violence bill and sent it to the senate. It was a half victory for women. The Dc and the Msi had been pressured to acknowledge sexual violence as a crime against a person, but they tacked amendments to the bill which enraged feminists. Sexual violence was legally defined as a grave crime against the person punishable by the government—but carefully excluded from punishment were husbands or lovers. For feminists this leaves the family a "free zone" for violence, protecting not the victim but the perpetrator. Another amendment makes it a crime for consenting teenagers to engage in sex.

The anger of feminists was sharpened by the behavior of the parties. The lay parties (Pri, Pli, and Psdi) voted with the Dc and the Msi. The Pr, heretofore the paladin of civil liberties, abstained from the vote. The Psi also abstained.[10] After the crippling amendments, the Pci, the Pdup, and the independent left also abstained from voting for the bill they had earlier supported. In the spring of 1985 the issue continues to roil Italian politics. The clout of the feminist vote is suggested in the tacit agreement of women to accept postponement of a senate vote on the measure until after the May 1985 administrative elections; male politicians are fearful that women will vote in reprisal. Feminists have tacitly accepted this peacemaking measure, perhaps as a bargaining chip.[11]

nuclear violence

The pattern of individuals converging autonomously also marked the beginning of the contemporary antinuclear movement in Italy on October 24, 1981, when a throng of 300,000 to 500,000 people serpentined through Rome with banners reading: "No to the missiles—PEACE." [12] The parties of the left were all present, but most demonstrators had gone into the streets spontaneously. The people outside the parties included men, women, and young people identified with schools, with *comunità di base*, with neighborhoods, cultural associations, leagues for the defense of the environment, and with factory councils. Present in the demonstration, thought an observer, was "civil society in all its multiplicity." [13]

The Italian peace movement represents more than the fear of becoming a theater of nuclear war. For a large arc of people, "It is the desire to construct a society and a future in which there is no longer space for violence and for oppression, no need for any type of weapons." One newspaper account evaluated the Italian peace movement as a notification by women, and young communists of both sexes, that the revolution is not made by armed force. [14] The many dimensions of the Italian peace movement are discussed in this chapter; a detailed analysis of the relation of feminists to what has become the cynosure of the Italian peace movement—nuclear missiles at Comiso, Sicily—is found in chapter 16.

violence to the environment

The utopian impulse that wants to have done with violence and to get on with building a new society has drawn feminists into many movements against violence although some feminists fear that concerns specific to women may thereby be swept away. Yet there are clear affinities between feminism and all movements opposed to violence. The feminist and ecological movements, for example, were born in Italy at about the same time, although the reach of feminism was wider. There was an early convergence of feminist and ecological concerns when the pollution from an industrial accident at Seveso in 1976 caused women to abort involuntarily. [15]

The political left and the ecology movement agree in their opposition to the capitalist model of development—regarded by ecologists as exploitative of nature; placards in demonstrations of the seventies and eighties demanded a new model of economic development. Both feminism and ecology point to a nonviolent civilization. In the mid-seventies a feminist ecology group connected with *effe* issued a manifesto stating that feminism not only strives to change the condition of women but also the conditions of life. They work for a nonhostile city and a nonpolluted environment.[16] Many catholic organizations, as well as *comunità di base*, have ecological orientations. In March 1983, Arci, the leisure organization of communists and socialists, demonstrated for ecology and feminism.[17] The melding of feminism into movements for peace and ecology was evident in women's day celebrations in March 1983. In the demonstration against sexual violence at Rome in February 1983 there were ecological banners: *"donna è verde"* (woman is green); *"cambiare la citta"* (to change the city). Feminism fits well with "green" themes of peace, disarmament, and opposition to missiles and a war economy. Feminists said that it was unlikely that a "green" political movement (like that of Germany) would emerge in Italy for the simple reason that "the entire women's movement" supports ecological concerns.[18]

In 1984 and 1985 a green movement has emerged in Italy, as part of the contemporary Italian process of particularist identification. The greens of Italy share concerns with the libertarian left and the new left—but there are tensions. For the new left, Dp, which wants to open the party to the concerns of *"ecopacifisti,"* prior premises are "You are not red if you are not green" and "You are not green if you are not red." The first Italian conference of greens was held at Florence in December 1984. For these greens the immediate problem is to "overcome" categories of right and left. An analysis of greens in Italy indicated that 45 percent voted for the Pci in 1984, followed by 24 percent for the Dp. The Italian green network is considerably smaller than that of Germany, but there is ecological presence in feminist cooperatives and in nonviolence and antinuclear groups. The affinity of the greens with Italian feminism was indicated in the themes of the Florence conference: greens identify with a "pragmatic utopianism" grounded on personal commitment, direct experience, day-to-day involvement, and an apparent distrust of political parties.[19]

violence of the mafia

In the south of Italy, the subject of peace turned attention to the violence of the mafia—and its analogues in Naples and Calabria. National attention was focused on what had been regarded earlier as a phenomenon appropriate to the "backwardness" of southern Italy. A 1983 article analyzed "Why all of Italy is a mafia."[20] Southern Italian feminists had early focused on the mafia because they regard the organization as the epitome of male violence. In the North, feminists working against drug use among youth looked to the source of the drug traffic. Parties of the left printed exposés of ties between the Dc and the mafia.

In its convoluted history the mafia had been crushed by the fascists but given new life by the U. S. in world war II to help in the war against the nazis. The mafia is considered by careful analysts to be a greater threat to the legal order than is terrorism. Simona Mafai, communist and feminist, notes that the mafia is the clearest example of the deterioration of Italian democracy because it is a hidden power. Controlling wholesale agricultural markets, operating a protection racket against small businesses, the mafia, Frederic Spotts has concluded, can also "manipulate bids on public works projects and extort kick-backs on their construction, fiddle interest rates, fix sporting events, operate prostitution rings, smuggle cigarettes, jewels, and weapons, and kidnap for ransom."[21] Sitting athwart a major center of the world drug trade, the mafia has become a large economic power. Mafia methods include blackmail, extortion, rake-offs, intimidation, and murder. At the end of the seventies, mafia murders escalated: assassinated in those years were the prefect of Palermo, the president of the Sicilian regional government, the head of the Sicilian Pci, the head of the Dc in Palermo, as well as police chiefs, investigating judges, and journalists.[22]

Insulated from justice by the code of silence (*omertà*) the mafia was finally challenged when feminists began defying it. In the civic center of Palermo in September 1979 feminists from the *festa della donna* denounced the murder of an investigating judge. The Pci took the campaign against the mafia as its own cause, initiating dramatic actions (for example, proposing that the Calabrian parliament be dissolved because there were mafia irregularities involved in legislative proceedings).

The pages of *noidonne* are full of accounts of women defying the mafia and the camorra (its counterpart in Naples). A Neapolitan group of women connects the increase in cases of sexual violence against women, as well as incest, with the archaic and violent "maschilismo" of the camorra, the mafia, and their ilk. Neapolitan women blame the mafia for corrupting masculine values so that brutality is considered courage and aggression regarded as enterprising. Neapolitan women against the camorra have connected with Sicilian women against the mafia and women of Calabria against the 'ndrangheta.[23]

Women are directly concerned about the mafia not only because it represents male brutality but also because the camorra, for example, controls the Naples economy of *lavoro nero*—in which women work to produce more gloves and shoes than any place else in the world.[24] Whatever Robin Hood–like attributes it may have had earlier, by the eighties the mafia (and its cohorts) was a brutal, heartless organization exploiting women, the poor, and victims of natural cataclysm.[25] On February 5, 1983, while women were protesting in Rome against the "shameful act of Parliament" that sidled over the meaning of the crime of rape, 100,000 young men and women protested in Naples against the camorra; shopkeepers rolled down their shutters in support.[26]

an autonomous and decentralized peace movement

The January 1983 national conference at Rome of all Italian peace groups revealed the large presence of women. A woman representative of the committee of October 24 (the ongoing coordinating peace committee connected with a *com-nuovi tempi* group of women and men) welcomed seven hundred delegates representing ninety-seven committees from all of Italy. There was heavy representation from Sicily; from the Naples region, where ecological concern for the destruction of the landscape combines with opposition to nuclear activities in the Bay of Naples; and from the northern industrial triangle, where the worker movement of Italy demonstrated, in the first months of 1983, against the government's economic policies.[27] Similar to the 1982 Udi conference, the January 1983 peace meeting insisted on autonomy from political parties and self-financing. Most delegates registered as students or as workers (paid and unpaid). Ages ranged from young to old, but most were young people in their teens to their thirties.

There are good reasons for the Italian peace movement to declare independence from the parties. Both the Pci and Psi have held equivocal positions on peace. The Pci repudiated the soviet model in 1981 but upheld NATO missile policy and defended increased military expenditures. The Psi, as part of the governing coalition of Italy, accepted NATO plans to install cruise missiles at Comiso. There are many communists and socialists in the Italian peace movement but they are intent on independence from the policies of their parties.[28] The major peace periodical, *pace e guerra*, was founded by independent communists and socialists. By the date of the large October 1983 demonstration, the Pci had visibly been influenced by Italian peace groups: party workers distributed stickers with a peace dove declaring: "No to all missiles"—those of the Warsaw Pact nations and those of NATO. In opposing both the weapons of Warsaw Pact nations and those of NATO, the sticker underlined the Pci's autonomy of the soviets and of the United States.

Insofar as there is a political dimension in the Italian peace movement, it may be that enunciated by the small new left Pdup, the autonomous communist party identified with criticism of both superpowers. Pdup's break with the Pci in 1969 was occasioned in part by soviet aggression in Czechoslovakia. Pdup did not as early as Pr demand that Italy leave NATO, but it denounced the aggrandizement of both blocs in the third world. Emphasizing the decentralization of all institutions, Pdup has tapped an Italian strain of opposition to authority in insisting on the right of Europe—and of Italy within Europe—to determine its own destiny. This theme of autonomy, central to Italian feminism, has ignited the Italian peace movement.[29]

Pr, founded on independence of the catholic church and of the communist party, stated early in the peace movement that it would not participate in peace events coordinated by communists because of what it regarded as the Pci's hypocrisy in calling for peace while supporting increased military expenditures.[30] Pr was the first party in the 1970s to move beyond abstractions about world peace to emphasize specific themes of world injustice, such as hunger.

The mainstream Italian peace movement regards itself as realistic as well as utopian. The group lotta per la pace, which wants Italy to leave NATO and to adopt unilateral disarmament, was marginal at the January 1983 peace conference. A familiar sign in Italian peace demonstrations conveys the movement's realism: "We are for disarmament, but we are not disposed to be conquered."[31] The mixture of utopian goals and realistic strategy was evident in the structure of the peace committees at the January 1983 conference. Like the restructured Udi, peace committees are self-financed and "davvero autonomi dai partiti" (truly independent of the parties).[32] They do not believe in the premise of a balance of terror, but the mainstream peace movement is not pacifist: there are few illusions about the peaceful nature of the Soviet Union. Their perspective is reflected in demonstration placards that state that two-thirds of humanity is on the edge of starvation because the resources of the planet are robbed by military spending and scientific research is devoted to death rather than life.[33]

Activists in the peace movement depend on autonomous initiatives rising from the base; an example is pax christi, founded by the radical archbishop Luigi Bettazzi, who encourages the women's movement and who shares many of the beliefs of the cdb. Pax christi has devised a peace timetable of what needs to be accomplished by 1990: (1) creation of nonnuclear zones, with nonnuclear defense forces; (2) dismantling of all extraterritorial military bases of the major powers; (3) more autonomy for Western European allies of the U.S. and Eastern European allies of the Soviet Union; (4) redistribution of armament funds (under the direction of the UN) in a world program of economic development to aid poorer countries; (5) conversion of military industry to production for peace. This is not a Eurocentric strategy; nonnuclear zones are to be created not only in Europe but in the Middle East, Africa, and the Indian ocean.[34] Pax christi aims to block not only nuclear arms, but also chemical and biological weapons. Its immediate aims are moderate: not a ban on all weapons now, but a prohibition of nuclear testing and a reduction of military expenditures by 5 percent, 4 percent of which is to be directed to world peace research.[35]

women and movements against violence

The revulsion against violence is a feeling that engages the consciences of many Italians, women and men. When feminists turn to doing something about violence, they sometimes find they are among women who had not hitherto called themselves feminists. This was first evident in the referendum campaign against sexual violence, when spontaneous committees arose to secure signatures for the referendum. In Italy there has been a double standard as to who can exercise violence. Among traditional prerogatives of the Italian male has been the right to act violently in the home; traditionally women were not allowed to be violent; they rarely were, except verbally.

Women in the Italian peace movement speak of building a culture for peace. There is discussion of a women's strike against giving birth until genuine peace initiatives are secured,[36] and of diversion of military expenditures into schools, child care, health centers—a better quality of life. Perhaps the most significant contribution of feminism to the Italian peace movement is the affirmation of direct democracy for vital issues: a woman cannot delegate to anyone else a decision governing her own body, and people cannot delegate life or death decisions to outside authorities. Feminists in the Italian peace movement have again embraced *doppio militanza* (double militancy), working autonomously on specific women's issues and together with men on vital issues that refer to humanity.

The Italian peace movement, as we have seen, is wide in its reach, yet specifically located on Italian soil after the 1979 parliamentary decision to put NATO nuclear missiles at Comiso, Sicily. The Italian base is one of the crisis points of Europe, like Greenham Commons in England; Florennes, Belgium; and the resistance of the greens in Germany. (The centrality of the Sicilian base in particularist feminist thinking will be analyzed in the next chapter. The focus of this chapter is on the convergence of feminism with the Italian national peace movement.)

In December 1982 a march from Milan to Comiso initiated by intellectuals and writers became a long march that swept Italian feminists into the thickness of Italian public life.[37] In the journey to the South, Dc and Pci mayors found themselves on the same platform calling for disarmament. Local poets prefaced their pieces with declamations that they were not communists or socialists but they were for peace. In a geographical reversal of the Allied march up the Italian peninsula, peace marchers going down the Italian boot to Comiso were greeted with wine and *biscotti*. They were joined by hitchhiking priests, greeted by schoolchildren, lodged in nursery schools, and invited by workers to meet factory peace committees. Arriving at Comiso at christmas time, marchers joined protesters at the international encampment and participated in candlelight marches and fasts promoted by local committees.[38]

Luciana Castellina, a Pdup delegate to parliament, Italian representative in the European Economic Community, and long-time member of Udi, discussed the antinuclear movement in the perspective of national autonomy at the end of March 1983. Women protesters had just been arrested at Comiso. Europe, she felt, must seize this moment to effect its autonomy (in money as well as missiles) of the United States and of the USSR, or it never would. For Castellina, the denuclearization of Europe is the first step in the recovery of European autonomy.[39] Comiso is a key to the denuclearization of Europe. On Good Friday 1983, women and men walked the way of the cross from church to church in Comiso, ending at the missile site. In the demonstration, promoted by many catholic groups, including pax christi, and *comunità di base*, women and men vowed that they would continue to demonstrate, with all nonviolent means, until parliament revokes the decision (regarded as a violation of the Italian constitution's prohibition against offensive war) to install nuclear missiles at Comiso.[40]

The issue of women's autonomy made participation in the peace movement problematic for some Italian feminists. By women's day 1984 abstract contradictions between feminism and the peace movement were put aside by a few well-known feminists who took matters into their own hands and organized "women's peace demonstrations." Among them were Adriana Zarri, the feminist theologian and nun; Pia Bruzzichelli, spokesperson for left catholics associated with *noidonne*; Franca Pieroni Bortolotti, a historian of Italian feminism; and Natalia Ginsburg, the woman novelist now in parliament.

Women believers distributed a leaflet at the October 22, 1983, peace demonstration at Rome, declaring that they were committed "as believers and as women" to "intransigent education for peace" in the schools, in the family, in all groups. These women supported conscientious objection (with alternative civil tasks) to military service. They also encouraged ("in the churches to which we belong") a reflection on the invitation of the protestant theologian Helmut Gollwitzer to live as a church "without the protection of arms." Aiming for conversion of military industry to enterprises of peace, opposing the nuclear base at Comiso, and supporting those who refuse to work for military industry, women *credenti* consider peace activism part of their work for full equality and full liberty—and part of their commitment "against all the forces of death" that produce injustice, violence, and war.[41] Their leaflet at the October 1983 manifestation declared: "We refuse to accept that the well-being of developed countries is founded in part on war industry, on the sale of arms, on indifference, on the exploitation of weaker countries." Disarmament, East as well as West, is the first step "toward an international situation capable of confronting, in a new climate, the fundamental problems of injustice."[42]

The feminist movement and the movements against violence converged; the intersection can be seen in independent catholic organizations, in the work of *comunità di base* and in the preaching of liberation theologians. An account of the 1983 peace demonstration at Rome described a pattern (like that of the feminist movement) of differences within unity: "Revolutionary favorites mixed with religious hymns as the most diverse socio-political groups came together, accepting to join each other in protest while remaining different." The striking new note in this demonstration was the "massive presence of catholics" carrying "olive branches, white doves, and white flags." The most applauded groups were those of nuns and priests with signs that read, "Either with Christ or with the Bomb." Franciscans, Augustinians, Franciscan Missionaries of Mary, Sisters of Divine Will, Orsolines from Verona, and many other catholic orders were present.

Catholic peace groups making their own decisions about peace point to an actual pluralism within catholicism. Acli is an example; having originated as a postwar anticommunist auxiliary of the papacy, Acli in recent years has taken a position of autonomy grounded on conscience, changing its name from "catholic" to "christian" in a move toward independence of the papacy. Sharing a pattern that has become widespread, Acli aims to hold to a path independent of political parties in its work for democracy from the base. Claiming a legacy from John XXIII, Acli states, "Every man and woman is our brother and sister. Our only enemies are the infernal weapons of nuclear war, such as those to be deployed here at Comiso."[43]

For Giulio Girardi, the widely read liberation theologian, the world order of war is sustained by a culture of violence—the violence that he considers to be the dynamic of capitalism and the violence that has betrayed "existing socialist nations."[44] For Girardi, the struggle for disarmament involves a large dismantling effort: dismantling the legitimacy of a culture of classes, dismantling violence in the family, dismantling violence in relationships of men and women, dismantling violence in the interactions of majority and minority ethnic groups, dismantling violence in revolutionary culture, "dismantling violence in religion itself." Demilitarizing humanity, states Girardi, is a great enterprise of reeducation so that "a culture of peace, of love, and of liberty can be born."[45]

Gianni Baget Bozzo, a former member of the Dc and today a liberation theogian, places feminist issues and world disarmament in perspective. He has said that the Italian peace movement posed "the right and duty of people not to destroy the life of humanity, of not uncreating the world . . . the right of small nations not to become mere spaces at the disposition of the superpowers . . . the right of young people not to be sent to die without reason, the right of parents to protect the life that they have created with responsible parenthood."[46]

part three   a women's movement

DONNA
UN NOME
UNA FAMIGLIA
NON PUÒ
APPENDICE
NON
VOGLIAMO
PIU' ESSERE
LA COSTOLA DI ADAMO

16

femminismo inedito—differenze

unedited feminism—differences

By the spring of 1983 Italian women had set out on a journey with many different paths and different vistas. The backdrop was an Italy that seemed to verify Alberto Ronchey's statement that in a country with *cattolici anomali* and *comunisti anomali* "anything is possible." In spite of turmoil, Italy remained the world's seventh greatest economic producer. In spite of high unemployment, high inflation, high interest rates, very high labor costs and very large public expenditures, Italian exports returned to earlier levels, industry was continually modernized, and productivity was particularly marked in small- and medium-sized enterprises.[1]

What earlier was called feminism had become a women's movement. The provocative feminist journal of the early seventies, *effe*, ceased publication because "other things were beginning."[2] The *casa della donna* at Rome was scheduled to move from Governo Vecchio to the *palazzo* of the *buon pastore*, an old refuge for *donne perdute* (lost women). The center of gravity symbolically shifted to the journal of the women's union when the cooperative of *noidonne* founded its own women's center at Rome, sala Anna Maria Mozzoni.[3]

Cultural as well as political themes were apparent in the decentralized feminist activities noted by the *noidonne* supplement of March 1983. At Bologna a regional assembly held a conference on the Emilian patriarchate, a term that was used to comprise all institutions of the power structure. At Milan a journal was dedicated to the unjust treatment of women in the courts. In the Veneto a women's group studied sentences for crimes of sexual violence. At Sassari, Sardinia, a women's legal clinic addressed itself to violence against women, abortion, separation and divorce, adoption, protective legislation for workers, new family rights, the home. A Roman collective held a discussion on adult fears regarding adolescent sexuality. At Taranto, a Udi group presented the poetry of Sylvia Plath and performances by a feminist mime troupe from Milan. A series was broadcast on Italian television on "masculine and feminine in the schools." The women's cultural center at Rome called Zanzibar announced a continuing series, *video donna;* the first tape was of the February demonstration against sexual violence. At Orvieto women called a national conference on child care centers.[4] Lectures at the new location of Centro Virginia Woolf focused on international themes such as the eighteenth century English debate on workers' protective legislation and the plays of Racine.

The end of one era and beginning of another was apparent in the founding of a women's library at Siena. By 1983 women were successfully involving city governments in their concerns. Naples funded archives on materials relating to the condition of women in the South and the islands. Milan sponsored a large exhibit, *Existere come donna* (How women live).[5] The theme of self-determination was evident in the national conference on the relationship between Udi and its periodical, *noidonne,* and in another conference on new forms of participation in women's health clinics. Women's culture announced itself in a feminist futurist art exhibit and a women's cooperative gallery at Rome, as well as in seminars in many cities on humanizing the birth process, in the *noidonne* literary conference encouraging short novels and short stories, in an experimental feminist drama troupe at Bergamo, and in an inquiry group of Udi women (and other citizens) reporting on women's treatment in the Bologna hospital San 'Orsola. Women in the March 1983 supplement suggested that Udi groups discuss the question, "If men have done so much wrong, why do we give them our hearts?"[6]

By 1983 it was apparent that the color feminists were settling upon as their unifying color was pink—connoting traditional femininity. *Noidonne* encouraged a pink postcard campaign to parliament urging immediate passage, without amendment, of the sexual violence bill.[7] Articles and interviews revealed that feminists have chosen pink not only because it is unifying but because pink is a shade of red.

Pci discussions of housing had made it evident that several feminist messages had been heard by the men of the party. They referred to the home as the matrix of a "revolution in behavior" and acknowledged that "traditional roles have changed"—women no longer wish to be "dependent and segregated" in the house. The pattern of authority and obedience that had determined not only domestic but social space, said a Pci spokesman, no longer existed. The home needed to be considered in alternative terms: instead of family hierarchy, individual liberation; instead of obedience, deciding together, collaborating on communal projects. In place of the isolated nuclear family, a new society was emerging: a rich network of relationships between the home and political or cultural groups and movements, including churches and political parties.[8]

Nonetheless, women were intent on viewing the problem of housing (and other matters) with their own perspectives. At Milan in the early eighties, women came together to consider the high cost of housing and the large number of people without homes. Housing may be everybody's problem, but it is also a specific women's concern because women spend more time in the house than do men. Women considered a campaign for more housing, but decided the problem extended beyond this. Conventional house design perpetuates the subordinate role of woman by showing little regard for women's need for autonomous space. Furthermore, conventional housing plans focus on the traditional nuclear family without taking into account statistics demonstrating that many contemporary families are composed of women with children, or women living with other women. The nuclear family in Italy is increasingly being replaced by other configurations, including a return to an earlier pattern of several generations living together.[9] In feminist circles in the last few years, there

has been growing consensus that the cooperative is a feminist institution.[10] Women of Milan formed a housing cooperative which they
called "*la casa matta*" (the mad house).[11]

La casa matta offered its experience in creating a women's housing
cooperative to readers of *noidonne*. The process revealed what Italians
call "capillarity"—the organic process of initiatives beginning at the
base, extending upward throughout the society, and then realized at
the base. Women's collectives first discussed the idea and then formed
the cooperative la casa matta. Next steps were consulting with city
administrators and joining the league of Italian coops, which helped
with financing. More women joined the coop. Milanese neighborhood groups discussed the idea. The city of Milan was asked for—
and gave—a building to be used as an office. Media discussion of la
casa matta (enlivened by puns about the name) publicized the project. Members met, established rules for assigning apartments, and
assigned priority to women who needed housing—specifically, single
women, or single mothers with children.[12]

Milan's feminist housing coop is a new structure, designed by
women, of apartments, with public spaces and connected public
buildings: a gymnastic space, an educational center, a hotel for visi-
tors, public shops, a restaurant, and a bar. Feminists of la casa matta
are conscious that they are simultaneously contemporary and harking back to preindustrial peasant communalism: there is a contemporary communal courtyard and a cooperative restaurant which the
women have named le allegre comari—the "happy godmothers."[13]

"*più donne che uomini*"
(more womanly than masculine)

In 1983 a group of northern feminists involved in the movement
since 1968 added up the tolls of the movement and evaluated wom-
en's condition: "We have efficiently struggled against the social misery of woman's condition. We have discovered the originality in the
fact of being women, the practical politics of relations among women,
meeting together, loving one another." What remained to be done
was finding "the means of translating into social experience the wisdom and value of being women."[14]

Instead of self-confidence the women felt a deepening *disagio* (unease) caused by conflicting desires: the desire for feminist autonomy

and the desire to be "more womanly than masculine."[15] In this widely discussed essay, the sottosopra group of Milan feminists said that it was no longer a matter of discrimination against women: women were not checkmated by others, but by their own unwillingness to win. The desire to win, when it does not intimidate, comes to seem a "virile" aspiration; this, rather than any discrimination, "has made us understand that society is masculine." For women who compete successfully with men, there is "always the risk of mutilation of one's self."[16]

Society, said these feminists, is a competition among men. When there is less discrimination, women can enter the tourney, but it always remains a "joust of men" in which the women participants play "with words and desires not ours."[17] Even a massive entry of women into social life does not automatically modify this situation— women tend to assimilate the male model.

By 1983 Italian feminists could appreciate women who did not choose to be feminists: women who stood to one side not taking the path of emancipation were in a sense affirming their integrity by their unwillingness to be assimilated. The concession of some public space to women is the answer to an obvious injustice: society is made by women, yet directed almost exclusively by men. But the space conceded to women turns out, these feminists felt, to be costly.[18]

The Milanese feminists tried to clarify the issue of separatism. Those of us, they wrote, "who have chosen to stay apart, separate from this society dominated by men" do so not to exalt our marginality—"which can be desperate"—but as a strategy, not as an optimal arrangement of women's relationships to men. Resistance, they noted, rather than separation, has historically been women's preferred strategy.[19] Women's solidarity also needed rethinking, because "we need to let diversity enter the game as a richness and not as a threat."[20]

a diverse perspective: Sicilian women

In the early eighties it was impossible for Sicilian women to think about self-determination without worrying about the nuclear base at Comiso. A town of 27,000 people situated in the south of Sicily, Comiso was the site selected in 1979 to carry out NATO plans for a cruise missile base—putting countries of Africa and the Middle East within range of Comiso missiles. A local peace committee and an international peace encampment were formed; as mentioned earlier there have been marches, fasts, and nonviolent resistance events at the base. A resident international group of women at Comiso, la ragnatela (the spider web), affirmed solidarity with women resisting at Greenham Commons, England, and elsewhere in Europe.

Specifically feminist in its orientation was the coordinamento per l'autodeterminazione della donna (coordinating committee for the self-determination of women) of Catania.[21] This committee put nuclear resistance in feminist context and demonstrated the possibilities of Italian feminist emphasis on differences, in this case joining regional as well as gender differences.

Sicilian women, to a greater degree than women in the north of Italy (and more so, maybe, under twentieth-century conditions than earlier) were kept under male control—by the use of actual or implicit violence. The Sicilian code of honor gave a husband the prerogative of killing a wife and her lover if they were found together.[22] A man who wished to marry a woman who did not want him could do so by raping her: under the code of honor she had to marry him. Women were regarded as prey; this was the rationale for segregating them in the house. Most women were dominated first by their fathers and then by their husbands. If a woman remained unmarried, she was controlled by all the males of the family.[23]

This is not to imply that all Sicilian men were oppressive or that all Sicilian women were passive. Just as many men showed gentleness, so did many women demonstrate their resistance to prevailing mores by appropriating family power. Southern women's resistance to church doctrine had historically been evident in their practice of the occult, as healers. In the 1890s Sicilian women carried their resistance into the public sphere in rebellions of socialist leagues and after each world war in the twentieth century they went beyond resistance in occupations of unused lands.

Yet social and economic conditions were not favorable to women's advancement in the South and the islands of Sicily and Sardinia: economic subordination of the South was institutionalized after unification. There was a movement for Sicilian independence after world war II but the issue of Sicilian autonomy subsided until the seventies, when banners in worker and feminist demonstrations declared, "Sicily is not a colony!" The subordinated region that Sicily had become was in a sense a woman's colony. When men began leaving to find work elsewhere at the turn of the twentieth century, women were often left alone. The code of honor fell even more heavily on a woman with an absent husband; her social behavior was closely scrutinized not only by her mother-in-law but by the entire village.

When Sicilian women began actively participating in the feminist movement in the early 1970s, Sicilian men became upset. Leonardo Sciascia, a writer of the independent left, avowed he could not understand what Sicilian women wanted since they had always exercised power within the family; indeed the close relationship of Sicilian mothers to their sons had in a sense, he charged, nurtured the immature criminal behavior of the mafia.[24]

Feminists responded to Sciascia in language sometimes unprintable. Lina Noto of Palermo raged that a Sicilian woman had never possessed her own body, much less her own spirit; she pointed out that the language of Sicilian men daily separated women into *puttane* (whores) and other women.[25] Feminists were early called *puttane* by some Sicilian men.[26]

The violence inherent in patriarchalism is visible in Sicily. When a young woman was seen by her father in a demonstration of farm workers at Corleone, he locked her up and beat her; when she tried to escape with a ladder of knotted bedsheets she fell to her death.[27] I have been told by Sicilian women that they have been forbidden by fathers and husbands to engage in or even to discuss politics, because they fear mafia reprisal.

An iron web has, until recently, kept Sicilian women and men constricted. The cult of virility of the Sicilian male is a violent one, epitomized in the mafia and translated into everyday abuse of women. A husband who beats his wife is not exceptional. Women accept beatings because in conditions of poverty, a violent husband is regarded as better than no man at all. Physical violence generates fear, so that even when a husband has emigrated, his threats keep his wife under control. Within Sicilian social control, a woman's life was held hostage to church and party prohibitions against divorce, birth control, and legal abortion. When Sicilian women voted for divorce in 1974 and then for legalized abortion in 1981, it was evident that a new era had begun.

Of all the regions of Italy, Sicily has the lowest percentage of

women working outside the home. Before 1900 women worked outside the home (primarily at harvest time, in orchards and fields) but
in the contorted social and economic development of the island in
the twentieth century women were returned to the home to work in
lavoro nero, an exploitation that enables a man to pat his honor and
takes advantage of women's concern to stay with their children.[28] In
Sicilian *lavoro nero*, women embroider until their eyes dim, knit until
their arms fall—weaving carpets ceaselessly, twining flowers endlessly,
working in foul home conditions for the fishing industry—without
the guarantees of factory workers. A Sicilian woman, Maria Rosa Cutrufelli, has analyzed the hidden, uncounted work of southern
women. Documenting Mariarosa Dalla Costa's thesis, Cutrufelli argues that the women of the South not only constitute a reserve army
of labor themselves, but they produce the forced labor (the future
workers) for the industrialized North.[29]

In the nineteen-seventies and eighties Sicilian women have awakened. Franca Viola refused to marry the man who raped her, force-
fully breaking the code of honor by sending him to jail instead. In
the deteriorating relationships between men and women of that submerged island, when women spill into the piazza on international
women's day, this is an act of courage. When women demonstrated
to support workers who occupied a closed-down *cannoli* factory, men
threw eggs at them; men have also vandalized Udi offices.[30] Yet wom-
en's efforts to improve their lot continue. In Alia, in the heart of
Sicily, weavers founded a cooperative by asking women to come together to weave after they had finished their housework. In Santa
Caterina di Villarmosa, a village populated by women, children, and
old people (since the men have all migrated to the North), where
women embroider from the age of ten until they lose their eyesight,
women have organized a cooperative.[31] A pattern has emerged of
radical mothers and children defying the fathers.

When the plan for NATO missiles at Comiso was announced, Sicilian women asked that the matter be placed on the agenda of the
national Udi conference in May 1982, but the proposal was side-
stepped by other Udi women.[32] Long-time Udi activists who remember the peace movement of the 1950s worry that today's peace
movement will push specifically feminist measures to one side. Sicilian women are also concerned about the future of the women's
movement, but they are alarmed about the nuclear danger on their

island. Early on, even in the heated atmosphere of the abortion campaign in 1981, Sicilian women said they would not descend into the
piazza to demonstrate for legalized abortion without also addressing
other contradictions of a sexist society—notably the nuclear base.

Feminists living elsewhere in Italy posed to Sicilian women the
question of whether it was possible to think about war and peace
specifically as women. Sicilian women responded in a document that
outlines a feminist perspective on violence, with specific reference to
the contemporary nuclear crisis. Translated into French, German,
and English, the Sicilian document has been taken to international
disarmament conferences and may be the clearest Italian feminist
summation of a decade and a half of agitation.[33]

The inclusive category for women, said Sicilian feminists, is "quality of life"—not more consumer goods, nor more social services, but
rather "respect for nature." Respect for quality of life is the underlying basis for campaigns against pollution, against private ownership
of natural resources, campaigns for clean energy, the right to health
and prevention of illnesses, a house for everyone, liberated work, the
rights of old people, children, young people, and the handicapped—
and the abolition of gender discrimination in laws and in behavior.
Quality of life is attained by "solidarity among the exploited." To
attain quality of life, peace is indispensable.[34]

The peace that Sicilian feminists have in mind is not one that
sedates conscience by ignoring world hunger and exploitation, but a
peace understood in the context of women's condition: "Women
undergo in all societies and in all social classes the specific exploitation inherent in their being women: sexual work, maternal work, domestic work, *lavoro nero*, underpaid work."[35] Tying concern for wom-
en's lot with concern for the world, Sicilian feminists said that their
no to war was part of their struggle for liberation; to these feminists
of an island whose history has been conquest and rapine (Phoenicians, Greeks, Romans, Germanic tribes, Moslems, Normans, Angevins, Bourbons, Northern Italians et.al.) the connection between nuclear escalation, the violence of war, and the violence of rape is clear.
The traditional relationship between the sexes, Sicilian women know
from their own history, was grounded on the historic pattern of the
male at war: aggression, conquest, possession, "control of a woman
or of a territory."[36]

Emphatically rejecting the traditional role of subordinate godmothers, Sicilian feminists of the eighties consider themselves "in the vanguard of a movement of struggle for peace," a peace which they define as a multibranched "struggle for self-determination": "against oppression and exploitation of one people over another, one class over another, one sex over another."[37]

Particular, or separatist, feminist focus rendered Sicilian women more radical than the mainstream Italian peace movement; they demand "unilateral disarmament now." They are simultaneously utopian and unprepossessing: "We believe firmly in the utopia of good sense, in courage without banners, in the fecundity of giving before receiving, in the uniqueness and beauty of human life." This, say Sicilian women, "is the culture of women."[38]

For Sicilian feminists, the culture of women was lost in the din of warlike preparations for a hypocritical peace, as well as in the wooliness of the "abstract pacifism of the left." Viewed from the perspective of the culture of women, war is neither natural nor inevitable. If this were so, women would not value motherhood, which is, "for many of us, our only source of identity and our only creative experience." For Sicilian feminists—whose Greek heritage is visible in the monuments of the island—the Lysistrata strategy could be deepened by declaring "conscientious objection to giving life" until military funding was transferred to projects funding a better quality of life.[39]

Other Italian women had supported this feminist interpretation of unilateral nuclear disarmament. In the early eighties a committee was formed to connect with other European women; a radio channel was dedicated to women and peace; at Cagliari, Sardinia, the Udi office became a women's peace center. But the drive to throw back the referendum to repeal the abortion law swept the peace issue aside for Italian women in 1981.[40]

The women's committee at Catania continued to press, demanding that the municipal government declare Catania a nonnuclear zone, that similar declarations be taken up in all cities of Italy, that military expenditures immediately be converted to social services. In December 1982 the committee invited all Italian women to make a great circle of peace with the women at Greenham Commons, England, to protest the "macabre iron embrace between the U.S.A. and the U.S.S.R." Was it possible to live with the base at Comiso? "Let us imagine it," said the women. "streets full of military colonizers, male as well as female prostitution, drugs, enormous inflation." In the event of war, Comiso as a nuclear target would be destroyed in a few minutes. Sicilian hospitals could not possibly care for the great number of injured people.

At the February 1983 feminist demonstration against sexual violence at Rome, women of Catania distributed an invitation to come to Comiso for 1983 international women's day. "Today is but the beginning of a long struggle that will bring our liberation," it read. Women, "like all oppressed peoples, like the slaves, like black people today, are in revolt." It is a revolt without bloodshed and without death, because "we are life."

Inviting women of the world to join them, the women described separatism as a "global vision" in which women "no longer intend to delegate the control of our lives" but to assume full responsibility for it. Women's rebellion against sexual violence, for Sicilian feminists, was also a rebellion against "militarism, racism, clericalism, hierarchy, and exploitation."[41]

As against the "destructive" forces of patriarchal society, women put the "creative force of our desire for life." To break the circle of violence, Sicilian women propose to take advantage of the fact women have historically been conditioned to be nonviolent. They propose to use this as a point of strength in denouncing "hierarchy, competitiveness, authoritarianism," which they consider the chief characteristics of a militarized society.

In their unedited marxism, Sicilian women put the "materiality of women's everyday lives" against abstract principles; abstract principles, the women felt, had historically been translated into actual holocaust. With the rhythm of marxist analyses, women said that the history of nuclear death began with the first male act of violent possession of a woman "and will end with our liberation."[42] Calling for the solidarity of women of the world in striving for self-determination, a nuclear-free world, liberated work, a clean environment, and responsibility for one's life, they declared: "We do not delegate our future to politicians, generals, lords of war of any sort, rapists, or *maschi-padroni*.[43]

International women's day of 1983 was festive at Comiso, with dancing encircling the base and parades; delegations from other European countries and the United States witnessed against sexual violence and the violence of nuclear weapons. The next day, the festive atmosphere was destroyed. When women adopted direct, nonviolent action and impeded entry of trucks to the missile base, police violently dragged them away. On the following day women seated in front of the main gate were pulled away, some by the hair. Women kept returning and police became more violent. The authorities, noted *il manifesto*, were more afraid of a few determined, nonviolent women than they were of nuclear holocaust.[44]

feminist diversity and solidarity

At the national manifestation for peace at Rome on October 22, 1983, the solidarity of Italian women across their differences was strikingly apparent. Parade organizers were initially perplexed as to whether to put prostitutes for peace or nuns for peace first, but as it turned out, many different groups led several beginnings of the largely spontaneous demonstration of 700,000 Italians for peace.[45] Sicilian women designed the large banner, stretching part of a city block, whose different colors represented the different components of the Italian peace movement: feminists, environmentalists, catholics, evangelicals, independent communists and socialists, labor unions and anarchists, christian democrats, radicals et al. The banner was held horizontally—with fresh flowers at the center—by women from all parts of Italy, suggesting the Italian feminist conception of cultural and political change: initiatives from everyone, supported by everyone. The feminist theme of equality of all human beings joined the theme of peace with justice; a Roman women's peace committee held a poster that read, "Since all human beings are equal participants in creation, we believe that all have the right to participate in an equal distribution of the resources of the earth."[46]

Woman as brooding hen
Caricature by Lydia Sansoni, by courtesy of effe *(July–August 1975)*

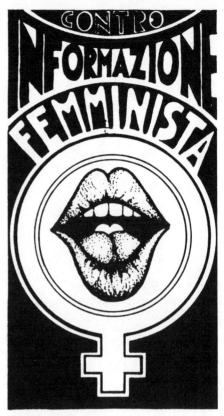

"Abortion Faced by Us": Cisa and Mld propose free and safe abortions. The triangle formed by two hands is a symbol of the women's movement.

"Feminist counter-information," *effe* logo.

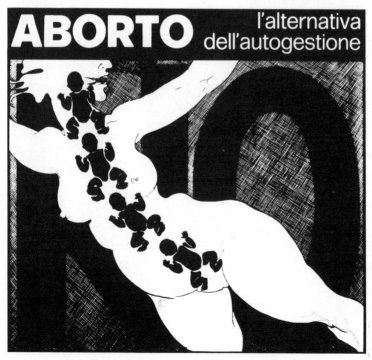

"The Alternative of self-management"
Courtesy of effe,
(July–Aug. 1975)

"As a pear tree belongs to the owner of the pears, so a woman is owned by the man, whose children she bears": Caricature illustrating a quotation from Napoleon in the *Antologia del delirio*
Drawing by Lydia Sansoni, by courtesy of effe, *(April–May 1974)*

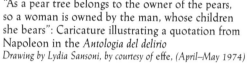

"Patient" and "doctor" at rally for abortion
Courtesy of siamo in tante . . . , © *1975*

"Legal regulation of abortion/From individual tragedy to collective responsibility": Udi rally, Rome, January 1977
Courtesy of noi donne *(Feb. 1977)*

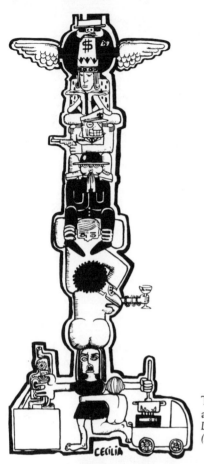

"When the cook knows how to govern and the one who governs knows how to cook, then we will have a socialist society."
Courtesy of effe (April–May 1974)

The patriarchal totem pole, with the wife and mother at the bottom
Drawing by Cecilia Capuana, by courtesy of effe (April–May 1974)

"We are fed up with being the crutch of masculine power":
Roman Feminist Movement
Courtesy of siamo in tante . . . , © 1975

Casa della donna graffiti

PARTECIPAZIONE

QUESTA DELLE CASA DONNE È

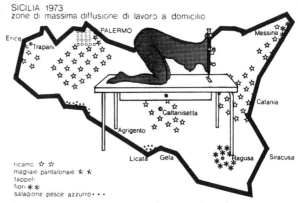

SICILIA 1973
zone di massima diffusione di lavoro a domicilio

ricamo ☆ ☆
magliaie pantalonaie ✷ ✷
tappeti
fiori ✷ ✷
salagione pesce azzurro • • •

Regions of Sicily of expansion of *lavoro a domicilio*
(work in the home)
By permission, from Maria Rosa Cutrufelli, Disoccupata con onore,
© 1975 Gabrielle Mazzota editore

Fiat autoworker at protest against unsafe conditions
for women workers: Turin, September 1980
Courtesy of noi donne *(September 1980)*

Lavoro a domicilio: Women embroidering
Courtesy of effe *(July–Aug. 1974)*

Women form a circle in front of ancient wall in Rome *Courtesy of* noidonne

Vigil protesting violence, Naples, 1976 (Among the signs: "violence! is the division of roles between men and women"; "violence! is being afraid"; "violence! is prostitution"; "violence! is conjugal duty!!!"; "violence! is part-time work"; "violence! is to abort" ...) *Courtesy of* effe *(Jan. 1977)*

8 marzo 1983
INCONTRO INTERNAZIONALE
COMISO 6-7-8 MARZO

" *Donne e disarmo: una parola in più* "

disarmo unilaterale

Comiso

CONTRO	PER
gerarchia	autodeterminazione
militarismo	denuclearizzazione
sfruttamento	lavoro liberato
violenza sessuale	spazi per incontrarci
disastro ecologico	mare pulito
forza distruttiva	forza creativa
....	....
delega della vita	responsabilità della vita

Comiso Catania Bruxelles Greenham Common Washington

coordinamento per l'autodeterminazione della donna · Catania
coordinamento donne di Comiso
donne del campo internazionale di Comiso

"Women and disarmament . . . *against* hierarchy, militarism, exploitation, sexual violence, ecological disaster . . . *for* self-determination, denuclearization, liberated work, space for encounters, unpolluted seas . . .": 1983 poster for Comiso rally for unilateral disarmament and International Women's Day

"Comiso wants to live/NO to the missiles, NO to the Mafia": Rally in Comiso, March 1983
Photograph by the author

17

io sono mia
siamo in tante

I am my own person
we are many

Italian feminist emphasis on being different from men was made visually clear to me at a conference I attended at the cittadella christiana at Assisi in 1983. Patrizia Magli, a professor of semiotics, held up a painting of an ancient Egyptian king—a woman with an artificial beard. Italian feminists assume political equality, aim for a society with economic equality, but insist on women's gender differences as indispensable for the humane society they envision.

Feminism can be understood, said Magli, as a replacement of Descarte's postulate, "Cogito, ergo sum" (I think, therefore I am), a paradigm feminists associate with male rationalism. Instead of knowing one's self because one thinks, Italian feminists say, "Io sono mia"—I am my own person. Italian women know themselves, as has been discussed earlier, by looking within, and by looking at others.

Separatism, said Magli, is women speaking among themselves. She admitted that separatism "puts men into crisis." A man in the audience, in a beam of recognition, responded: "Siamo tutti entrati in crisi" (all of us have entered into crisis). The metaphor of *other*, she explained, has positive connotations implying a society with plural differences. It may also, said Magli, connote *stranger.* A man asked, "Are women the only strangers?" She responded, "No. There are always strangers coming from the South," alluding to the poor of the southern half of the globe.[1]

A combined old and new left campaign in June 1983 for *l'alternativa*—a slogan that connoted an alternative way to socialism aligned with significant social movements of women, ecology, and peace—resulted in the Dc losing six percentage points and a vote that was close to a draw for Italy's two major parties. In elections of June 1984 for the European parliament (regarded as a referendum on the policies of its constituent national governments), the Pci for the first time received a few more votes than the Dc. The party with the "largest women's consensus" received 33.3 percent of the vote; the anticommunist political party of papal catholicism and constrictive views of women received 32.9 percent.[2] U.S. analysts argued that the gain of the Pci represented a sympathy vote for the death in June 1984 of the party secretary, Enrico Berlinguer.[3]

Women claim to have exercised pivotal leverage in the decline of the Dc beginning with the "earthquake" vote of 1974 sustaining the right of divorce in the face of papal and Dc opposition. The 1981 vote sustaining legal abortion was another blow to the Dc. Early in 1983 a large wave of women's indignation crested over what was regarded as Dc manhandling of the bill against sexual violence.

Although the Pci receives most of their votes, feminists have put the party on notice. They claim credit for the growth of the Pci in the early seventies; their disaffection was registered in lower party percentages in 1979. Although the party helped to secure the large 1981 vote that sustained the abortion law, Udi's declaration of independence in 1982 was a signal that Italian women of the left are not in the pocket of the Pci.

Several women were elected as independents in the 1983 united campaign of Pci and Pdup for *l'alternativa*. Although they were supported by Pci, these women do not consider themselves bound to Pci policies. The emergence of a significant Italian independent left was marked by the 1983 accord of Pci, Pdup, and the independent league of socialists that the Pci would support independent leftists on party ballots, but the candidates would not be tied to Pci in parliament. The Italian independent left is a kaleidoscope of different people with different points of view; the bond is a desire for an alternative way to socialism stressing nonviolence, pluralism, decentralization, conscience, and self-management. These are feminist values, although the independent left consensus has been created by many currents—notably the ferment of left catholicism—in contemporary Italy.

The 1983 campaign posters for an alternative suggested all the changes in the thinking of the Pci since 1968; posters referring to the traditional Italian national colors called for "more green," "more red," and "less white" (in rough chromatic translation: more ecology, more nonviolence, more equality and justice, and less church doctrine—in an alternative mode of politics determined by women's issues and issues of peace and ecology). A women's parliamentary *gruppo* (caucus) was formed where women independents elected on Pci slates and women communists in the Pci can discuss and make voting decisions on women's issues.

Independent women elected to parliament with Pci support have a variety of perspectives. They include a psychiatrist from the Veneto who opposes authoritarian psychology, a woman identified with liberation theology and third-world concerns, a woman whose chief concern is support of unilateral disarmament and European and Italian autonomy of the superpowers, a renowned writer whose novels limn changing relationships between men and women. There is also a sociologist who has studied the changing Italian family; a woman whose expertise is the crisis of welfare states; the president of the Lega dei diritti humani (League of human rights), which opposes the policies of the soviets in Afghanistan and of the United States in Central America; an officer of the league of Italian cooperatives; women journalists; and a young woman who has written on the electoral disaffection of Italian youth.[4]

feminism and the "transformation" of Italian communism

Luciana Castellina, a Pdup feminist who was returned to her parliamentary seat, wrote an article in June 1983 on the campaign. Sometimes a political discussion of *l'alternativa* in a piazza, said Castellina, became an exploration of how feminism has "transformed" the nature of being communist. With an awareness of the ancient roots of Italian feminism, Castellina said that the contemporary women's movement could be likened to a diffuse, long-submerged "subterranean force" that touches all of Italian culture.[5]

After the 1981 declaration of autonomy of the soviets, the party addressed itself to new left feminist criticism of democratic centralism. Feminist decentralization of their own union was one of several prods that pushed the Pci in a democratic direction. At the March 1983 party congress the Pci adopted a policy of a "democratic alternative." All parties were invited to participate in the communist conference; more democracy in the party was institutionalized, beginning with "transparency" of central committee debates. Berlinguer announced that the party would relate to independent movements regarded as "major agents of social transformation"—the women's movement and movements for ecology and peace. Responding to the peace movement, the party endorsed local peace initiatives, including declarations of nuclear-free zones. Women, said the Pci secretary, are "carriers of a new mode of doing politics and a new rapport between culture and politics."[6]

At the March 1984 conference of women communists of the Pci the insistent refrain was that being a feminist and a woman communist are not the same. Berlinguer agreed, castigated men communists for "diffuse masculinism" and reminded them that "without women, nothing changes."[7] Women inside the Pci have suggested structural changes to insure women's autonomy in the party; one idea that has been implemented is the women's group in parliament to which women communists belong in a role autonomous of the party. Another proposal, encouraged by Berlinguer, aims to assure the autonomy of women in the central committee. More women in parliament and on the central committee are important, feminists agree, but the issue is more complex than a matter of numbers.[8]

Are women in the Pci feminists, or communists, first—or autonomous women? Ida Dominijanni considered the question in a report on the March 1984 conference of women communists. Feminism, she concluded, had entered these women's lives, "if by feminism is meant a certain scale of priorities, an open research into women's identity, personal and collective, a new way of social living constructed on everyday relations of women among themselves, an interrogation of the contents, forms and ends of politics."[9] Dominijanni posed questions: Were women of the Pci practicing *doppiezza* (dissimulation) with one foot in the feminist movement and another in the party? Or was it astuteness to seem enthusiastic while holding mental reservations? Dominijanni concluded that maybe it was all of these—and maybe none. Perhaps the question of whether these women are feminists or communists first is not meaningful. As Luciana Castellina pointed out, the effect of feminism has been to change the nature of Italian communism.

In a speech given a few months before he died in June 1984, Berlinguer said that since 1976 women had become "protagonists" in Italy, causing "one government after another" to fall on women's issues.[10] Berlinguer's successor, Alessandro Natta, is expected to carry on his predecessor's policies during the transitional period prior to the ascendancy of the youth generation of 1968.

The "years of Berlinguer," whose tenure in the post of Pci party secretary spanned a decade and a half of feminist activism, have been called by Paolo Spriano a "season of great innovations" with an "element of utopia" that was visible in his sensibility on the woman question. Spriano explained, "He invited communists to 'overcome those cultural orientations, those mental and practical attitudes, those usages of a society and a culture constructed in the name of a pretended male supremacy'" and thereby manifested the indispensable sign of a revolutionary—the "ability to see to the roots" of issues.[11]

A 1980 survey of attitudes of young men and women in a seaside community south of Rome indicated that feminism may have changed traditional priorities of young women and men and may have helped to equalize gender relationships. Both women and men in this survey considered the "struggle for an equalitarian society" their main task, but young women put "struggle for justice" prior to harmony in a relationship or marriage while young men ranked a "happy marriage" ahead of the struggle for justice—an upturning of the age-old truism that men seek their destiny in the world and women find fulfillment in the home.[12] In the October 1983 peace demonstration young women and men danced on garden walls and chanted, "vogliamo socialismo!" The socialism they apparently want is an "alternative" one grounded on an unedited reading of Marx.

For the centenary of Marx, Arci, the organization connected with the Pci and the Psi, distributed a cartoon book reflecting the unedited marxism that has become characteristic of the Italian left. *Il Grande Karl*, the great German theoretician, in this Italian translation becomes Carlo Marx, boy and man. One cartoon depicts Carlo as a boy in a schoolroom with a nun reciting a poem, "God does not exist and if he does, he exists in a corner eating hazelnuts"; the drawing is credited to "Foto Wojtyla." Another cartoon is of God, who "did not believe in the existence of Carlo Marx." There is a picture of Marx the day he graduated from the University of Bologna with a thesis on "communism and ragù." A cartoon of Marx in his library fixes on a feminist study, *Saffo-Clito superstar*, and a volume by the pope on Polish stamps. The caption under a cartoon of Carlo's cat advises that the cat never learned to catch mice, although he could recite the complete works of Shakespeare.[13] Behind the humor are important premises of the unedited marxist beliefs of many Italians. Marx is depicted as a participant in an international soccer match; other players include Mao, Che Guevara, Lassalle, Abraham Lincoln, an anarchist ("probably individualist"), Lenin, Gramsci, Trotsky, and an infiltrator of the czarist police.

On the centenary of his death, *noidonne* humorously dedicated an issue to Marx—"The Metro Golden Marx presents everything you wanted to know about Marx and dared not ask"—supplemented with serious thinking on the connection between feminism and marxism.[14] "Pulling the beard of the prophet," feminist cartoons depict Marx saying, "I was always among the first to uphold the necessity of women's liberation!" In another, "Women are the Engels of the hearth!" In another, a woman rewrites a traditional marxist theorem, saying, "My husband reproduces at home the same patterns as at the factory." How? "At night he is always on strike." A feminist declares: "Io sono mia!" An excessively rationalist male marxist answers: "Foolishness! Private property does not exist!"[15]

The celebration issue featured an article by Rossana Rossanda, the new left theorist who had pondered the relationship of feminism to marxism for a decade and a half. The two perspectives, said Rossanda, should be regarded as traveling in two different orbits. Assuming marxism and feminism do not aspire to be totalizing theories, this is valuable for anyone who does not want to encase the multiformity of social and individual experience into one system. This does not mean incommunicability between the two: marxism and feminism intersect when marxism refers to liberation of people and when feminism is concerned with the material ground of liberation. Any attempt of either of the two perspectives to absorb the other, for Rossanda, will make the two less productive as theories and as movements.

Indicating that her own thinking had shifted ground since 1968, Rossanda said that feminists had gone farther up, and farther down, the terrain traversed by Marx. The feminist theory of differences implies that there are diverse, true, and irreducible ways of life and interpretations of reality, with different priorities. For a decade Rossanda had criticized feminists with a marxist lens; in 1983 she criticised marxists with a feminist question: Why, asked Rossanda, would marxists want to negate this value of difference? [16]

Demonstrating the dialectical process implicit in unedited marxism, Anna Maria Crispino criticized, in the same issue of *nd*, Rossanda's "dualism." For Crispino, marxist thinkers are more relevant to feminism than Rossanda's two-orbit theory implies;[17] she quoted Gramsci as saying that it would be impossible to untie the knot of the woman question until women were independent and thought of themselves differently in sexual relationships.[18]

"what it means to be a communist today"

Capping a decade and a half of new left insistence on defining communism for itself—and also revealing the convergence of feminism with new left thinking—Lidia Menapace presented her perspective on "what it means to be a communist today" at a fall 1983 Pdup regional conference. She assured men of the left that feminism does not mean replacing a male with a female vanguard; it does mean that traditional marxist dialectic must be stretched into a "multipolar dialectic" that "can change reality." To be a communist today, said Menapace, means accepting a multipolar dialectic in which the first contradiction is that posed by feminism which emphasizes "quality of life" rather than economics alone.

Other contradictions are planetary in scope—between survival and resources, between peace and war, between the North and South of the globe. These contradictions entail new thinking about the goals of production; when considered together with the traditional marxist contradiction between capital and labor, it becomes obvious that new thinking is needed about how change comes about, as well as the role of the state. In an era of multiple contradictions and universal autonomy, said Menapace, delegated representation can no longer exist. We can no longer "pretend" to govern in the name of the working class, of women, of youth, of old people, or of the masses.

Contradictions expressed by the various green movements—ecological, antinuclear, and pacifist—bring into view the possibility of a political economy with new values. Multipolarity implies, said Menapace, that a gradualist strategy—first we'll construct socialism, then we'll take women's liberation into account, and then we'll look into the relationship of the earth's resources and the survival of the planet—is no longer tenable.[19]

crisis, or cultural revolution?

"Our civilization is in crisis," said Sabino Acquaviva in 1983. Since 1968, "Italy has changed completely." The sociologist pointed to unprecedented change in the "family, religion, and politics."[20] Twenty years ago, said Acquaviva, there was a clear difference between a catholic and someone who was not; now Italians speak of a catholic-communist continuum. There are Italians about whom "we, honestly, cannot say if they are catholics or not, if they are marxists or not, if they are atheists or not, if they are *credenti* or not." And there are others, he pointed out, who will reply differently at different times and places to a query about their beliefs. There has been, said Acquaviva, a "revolution inside of ourselves." He likened the large change to the one that occurred at the time of Saint Francis, at the end of the Middle Ages and the dawn of the modern era, when people began thinking differently about themselves and about the world. In our time, said Acquaviva, a similar phenomenon is happening—among women and men.[21]

If there is, by the. mid-eighties, no longer a clear demarcation in Italy between catholics and communists, the line between feminists and other women is even harder to discern. Conservative catholic women held conferences on how had it happened that they had let themselves be cut off from "the richest social militance of the 70s." They invited Betty Friedan from the U.S. to explain feminism and asked the editor of *noidonne*, "Is it true that feminists have a theology?"[22]

In a round table on the subject, feminist communists tried to measure the phenomenon. Grazia Francescato said that feminist consciousness was so pervasive in Italy that the question of who was, and who was not, a feminist was meaningless. The ground of feminism, said Francescato, was the utopian hope; the task was to work for this vision with the awareness that each woman brings her own history to the common enterprise.[23]

To Giglia Tedesco, it was clear that "women had changed" and that a women's "collective consciousness" existed in Italy: "the most peripheral housewife has attained a consciousness of herself and of her rights." One can approximate the reach of Italian feminism, said Tedesco, if one thinks about twelve million housewives carrying on the battle inside the house and going outside into the piazza to change society.[24]

on differences among men

Via their own paths, some men arrived at conclusions by the mid-eighties similar to those of feminists. Massimo Cacciari, a professor of theoretical philosophy, a political consultant to the Pci, and a utopian, shares the feminist epistemological premise that to know anything one must be a participant. An advocate of decentralized socialism, Cacciari discerned a "multiverse of politics" on the horizon. The crisis of identity and obligation, from Cacciari's perspective, can be resolved by "localization." Politics should not be seen as the activities of the state; in our time "politics are the dynamics that are destroying the state." The future is that of "polyarchy, not autarchy." This thinking, according to Cacciari, is "utopian and realistic" because contemporary state politics are not realistic. Democracy is to be reconstituted as polycentrism, with different rules from those of classical political theory. The point is that "we are in transition from metaphysics to a new construction of participatory democracy." The immediate program is to give free rein to the creativity of everyone. Decentralization implies the empowerment of everybody and the recognition that the citizen, not the state, is authoritative.[25]

By the middle of the decade, it was no longer a matter of women finding their voices but of some men remaining so absorbed in their own abstractions that they could not hear. This was clearest at the top of the pyramid that Italian women call the *gerarchia* (hierarchy). As the vatican negotiated with the Italian government for a renewal of the 1929 lateran pact, it was apparent that the church was anxiously approaching a relinquishing of its privileged status in Italy. Under the accord that was signed early in 1984, catholic religious instruction in the schools has become voluntary. The privileged status of the church in Italy remains, but the privilege has been considerably diminished.

Anxiety may have been expressed as intransigence at the top of the hierarchy; in September 1983 Pope John Paul II said that the teaching of the church on contraception was "one of the essential points of the christian doctrine of matrimony."[26] When the couple subtracts procreative potential from the sexual act, they are attributing to themselves a power that belongs solely to God. Later that month he addressed U.S. bishops, saying that they must reaffirm church stands against contraception, divorce, homosexuality, premarital sex, and abortion.

Annamaria Guadagni, the editor of *noidonne*, responded. She analyzed the pope's description of the use of contraception as a form of "moral disorder," as a sin against chastity, and ultimately as a sin against religion and faith itself. The image of woman that emerges from the pope's speeches, said Guadagni, is of "a machine for reproduction without human ability to choose." The present pope, she said, is embarked in a direction radically different from that of "papa Giovanni," who had wanted to distinguish between "error and the person who erred, between sin and the sinner." John Paul II's description of birth control leaves woman "a being condemned to an existence essentially naturalistic and therefore, and conclusively, an animal being." Eighty percent of catholic women in the United States use artificial contraception; a survey in Italy, said Guadagni, indicated similar data.[27]

In August 1984 a catholic priest and sociologist in the United States, Andrew M. Greeley, publicized findings that "as many as 85 percent of catholics" agree with U.S. protestants that abortions should be available to women whose health is endangered by a pregnancy, 80 percent of catholics approve of abortion for rape victims.

On the other hand, only 30 percent of U.S. catholics (and protestants) approve of abortion on demand. Greeley called this a "nuanced" approach that is neither that of prochoice nor of prolife forces.[28]

Neither is this "nuanced" perspective of catholics in agreement with the views of the pope. We may be seeing, in Italy and the United States, an attitude on the part of many catholics that refers moral decisions to individual conscience. This ancient peasant stance toward the church, an antinomian perspective articulated by Pope John XXIII in the 1960s, may have become the nub of doctrinal controversy by mid-decade, but it may also be a sign of a shift in the actual beliefs of catholics.

The issue extends beyond contraception and abortion. In 1984 Pope John Paul II summoned liberation theologians—whose beliefs are grounded on an unedited gospel and who adopt Marxist analysis—to Rome for censure; shortly thereafter the pope demanded that U.S. nuns who had published a paper maintaining that "a large number of Catholic theologians hold that even direct abortion, though tragic, can sometimes be a moral choice" retract their statement or leave their religious communities. For the feminist theologian Rosemary Ruether this is a return to the days before vatican council II when the papacy resembled a "top-down monarchy" in which nuns were important in the hierarchical scheme because "they are at the bottom of the chain of command but have the essential role of passing on commands to the laity."[29] In January 1985 John Paul II announced a synod to reconsider vatican council II.

On Enrico Berlinguer's death, the editor of *noidonne* evaluated a decade and a half of feminist challenge to men of the Pci. "All of us remember the feet of lead with which the Pci addressed itself to the referendum on divorce and then on abortion."[30] Yet Annamaria Guadagni credited the momentum of the party, once it was in gear, for helping to secure feminist gains. She also noted that some men of the Pci were not convinced until electoral evidence rained on them.

Reflecting on differences among men, she said of Berlinguer's kindness, discretion, and balance: "He was a moral man." Not only, in a political system wracked by scandals of corruption, did he head a party that had "clean hands," he was a moral man, for Guadagni, because he viewed politics as engagement in moral tension. For Ber-

linguer, communists had to be simultaneously conservatives and revolutionaries. He had severed the party's umbilical cord with Moscow,
said Guadagni, and guided the party to a position, "alone among
communist parties," that recognized exploitation of gender as well as
class, agreeing with feminists that there cannot be revolution without liberation of women. This conviction, according to Guadagni,
led the Pci to question democratic centralism and to recognize "the
equal legitimacy of all positions." [31]

The influence of fifteen years of feminist activism was marked in
the concluding chapter of a definitive history of Italian socialism in
1980. Giorgio Galli entitled this chapter "La storia e le streghe" (History and witches). [32] In the history of marxism, said Galli, theorists
had analyzed the oppression of people from slaves to proletarians—
yet women as a subordinated group had been left out. [33]

Feminists, since 1968, according to Galli, have been the embryo
of an alternative culture, replacing one predominantly masculine
with another. Galli read the nineteenth century theorist J. J. Bachofen who had analyzed the women deities who preceded judeo-
christianity. Galli noted the criticism engendered by scholars who
studied topics of an alternative women's culture: earth-mother deities, women gnostics, witches, healers, and feminists. Matriarchal culture, said Galli, is characterized by bonds of kinship, ties to the earth,
and acceptance of natural phenomena. In contrast, patriarchal culture is characterized by human laws, the dominance of rationalist
thought, and the belief that men can control nature. He analyzed
the political implications of the two cultures: "According to matriarchal conception, all humans are equal" [34] and attention is on human
life now. [35] In patriarchy, said Galli, there is a tendency to leave everyday reality for abstractions, and there is "always the favored son."

Alternative women's culture, Galli continued, has historically been
branded by men as unbridled eroticism and men have historically
used violence to subdue women. Would this pattern be repeated at
the end of the second millenary? Galli, an Italian man of the left,
dedicated his history of Italian socialism to "una ribelle vera questa
storia di una ribellione incompiuta" (to a particular woman rebel in
an unfinished rebellion). [36]

Italian feminists kept their own history in the lullabies they sang
to their children and in their songs at demonstrations. The tie with
their peasant past was woven in "Dirindina la malcontenta," an old

Tuscan lullaby: "babbo gode e mamma stenta/ babbo mangia li fagioli mamma tribola co'figlioli."[37] Women's militancy, as well as resistance, are commemorated in many songs. Everybody sings, at all demonstrations, a song of women rice workers that became the song of the partisans, "Bella ciao."

The cover of a collection of peasant and feminist songs entitled *Siamo in tante* (We are many) has a representation of the earth mother. In a song they particularly like, Italian feminists convey a timeless sense of self:

"I am woman, where everything ends and everything begins again."[38]

> *Siamo in tante siam più della metà*
> *lo siamo sempre state in questa umanità.*
> *Siamo intante siam più della metà*
> *ma non contiamo niente in questa società.*
>
> *E se siam separate ciascuna a casa sua*
> *allora siam fregate e senza liberta*
> *se noi ci nascondiamo ognuna nella cella*
> *sprechiam la nostra vita che presto finirà*
>
> > *Siamo in tante siam più della metà . . .*
>
> *Ma se ci uniamo insieme e respiriamo forte*
> *allor vediam le altre e ci riconosciam*
> *una speranza abbiamo che tutto può cambiare*
> *e chi diciamo basta alla vecchia realtà.*
>
> > *Siamo in tante siam più della metà . . .*[39]

afterword

Offering a mirror to other women's movements, feminists of Italy have drawn on a long history for their vision of a new society where terrorists "of all types" throw away arms and abuse gives way to respect for the beauty and diversity of human life. The continuing vitality of the Italian movement may be related to having tapped subterranean as well as rational beliefs. Figures on the sash of this ancient and advanced feminism fuse into one another: the primordial earth mother, Graeco-Roman goddesses, early judeo-christian women, popular madonnas, familiar saints, persecuted witches and healers, peasant godmothers, peasant women socialists, feminist socialists, women marxists, antifascist women partisans—and contemporary feminists, who are a galaxy of different women from catholic matrons and housewives to prostitutes, lesbians, nuns, and others. From Hybla to Maddalena, Demetra and Proserpina to *parteggiane*, peasant premillenialists to feminists who study the judeo-christian gospel, marxist philosophy, and the history of women with an unedited perspective they have proceeded from "L'utero è mio e me lo gestisco io" to a vision of a decentralized, libertarian, self-managed socialism in a world of equality, justice, and peace: "Since all human beings are equal participants in creation all have a right to participate in the world's resources."

Ancient and advanced, realist and visionary, they also have seasons of fatigue. A history of Italian feminism from 1965 to the 1980s concludes that this has been a history from a feminist movement to *"femminismo diffuso"* (diffuse feminism)."[1] The 1985 volume, written by Laura Grasso and Annarita Calabro, is based on interviews in the Lombardy region; the study emphasizes the difficulties in a movement based on differences among Italian women and the doubts that have arisen over the choice feminists made in the early eighties to dissolve their political identity into something other. Lea Melandri's review of the book (and of the movement) concludes that the "heart counts, but . . . a heart without a head is not worth much" and the point may be to recover the head. She added that Italian women were more than ever active in society and politics and this activism is accompanied by a renewed interest in motherhood, living with men, and looking inward; for Melandri, the two spheres of the political and the private, in Italy, have become one.

The ancient and advanced qualities of Italian feminists may be suggested in two instances. The smallest political *circoscrizione* of Rome is number 17, whose administrative president is Daniela Valentini. A writer for *il manifesto* sought her out to find out how that neighborhood group had voted itself a denuclearized zone. Not yet forty, Valentini laughs a lot and told the interviewer she honestly did not know how the vote had come about—she does not feel that she is "committed politically." Pressed by questions, she said that her politics could be traced to her catholic beliefs, that she had been "seduced" by the events of 1968. Thereafter she was "trascinata" (carried away) but she was "felice e apppasionata" (happy and committed). In the seventies she lived (with her husband and eventually three children) in a *comunità di base*; in 1973 she joined the Pci, a party she considers close to the people and able to resolve problems. In 1981 her neighborhood turned from the Dc and the Msi to the left; Valentini, who had worked in problem areas that referred to schools, was elected president of the *circoscrizione*. She has governed in a coalition of parties and has attempted to take into account the interests of businessmen, old people, people without homes, and the young. There are military barracks in her neighborhood that she is trying to turn to civil use. While Valentini was being interviewed, an old woman came in without knocking and, in a nurturant gesture, said she had brought the younger woman, *"un po' di pizza con la ricotta"* and left.[2]

Noidonne, encouraging unedited feminism, gave several pages in the mid-eighties to a Sicilian group of feminists active in resistance to the Comiso nuclear base. The women have named their group Demetra—connecting their concern to preserve life on earth with the ancient Greek and Roman goddess of fecundity. For their autonomous pages in the journal, the women printed a representation of the earth mother and the words of a song of Colombian Indians. The song was addressed to the "mother of all"—of all the rivers, and of all the trees, and of all human tribes.[3]

No existing socialism has been able to translate marxist philosophy into a society that is libertarian and genuinely equalitarian. In Italy where traces persist of the ancient Mediterranean earth mother who nurtured diverse peoples and a multiplicity of beliefs, where pluralism mixes beliefs of an unedited gospel with an unedited marxism and feminists laugh as well as rage, the vision is as real as the dark wheat and red poppies of Sicily.

appendixes

notes

glossary

bibliographical essay

index

appendix a: chronology

1870   Culmination of risorgimento in completion of unification of Italy. Pope ceases to be a temporal sovereign, forbids catholics to hold public office or to vote.

1881   Anna Maria Mozzoni founds Lega promotrice degli interessi femminili.

1891   Mozzoni helps to found partito socialista.

Leo XIII, in encyclical *Rerum novarum*, opposes socialism and asserts that women, as the weaker sex, are made for domestic work.

1892   Mozzoni criticizes attitudes of male socialists in "I socialisti e l'emancipazione della donna."

1893 −94   Women participate in socialist demonstrations of *fasci Siciliani.*

1904   In cases of southern "crimes of honor" (*delitti d'onore*) magistrates absolve fathers, brothers, and husbands who kill daughters, sisters, and wives found in *delicto flagrante.*

1915   Women demonstrate for "pace e lavoro."

1921   Partito comunista italiano (Pci) formed at Livorno.

Antonio Gramsci's article "Il nostro femminismo" appears in Pci newspaper, *Ordine Nuovi.*

Camilla Ravera edits *Tribuna delle donne.*

Southern men and women peasants occupy lands.

1923   Fascist dissolution of worker associations, parties, and press and revocation
–26   of lands held by peasants.

1924   Murder of Matteotti, critic of fascists, in parliament.

1926   Arrest and incarceration of Gramsci.

1927   Strikes of women rice workers.

1928   Catholic associations outline women's duties.

1929   Fascists conclude lateran pacts with papacy.
        Compulsory religious education in the schools.

1930   Papal encyclical *Casti connubi* defines women's work outside the home as a
        corruption of maternal dignity and a perversion of the family.
        Fascist penal code (Rocco) confirms disparities between men and women,
        institutionalizes *delitto d'onore.*

1931   Papal encyclical *Quadragesimo anno* restates that women's work is inside the
        home.
        Subsequent fascist measures against women's outside employment; fascist
        campaign to encourage women remaining in the home and to lift the birth
        rate to ideal fascist family of twelve children.
        Ecclesiastical courts hold jurisdiction over dissolution of marriages.

1935   Mussolini asks women for their wedding rings for imperial war expenses.

1936   *Unione donne italiane* organizes in France.

1937   *Noi Donne* published in France as Udi journal.

1942   Fascist legislation underlines women's subordination to husbands, hus-
        band's right to "correct" his wife's behavior.

1943   Women demonstrate against the war. Strikes.
        Women's resistance organized as *gruppi di difesa della donna e per l'assistanenza*
        ai volontari della liberta.

1944   Women's strikes in fields and factories.
        Women partisan soldiers.
        Noi Donne published in Italy.
        Unione donne italiane founded.
        Formation of catholic workers' association, Acli, to protect interests of
        catholic workers in the communist and socialist trade union, Cgil. When
        catholics form their own union, Cisl, Acli turns to political work supporting
        Dc.

1945   Women's vote.

1945   Women and men occupy lands in the South.
–46

1945   Over four million southerners migrate to northern Italian cities, European
–75   countries, and overseas.

1946   Centro italiano femminile (Cif), catholic, anticommunist women's organi-
        zation is founded, supporting the papacy and the christian democratic
        party (Dc).

1947   Women and men in Calabria occupy uncultivated fields.

Udi congress, "For a happy family, peace, and work."

Udi petition for disarmament and prohibition of atomic bomb.

Pci and Psi excluded from participation in government.

1948   Italian republican constitution: "All citizens have equal social dignity and are equal before the law without distinction of sex, of race, of language, of religion, of political opinion, of personal and social condition." Women's right to work outside the home. Equality of marriage partners.

Dc campaign: "A vote for left parties is a sin."

After successful election of 1948, beginning of Dc hegemony over Italian politics, a church-state relationship of practicing catholics who govern Italy with an anticommunist orientation that includes constrictive views on women.

Dc government denies proposal for women's protective legislation.

1949   Pope excommunicates catholics who support Pci or Psi.

Italy joins NATO.

1949 –50   Women and men occupy untilled lands in the South.

1950   Modest Dc land reform program; continued migration of peasants to the North.

Dc criticizes women working outside the home as wanting "to buy silk stockings."

Protective legislation for working mothers.

Large growth of Catholic Action, religious support group of Dc.

1950 –63   Years of rapid economic growth. Italian GNP rises at an annual rate of 7 percent (against a European average of 4.5 percent); peasants become urban proletariat, peasant women and children become subproletariat.

1954   Women demonstrating for water at Mussomeli, Sicily, are assaulted by police; three are killed, many wounded.

1955   Udi proposes salaries to housewives.

1956   Parliament approves principle of salary equality for women.

Udi espouses themes pertaining to birth control, prostitution, family law, rights of illegitimate children.

1957   Italy enters European Economic Community, with lowest wage rate of EEC countries. Exports do well in international competition.

1958   Law (promoted by Udi) abolishes state benefits derived from legal prostitution.

1958 –63   Papacy of John XXIII. Openings to the left. Women's advancement, like advancement of workers and colonial efforts for independence, regarded as "signs of the times." In encyclicals *Mater et magistra* and *Pacem in terris*, the church addresses itself to all men of good will, looks to problems of the poor, of poorer nations, and peace.

1959   Strikes of women clothing workers for salary equality.

1960   Clothing industry accepts principle of women's salary equality.

1962   Vatican council II; the church relates to the modern world. Encyclical *Gau-*
−65   *dium et spes* condemns discrimination against women.

1963   Law prohibits firing women on account of marriage.
In new catholic atmosphere, Dc accepts Psi entry in government coalition.
Law posits free access of women to all professions, including the magistracy.

1964   Law positing equality of women's work in agrarian contracts.
Perspectives encouraged by John XXIII develop into liberation theology.

1968   Encyclical of Paul VI, *Humanae vitae*, condemns artificial contraception.
Abolition of civil law punishing "the unfaithful wife."
Women join men students in strikes, occupations, confrontations.

1969   Women workers participate in large strikes of the "hot autumn" involving
five million workers. Factory councils.
Bombings of Piazza Fontana. Anarchists charged; ten years later neofascists
found guilty.
Women's collectives propose women's role in the "revolutionary process."
Universities opened, free to all high school graduates; large enrollment of
women.

1970   Divorce law.
Movimento di liberazione della donna (Mld), affiliated with radical party
(Pr), agitates for legalized abortion, arranges safe abortions for women.
Rivolta femminile, Milan, issues feminist manifestos.
First elections under law implementing constitutional decentralization into
regions and provinces enables left parties to govern on regional level.
Italy ranked seventh industrial nation of the world; farm population has
declined to 20 percent.
"Statute of workers' rights" greatly strengthens unions, forbids records of
political affiliation, guarantees freedom of assembly and speech on shop
floor. Italian unions in the seventies negotiated wage agreements that included education of workers and others, health care, rent control, housing,
pensions, and other social measures.

1970   Italy has highest strike record in Europe.
−77

1971   Nursery schools law (subsidized by national government).
−72

1972   Abolition of law forbidding birth control information.
Protective legislation for working mothers.
Mld promotes referendum campaign for repeal of punitive abortion law.
Wages for housewives conference, Padua.
Labor unions include stipulation for "150-hour classes" in contracts, en-
abling factory and clerical workers and housewives to take women's studies
classes.

1973   Protective legislation for women in cottage industries.

Women's theatre, la Maddalena, founded.

Udi conference on gender division of roles.

1974   Papal and Dc referendum to annul divorce law defeated decisively (20 million votes against the referendum to 13 million for).

First *festa della donna* organized by Udi and Pci.

Right-wing bombing of antifascist meeting; train *Italicus* bombed. *Bologna*

1975   50,000 women demonstrate in Rome for approval of equal family rights law, approved in May.

Constitutional court removes penalty for therapeutic abortions.

Large industrialists urge cooperation of unions, Pci, government to control wages.

1976   Law for women's health clinics (birth control information).

Demonstration of 20,000 women for legalized abortion.

Pci receives highest historical vote, 34.4 percent, largely because of entry of young people and women into party.

✓ First woman cabinet minister (Dc).

Women's demonstrations throughout Italy for Lysistrata strategy, "Let's take back the night."

Papacy denies possibility of women in the priesthood, reaffirms men as the norm in social life.

Pci in working coalition with Dc (1976–79), a "historic compromise." Threatened withdrawal of feminists from politics: "the personal is political."

Red brigades' kidnappings and shootings.

1977   *Casa della donna* founded at Rome.

50,000 women demonstrate in Rome for legalized abortion.

Law clarifying equality for women in pay, accessibility to all careers.

1978   Law 194, legalizing "voluntary interruption of pregnancy."

John Paul II ascends to papacy (first non-Italian since the 16th century).

Labor union accord accepting wage restraint and fiscal austerity in return for economic development, particularly in South.

Red brigades kidnap and murder Aldo Moro, symbolic leader of the Dc and of the historic compromise. Parties of left as well as right refuse to negotiate with terrorists for his life. Sweep against terrorists.

Women's demonstrations against terrorism of left and of right.

1979 –80   Antiterrorist legislation stipulates preventive detention.

1979   University for women, Centro culturale Virginia Woolf, founded at Rome.

Referendum campaign for law against sexual violence.

Italian inflation rate in late 1970s and early 1980s reaches highest level of Europe; unemployment (three-quarters reflecting young people under thirty) increases to 10 percent.

Pci party theses declare communist members may be practicing catholics, need not be marxists.

Reform of national health system, but doctor and patient dissatisfaction.

Acceptance by a socialist defense minister of proposed NATO nuclear site at Comiso, Sicily. Surveys indicate that only one-third of Italians support participation in NATO.

Women present referendum with 300,000 signatures against sexual violence (including marital rape) to parliament.

Church and Dc sponsor referendum to repeal Law 194 (legalized abortion).

Right-wing bombing of Bologna train station.

1980 −84 Italy in the 1980s, with a population of 55 million, remains the world's seventh economic power.

1981 50,000 women demonstrate in defense of abortion law.

On international women's day, March 8, 1981, women of all ages and social status, throughout Italy go into the piazza to support law legalizing abortion.

Abortion law of 1978 sustained by every province but one with large pluralities (national average of 70%) defeating catholic referendum to repeal and Pr referendum to liberalize.

Women participate in peace demonstration of 250,000 against nuclear missiles in Europe.

Revelation of secret P2 plot involving men in every party but Pci and Pr in ambiguous complicity with right-wing terrorism.

Pci openly declares independence of Soviet Union, repudiates soviet model, affirms the "many socialisms" developing in the world.

1982 Udi declares, and effects, independence of Pci, refounds the women's union as a decentralized and autonomous women's movement.

Continued murders by mafia stimulate government moves against mafia, feminist defiance, unprecedented citizen resistance.

1983 50,000 women spontaneously demonstrate against Dc definition of rape as a crime against "social morality" instead of crime against a person.

Demonstrations and work throughout Italy oppose fascist violence, violent revolution, violence to the environment, violence of mafia, nuclear violence, and violence against women.

Papacy restates opposition to premarital sex, contraception, homosexuality, women in the priesthood, politically committed priests and nuns, abortion, and liberation theologies.

700,000 women, men, and children, priests and nuns, worker associations, unions, catholics, evangelicals, environmentalists et al. demonstrate at Rome against NATO and soviet nuclear missiles and for a variety of concerns against violence.

Pci democratizes structure, declares opposition "a tutti i missili" and aligns party with "movements of transformation"—of women, peace, and ecology.

1984 Renewal of lateran pacts with papacy with proviso that religious instruction in schools is now voluntary.

Women who live at the *casa della donna* after feminist activities have moved elsewhere are arrested for prostitution.

Bomb in train tunnel near Bologna attributed to right-wing terrorists.

Bill against sexual violence passes house of deputies. It recognizes rape as a crime against a person but excludes husbands and lovers from possible prosecution.

1985   Pope calls synod to reconsider vatican council II; restates opposition to birth control, abortion, premarital sex, homosexuality, women in the clergy, and liberation theologies.

appendix b:
major organizations and periodicals

organizations (political parties and women's groups)

Dc (democrazia cristiana): The Christian democratic party, formed in the postwar era. The dominant party of Italy after 1948. Associated with defense of the catholic church and anticommunism, and alignment with NATO and the European Common Market. A party of disparate groups (peasants, workers, landholders, industrial entrepreneurs, shopkeepers, white-collar employees) held together by political catholicism. Dc hegemony was weakened by the votes on women's issues in the 1970s and 1980s. In the May 1985 elections the Dc recovered some of its strength, remaining the first party of Italy with 34 percent of the electorate.

Dp (democrazia proletaria): Radical offshoot of Pdup. A new left party aiming to speak for ecologists, pacifists, and feminists. In May 1985 it won city council seats in almost every city in which it appeared on the ballot.

Pci (partito comunista italiano): The Italian communist party, founded in 1921. After 1948 it became the second party of Italy. In 1984 it attained a slight majority over the Dc; in the May 1985 administrative elections, the party dropped back to 30 percent of the electorate. It has been an autonomous communist party since 1981 and is the largest communist party in the West. It may be the only communist party that enables members to hold religious belief prior to political identification and that recognizes the women's movement as an agency of "social transformation."

Pdup (partito di unità proletaria per il comunismo): A new left autonomous party for communism, formed from the dissenting *il manifesto* group that was "radiated" out of the Pci in 1969; in the 1980s the new left party for communism is supported by the Pci on electoral ballots. Important source of critical support for feminists.

Pli (partito liberale): The liberal party, a small lay party in the Psi and Dc governing coalition of the eighties.

Pr (partito radicale): Radical party independent of the ideologies of catholicism and communism. In the 1970s, it was the first party to promote feminist issues and to focus attention on world peace. In the 1980s it has defended the civil rights of revolutionaries and supported free abortion on demand.

Pri (partito repubblicano): The republican party, a small lay party emphasizing business and internationalism that forms part of the *pentapartito* of the 1980s with the Dc and Psi.

Psi (partito socialista italiano): Italian socialist party, founded in 1891. The Psi was part of the antifascist coalition, expelled with the Pci from government in 1947. In the early 1960s it joined the Dc in a governing coalition; in the 1980s, Italy elected its first socialist prime minister, Bettino Craxi, who is appreciated by the right and criticized by the left for accommodating the interests of NATO. Psi totals rose to 13 percent in the elections of May 1985.

verdi: The "greens" of Italy, who appeared on independent electoral lists in 1985.

Cif (Centro italiano femminile): Italian catholic women's organization founded after 1945 as a political support group for the papacy and the Dc. In the 1970s disagreed with feminists over divorce and abortion, but evinced considerable agreement on other issues; in the 1980s maintained stronger identification with other women than with abstractions, and controversial issues like abortion were remanded, in effect, to the private conscience of each woman.

Mld (Movimento di la liberazione della donna): Umbrella organization of Roman feminist collectives that took the lead on the abortion issue. In the early 1970s, associated with Partito radicale in launching a referendum to repeal the punitive abortion law, in mobilizing women's support for defeat of the papal and Dc attempt to repeal divorce law, and in founding the *casa della donna* at Rome.

Udi (*Unione donne italiane*): Women's union founded in 1944 as part of the partisan resistance against fascism. As an auxiliary of the Pci, it worked for protective legislation for women and implementation of the equality provisions of Italy's 1948 constitution. Criticized by neofeminists after 1968 for subordinate status in the Pci. Refounded in 1982 as an autonomous, decentralized women's movement.

periodicals

com-nuovi tempi (*cnt*): Postconciliar journal of Italian protestants, catholics, Jews, believers, and *comunità di base*. Major source of feminist support.

differenze: Unedited journal of Roman feminist collectives in the 1970s.

donnawomanfemme (*dwf*): International Italian women's academic journal.

donne e politica: Journal of women in the Pci.

effe: Italian cultural feminist periodical of the early 1970s, subsidized by Psi; *effe* took the lead in cultural feminist issues.

memoria: Intellectual journal of Italian feminism.

noidonne (nd): Udi journal which, reflecting the changing nature of the Italian women's movement, went from a partisan periodical in 1937 to a feminist journal in critical relationship with the Pci in the 1970s, to an autonomous periodical of the decentralized women's movement in the 1980s.

quotidiano donna (qd): Daily feminist newspaper of the 1980s which disseminated feminist issues to a wide audience.

rocca: Journal of left catholics, originating from the *cittadella christiana* at Assisi. Major source of feminist support.

sottosopra: Journal of Milanese feminists. Important for feminist theory.

notes

preface

1. Elizabeth Schussler Fiorenza, *In Memory of Her: A Feminist Theological Reconstruction of Christian Origins* (New York, 1983), xvii.
2. See discussion of Patrizia Magli and Massimo Cacciari, chapter 17, this work. See also Robert N. Bellah et al., *Habits of the Heart: Individualism and Commitment in American Life.* (Berkeley and Los Angeles, 1985), Appendix: "Social Science as Public Philosophy," 297–307.
3. Antonio Gramsci, "The Southern Question" in *The Modern Prince and Other Writings* (New York, 1957).
4. Leonardo Sciascia, *La Sicilia come metafora: Intervista di Marcelle Padovani* (Rome, 1979). "The problems of Sicily are those of Italy, and I do not believe that it is possible to resolve them without resolving the problems of Italy" (p. 52) and "I am convinced that Sicily offers an image of so many problems, of so many contradictions, not only Italian but also European, that Sicily may constitute a metaphor for today's world" (p. 78).
5. Gramsci, "The Southern Question," 31.
6. Ibid.   7. Ibid.
8. Robert N. Bellah and Phillip E. Hammond, *Varieties of Civil Religion* (San Francisco, 1980), chap. 4, Bellah, "The Five Religions of Modern Italy," 90–94.
9. Bellah, "Five Religions," 92.
10. Ibid.   11. Ibid.
12. Bellah, "Five Religions," 93.
13. For discussion of "red christs" in southern Italian folklore, see "Simbolo, religione, politica" (a round-table discussion with the following participants: Tullio Tentori, Alberto Izzo, Alfonso M. Di Nola, Carlo Molari, Arnaldo Nesti, Roberto Cipriani, Maria Immacolata Macioti, Vincenzo Padiglione, Giovanni Rinaldi), *idoc internazionale*, May 1981.

14. R. Cipriani, G. Rinaldi, P. Sobrero, *Il simbolo conteso: simbolismo politico e religioso nelle culture di base meridionali* (Rome, 1979). See page 32 for May day festivities in southern Italy featuring figures of the madonna and of *cristi rossi*. For a 1976 photo of a *cristo rosso* in the easter week ritual of the mother looking for her son, see page 81. For the high valence of the madonna in these christian/communist beliefs, see the chapter "La cavalcata degli angeli." The impression these southern Italian rituals give is of a mother with several red sons (*cristi rossi*). Italian feminist response to these images is suggested in Chapters 7, 8, 9, and 17 of this work.
15. See Bibliographical Essay.
16. See Chapter 16.

1 *la gran madre mediterranea, madrine, e socialiste*
the great Mediterranean earth mother, godmothers, and socialists

1. For prehistoric Italy, see Pierre Grimal, *In Search of Ancient Italy*, trans. P. D. Cummins (New York, 1964).
2. Apuleius is quoted in Lawrence Di Stasi, *Mal Occhio: The Underside of Vision* (Berkeley, 1981), 87. See also chapter 4 on the mother goddess, her many manifestations, and her connection with the peasant woman's ritual of exorcising "mal occhio." This ritual, condemned by the church as superstition, was practiced by Italian peasant women from time immemorial and carried to the United States by Italian women emigrants. This study is the definitive book on the subject.
3. Di Stasi, *Mal Occhio*, 90.
4. Di Stasi, *Mal Occhio*, 107. See also Eric Pace, "Women's Cults of Antiquity: The Veil Rises," *New York Times*, 30 April, 1985, Science section. Recent excavations in southern Italy have found the shrine of a goddess cult related to the earth mother, Demeter, dating from the sixth century B.C. to ca. the third century after Jesus. Archeologists discussing this excavation point out that many earth goddesses of fertility were also related to goddesses of love: Aphrodite for the Greeks, Venus for the Romans.
5. Sarah B. Pomeroy, "A Classical Scholar's Perspective on Matriarchy" in *Liberating Women's History: Theoretical and Critical Essays*, ed. Berenice A. Carroll (Urbana, 1976).
6. Pomeroy, "A Classical Scholar's Perspective," 218.
7. Ibid., 220; cf. Susan Moller Okin, *Women in Western Political Thought* (Princeton, N.J., 1979).
8. Pomeroy, "A Classical Scholar's Perspective," 221.
9. Ibid.
10. See Pomeroy, *Goddesses, Whores, Wives and Slaves: Women in Classical Antiquity* (New York, 1975); cf. Okin, *Women*. See Bibliographical Essay, this work.
11. An Italian scholar's study of archeological traces of prehistoric women deities is Eugenio Manni, *Sicilia pagana* (Palermo, 1963).
12. See Vincent Cronin, *The Golden Honeycomb*, 2nd ed., (London, 1980).
13. For Hybla Heraia, see "Ragusa," *Sicilia: Guida d'Italia del Touring Club Italiano* (Milan, 1968), 683.
14. See Afterword.
15. Di Stasi, *Mal Occhio*, 123.

16. Gilles Quispel, presentation to C. G. Jung Institute, San Francisco, California, 28 September 1984.
17. See Lucia Chiavola Birnbaum, *La religione e le donne sicule americane* (Siracusa, Italy, 1981)
18. Salvatore Salomone-Marino, *Costumi ed usanze dei contadini di Sicilia* (Palermo, 1879), 13–19.
19. Salomone-Marino, *Costumi*, 9. For the historical roots of the contemporary Sicilian political economy, see Jane Schneider and Peter Schneider, *Culture and Political Economy in Western Sicily* (New York, 1976). For the modern history of Italy from a woman's viewpoint, see Camilla Ravera, *Breve storia del movimento femminile in Italia* (Rome, 1978) particularly 13ff. Also see Bibliographical Essay.

    This section of this chapter is based on research originally undertaken for an essay on religion in the United States for a proposed festschrift in honor of Henry Farnham May. Subsequently the manuscript was translated into Italian and published by Minori Cappuccini, a franciscan publishing house, under the title, *La religione e le donne sicule americane*. The little book has been distributed by the franciscan family periodical *il focolare: mensile della famiglia* in Sicily as part of the postconciliar enterprise of recovering the religious beliefs of the people. The research was also the basis of an invited paper, "Religious and Political Beliefs of Sicilian and Sicilian American Women, 1890–Present," for the conference of the American Historical Association, San Francisco, 30 December 1983, session of the Immigration History Society, "Sicilians and Sicilian Americans."
20. See Chapter 16, this work.
21. Giovanni Verga's *La lupa* was published in 1880. See Giovanni Cecchetti, *The She-wolf and other Stories*, 2nd ed. (Berkeley and Los Angeles, 1973).

    She was tall, thin; she had the firm and vigorous breasts of the olive-skinned— and yet she was no longer young; she was pale, as if always plagued by malaria, and in that pallor, two enormous eyes, and fresh red lips which devoured you.
    In the village they called her the She-wolf, because she never had enough—of anything. The women made the sign of the cross when they saw her pass, alone as a wild bitch, prowling about suspiciously like a famished wolf; with her red lips she sucked the blood of their sons and husbands in a flash, and pulled them behind her skirt with a single glance of those devilish eyes, even if they were before the altar of Saint Agrippina. Fortunately, the She-wolf never went to church, not at Easter, not at Christmas, not to hear Mass, not for confession.— Father Angiolino of Saint Mary of Jesus, a true servant of God, had lost his soul on account of her. (P. 3)

22. See Chapter 12, this work. See also Judith Jeffrey Howard, "Patriot Mothers in the Post Risorgimento," in Carol R. Berkin and Clara M. Lovett, eds., *Women, War, and Revolution* (New York, 1980).
23. See Bibliographical Essay, this work.
24. Sciascia, *La Sicilia*, 37ff. Compare Marina Warner, *Sola fra le donne: Mito e culto di Maria Vergine* (Palermo, 1976).
25. Di Stasi, *Mal Occhio*, chap. 4.
26. Salomone-Marino, *Costumi*, 172, 26–28, 40–41, 31, 34, 35, 19.
27. Ibid., 9; Serafino Amabile Guastella, *Le parità morali* (1883), 205, chap. 24.
28. Guastella, *Le parità morali*, 205, chap. 24. See Lucia Chiavola Birnbaum, Sicilian Women on the Eve of Emigration: Images in the Literature of Verga, Capuana, Pitré, and Sicilian Folklore, Paper delivered at the Conference of the California

Chapters of the American Studies Association, San Jose State University, 25 February 1979. Also Lucia Chiavola Birnbaum, Political Economy of Oppression and Folklore Nurturing Rebellion: Sicily in the 1890s, Paper delivered at the Spring Conference, West Coast Association of Women Historians, Mills College, Oakland, 21 April 1979.

29. See Charles Tilly, Louise Tilly, and Richard Tilly, *The Rebellious Century, 1830–1930*, chap. 3, "Italy" (Cambridge, Mass. 1975). See also Eleanor S. Riemer and John C. Fout, eds., *European Women: A Documentary HIstory, 1789–1945*, with an English language bibliography (New York, 1980).

30. E. J. Hobsbawm, *Primitive Rebels: Studies in Archaic Forms of Social Movements in the 19th and 20th Centuries* (New York 1959), chap. 6. The statement of the peasant socialist woman is printed in full in Appendix 5, 183.

31. Ibid.

32. Quoted in Tilly, *Rebellious Century*, 101.

33. Ibid., 102.

34. See Chapter 9.

35. A good description of working conditions for women in the Italy of this period can be found in Teresa Noce's autobiographical novel, *gioventù senze sole* (Rome, 1973), 15–36. See also "Organizing a women's union, Italy, 1903" in Riemer and Fout, *European Women*, 27. For legislation that fixed the characterization of "weaker sex" on women, see Annamaria Galoppini, *Il lungo viaggio verso la parità: i diritti civili e politici delle donne dall'unità ad oggi* (Bologna, 1980), 1–67.

36. Noce, *gioventù*, 86–98.

37. Ibid.   38. Ibid., 99–121   39. Ibid., 99.   40. Ibid., 98–121.

41. Frederick Engels in *The Origin of the Family*, quoted in *The Woman Question: Selections from the Writings of Karl Marx, Frederick Engels, V. I. Lenin, Joseph Stalin* (New York, 1951).

42. Engels, *Origin of the Family*, quoted in *Woman Question*, 17ff.

43. Engels, *Origin of the Family*, quoted in *Woman Question*, 17.

44. Engels, *Origin of the Family*, quoted in *Woman Question*, 39.

45. See Chapter 12. Also see Luisa Abba et al., *coscienza di sfruttata* (Milan, 1972), 28–43.

46. An historical analysis of this subject from the perspective of a critical Italian feminist is that of Maria Antonietta Macciocchi, "Quelques themes autour du marxisme et des femmes," *Les femmes et leurs maitres* (Paris, 1978), 387–441. See also Bibliographical Essay, this work.

47. Anna Maria Mozzoni, *La liberazione della donna*, ed. Franca Pieroni Bortolotti (Milan, 1975), introduzione.

48. Mozzoni, "I socialisti . . ." in *La liberazione*, 214, 209, 216.

2   *donna, guerra, e rivoluzione:*
women, world war I, and revolution

1. See Tilly, Tilly, and Tilly, *Rebellious Century*. For the intellectual background of the prewar period, see E. M. Standing, *Maria Montessori: Her Life and Work* (New York, 1957). This catholic educator, whose influence has been profound in Italy and elsewhere, held the view that a child who is given "unlimited freedom to do right" prefers work to play, a view similar to that of libertarian feminists after 1968.

2. Tilly, *Rebellious Century*, chap. 3. See also James Joll, *The Anarchists* (New York,

1964), chap. 8. For a contemporary new left evaluation of anarchism, see Howard J. Ehrlich *et al.*, eds., *Reinventing Anarchy. What are Anarchists Thinking These Days?* (London, 1979). For contemporary Italian anarchism, see *bollettino del centro di documentazione anarchica* (Rome, spring, 1983) which lists relevant contemporary anarchist books.

3. For women's resistance to war, see Ravera, *Breve storia*, 80–116. See also Tilly, *Rebellious Century*, chap. 3.

4. Ravera, *Breve storia*, 88–90.

5. Jole Calapso, *Donne ribelli: un secolo di lotte femminili in Sicilia* (Palermo, 1980) 140–172.

6. Ravera, *Breve storia*, 90. See Tilly, *Rebellious Century*, 164–175.

7. Ravera, *Breve storia*, 91–99.

8. Calapso, *Donne ribelli*, 175–191.

9. Ravera, *Breve storia*, 93–97.

10. Marie Marmo Mullaney, "Alexandra Kollontai: The Female Revolutionary as Visionary," *Revolutionary Women: Gender and the Socialist Revolutionary Role*, (New York, 1983), 99–146. See also Esther Kingston-Mann, *Lenin and the Problem of Marxist Peasant Revolution* (New York, 1983).

11. For Luxemburg, see Mullaney, *Revolutionary Women*, 144–46. See also Ravera, *Breve storia*, 99–104, and Raya Dujanayevskaya, *Rosa Luxemburg, Women's Liberation, and Marx's Philosophy of Revolution* (Atlantic Highlands, N.J., 1982). In a careful study of the notebooks of Luxemburg and of Marx, Dujanayevskaya concludes that "his attack on colonialism, racism, as well as discrimination against women, is relentless." (184). Marx saw the possibility of new human relations emerging "from a new type of revolution" (190).

12. Ravera, *Breve storia*, 104.

13. Ibid., 104–7. Mullaney, *Revolutionary Women*, 89.

14. Mullaney, *Revolutionary Women*, 53–96.

15. Ibid.   16. Ibid., 89.

17. See chapter 16, "Workers Opposition," in Cathy Porter, *Alexandra Kollontai. The Lonely Struggle of the Woman who Defied Lenin* (New York, 1980).

18. Alexandra Kollontai, "The Workers' Opposition in Russia" (1921) reprinted in Branko Horvat, Mihailo Markovic, and Rudi Supek, eds., *A Reader of Self-Governing Socialism*, vol 1 (White Plains, New York, 1975). See review by Beatrice Farnsworth of *Aleksandra Kollontai: Socialism, Feminism and the Bolshevik Revolution* (Stanford, 1980) and Cathy Porter, *Alexandra Kollontai: The Lonely Struggle of the Woman Who Defied Lenin* (New York, 1980) in *Signs*, (Autumn 1981). Alexandra Kollontai, *Love of Worker Bees* (Chicago, Illinois, 1977) is important. See also Rose Glickman, *Russian Factory Women* (Berkeley, California, 1984).

19. Ravera, *Breve storia*, 117.

20. Antonio Gramsci, *Selections from the Prison Notebooks*, ed. and tr. Quintin Hoare and Geoffrey Nowell Smith. (New York, 1971).

21. Ibid.

22. See Martin Clark, *Antonio Gramsci and the Revolution that Failed* (New Haven, 1977).

23. See also Giuseppe Fiori, *Antonio Gramsci: Life of a Revolutionary.* (New York, 1973); Hugues Portelli, *Gramsci e la questione religiosa* (Milan, 1974); Anne Showstack Sassoon, *Approaches to Gramsci* (London, 1982); John Cammett, *Antonio Gramsci and the Origins of Italian Communism* (Stanford, California, 1967); and Eugene Genovese, "On Antonio Gramsci," *Studies on the Left* 7(1967):2. In chap. 4 of

Bellah and Hammond, *Varieties of Civil Religion*, Bellah analyzes Gramsci's view of religion not in the confessional sense "but in the secular sense of a unity of faith between a conception of the world and a corresponding norm of conduct" (89). (See 92 ff. for analysis of the "religious ground bass" of Italy mentioned in Preface, this work.)

3   *donne sotto fascismo:*
women under fascism

1. Tilly, Tilly, and Tilly, *Rebellious Century*, 164.
2. Ibid.   3. Ibid., 168.   4. Ibid., 168–69.
5. Ibid., 168–72.   6. Ibid., 176.
7. Alexander De Grand, *Italian Fascism: Its Origins and Development* (Lincoln, Nebraska, 1982), 23; cf. Palmiro Togliatti, *Lectures on Fascism* (New York, 1976). Fascist documents are reprinted in Charles F. Delzell, *Mediterranean Fascism, 1919–1945* (New York, 1970). See also Herman Finer, *Mussolini's Italy: A Classic Study of the Non-communist, One-party State* (first published 1935, reprinted New York, 1965) and Richard Webster, *The Cross and the Fasces* (Stanford, 1960).
8. Quoted in Tilly, Tilly, and Tilly, *Rebellious Century*, 190.
9. De Grand, *Italian Fascism*, 54ff.
10. Ibid.
11. De Grand, *Italian Fascism*, 90–91.
12. Roland Sarti, ed., *The Ax Within: Italian Fascism in Action* (New York, 1974), chapter 10. For Italian Jews, see Giorgio Bassani, *Il giardino dei Finzi-Contini* (Turin, 1962), a portrait that is balanced by Primo Levi's *If Not Now, When?* (New York, 1985). See also Chapter 4 of the present work.
13. Right Wing Women in France and Germany in the 1920s, Paper delivered at the Sixth Berkshire Conference on the History of Women, 1,2,3 June 1984, Smith College, Northampton, Mass. See "La legislazione fascista e la condizione femminile" in Annamaria Galoppini, *Il lungo viaggio verso la parità: I diritti civili e politici delle donne dall'unita ad oggi* (Bologna, 1980). See also Frank Rosengarten, *The Italian Anti-Fascist Press, 1919–1945* (Cleveland, Ohio, 1968).
14. Kari Elisabeth Borresen, *Natura e ruolo della donna in Agostino e Tommaso d'Aquino* (Assisi, 1979), is a critical study of catholic doctrine encouraged by the cittadella christiana at Assisi; see chapters "Agostino e la donna," "L'ordine della creazione," "La pena del peccato," "L'ordine della salvezza," and "I tre stati di vita della donna."
15. Borresen, *Natura e ruolo*, parte seconda, "L'ordine della creazione."
16. Ibid., "Antropologia e androcentrismo."
17. Camilla Ravera, *Breve storia*, 109.
18. Ravera's account of fascism is written from the standpoint of women. See also Denis Mack Smith, *Mussolini: A Biography* (New York, 1983), 159–160, 161, 209–10. For a discussion of catholic women's associations by an Italian feminist scholar, see Paola Di Cori, "Storia, sentimenti, solidarietà nelle organizzazioni femmili cattoliche dall'età giolittiana al fascismo," *donnawomanfemme*, January-June 1979. For an analysis of an important aspect of fascist culture, see Victoria De Grazia, *The Culture of Consent: Mass Organization of Leisure in Fascist Italy* (Cambridge, 1981). Also Victoria De Grazia, "Il fascino del priapo: Margherita Sarfatti biografa del duce," *memoria*, June 1982.
19. Quoted in Ravera, *Breve storia*, 129–30.

20. Ibid., "La donna italiana durante il fascismo."
21. All salaries declined in the fascist era, but the difference between men's and women's salaries was sharp. Italian women in the 1930s earned on average one-half of the salary men received for the same work. See Ravera, *Breve storia*, "La donna italiana durante il fascismo."
22. Smith, *Mussolini*, 160.
23. Ibid.
24. Smith, *Mussolini*, 159–63.
25. Maria Antonietta Macciocchi, *La donna 'nera', 'consenso' femminile e fascismo* (Milan, 1976), chap. 4.
26. Ibid. See also Oria Gargano, "Le signore d'Italia," *effe*, July/August 1982, whose descriptions of women who supported fascism are similar to Iris Origo's description of them as the "smart young women" who frequented the Hotel Excelsior in Rome (see chapter 4, this work).
27. Smith, *Mussolini*, 210.
28. Smith, *Mussolini*, 160.
29. Calapso, *Donne ribelli*, 197–98.
30. Ibid., 195–224.
31. Discussion in the session on Resistance and Revolution, Conference of the Western Association of Women Historians, 12 May 1985.
32. Calapso, 200, 206–223.
33. Elio Vittorini, *In Sicily* (New York, 1949), 81. This parable not only reverses the Sicilian theme of the mother looking for her son but has the son, instead of asking something of his mother, listen to her views.
34. See discussion of the gnostic gospels, Chapter 9 of the present work.

4   *resistenza:*
resistance

1. Iris Origo, *An Italian War Diary, 1943–1944* (1947; reprinted in Boston, 1984), introduction, preface, 13.
2. Ibid. See also Rosengarten, *Italian Anti-Fascist Press:* "Of all the countries ruled by rightist totalitarian regimes, Italy was the one in which the forces of resistance waged the most successful and organized campaign in both a political and a military sense" (xv).
3. Origo, *Italian War Diary*, 37.
4. James D. Wilkinson, *The Intellectual Resistance in Europe* (Cambridge, Massachusetts, 1981), pt. 3, "Italy."
5. Origo, *Italian War Diary*, 40.
6. Ibid., 49.   7. Ibid., 77.
8. Ibid., 83. Toward the end of the war enlistments were obtained under the threat of deportation to Germany (89).
9. Origo, *Italian War Diary*, 93.
10. Ibid., 96.
11. Ivo Herzer, Italy and the Jews, World War II, Paper read at Conference of the American Italian Historical Association, Washington D. C., 11 November 1984. See also Andrew M. Canepa, "Reflections on Antisemitism in Liberal Italy," *Wiener Library Bulletin* n.s., vol. 30, 47/48 (1978).
12. Origo, *Italian War Diary*, 144.
13. Ibid., 186.   14. Ibid., 222–23.

15. Herzer, Italy and the Jews.
16. Ibid.
17. P. Levi, *If Not Now When?*, 324.
18. Ibid., 325.
19. Jane Slaughter, Women's Politics and Women's Culture: The Case of Women in the Italian Resistance, Paper read at the Sixth Berkshire Conference on the History of Women, 3 June 1984, Smith College, Northampton, Massachusetts.
20. Ibid.   21. Ibid.
22. Ravera, *Breve storia*, "Il secondo Risorgimento."
23. Slaughter, Women's Politics.
24. Communication from Margherita Repetto Alaia, 13 December 1984. See Maria Michetti, Margherita Repetto and Luciana Viviani, *l'Udi: laboratorio di politica delle donne: Idee e materiali per una storia* (Rome, 1985). Also Vania Chiurlotto, "Una memoria amorosa," *noidonne*, July 1984.
25. Communication from Margherita Repetto Alaia, 13 December 1984. See also Margherita Repetto Alaia, The Unione Donne Italiane: Women's Liberation and the Italian Workers Movement, 1945–1980, Paper read at the Sixth Berkshire Conference on the History of Women, 3 June 1984, Smith College, Northampton, Massachusetts.
26. Ravera, *Breve storia*, "Il contributo delle donne per la rinascità del paese."
27. See chapter 14 of this work.
28. Relevant Togliatti speeches and writings on women: to the Neapolitan communist cadres, 11 April 1944; "on socialism and democracy," *Rinascità*, April 1961; in Reggio Emilia, 24 September 1946; to the Eighth congress of the Pci, December 1956; to the ninth Congress of the Pci, 30 January to 4 February 1960; in parliament, *l'Unità*, 10 July 1963 (Reprinted in Peter Lange and Maurizio Vannicelli, eds., *The Communist Parties of Italy, France and Spain: Postwar Change and Continuity: A Casebook* [Birmingham, England, 1981]). Togliatti's speech of June 1945 at Rome, addressed to women, is discussed in Ravera, *Breve storia*, 172.
29. Roberto Battaglia, *Storia della resistenza italiana* (Turin, 1964) 492. See also Vincenzo Mauro, *Lotte contadine e repressione nel Sud*, Appendix:"rassegna della stampa 1943–1944" (Milan, 1979).
30. Ravera, *Breve storia*, "il secondo Risorgimento," 149–73.

5   *dopoguerra e l'Unione donne italiane:* the postwar era and the Italian women's union, 1945–68

1. An excellent analysis of postwar Italy can be found in Wilkinson, *Intellectual Resistance* chap. 8. A good analysis of Italian postwar groups is Joseph La Palombara, *Interest Groups in Italian Politics* (Princeton, New Jersey, 1964); for a U.S. cold war–view of Udi, see 133–39, 143, 144, 150, 151, 153, 211, 405ff.
2. Wilkinson, *Intellectual Resistance*, 237. See Elio Vittorini, *Uomini e No* (Rome, 1945); *A Vittorini Omnibus: In Sicily; The Twilight of the Elephant; La Garibaldina* (New York, 1960); *Erica e i suoi fratelli; La garibaldina* (Turin, 1975); and *Le donne di Messina* (Milan, 1974).
3. Ibid., 245. See Carlo Levi, *Cristo si è fermato a Eboli* (first published Rome, 1945), 1979 edition.
4. Ibid., 7.   5. Ibid., 103.   6. Ibid., 104–5.   7. Ibid., 106.
8. Wilkinson, *Intellectual Resistance* 246–50.

9. Ibid., 253. See Ignazio Silone, *Fontamara* (New York, 1934); *Bread and Wine* (New York, 1937); and *Emergency Exit* (London, 1969). See also Salvatore Quasimodo, *Tutte le poesie* (Rome, 1960).

10. Margherita Repetto Alaia, "Unione Donne Italiane."

11. For a helpful chronology, see "l'Udi anno per anno," *com-nuovi tempi*, 17 October 1982.

12. See chapter 17, this work. A good way to study the condition of women in the *dopoguerra* is to examine the literature of the period. See the collection of postwar stories by Italo Calvino, *Difficult Loves*, trans. William Weaver *et al.* (San Diego, New York, and London, 1984). Alberto Moravia's treatment of women was criticized by feminists of the seventies and eighties as sexist; see *La romana* (first published in 1947; Milan, 1980). See the works of Natalia Ginsburg for a woman's perspective: *La strada che va in città* (Turin, 1942); *È stato così* (Turin, 1947); *Valentino* (Turin, 1957); *Ti ho sposato per allegria e altre commedie* (Turin, 1966). *The Advertisement* (1968) may be found in the anthology *Plays by and about Women*, ed. Victoria Sullivan and James Hatch (New York, 1973). Ginzburg was born in 1916 in Palermo. Her writings offer a cultural history of Italy since the 1940s. She is, in the 1980s, an independent left member of the Italian parliament.

13. Margherita Repetto Alaia, Unione Donne Italiane.

14. Ibid.

15. Miriam Mafai, *L'apprendistato della politica: le donne italiane nel dopoguerra* (Rome, 1979), 109, 115.

16. Ravera, *Breve storia*, 97ff.

17. "l'Udi anno per anno," *com-nuovi tempi*, 17 October 1982.

18. Communication from Margherita Repetto Alaia, 13 December 1984. See Michetti, Repetto, and Viviani, *l'udi*, chap. 8.

19. l'Udi anno per anno," *com-nuovi tempi*.

20. M. Mafai, *L'apprendistato*, 27.

21. M. Mafai, "La speranza e la fame," in *L'apprendistato*.

22. *noidonne 1944–1945, ristampa*, (Rome, 1978).

23. Lucia C. Birnbaum, "Women writers who have 'broken the sequence' in the recent history of Italian feminism, with particular attention to the Italian feminist press," *Proceedings*, International Symposium on Women Writers, Wellesley College, Wellesley, Massachusetts 2 May 1981.

24. la stampa femminista: *noi donne*, Paper read at the Conferenza sulla Storia, Biografia, Sociologia, University of Rome, 3–5 November 1981.

25. See Ravera, *Breve storia*, "Il contributo delle donne per la rinascità del paese."

26. M. Mafai, *L'apprendistato*, 185. For the postwar southern agrarian question, see Paul Ginsborg, "The Communist Party and the Agrarian Question in Southern Italy, 1943–48," *History Workshop*, Spring 1984. See 88ff. for the wave of peasant agitation that swept the South as the war ended. Peasant efforts, according to this analysis, were thwarted by the Pci policy of moderation, by the Allied hostility to social change, and by "fierce and hysterical resistance on the part of landowners" (93).

27. Ginsborg, *Agrarian Question*, 94–95.

28. Ibid, 100. A good analysis of the Dc is that of Mario Einaudi and Francois Goguel, *Christian Democracy in Italy and France* (First published in 1952. Reprint ed. South Bend, Indiana, 1969).

29. Michetti, Repetto, and Viviani, *l'udi*, pts. 4, 7, 8, 9, and 10.

30. J. Derek Holmes, *The Papacy in the Modern World 1914–1978* (New York, 1981), 174.
31. Ravera, *Breve storia*, 221.
32. Ibid.
33. Frederic Spotts and Theodor Wieser, *Italy: A Difficult Democracy* (New York, 1986), chap. 3.
34. Udi women would remember this when another peace movement arose in the late 1970s and early 1980s and some, at first, would consider work for peace incompatible with women's issues.
35. Interviews with Udi activists, October 1980.
36. Ibid.
37. See chapter 6, this work.
38. Grant Amyot, *The Italian Communist Party: The Crisis of the Popular Front Strategy.* (New York, 1981), 30–49. Compare Palombara; Spotts and Wieser; Ravera; and Michetti, Repetto, and Viviani.
39. Amyot, *Italian Communist Party*, 31ff.
40. Ibid., chap. 2.   41. Ibid.   42. Quoted in ibid., 54.
43. Ibid., 54–59.   44. Ibid., chap. 3.

6   *liberazione della donna e degli altri: segni dei tempi:* liberation of women and of others: signs of the times

1. Giancarlo Zizola, *L'utopia di Papa Giovanni*, seconda edizione (Assisi, 1974). "Come è nata la Pacem in terris," 16–44; "il papa della periferia."
2. Zizola, *L'utopia*, 17, 27.
3. Ibid., 29, 33–34.   4. Ibid., 35, 38–39, 40, 43.
5. Quoted in the exhibit Jews of Germany under Prussian Rule, sponsored by the Bildarchiv Preussischer Kulturbesitz, Berlin, in cooperation with the Leo Baeck Institute, New York. Quotation may be found in the unpaged booklet accompanying the exhibit at the Jewish Community Museum, San Francisco, California, May 12–August 25, 1985.
6. Thomas Sheehan, "Revolution in the Church," review of Hans Küng, *Eternal Life? Life after Death as a Medical, Philosophical, and Theological Problem* (New York, 1984), in the *New York Review of Books*, 14 June 1984.
7. Ibid.
8. Ibid. A good example of contemporary liberal biblical criticism from a woman's perspective is Fiorenza, *In Memory of Her.*
9. Two recent feminist theological studies that incorporate this perspective are Elizabeth Schussler Fiorenza, *Bread Not Stone: The Challenge of Feminist Biblical Interpretation* (Boston, 1984) and Rosemary Radford Ruether, *Womanguides: Readings Toward a Feminist Theology* (Boston, 1985).
10. Jean Marie Aubert, *La donna: antifemminismo e cristianesimo* (Assisi, 1978).
11. Ibid., capitolo sesto, "la donna interpella la chiesa," 171ff.
12. Zizola, *L'utopia*, 153–56. See also *The Documents of Vatican II* [Sixteen official texts promulgated by the ecumenical council 1963–1965], ed. Walter M. Abbott, S.J. (Piscataway, New Jersey, 1966).
13. Zizola, *L'utopia*, 359–61, capitolo quarto, capitolo nono.
14. Giulio Girardi's books were translated into French, English, German, Portuguese, Spanish, Catalan, and Japanese. In Italy they were published by the franciscan

cittadella christiana at Assisi, important center of support for feminist issues. Girardi's books found a wide audience in the Italy of the late sixties, seventies, and eighties. Topics included: marxism and christianity, believers and nonbelievers for a new world, christianity as human liberation, education for which society?, christians for socialism, and contemporary atheism. The books sold in multiple editions. The context for 1968 in Italy is suggested by Girardi's *Credenti e non credenti per un mondo nuovo* (believers and nonbelievers for a new world) which was written in 1968, published in 1969.

15. Giulio Girardi, *Credenti e non credenti per un mondo nuovo* (Assisi, terza edizione, 1976).

16. Girardi, *Credenti*, 81

17. Ibid, 193–208.   18. Ibid, 180–90.

19. Ibid, "Dialogo e rivoluzione," 209–72.

20. Ibid, 240.   21. Ibid, 234.   22. Ibid, 146.

23. Ibid, "Prospettive del dialogo," 256–72.

24. Gian Enrico Rusconi and Sergio Scamuzzi, "Trend Report: Italy: An Eccentric Society" in *Italy Today: An Eccentric Society* (International Sociological Association: 1981).

25. Ibid, 20.   26. Ibid, 27.

27. Ibid, 28. See also Amyot, *Italian Communist Party.*

28. S. S. Acquaviva and M. Santuccio, *Social Structure in Italy: Crisis of a System.* (Boulder, Colorado, 1976), 81–84, 101–10.

29. Ibid, 25. See also Ann Cornelisen, *Strangers and Pilgrims: The Last Italian Migration* (New York, 1980).

30. Acquaviva and Santuccio, *Social structure*, 83. See also Giorgio Galli and Alessandra Nannei, *Il capitalismo assistenziale: ascesa e declino del sistema economico italiano 1960–1975* (Milan, 1976).

31. See Corriere del Friuli, *Pasolini in Friuli, 1943–1949* (Udine, 1976).

32. Enzo Siciliano, *Pasolini: A biography,* trans. John Shepley (New York 1982), 81.

33. Ibid, 91.   34. Ibid, 106.   35. Ibid, 118.

36. Ibid, 136–39.   37. Ibid, 162.   38. Ibid, 211.

39. Ibid, 226. For Pasolini films, see Claudia G. Fava and Aldo Vigano, *The Films of Federico Fellini* (Secaucus, New Jersey, 1981).

40. Ibid, 266. See also Pier Paolo Pasolini, *Le ceneri di Gramsci: poemetti* (Turin 1957, reprint ed. Turin, 1981) and Pasolini, *Una vita violenta* (Rome, 1959). Dacia Maraini has chronicled this period from a woman's perspective in *La vacanza: l'adolescenza di una donna-oggetto* (Milan, 1962).

41. Maraini, *La vacanza,* 271. See Giuseppe Angione, *La città del sole: realtà e sogno di un bracciante,* ed. Giovanni Rinaldi e Paola Sobrero (Foggia, 1982), for documentation of Pasolini's insight about the hidden utopian dreams of peasants. In Angione's utopian anarcho-communism, Jesus loses his divine attributes to become a revolutionary organizer for an equalitarian society.

42. See Autori vari, *Per Pasolini* (Milan, 1982) for a collection of essays by Italians about what Pasolini's life meant to them. Oriana Fallaci's "Lettera a Pier Paolo" is particularly perceptive, referring to Pasolini's conversations with her about Jesus and Saint Francis (p. 14). In the lengthy list of Pasolini's work, these are especially relevant to this study: *Poesie a Casarsa* (Bologna, 1942); *Le ceneri di Gramsci* (Turin, 1957); *L'usignolo della Chiesa Cattolica* (Milan, 1958); *Ragazzi di vita* (Milan, 1955); *Passione e ideologia* (Milan, 1960). Among the Pasolini films, see

Accattone (Rome, 1961); *La commare secca* (Milan, 1962); *Il Vangelo secondo Matteo* (Milan, 1964); *Edipo re* (Milan, 1967); *Medea* (Milan, 1970); *Ostia* (Milan, 1971); *San Paolo* (Turin, 1977).

7   *sessantotto:*
1968

1. For the extraparliamentary left, see Luigi Bobbio, *Lotta continua: storia di una organizzazione rivoluzionaria: Dalla fondazione del partito al congresso di 'autoscioglimento' di Rimini* (Rome, 1979). For the new left political party Pdup, see Marco Calabria, Michele Melillo, Gianni Riotta, eds., *Le interviste del manifesto 1971/1982* (Roma, 1983). See also Herbert Marcuse, *One Dimensional Man: Studies in the Ideology of Advanced Industrial Society* (Boston, 1964).
2. See Marina Romello, ed., *La stregoneria in Europa,* (Bologna, 1975). Women (and a few men) were accused of witchcraft and persecuted in Italy in the fourteenth, fifteenth, and sixteenth centuries. Witchcraft was identified with the "feminine element," with the allusion that witches engaged in sexual union with demons. The area of catholic witch persecution extended from northern Italy to northern Spain, to France, Holland, Bohemia, and Poland. In the period of the protestant reformation, Luther and Calvin exhibited a similar zeal against witches. (See *La stregoneria,* introduzione. See also Jeffrey B. Russell, *A History of Witchcraft: Sorcerers, Heretics and Pagans* (London, 1980). See discussion of Margaret Murray's 1921 work, *Witch-Cult in Western Europe,* in which she argued that European witchcraft was an ancient fertility religion based on worship of the horned god Dianus. Anton Meyer has argued that the ancient fertility religion emphasized the earth goddess more than the horned god (pp. 40 ff). Compare Giorgio Galli, *Storia del socialismo italiano* (Rome and Bari, 1980) "Le streghe e la storia." See also chapter 17, this work. For the church and heretics and witches, see Cecil Roth, *The Spanish Inquisition* (New York, 1964).
3. Anna Riva, *La rabbia femminista* (Rome, 1981), 1.
4. Ibid., 1–21.   5. Ibid., 54–57.
6. Dario Fo, *Morte accidentale di un anarchico. Accidental death of an anarchist: a farce* (London, 1980).
7. Riva, 55.
8. The quotation regarding caring is found in Riva, 60.
9. For contemporary communist epistemology, see chapter 17, this work. Also see Ignazio Silone, *Emergency Exit* (London, 1969).
10. See chapter 8, this work.   11. See chapter 10, this work.
12. Lonzi, *Sputiamo,* 57. See also Abba *et al., La coscienza,* for feminist essays emphasizing "the limits of reason," "hidden antagonism," and an analysis of Proudhon, Fourier, Marx and Engels, Bebel, and Lenin in light of feminist concerns. The role of women under fascism and nazism and the connection of racism and sexism are examined. See also Lieta Harrison, *La donna sposata: mille mogli accusano* (Milan, 1972), an investigation of women of Milan, Rome, and Palermo on the realities behind the Dc slogan "la famiglia italiana." Harrison was born in Ragusa of a Sicilian father and English mother and brings a marginal, perceptive view to the subject.

8 *femminismo e rivoluzione:* feminist cultural and political revolution

1. For Italy in the seventies and the eighties, two indispensable books are Spotts and Wieser, *Italy: A Difficult Democracy* and Galli and Nanei, *Il capitalismo assistenziale.*

2. Adriana Sartogo, ed., *Le donne al muro: L'immagine femminile nel manifesto politico italiano 1945/77.* (Rome, 1977). See preface and chapter 8. See also Galoppini, *Il lungo viaggio,* chapter 7. For health clinics and abortion legislation, see Liliana Barca *et al., Chi ha paura del consultorio* (Rome, 1981) and *Aborto: Norme per la tutela sociale della maternità e sull'interruzione volontaria della gravidanza* (Perugia, 1978). See Julienne Travers, *10 donne anticonformiste* (Bari, 1968), for changing attitudes of Italian women as revealed in interviews. An early anthology of feminist writings is that edited by Lidia Menapace, *Per un movimento politico di liberazione della donna: Saggi e documenti* (Verona, 1972); this is an important source because it contains essays by U.S. and other world feminists, as well as a provocative essay by Menapace suggesting that emancipation is not an adequate feminist aim. An account of an encounter between the U.S. feminist Betty Friedan and Italian feminists highlights differing assumptions. A helpful study that places Italian feminists in European context is Vera Squarcialupi, *Donne in Europa* (Rome, 1979). Surveys of the topic include a Rai television program on the history of feminism by Ginevra Conti Odorisio, *Storia dell'idea femminista in Italia* (Roma, 1980), and a social anthropological study of women in the city by Matilde Callari Galli, *Il tempo delle donne* (Bologna, 1979). Among memoirs, see Laura Gemini, *Dossier di una femminista* (Milan, 1973). For collections of interviews, see Guido Gerosa, *Le compagne: Venti protagoniste delle lotte del Pci dal Comintern a oggi narrano la loro storia* (Milan, 1979). For collections of documents, see *Per l'emancipazione della donna: 3 anni di lavoro, di dibattito, di lotta,* ed. Sezione Femminile del Pci (Rome, 1976), which is particularly good for differing views of feminism by women within the Pci. See also the Bibliographical Essay in the present work.

3. A helpful chronology, with numbers of people in demonstrations, etc., is "Sessant'anni: il nostro cammino" in *donne e politica,* January–February, 1981. See chapter 17, this work.

4. Spotts and Wieser, *Italy,* chap. 2. See also *Italy at the Polls, 1979: A Study of the Parliamentary Elections* (Washington, D. C., and London, 1981), chap. 3 by Douglas A. Wertman on the Dc, chap. 4 by Joseph LaPalombara on the Pci, chap. 5 by Gianfranco Pasquino on the Psi, chap. 6 by Robert Leonardi on the smaller parties, and chap. 9 by Karen Beckwith, "Women and Parliamentary Politics in Italy, 1946–1979."

5. Spotts and Wieser, *Italy,* chap. 2. For women in the Dc, see analyses of Cif conferences in chapter 13 of this work. For the convergence of feminist and catholic women on the subject of family rights and the rights of illegitimate children, see "I figli illegittimi: l'amara 'storia' del piccolo Luca," *il focolare: mensile della famiglia,* April 1975.

6. Spotts and Wieser, *Italy,* chap. 2.

7. Possibly the best interpreter of the Dc is Gianni Baget-Bozzo, a priest who shifted from catholic activism in the Dc to liberation theology and the political left. See his *Il partito cristiano e l'apertura a sinistra: la Dc di Fanfani di Moro, 1954–1962.* (Florence, 1977), his *Questi cattolici, la Dc, la Chiesa, la coscienza religiosa*

1962. (Florence, 1977), his *Questi cattolici, la Dc, la Chiesa, la coscienza religiosa davanti alla crisi contemporanea* (Rome, 1979), and his *Tesi sulla Dc: rinasce la questione nazionale* (Bologna, 1980).

8. Spotts and Wieser, *Italy*, chap. 2.

9. See chapter 17, this work.

10. See Leonardo Sciascia, *L'affaire Moro* (Palermo, 1978). Pr, which urged negotiation with the red brigades to save Moro's life, secured an all-time high vote in 1979 (3.5 percent).

11. Spotts and Wieser, *Italy*, chap. 3.

12. Ibid. See essays by Aldo Garosci in *Communism in Western Europe*, ed. Mario Einaudi, Jean-Marie Domenach, and Aldo Garosci (Ithaca, New York, 1951. Reprint ed. 1971).

13. Spotts and Wieser, *Italy*, chap. 3. See also Carl Marzani, *The Promise of Eurocommunism*, Introduction by John Cammett (Westport, Connecticut, 1980).

14. See chapter 17, this work.

15. Spotts and Wieser, *Italy*, chap. 3; cf. Carl Boggs and David Plotke, eds., *The Politics of Eurocommunism: Socialism in Transition* (Boston, 1980). For the Pci at a local level, see Max Jaggi, Roger Muller, and Sil Schmid, *Red Bologna* (London, 1977). For the Pci and the catholic church, see "The Church and The Party: Documents on the Catholic-Communist Dialogue in Italy," *Marxist Perspectives*, Fall 1979.

16. Joanne Barkan, *Visions of Emancipation: The Italian Workers' Movement Since 1945* (New York, 1984), interview with Diego Novelli.

17. See chapter 14, this work. See also *Noi Donne 1944–1945, ristampa,* (Rome, 1978).

18. See chapter 17, this work. See programs of *feste nazionale delle donne*; for example, the women's festival in September 1979 at Palermo featured play space with a puppet show for children, an African percussion band, an open debate on women in Italian society with women of the Pci, Udi, Pdup, Psi, and Dc and an independent feminist. Discussion of the referendum on sexual violence was conducted by women of the Pci, the Psi, Udi, and the independent feminist organization Mld. Poetry was presented by Latin American women, women's health clinics were discussed, and the first woman to head the house of deputies, Nilde Jotti, met the press. Evolution of the women's movement is suggested by comparing the 1979 festival program with one of 1976; the earlier women's festival stressed political rather more than cultural change, and there were more men interpreters: see *festival nazionale de l'unità per la donna*, La Spezia 17–25 July 1976.

19. Spotts and Wieser, *Italy*, chap. 4.

20. Ibid., chap. 5.

21. Carla Lonzi, *Sputiamo su Hegel. La Donna Clitoridea e la donna vaginale. e altri scritti di Rivolta Femminile,1, 2, 3* (1970), 29.

22. Communication from Margherita Repetto Alaia, 13 December 1984.

23. *L'altra chiesa in Italia*, a cura di Arnaldo Nesti (Rome, 1970).

24. For the family rights law see Ravera, *Breve storia*, 331–49. For Ravera's appointment as senator for life, see "Carissima Camilla," *noidonne* 22, January 1982. See also "Partigiane della libertà," *donne e politica.* January–February 1981.

25. Communication from Margherita Repetto Alaia, 13 December 1984.

26. "La donna clitoridea e la donna vaginale" in Lonzi, *Sputiamo.* Among the reasons this essay shocked some bystanders was that it featured drawings of male and female genitalia. This essay analyzed the roots of woman's subordination to the

traditional sexual act, wherein woman is passive, man's supremacy is considered "natural," and patriarchy is thereby given its major support. "The vaginal woman is the carrier of this culture: she is the woman of the patriarchy and the source of every maternal myth, a woman slave who transmits the chains of subjection rendering secure masculine domination in every historical change" (p. 140 in the 1974 edition).

27. Fausta Cecchini *et al.*, *Sesso amaro, trentamila donne rispondono su maternità sessualità aborto*, (Rome, 1977). For an analysis of the abortion law by the Pci woman who carried it through parliament, see Simona Mafai, "Una vittoria delle donne e delle democrazia," *donne e politica*, January–February 1978.

28. Yasmin Ergas, "1968–79—Feminism and the Italian Party System: Women's Politics in a Decade of Turmoil," *Comparative Politics*, April 1982. This is an important evaluation of the movement for the period noted, reflecting some of the pessimism of the late seventies. Ergas's analysis is excellent for documenting the sharp decline in membership of catholic women's associations: "With the decline of female membership in *Azione Catttolica* (from 1963 to 1969 women's enrollment fell 66.8 percent—from a total of 1,895,000 to 630,000), female registration in the Christian Democratic party suffered proportionately" (257–58). Ergas's explanation for the eruption of the feminist movement in the late sixties stresses the importance of the first generation of women who had reached maturity and a high level of education after the guarantee of equality in the 1948 constitution. Ergas also emphasizes the significance for feminist consciousness of the accessibility of new contraceptive methods and the university setting for feminist revolt; she cites the rise in the percentage of women in the universities from 26.5 in 1952–53 to 36.1 in 1967–68 (276).

29. Barkan, *Visions of Emancipation*, 34ff.

30. Interviews with Italian women, 1979–1983. See chap. 16, n. 4, this work.

31. See "Creatività," *effe*, July–August, 1974.

32. Documento del comitato per l'aborto e la contraccezione," *effe*, June 1975. See also Lidia Menapace "L'autogestione è il nostro obiettivo," *effe*, September 1975.

33. See "I nostri lavori forzati," *effe*, October–November 1975.

34. "Denuncia la violenza contro le donne," *effe*, October–November 1975. For *effe*, see Birnbaum, "Women writers." See also Marella Regoli, La stampa femminista: *effe*, Paper read at the Conferenza sulla Storia, Biografia, Sociologia, University of Rome, 3–5 November 1981.

35. *Lessico politico delle donne: teorie del femminismo* (Milan, 1978), 95.

36. See collection of documents in *La politica del femminismo: il movimento femminista, l'Unione delle donne italiane, le forze politiche di sinistra di fronte al femminismo nei documenti (1973–76)* (Rome, 1978).

37. Ibid.

38. See Noce's autobiography, *gioventò senza sole*. See also Erica Scroppo, *Donna, privato e politico: storie personali di 21 donne del Pci* (Milan, 1979), "Teresa Noce."

39. Scroppo, *Donna*, "Angela Migliasso."

40. Ibid., "Grazia Zuffa."

41. Ibid., "Fiamma Nirenstein."

42. Ibid., "Daniela Baccaci."

43. Ibid., "Anna Casella."

44. Ibid., "Angela Francese."

45. Ibid., "Giovanna Filippini."

46. Ibid., "Maria Grazia Gianmarinaro."
47. Ibid., "Livia Turco." See also Laura Lilli and Chiara Valentini, *Care compagne: il femminismo nel Pci e nelle organizzazione di massa* (Rome, 1979), and Simonetta Piccone Stella, *Ragazze del sud* (Rome, 1979).
48. Barkan, *Visions of Emancipation*, 140–41.

9 *cattoliche, credenti, e femministe:* catholics, believers, and feminists

1. This chapter was originally presented to the Third WHOM Conference on the History of Women, 30 April–2 May 1982, College of St. Catherine, St. Paul, Minnesota. In an earlier form, it was published in the *Stanford Italian Review,* Spring 1983. See Bibliographical Essay for extensive bibliography pertaining to this chapter.
2. See accounts in Lilli and Valentini, *Care compagne.* See also "sacro e profano" issue of *memoria,* November 1982 (e.g., Paolo Di Cori, "Rosso e bianco: la devozione al Sacro Cuore di Gesù nel primo dopoguerra.") Arnaldo Nesti, *Una cultura del privato: morfologia e significato della stampa devozionale italiana* (Turin, 1980), is a study of catholic devotional literature.
3. See account of Mary Magdalen in Elaine Pagels, *The Gnostic Gospels* (New York, 1979), and in part 2 of Fiorenza, *In Memory of Her.* The study of the gnostic gospels today is in part an excavation endeavor; e.g., Gilles Quispel has discovered an "other" Jesus in the gnostic gospels, one whose sayings resemble Zen koans and seem to imply psychoanalytic wisdom (Jesus said, "If you do not bring forth what is within you, what you do not bring forth will destroy you."). See Elaine Pagels, *The Gnostic Gospels* (New York, 1979) Introduction, xv, xvii, xix, xxxv, 25, 57, 60–61, 73.
4. See chapter 17, this work.
5. Dacia Maraini, "Quale cultura per la donna," in *Donna, cultura e tradizione,* ed. Pia Bruzzichelli and Maria Luisa Algini (Milan, 1976), 62.
6. Ibid., 60–66. See Di Cori, "Storia, sentimenti, solidarietà." Marina Terragni, *Vergine e piena di grazia: la donna secondo la pubblicistica di Santa Romana Chiesa* (Milan, 1981), a study of the role of women in the official press of the church.
7. Maraini, "Quale cultura," 63. See also Aubert, *La donna.*
8. Maraini, "Quale cultura," 64.
9. Ibid.   10. Ibid.
11. Bruzzichelli and Algini, *Donna, cultura e tradizione,* 7, 15.
12. Roberta Fossati, *E Dio creò la donna: Chiesa, religione e condizione femminile* (Milan, 1977).
13. Alfredo Fierro, *introduzione alle teologie politiche* (Assisi, 1974). See Bibliographical Essay for other works of liberation theology.
14. Lidia Menapace, "una fase di precarietà," in *I cattolici e la sinistra: dibattito aperto* (Assisi, 1977), 19–23.
15. Ibid., 23–25.
16. Ibid. Also "Maturità non è autosufficienza" in Menapace, *I cattolici,* 99–104.
17. Ibid., 103.
18. Ibid. See also "Cuba: l'ultimo idolo infranto" in *Quale socialismo? Dibattito aperto* (Assisi, 1980).
✓ 19. Franca Long and Rita Pierro, *L'altra metà della chiesa: essere femministe e cristiane* (Rome, 1981), introduzione.

20. Ibid., 97.   21. Ibid., 105.   22. Ibid., 109.
23. See chapter 17, this work.
24. Rossana Rossanda, "L'estinzione dello stato," in *Quale socialismo?*
25. Rossana Rossanda, *Le altre: conversazioni a Radiotrè sui rapporti tra donne e politica, libertà, fraternità, uguaglianza, democrazia, fascismo, resistenza, stato, partito, rivoluzione, femminismo* (Milan, 1979), chapter 12.
26. Claudio Santoro, "Il ruolo delle communità di base," in Menapace, *I cattolici*, 70. For comunità di base, *La Chiesa cresce dal basso* (Turin, 1976) and Sandro Magister, "Come ai tempi di Frate Leone," *L'Espresso*, 2 May 1982. For an analysis of these "new catholics," see Giovanni Bianchi and Renzo Salvi, "I nuovi cattolici: oltre il dissenso e oltre le sette," *rocca*, 15 December 1984.
27. For women, in this swing away from groups associated with the Dc, see analysis by Yasmin Ergas discussion in chapter 8, this work.
28. Santoro, "Il ruolo."
29. Ibid., 71.   30. Ibid., 72.
31. See comunità cristiana di base di piazza del Luogo Pio, Livorno, *Siamo Chiesa: Il cammino di una comunità nella riappropriazione dei sacramenti, com-nuovi tempi*/documenti 12, Supplemento a *com-nuovi tempo*, n. 27, 15 July 1979.
32. Ibid.
33. Conversations with Marcello Vigli, October–November 1983.
34. Four hundred cdb were represented at the national conference of cdb at Livorno in which I participated in December 1983. Magister, "Come ai tempi," analyzes a census of cdb sponsored by the Agnelli Foundation. More than 8,000 catholic base groups were counted involving 300,000 predominantly young people. Only 2 percent said they dissented from the church (they say, "we are church"). Their largest aggregation is in the Lombardy-Veneto area, a region formerly identified with the conservative church group Catholic Action. In the south of Italy *comunità ecclesiale di base* are more characteristic, representing clergy working alongside their parishioners for a better life, notably in work against all forms of violence—revolutionary violence, mafia violence, fascist violence, environmental violence, violence against women.
35. Mario Pancera, *Conversazioni con Bettazzi: la rivoluzione cattolica* (Vicenza, 1978).
36. See Fiorenza, *In Memory of Her*, for feminine presence in early christianity; also Pagels, *Gnostic Gospels*, Introduction and chap. 3.
37. See Robert Bellah's discussion of Italy's "real" religion, Preface, this work.
38. See Pancera, *Conversazioni con Bettazzi*, 10.
39. National conference of cdb, Livorno, December 1983.
40. Gianna Sciclone, "La sfida della teologia femminista," *idoc internazionale*, February 1982.
41. The waldensian church is the oldest extant protestant group in the world today, dating back to three hundred years before Luther. In 1979 waldensians were integrated with the methodist church in Italy in a synod that numbers circa twenty-five thousand adults in two hundred Italian communities. Waldensians are close to the beliefs of cdb and highly visible in movements against violence. The waldensian spirit converges with left catholic emphasis on an unedited gospel and the church of the poor of liberation theology. Waldo, a rich merchant of Lyons, France, on reading the gospel in 1174 determined to make the scriptures available in native languages and launched a movement of people who called themselves "the poor" in France and northern Italy and who were determined to live as apostles. They were excommunicated but not suppressed. In 1532 they

adhered to the Geneva Reformation in a confession of faith similar to Calvin's. *Com-nuovi tempi* is the best source for waldensian activity in Italy. See Giorgio Girardet *Protestanti perchè?* (Turin, 1983) and Giorgio Tourn, *I valdesi: la singolare vicenda di un popolo-chiesa* (Turin, 1977). The Jews of Italy were discussed in chapter 5 of this work. See also Edith Bruck, "Gli ebrei come le donne: un plurale oltraggioso," *noidonne*, August 1982 and Andrew Canepa, "Jews of Italy," manuscript in progress. P. Levi, *If Not Now, When?* is a true story of partisan Jews with an excellent discussion of Jews in Italy and the compatibility of their beliefs with those of Italian catholics (see discussion in chapter 5, this work).

42. "Against abortion—in defense of the law," *com-nuovi tempi supplemento*, 1981.
43. Ibid.
44. La famiglia: una tradizione cristiana che scompare," *il focolare: mensile della famiglia*, January 1982. See also "L'emancipazione della donna" in same edition of *il focolare* and "Vocazione in famiglia," *il focolare*, November–December 1981, and "Problemi della donna: le consulte femminili per un'autentica promozione della donna," *il focolare* November–December 1981.
45. Arnaldo Nesti ed., *L'altra chiesa in Italia*, (Rome, 1970).
46. Oliviereo Ferrari, "Preti operai: Una pagina di Vangelo a Lodi," *com-nuovi tempi*, 16 December 1984. See *dimensioni sacerdotali*, a priests' journal that reports on thinking and activities of *comunità di base*.
47. *Una chiesa senza preti? ricerca teologica sulla presenza dell'eucarestia promossa dalle comunità di base italiane* (Rome, 1981).
48. See Jose Ramos Regidor, " 'Pericolosi per la fede': Non piacciono al cardinale i teologi della liberazione," *il manifesto*, 19 April 1984. The anomalous nature of the Pci was highlighted in 1984–85 discussion of the pope's censure of liberation theology: the communist party defended liberation theologians who identify the message of Jesus with the resistance of the poor (see issues of *Rinascità* after September 1984). For cdb and papal censure of liberation theologies, see "Le comunità di base italiane contro il documento Ratzinger," *com-nuovi tempi*, 30 September 1984. See also Diana Johnstone, "New Inquisition on Liberation Theology," *In These Times*, Nov. 21–Dec. 4, 1984.
49. Adriana Zarri, *I guardiani del sabato: riflessioni sulla chiesa italiana dopo il referendum sull'aborto* (societa cooperativa *com-nuovi tempi*, 1981).
50. Zarri, "quasi una prefazione."
51. Ibid.   52. Ibid.
53. Zarri, *I guardiani*, 28ff.
54. Ibid, 30.
55. Zarri, *I guardiani*, 111–23.
56. Zarri, *I guardiani*, 129–33.
57. Zarri, *I guardiani*, 100–110. See "Adriana Zarri, Teologa" in evaluations of the papacy of John Paul II by several women in *com-nuovi tempi*, 23 October 1983.
58. Zarri, *I guardiani*, 100.
59. Adriana Zarri, *Nostro signore del deserto: teologia e antropologia della preghiera*. (Assisi, 1978).
60. Zarri, *Nostro signore*. For an example of the contemporary enterprise of recovering the actual beliefs held historically by Italians, see Birnbaum, *La religione*. See also Nesti, *Una cultura* and "The Five Religions of Modern Italy" in Bellah and Hammond, *Varieties of Civil Religion*. See also Bibliographical Essay, this work.
61. For Teresa, see Rosa Rossi, *Teresa d'Avila: Biografia di una scrittrice* (Rome, 1983). Also see Rossi's *Le parole delle donne* (Rome, 1978): "Teresa was one of the first

women to describe women's erotic experience . . . a woman who used language with such force that she can easily be placed alongside Kafka or Montaigne" (103–110); St. Teresa of Avila, *Collected Works*, 2 vols. (Washington, D. C., 1976 and 1980); E. Allison Peers, *Mother of Carmel: A Portrait of St. Teresa of Jesus* (Wilton, Connecticut, 1944); E. Alison Peers, trans. and ed., *The Way of Perfection: St. Teresa of Avila* (Garden City, N. Y., 1964); and *La monaca inquieta e disobbediente: edition of "Le Fondazioni" di S. Teresa d'Avila*, ed. Padri Carmelitani Scalzi della Provincia Veneta (1970). Also see chapter 3 in *Woman as Revolutionary*, ed. Frederick C. Giffin (New York, 1973) (for Teresa's statement about men in a crisis crumbling like dried parsley, see p. 43).

62. Rossi, *Teresa d'Avila*, and *Le parole. St Teresa of Avila. Collected Works.* 2 vols. (Washington, D. C., 1976 and 1980).
63. Rossi, *Teresa d'Avila*, 147.
64. Ibid., 184, 52.
65. Fiorenza, *In Memory of Her*, 105 ff. See also Fiorenza, *Bread Not Stone*, chap. 1. Also Ruether, *Womanguides*, chap. 1.
66. Fiorenza, *In Memory of Her*, 285 ff.
67. "Gli operatori del consultorio," *donne e politica*, November–December 1979.
68. Pagels, *Gnostic Gospels*, xvii.

**10   *casalinga:*
Italian feminists and unedited marxist theory: unpaid work of the housewife as a lever of social subversion**

1. Mariarosa Dalla Costa, "Donne e sovversione sociale," in *Potere femminile e sovversione sociale* (Padua, 1972). See "Lavoro/non lavoro: per un'economia politica della liberazione della donna," *donnawomanfemme*, July–December 1979.
2. *Le operaie della casa*, ed. collettivo internazionale femminista (Padua, 1975).
3. See pt. 8, "Motherhood and Housework," in *German Feminism: Readings in Politics and Literature*, ed. Edith Hoshino Altbach *et al.* (Albany, 1984).
4. *Le operaie*, 19–24. See also 7, 11–15, 27–39, 43–78.
5. See discussion of Cif, chapter 13.
6. *Le operaie*, 24–34.
7. *Le operaie*, 21–22.
8. *Le operaie*, 34–55.
9. *Le operaie*, 55–56, 57–78.
10. See "Lavoro/non lavoro."
11. Ibid.
12. The issue held considerable strength by the eighties. There were twelve million housewives in 1980, their national association was Andic. Andic's proposal for a stipend for housewives was accompanied by an effort to encourage housewives to form cooperatives to carry out essential services like assistance to the sick, old people, and children. This was similar to the recommendation of Cif for an "open family," but the traditional burdens placed on women were in the Andic proposal to be shared in coops.
13. Communication from Margherita Repetto Alaia, 13 December 1984.
14. The issue was debated in all the women's journals. See *quotidiano donna, effe, noi donne*, and *com-nuovi tempi*, particularly after 1979 when the Dc proposal was made. One interesting aspect of this debate was the different arguments women

used. An article that attempts to synthesize thinking on the subject is "Lavoro/ non lavoro."

15. An exhaustive analysis of the implications of computer technology may be found in the January–February 1985 issue of *idoc internazionale*. The implications are analyzed for all those hitherto silenced, notably people of the third world.

16. See "Sconfiggerela casalinghità," *noi donne*, 1 May 1977.

17. See chapter 17, this work.

18. Ibid.

19. Mariarosa Dalla Costa and Leopoldina Fortunati, *Brutto ciao: direzione di marcia delle donne negli ultimi 30 anni* (Rome, 1976), 57–70.

20. For radical mothers and children, see Simona Mafai *et al.*, *Essere donna in Sicilia* (Rome, 1976), 7–83.

21. Dalla Costa and Fortunati, *Brutto ciao* 39.

22. The best documentation of racist attitudes of northern Italians toward southerners, perhaps, is to be found in the films of Lina Wertmuller.

23. Claudia von Werlhof, "The Proletariat is Dead: Long Live the Housewife!" (In German, "Die Krise: Hausfrauisierung der Arbeit,") *Courage*, March 1982.

24. The best analysis in English of the literature of housework from a feminist perspective is that of Nona Glazer-Malbin, "House-work," a review essay in *Signs*, Summer, 1976. See also Glazer, "The Invisible Intersection: Involuntary Unpaid Labor Outside the Household and Women Workers," Center for the Study, Education and Advancement of Women, University of California (Berkeley, 1982); Susan Strasser, *Never Done: A History of American Housework* (New York, 1982); Alice Kessler-Harris, *Out to Work: A History of Wage-Earning Women in the United States* (New York, 1982). An excellent anthology of essays on women's work is Rachel Kahn-Hut, Arlene Kaplan Daniels, and Richard Colvard eds., *Women and Work: Problems and Perspectives* (New York, 1982). Proceedings of the important international conference on women's work in Turin in 1984 are published as *Produrre e riprodurre, cambiamenti nel rapporto tra donne e lavoro*, Primo convegno internazionale delle donne dei paesi industrializzati promosso dal movimento delle donne di Torino (Turin, 1984).

11 *casa della donna:*
"this house belongs to all women in struggle"

1. Giuseppe Di Palma, *Surviving Without Governing: The Italian Parties in Parliament* (Berkeley and Los Angeles, 1977), xi.

2. Di Palma, *Surviving*, chap. 7.

3. A good source for differing evaluations of Italy in the seventies is the essay "Italy: Crisis, Crises or Transition?" in *Italy in Transition: Conflict and Consensus*, ed. Peter Lange and Sidney Tarrow (Bournemouth, England, 1980).

4. Ibid.   5. Ibid.

6. See introduzione, *Il mio segno: la mia parola. rabbia, amore, confessioni, appuntamenti, disegni nella casa della donna in via del governo vecchio*. (Rome, 1979).

7. See *Contro la violenza sessuale. le donne, la legge. Incontro aperto di donne. atti del convegno tenuto a Milano, 27–28, 1979*. See chapter 17, this work.

8. See *Contro la violenza sessuale.*

9. *Il mio segno*, introduzione.

10. Ibid.   11. Ibid.   12. Ibid.

13. Rossana Rossanda, *Le altre*, 7, 9.

14. For Rossanda's biography, see her *Un viaggio inutile: o della politica come educazione sentimentale* (Milan, 1981). Also *Le altre*, introduction, 11, 13, 14–17, 22, 23, 26, 29, 31, 34.

15. *Le altre*, "politica 1," 52–53.

16. Ibid., 54.

17. Ibid., "politica 1," 54–55, 59, 61.

18. Ibid., 56–57.

19. Ibid., "politica 2," 69–70.

20. Ibid., 71

21. Ibid., (libertà) 76–115, 66, 68, 69, 71, 72, 74–75; ("uguaglianza") 77–81, 83, 85, 87–88; ("fraternità") 89, 90, 93, 99–100, 103, 109.

22. *Le altre*, "fraternità," 89–104.

23. Ibid., "resistenza," 144–55, 156.

24. Ibid., "partito," 170–85, 172–73, 175–80, 183. See also "stato," 157–70, 158, 167.

25. Ibid., "partito," 175.

26. Ibid., 174.   27. Ibid.

28. Ibid.,"democrazia," 125.

29. Ibid., "democrazia," 116–33, 120.

30. Ibid.   31. Ibid., 179, 187.

32. Ibid., "rivoluzione," 185–200, 187.

33. *Ibid.*, 188.   34. Ibid.   35. Ibid.   36. Ibid., 190–96, 192.

37. Ibid., "femminismo," 200–215, 200.

38. Ibid., 202.   39. Ibid., 201–4.

40. Ibid., "stato," 157–69.

41. Ibid., 222.

42. "La bobina che non si lasciava trasmettere," an appendix to *Le altre*, reflects the fatigue and disillusionment of some northern feminists at the end of the seventies.

43. See Karen Beckwith, "Women and Parliamentary Politics in Italy, 1946–1979," in *Italy at the Polls, 1979: A Study of the Parliamentary Elections*, (American Enterprise Institute for Public Policy Research: Washington, D. C. and London, 1979).

44. Adriana Seroni, *La questione femminile in Italia 1970–1977* (Rome, 1977). See "conversazione introduttiva."

45. Ibid.   46. Ibid.

47. Interviews and correspondence with Simona Mafai, 1976–85. See Gerosa, *Le compagne*, and Scroppo, *Donna, privato e politico*, "Simona Mafai." For Mafai's role in the passage of the abortion law, see *Aborto*, 49. See also her sister's account of the postwar period, which was also Simona's apprenticeship to politics: M. Mafai, *L'apprendistato*. For Mafai's work in Sicily, see S. Mafai et al., *Essere donne in Sicilia*.

48. Scroppo, *Donna*, "Simona Mafai"; interviews.

49. Ibid. Also Gerosa, *Le compagne*, "Simona Mafai."

50. Ibid. Interviews, 1977, 1979, 1981, 1983; correspondence.

51. Ibid.

52. Gigliola Lo Cascio, *Occupate e casalinghe* (Rome, 1979), chap. 7. Also interviews.

53. Interviews, September 1979.

54. Interviews, September 1979.

55. Interviews, September 1979.

56. "Maria Rosa Cutrufelli" in *Che cos'è un marito?* autori vari (Milan, 1978). See 91 for Cutrufelli's discussion of Chesler.

57. See chapter 16, this work.
58. Interview, December 1983. For Maria Rosa Cutrufelli, see *Economia e politica dei sentimenti* (Rome, 1980); *Le donne protagoniste nel movimento cooperativo: la questione femminile in un'organizzazione produttiva democratica* (Milan, 1978); *L'invenzione della donna: miti e tecniche di uno sfruttamento* (Milan, 1974); *Il cliente: inchiesta sulla domanda di prostituzione* (Rome, 1981); conversations and interview, December 1983. Other Sicilian women, many of them journalists, have written on the lives of women of their island. See Giuliana Saladino, *Terra di rapina: come un contadino siciliano può diventare bandito* (Turin, 1977). For Saladino's article on our mutual interview, see "Una donna in cerca delle radici, trova dee e 'madrine' siciliane," *giornale di Sicilia*, 22 September 1979.

12 *"spacca la mela"*: literature of feminist cultural revolution

See Bibliographical Essay for women's studies in Italy. This enterprise of self-discovery by women was also occurring on a smaller scale among men coming from the South to the North (see Gavino Ledda, *Padre Padrone: The Education of a Shepherd* (Rome, 1975; New York, 1979).

1. *Agenda, 82: Spacca la mela* (Rome, 1982)
2. See Laura Balbo and Yasmine Ergas, *How Trade Unions, the Women's Movement, and the University Have Produced Women's Studies in Italy* (Old Westbury, New York, 1982). See also Yasmin Ergas, "Intervento, movimento e istituzioni," *donnawomanfemme*, October–December 1977. A good evaluation of the 150-hour classes is that of Lea Malandri, "Educazione degli adulti/150 ore: le ore nascoste: studie e vissuto di scolari senza età," *il manifesto*, 5 April 1984.
3. Balbo and Ergas, *Women's Studies in Italy.*
4. Ibid. The 150-hour classes in women's studies probably best indicate the difference between women's studies in Italy and in the United States—diffusing women's studies in the first instance, narrowing women's studies to the universities in the second.
5. Chiara Saraceno, *Uguali e diverse* (Bari, 1980).
6. Interviews with Italian women. See Radiotelevisione italiana, *Le reazioni di un campione di pubblico al programma storie allo specchio* (Rome, 1981), a survey of women's responses to a feminist television series.
7. Ibid.
8. Saraceno, *Uguali e diverse.*
9. Ibid.   10. Ibid.   11. Ibid.
12. Interview, November 1981.
13. Ibid.   14. Ibid.   15. Ibid.
16. *Agenda '82.*
17. Ibid.   18. Ibid.
19. *Il diario delle lune,* 1982 (Rome, 1982)
20. Quoted in Boggs and Plotke, *The Politics of Eurocommunism.* See chapter 7.
21. Margherita Repetto, "La nostra storia è appena cominciata: Note sul saggio di S. Rowbotham," *donnawomanfemme*, no. 14, 1980.
22. Ibid.
23. *memoria: rivista di storia delle donne.*
24. *memoria* has proved to have staying power in the period of disintegration of women's periodicals in the early eighties. The September 1983 issue was an explora-

tion of the theme of mothers and nonmothers. The controversial terrain of "family" was explored by Natalia Ginsburg in *Lessico famigliare* (Rome, 1963), in *Famiglia* (Rome, 1977), and in *La famiglia Manzoni* (Rome, 1983). In her documented biography of Manzoni (regarded as Italy's greatest catholic writer) Ginsburg views the writer with a feminist optic, describing him as a "great egoist" who impregnated his wife thirteen times. Ginsburg's last novel, *La città e la casa* (Rome, 1984), evokes the sense of velocity within ferocious silence. In a 1984 interview she spoke of men as lost, while women have grown stronger. "Intervista/Natalia Ginzburg parla del suo nuovo libro," *il manifesto*, 18 December 1984.

25. Interviews with Italian feminists, 1983.

26. Centro culturale Virginia Woolf, *programma 1981–82*, "L'ambiguo materno: ipotesi di ricerca" (Rome 1981). See Nadia Fusini, "L'ambiguo materno," *Rinascità*, 20 November 1981, and Anna-Marie Boetti, "Dove vola l'università delle donne: in cerca dell' 'ambiguo materno,'" *il manifesto*, 22 November 1981.

27. Centro culturale Virginia Woolf, *programma 1984*, "L'eccesso femminile." See Ida Dominijanni, "Femminismo/politica culturale: la donna per eccesso: il quinto anno di attività del centro culturale 'Virginia Woolf' di Roma," *il manifesto*, 22 February 1984. See Eva Cantarella, "Ragione d'amore: preistoria di un difetto femminile," *memoria*, March 1981.

28. Centro culturale Virginia Woolf, *programma 1984*, "L'eccesso femminile."

29. Ibid.   30. Ibid.

31. Ibid. In counterpoint to the 1984 theme of excess, the central idea of the 1985 program of Centro culturale Virginia Woolf was "Sul limite: il problema dei confini nell'esperienza femminile" (limits, or the problem of boundaries in women's experience). Among the workshops: psychological aspects of women's work, sex from the standpoint of nature and of culture, an analysis of "the obvious", guilt and the sense of guilt in women's existence, regression and discovery of self in women's monastic experience, women's work not only as exchange but as noneconomic use and pleasure, Maria—virgin and mother—in symbol and image in papal councils and peasant views, women's "difference" from Rousseau to Weininger, Marian devotion and women's identity in catholic institutions, Foucault's view of sex, a rereading of the early Italian feminist Sibilla Aleramo, the fragile solidarity of women in a 1589 witchcraft trial at Lucca, women's difference according to Ivan Illich, motherhood in different cultures, the law against sexual violence, and women's eroticism (Centro culturale Virginia Woolf, *Programma 1985* [Rome, 1985]). For the large interest in Foucault by the mid-80s, see Foucault, *The History of Sexuality*, trans. Robert Hurley (New York, 1978).

32. Maria Occhipinti, *Una donna di Ragusa* (Milan, 1957).

33. Interview, November 1981. Correspondence.

34. Ibid.

35. Adele Cambria, *Marx: la moglie e la fedele governante* (Padua, 1980).

36. Adele Cambria, *Il Lenin delle donne: dalla castrazione amorosa alla violenza terrorista* (Padua, 1981).

37. Ibid.   38. Ibid.

39. Adele Cambria, *Amore come rivoluzione: tre sorelle per un rivoluzionario: le lettere inedite della moglie e delle cognate di Antonio Gramsci*, con un testo teatrale, "Nonostante Gramsci" (Milan, 1976).

40. Ibid.

41. See Macciocchi, *La donna "nera,"* and *Les femmes et leurs maitres* (Paris, 1979), 1–9.

42. Macciocchi, *Les femmes*, 1–9.

43. Ibid.
44. Macciocchi, *Les femmes*, 387–432.
45. Macciocchi, *Les femmes*, 393, 395, 397, 419, 420, 421, 427 432.
46. Ibid.   47. Ibid.   48. Ibid.
49. Dacia Maraini, *Donna in guerra* (Milan, 1979).
50. Dacia Maraini, *Lettere a Marina* (Milan, 1981).
51. Piera Degli Esposti and Dacia Maraini, *Storia di Piera* (Milan, 1980).
52. See Dacia Maraini, *A Memoria* (Milan, 1968); *Memorie di una ladra* (Milan 1972). Theatrical works include *La famiglia normale; Il ricatto a teatro; Recitare e Venere; Viva l'Italia; La donna perfetta: Dialogo di una prostituta con un cliente; Suor Juana; Manifesto dal carcere; Don Juan;* and *I sogni di Clitennestra.*
53. Interview, November 1981. For Italian feminists and psychoanalysis, see gruppo donne e psicanalisi, *differenze 11* (Rome, 1980).
54. Interview, November 1981.
55. See Maraini, Writing and feminism in an experience of the theater, December 1980; Paper delivered at the International Symposium on Women Writers; Wellesley College; Wellesley, Massachusetts; May 1981.
56. Interview, November 1981. See foreword to Maraini's *La vacanza,* 3d. ed. (Milan, 1980), for the interweaving of her personal and professional life.
57. Interviews, 1979, 1981.
58. Oriana Fallaci, *Letter to a Child Never Born,* trans. John Shapley (New York, 1978). The book is dedicated to all women.
59. Ibid. See also Fallaci, *A Man: A Novel.* (New York, 1980). Also Fallaci, *Interview with History* (Boston, 1977). This book of interviews with Kissinger, Arafat, Indira Gandhi *et al.* is dedicated to her mother and "to all those who do not like power."
60. Fallaci, *Letter to a Child.* One of the ten points of a "feminist decalogue" I saw in Catania in 1981 was, "We want men—not boys."

13   *femministe e "le altre":* feminists and "others"

1. Cif Convegno reginale, March, *La donna oggi: realtà e prospettive* (Palermo, 1979)
2. Cardinale Salvatore Pappalardo, "Saluto," Cif convegno regionale, 1978, Palermo.
3. Mons. Alfredo Garcia, "La novità cristiana e la donna," Cif convegno regionale, 1978, Palermo.
4. Ibid.
5. Carlamaria Del Miglio, "Ambiguità e verità dell'essere donne," Cif convegno regionale, 1978, Palermo.
6. Ennio Pintacuda, "Ruolo della donna: Condizionamenti, valori, prospettive nel contesto socioculturale siciliano," Cif convegno regionale, 1978, Palermo.
7. Maria Eletta Martini, "La donna oggi realtà e prospettive," Cif convegno regionale, 1978, Palermo.
8. Mozione conclusiva," Cif convegno regionale, 1978, Palermo.
9. "Più spazio alla donna, per una famiglia nuova, per una società più umana," Cif convegno regionale, Palermo, 1981.
10. Ibid.
11. Intervento, Laura Barone. Cif convegno regionale, 1981, Palermo.
12. Maria Teresa Moscato, "Famiglia e condizione femminile oggi," Cif convegno regionale, 1981, Palermo.

13. Ibid.
14. Carlamaria Del Miglio, "Donna come?" Cif convegno regionale, 1981, Palermo.
15. Ibid.   16. Ibid.   17. Ibid.   18. Ibid.
19. Ibid. Many women in Cif belong also to Fidap, the Italian federation of women in business, the professions, and the arts. See handbook of Fidap, *La federazione italiana donne arti professioni affari: quarant'anni di vita associativa 1930–1970* (Naples, 1970).
20. See Laura Barone, "8 marzo: La festa della donna è entrata nel nostro costume ma la donna come sta?" *il focolare*, March 1984. For this catholic woman (and others) there was a tendency to do one's own thinking, yet not give up affiliation with the church. For example, Barone cherished Saint Francis, but she considered him a saint identified with the existing church (many left catholics and *credenti* identified Francis with the prophetic church). See Laura Barone, "L'insegnamento di S. Francesco e i giovani del nostro tempo," *il focolare*, August 1983. Also Laura Barone, "Famiglia, Chiesa e Società," *il focolare*, July 1983.
21. Valentina Savioli and Roberta Tatafiore, "L'inchiesta prostituzione: dove volano le lucciole," *noidonne*, April 1983.
22. *la lucciola*, October 1983.
23. Ibid.
24. "il triangolo della prostituta," *noi donne*, 6 February 1977; Savioli and Tatafiore, "L'inchiesta prostituzione; Roberta Tatafiore, "gli uomini pregano, pagano, poi disprezzano: conversazione con Pieke Biermann," *noidonne*, June 1984.
25. Ibid.
26. *noidonne*, supplemento, September 1983.
27. Ibid.   28. Ibid.
29. Earlier *effe* had taken up the issue of lesbianism in "mamma, amo una donna," *effe*, March 1981, and "Il continente sommerso," *effe*, April 1981. Italian feminists are highly interested in the writings of Adrienne Rich. See Marina Camboni, "Come pagine di un diario: i ghazals di Adrienne Rich," in E. Zolle, ed., *L'esotismo nelle letterature americane* (Rome, 1982).
30. Roberta Tatafiore, *noidonne*, September 1983.
31. *noidonne*, supplemento, October 1983.
32. Paola Zaccaria, "Italy: A Mortified Thirst for Living," in *Sisterhood is Global: The International Women's Movement Anthology*, ed. Robin Morgan (Garden City, New York, 1984).
33. Ibid.   34. Ibid.   35. Ibid.
36. Bernardi *et al.* (no first names), *La casalinga di Cristo* (Rome, 1976).
37. Ibid.   38. Ibid.   39. Ibid.
40. Interviews 1981–83.
41. The implications of the concept of difference are perceptively analyzed in Simona Morini and Giulio Giorello, "L'individualismo metodologico: Il primato della differenza," *1999 Italia: rivista trimestrale del club dei club*, December 1982. The author's interviews substantiated this point.
42. Cutrufelli, *Il cliente*, 61ff.
43. Ibid.

14 *unione donne italiane:*
the italian women's union ...

1. See chapter 5, this work; also "l'Udi anno per anno," *com-nuovi tempi*, 17 October 1982.

2. "l'Udi anno per anno."
3. Interviews, 1975–83, with Udi women. See Aida Tiso, "Il cammino dell'organizzazione," *donne e politico*, May–August 1982.
4. "l'Udi anno per anno."
5. Ibid.   6. Ibid.
7. Operazione congresso," *noi donne*, 19 February 1982; "Congresso Udi/il nome e la cosa," *effe*, June 1982. "Dal congresso in poi," *noidonne*, 23 July 1983.
8. Ibid. Also, communication from Margherita Repetto Alaia, 13 December 1984.
9. Ibid.   10. Ibid.
11. Interview, November 11, 1981.
12. Ibid.
13. Ibid. See also Repetto, "La nostra storia è appena cominciata," *donnawomanfemme*, no. 14, 1980.
14. Ibid.   15. Ibid.
16. For *noidonne*, see Birnbaum, "Women writers;" "La stampa femminista: *noi donne*," Conferenza sulla Storia, Biografia, Sociologia, University of Rome, 3–5 November 1981.
17. An analysis of the readers of *noidonne* in the issue of July 1980, "Lettrice, chi sei?" indicated that 60.2 percent were in the age range of twenty to forty-four. Regions with the most readers were Emilia, Lombardy, and Tuscany. Most are activists in Udi, unions, cooperatives, schools. In 70 percent of the cases, the militant women's magazine is read by other members of the family. White-collar workers and teachers composed 34.8 percent of the readership; women factory and farm workers were 16.6 percent; students were 14.8 percent; housewives were 15.0 percent; shopkeepers and artisans 5.8 percent; entrepreneurs and leaders, 1.2 percent, pensioners and others, 11.8 percent. Sixty percent of the readers were in the northeast; 22.6 percent, in the northwest; 11.0 percent, in the center; 6.4 percent, in the South and the islands. College graduates made up 9.9 percent of the readers; 40.2 percent were high school graduates; 27.4 percent had completed junior high school; and 22.5 percent had completed elementary school.
18. Birnbaum, "Women writers"; "La stampa femminista: *noidonne*." See also Conferenza sulla Storia, Rome, November 1981, Rome.
19. Ibid.
20. See Cecchini *et al.*, *Sesso amaro*.
21. The history of the movement of the seventies can be tracked in *noidonne* articles. Beginning in 1975, see this sampling: On women's love-hate relationship to the house: "Cara casa odiata," 25 May 1975. On an Udi demonstration for jobs: "Lavoro: tanto si licenzia da solo," 5 December 1976. Women's testimonies about motherhood and abortion: "Tutte lo fanno," 20 March 1977. Prostitutes: "Sesso e amore nella storia: le chiamavano 'donne perdute'" 9 January 1977. Women's demonstration for legal abortion: issue of 26 June 1977. Abortion: "Da Erode a Pilato," speciale sul aborto, 25 September 1977. Demonstration against sexual violence: "Più che una legge," 5 October 1979. Lesbians: 3 April 1981, 24 April 1981. Health clinics: "Consultori: bilancio di un anno," 4 September 1977. Sexual violence: "Violenza carnale," 2 January 1977. Women's work, "Sconfiggerela casalinghità," 1 May 1977. *No* on both 1981 abortion referendums (right-wing referendum to repeal 1978 legalized abortion law and libertarian referendum for

free and unrestricted abortions): "Aborto: prepariamoci ai referendum," March 1981.
On the 1981 electoral victory sustaining the abortion law: "Viva il maggio delle donne," 29 May 1981. Lesbianism: "Lei ama lei: inchiesta sul lesbismo," July 1981. On the referendum against sexual violence: "Alle nostre 300 mila firme contro la violenza sessuale il parlamento ha detto ni," 16 October 1981. Women's peace march from Perugia to Assisi preceding large national peace demonstration of October 24: "Donna in guerra/contro la guerra," 16 October 1981. Women's strike against giving birth until peace assured: 13 November 1981. Women and a culture of peace: 2 April 1982. Sexual molestation at the workplace: 16 July 1982. Bill against sexual violence: 10 September 1982. Women against the mafia: 22 October 1982. Sexual violence and the law: January 1983. Udi after decentralization: "Dal congresso in poi," 23 July 1983.

22. David I. Kertzer, "The liberation of Evelina Zaghi: the life of an Italian communist," *Signs*, Autumn, 1982.
23. Ibid.
24. See "Sempre più piccole le famiglie italiane," *memoria*, September 1983. The census indicated that the smallest families were in Liguria (2.5 persons) and the largest in the Campania and in Sardinia (3.5 persons). The average Italian family has become three persons, or one child per family. Since the sixties all western industrialized countries have experienced a decline in birth rate. Decline was slower in Mediterranean countries, but in 1981 Italy's birth rate of 1.56 children per woman resembled that of the rest of Europe. Conservatives have expressed alarm and pointed to legalized abortion as the cause for the decline. Feminists in this article state that the decline in number of births can be interpreted as lifting the quality of life for children that are born.
25. Interviews, 1982–3.
26. See "Dal congresso in poi," *noidonne*, 23 July 1983.
27. The *donne e politica* issue of May–August 1982 is devoted to an evaluation of the implications of the 1981 Udi congress by Pci women.
28. Lalla Trupia, "Un congresso non chiuso," *donne e politica*, May–August 1982.
29. Ibid.   30. Ibid.
31. See discussions by Grazia Francescato, Giglia Tedesco, and Elena Marinucci in the symposium of May–August 1982 in *donne e politica*. Interviews, 1982–84.
32. "Dal congresso in poi." "l'Udi è morta: viva l'Udi!" *pace e guerra*, June 1982. Interviews.
33. "Dal congresso in poi."
34. Ibid. Interviews 1982–84.
35. "Tra donne e politica," *donne e politica*, May–August 1982. See also Stefania Giorgi e Silvia Neonato, "Congresso dell'Udi: riusciranno le nostre eroine," *noidonne*, May 1982; Stefania Giorgi *et al.*, "Udi, che congresso questo congresso!" *noidonne*, June 1982; Anita Pasquali, "Perchè la nostra assemblea è muta?" *noidonne*, July 1983.
36. Repetto, "La nostra storia."
37. Ida Dominijanni, "Noi donne e voi lettrici," *il manifesto*, 17 January 1985.
38. Alberto Ronchey, *Diverso parere: Le opinioni sui temi più scottanti del nostro tempo a confronto con la verifica dei fatti e la critica dei lettori* (Milan, 1983), "Comunisti e cattolici senza più religione."
39. Ibid.   40. Ibid., 169.

41. Umberto Eco, *The Name of the Rose*, trans. William Weaver (San Diego and New York, 1983).
42. See Umberto Eco's essay in Sartogo, *Le donne al muro*.
43. Eco, *Name of the Rose*, introduction, 11, 14–16, 18–21, 53–56, 59–63, 68, 106. See also Umberto Eco, *Lector in fabula: la cooperazione interpretativa nei testi narrativi* Milan, 1979); and *Semiotics and the Philosophy of Language* (Bloomington, Indiana, 1984).
44. See Lucia Chiavola Birnbaum, Italian Political and Religious Beliefs in *The Name of the Rose*, Paper read at session of the American Italian Historical Association (WRC), conference of the Foreign Language Association of Northern California, Stanford University, 27 October 1984.
45. Eco, *Sette anni di desiderio: cronache 1977–1983* (Milan, 1983), 6, 11, 14–16, 18–21, 53–56, 59–63, 68, 106. See also Franco Ferrarotti, *Una teologia per atei* (Rome, 1983).
46. Eco, *Sette anni*, 19, 53–56; see "Colpire quale cuore?" and "Sette anni di rabbia."
47. Eco, *Sette anni*, introduzione, 14, 59–63; see "Gli amici della 'pravda.'"
48. Eco, *Sette anni*, 16, 68, 106. See "Gli orfani del Sessantotto"; "I preti spretati."
49. Eco, *Sette anni*, "Sulla crisi della crisi della ragione"; "Il sacro non è una moda."
50. Girardi, *Credente e non credente*. See chapter 6, this work.
51. Umberto Cerroni, *Il rapporto uomo-donna nella civiltà borghese* (Rome, 1975).
52. Giovanni Cesareo, *La contraddizione femminile* (Rome, 1977).
53. Ibid.
54. Eugenio Manca, "3 domande," *donne e politica*, May–August 1982.
55. Barkan, *Visions of Emancipation*, 3, 10, 23.
56. See Michetti, Repetto, and Viviani, l'udi.
57. Barkan, 10.
58. Ibid., 23.   59. Ibid., 31.   60. Ibid., 72.   61. Ibid., 85.
62. Ibid.   63. Ibid., 144.
64. Barkan, interviews, "Marisa."
65. Barkan, interviews, "woman in 150-hour class."
66. Barkan, interviews, "Maria."
67. Barkan, interviews, "Sondra."
68. Barkan, interviews, "Palmerio."
69. Barkan, interviews, "Tomasso."
70. Barkan, interviews, "Liliana."
71. Barkan, interviews, "Telesca."
72. Barkan, interviews, "taxi driver." For a glimpse into the complexity of the thinking of Fiat workers, see Brunello Mantelli and Marco Revelli, eds., *Operai senza politica: il caso Moro al Fiat e il 'qualunquismo operaio': Le risposte degli operai allo Stato e alle Br registrate ai cancelli della Fiat durante i 55 giorni del rapimento di Aldo Moro* (Rome, 1979). For the thinking of explicitly catholic workers, see survey in *il manifesto* in April 1984, particularly "Inchiesta/ il nuovo protagonismo politico dei cattolici/6: 'la nostra emozione per gli ultimi': Intervista a Bruno Manghi sull'anima della nuova Cisl."

15 *violenza e pace:* violence and peace

1. Spotts and Wieser, *Italy: A Difficult Democracy*, chap. 9. See September–October 1983 issue of *il mulino* for several articles on fascist, red, and institutionalized

violence in Italy. For the christmas 1984 bombing (attributed to fascists) placed in the context of other right-wing terrorism, see "Una strage impunita lunga quindici anni," *il manifesto*, 25 December 1984.   ♥

2. For the reach of *comunità di base*, see "come ai tempi di Frate Leone," *l'Espresso*, 2 May 1982 and chapter 9, this work. For the contemporary Italian belief in nonviolence, see *La strada è un'altra: dati e riflessioni per un'alternativa alla violenza*, a cura del gruppo ecclesiale "giovani zona 2" di Roma e di G. Martina e D. Mongillo (Assisi, 1981). For the European peace movement of the eighties, see Lucia Chiavola Birnbaum, "European disarmament movement: the next steps," *journal of women and religion*, Winter 1982. For the 1981 peace demonstration, see "Siamo oggi a Roma . . ." *com-nuovi tempi*, 22 November 1981, and "Essere per la pace non è solo essere contro la guerra," *rocca*, 15 November 1981. For the wide Italian view of peace, see Luciana Castellina, Biagio De Giovanni, and Valdo Spini, "Terzo mondo e questione cattolica nel dibattito sulla terza via," *idoc*, March–April 1982. See Giulio Girardi for the meaning of violence in Italian liberation theology ("In principio era la violenza" in *rocca*, September 1983). Journals whose main theme is nonviolence include: *azione nonviolenta, rivista mensile edita dal movimento nonviolento* and *alternativa nonviolenta* (see speciale *Fame*, 1983). *Cristiani nonviolenti*, a journal of Italian protestants, emphasizes dialogue, noncooperation, and civil disobedience grounded on conscience (see October 1983 issue).

3. See chapter 17, this work.

4. *Francesco: un pazzo di slegare* (Assisi, 1983). See Efrem Trettel, *Francis* (Chicago, 1975); Morris Bishop, *St. Francis of Assisi* (Boston, 1974).

5. See Diana Johnstone, "Communist Party Scraps Soviet Model," *In These Times*, 20–26 January 1982, and "Italy: Communists Turn to a 'Third Way'," *In These Times*, 31 March–6 April 1982.

6. "*Tremate! tremate! Le streghe son tornate!*" *rocca*, 1 March 1983; "Cinquantamila donne a Roma in piazza contro la morale democristiana," *com-nuovi tempi*, 13 February 1983; Carla Rodota, "Una comunista si è dimessa: per un principio: la violenza sessuale e un delitto contro la persona," *pace e guerra*, 10 February 1983. For an analysis of the Italian sexual violence bill, see Francesca Colli and Giusi Di Crescenzo, "La violenza sessuale e la legge," *noidonne*, January 1983.

7. See *contro la violenza sessuale: le donne. . . . la legge: incontro aperto di donne*, Milan, 27–28 October 1979, for differing attitudes toward the referendum against sexual violence. For provisions of the sexual violence bill, see Alida Castelli, "Violenza sessuale: cancellate anacronistiche definizione," *documentazione, donne e politica*, September–October 1982.

8. "Cinquantamila donne."

9. Ibid. For the October 1984 sexual violence bill passed by the camera, see "La legge sulla violenza sessuale e il voto contrario dei comunisti: Intervista a Lalla Trupia, I diritti conquistati i principi respinti," *Rinascità*, 3 November 1984. Also, Lidia Menapace, "Violenza sessuale/diario di viaggio: le forme di incontro delle donne e la giusta esclusione dell'uomo," *il manifesto*, 2 January 1985.

10. "La truffa del giovedì notte," *noidonne, supplemento* of November 1984.

11. "La legge sulla violenza sessuale." Also Menapace, "Violenza sessuale/diario di viaggio."

12. See Birnbaum, "European disarmament movement."

13. Giorgio Girardet, "Per i cristiani centrale il problema della pace," *com-nuovi tempi*, 8 November 1981; Laura Grassi, "Le donne per la pace, con un contributo spe-

cifico," *com-nuovi tempi,* 13 December 1981; "Non serve Plotino per interpretare il movimento pacifista," in "controgiornale," *pace e guerra,* 7 April 1983. For response to the action of parliament in March 1984 ratifying the installation of nuclear missiles at Comiso, see Raniero La Valle, "La svolta di marzo," March/April 1984, *bozze 84.*

14. See Pietro Columbo, "Oltre le chiacchiere velate, passare ai 'fatti' di pace," *com-nuovi tempi,* 17 January 1982. In the mid-eighties the movement against missiles at Comiso has widened to a campaign for denuclearized cities and against nuclear reactors. See "Sicilia/cruise: Capodanno pacifista, magistrati a convegno su missili e espropri," *il manifesto,* 22 December 1984, and "Nucleare/Carovigno/Avetrana: La campagna di Puglia contro la centrale, batterie di referendum," *il manifesto,* 22 December 1984. At a conference of young people in December 1983 addressing "Smilitarizzare l'uomo" (demilitarizing man), feminists pointed out the need to remove violence from all human relationships; see "Smilitarizzare l'uomo," *rocca,* 15 January 1984.

15. See "Mille modi nuovi per lavorare insieme," *com-nuovi tempi,* 5 December 1982. Pax christi, "No ai missili a Comiso!" Leaflet, 22 October 1983. Agenzia settimanale di informazione del Pdup, *Compagne e compagni,* 22 ottobre da Comiso a Roma: Per la pace. Per l'alternativa, Pamphlet, 22 October 1983. "Europa contro i missili. Mezzo millione di pacifisti sfila a Roma," *la Repubblica,* 23–24 October 1983. "Per la pace con gayezza!" Leaflet, 22 October 1983. Federazione donne evangeliche in Italia, "Donne per la pace: "il frutto della giustizia sarà la pace" Leaflet, 22 October 1983. "Oggi molta gente del mondo nega la cultura di guerra e le armi di ogni contrada che porta in grembo," *il manifesto,* 22 October 1983. Also, "Straordinaria marea pacifista. un millione e forse più dilaga nelle strade di Roma. si fa più forte la voce che dice no a tutti i missili," *l'Unità,* 23 October 1983.

For the large women's peace demonstration that was coordinated with women's day celebrations in March 1984, see Ida Dominijanni and Paola Tavella, "Per vivere e vivere in pace migliaia di donne in piazza a Roma," *il manifesto,* 11 March 1984. Men who joined this women's demonstration were not asked to leave, as had happened at times in the past. For large March demonstration of workers and other people protesting measures taken by Craxi, see "la manifestazione più grande" *il manifesto,* 25 March 1984.

16. This was Gruppo ambiente.

17. See Ellen Setteducati, "Toward a woman-centered environmentalism," M.A. thesis, University of California, Santa Cruz, 1982, 28–29. See Giovanni Forti, "Adesso il cigno vuole beccare," *pace e guerra,* 7 April 1983. See account of ecology conference at the site of an ancient earth mother (and love goddess) at Erice: "Convegno sull'ecologia ad Erice," *espresso sera,* 17 November 1983. Also, Grazia Francescato, "La donna è ecologa anche se no lo sa," *pace e guerra,* 31 March 1983.

18. "Il congresso della Lega ambiente Arci. ecologia: incidere nel modo di produrre," *com-nuovi tempi,* 3 April 1983. Ecological concerns are supported by all parties of the left as well as by a considerable band of the center-right in Italy. There are some ideological contradictions; see Enzo Riboni, "Ecco il partito eco-operaista. Ma com'è difficile conciliare Lenin e i verdi," *il manifesto,* 18 December 1984, an account of a conference of Dp (democrazia proletaria) the radical offshoot of the new left Pdup. For Dp, representing some of the generation of '68, there remains the problem of not renouncing leninist centralization, not renouncing the centrality of factory workers, yet opening the party to concerns of *ecopacifisti.*

This very small party (1.5 percent of the electorate) has adopted campaigns for jobs, for reducing the work-week to thirty-five hours, and for electing Dp people to city councils. In 1985 the little party was at the forefront of a campaign for denuclearized cities: "a commitment to disarmament and self-determination." A wider band of people concerned about ecological issues are men and women who campaign electorally on "green lists" independent of any party identification. See Alberto Poggi, "Dall'antinucleare all'arcipelago verde," *rocca*, January 1985, an account of the first Italian conference of greens at Florence in December, 1984. See also Fritjof Capra and Charlene Spretnak, *Green Politics. The Global Promise* (New York, 1984).

19. See Riboni, "Ecco il partito eco-operaista."

20. Roundtable, "Perchè l'Italia è tutta una mafia," *pace e guerra*, 31 March 1983. Turi Caggegi, "Tutta l'Italia mafiosa: i primi ma significativi dati di una legge mal applicata," *il manifesto*, 9 December 1984.

21. Spotts and Wieser, *Italy*, chap. 9.

22. Ibid.

23. "La camorra diffusa," *noidonne, supplemento* of November 1984.

24. Ibid.

25. In the early eighties the camorra manipulated relief funds that were sent for victims of the earthquake in the Naples area.

26. See article on a youth conference convoked on the problem of the mafia and the camorra, "Una società sfregiata dalla mafia e dalla camorra. il coraggio di parlare. la forza di cambiare," *rocca*, 15 February 1983. Also see "Una cultura contro la mafia," *noidonne*, May 1984, and Romolo Menighetti, "La lotta alla mafia nel quotidiano," *rocca*, 15 November 1984. For the campaign against the heroin traffic, see Mirella Alloisio, "Tutto su la mafia," *noidonne*, February 1982, Giovanni Pajetta, "1984, l'anno dell'eroina. i morti aumentati del 50%. nessuno sa perchè," *il manifesto*, 29 December 1984; Gabriella Lapasini, "Palermo affonda nell'eroina," *noidonne*, October 1983; Franco Prina and Gianpaolo Meucci, "Droga: il flagello del nostro tempo," *rocca*, 1 March 1984; "Giovani e giovanissimi al corteo di Roma contro la camorra," *il manifesto*, 6 May 1984.

27. Birnbaum, "European disarmament movement."

28. The best source for the independent position of people in the peace movement was *pace e guerra*, until it ceased publication in 1983 (when most of its editorial staff was elected to parliament). A good source of independent left thinking on violence and peace is *bozze* (e.g., Fabrizio Mastrofini, "La bomba come cosa visibile e nascosta," May/August 1984). *Bozze* is also a good source of left catholic thinking on contemporary issues; e.g., Daniele Menozzi, "La Chiesa e i poveri nella storia: Dalla povertà delle origini al dividendo sulle tasse;" "La ratifica del Concordato: documenti," September/October 1984. The wide range of principles comprised in the Italian peace movement is suggested in "Alcune considerazione sul movimento per la pace," *il manifesto*, 4 January 1985, in which Peppe Sini of the committees for peace of Viterbo recommends to all Italian peace committees the unifying theme peace/democracy/human rights, with a program of constructing a "new model of development" coordinated by movements of liberation. Feminist influence is indicated in Simi's prospectus stressing nonviolence, democracy, and respect for differences. The peace movement touches catholics inside and outside the church. See Laura Barone, "Necessità di una pedagogia della pace" in *il focolare*, September/October 1984; Barone, a Cif activist, urges a revision of school curricula to emphasize peace not war.

29. Best source for Pdup is its newspaper, *il manifesto.*
30. See "30 milione di persone muoiono ogni anno per fame. Armati di nonviolenza vivi alla pace," *notizie radicali,* numero 6, 1981, announcing Marco Pannella's hunger strike in witness to the 30 million people who die of hunger each year and the Pr demonstration of October 17, 1981, at Rome for life, peace, and development. The hunger fast and other Pr themes have been adopted by the mainstream Italian peace movement.
31. Birnbaum, "European disarmament movement."
32. "Movimento per la pace e comitati all'alba del 1983," *com-nuovi tempi,* 23 January 1983.
33. "Dopo il convegno nazionale delle cdb. come essere chiesa negli anni 1980," *com-nuovi tempi,* 16 January 1983. See Paolo Gentiloni, "Pacifisti in mezzo al guado," *pace e guerra,* 3 February 1983. See Associazione Culturale B. Brecht, Comiso, "Prima che sia troppo tardi" (Comiso, 1982); the first document in this collection is Bertolt Brecht's statement: "There are many methods of killing. One can put a knife in someone's chest, take bread away from people, not protect them from illness, put them in an unliveable house, kill them with work, force them to suicide, make them go to war. . . ."
34. See Birnbaum, "European disarmament movement." For Bettazzi and pax christi, see Pancera, *Conversazione.*
35. Pancera, *Conversazione.*
36. See discussion of Sicilian antinuclear women in chapter 16, this work.
37. Birnbaum, "European disarmament movement."
38. Ibid. See leaflet distributed by Sicilian committees for peace and disarmament: *Dossier contro la militarizzazione in Sicilia,* a detailed analysis of all military forces in Sicily. See pamphlet prepared by young people's sector of Pci at Rimini (Fgci) a pictorial projection of Rimini after a nuclear bomb has fallen, *Rimini nella bomba* (Rimini, 1983).
39. Luciana Castellina, *pace e guerra,* March 1983.
40. For the strategy of direct nonviolent action, see Paolo Gentiloni, "Azione diretta non violenta: la formula magica coniata dai pacifisti inglesi e rimbalzata fino a Comiso," *pace e guerra,* January 1983. For Christmas at Comiso, 1982, see Gianni Novelli, "Un Natale nel segno della pace: la chiesa meno diffidente verso chi protesta a Comiso," *com-nuovi tempi,* 9 January 1983. For the international context of the Italian peace movement, see Fabrizia Baduel Glorioso, "Comiso, Florennes, Greenham Commons anche al parlamento europeo," *pace e guerra,* 22–28 April 1983; and Ben Thompson, European Nuclear Disarmament (END), *special report: Comiso* (London 1982). An important analysis of the Italian peace movement is the special issue of *rocca* "Paura della pace," 15 February–1 March 1982. Information about the U.S. peace movement is publicized in Italy; see interview with Grace Paley, "Usa: mille rivoli contro la bomba," *Rinascità,* 7 January 1983.
41. Leaflet entitled, "As believers and as women," Rome peace demonstration, 22 October 1983.
42. Leaflet of *credenti,* Rome peace demonstration, 22 October 1983.
43. Italian Christian Workers Associations (Acli), *Before all else, peace* (Rome, 1983). See also "Manifesto appello a tutte le donne" of donne contro gli armamenti, Rome, 1982. The manifesto declares that the military economy destroys the civil economy, that as long as there are weapons and armies, there will be wars. Women are accomplices in this as long as they do not denounce militarized societies that allow 110,000 persons to die each day of hunger or from war in

underdeveloped countries. Appealing to Italy's constitution (which in Article 11 repudiates war as an instrument of offence), this women's committee of Rome demanded unilateral disarmament. See editorial, "I compiti attuali del movimento per la pace," *testimonianze, quaderni mensili*, August–November 1983.

44. See article "comunità di base" in *com-nuovi tempi*, 16 January 1983.
45. Giulio Girardi, "In principio era la violenza," *rocca*, September 1983.
46. Gianni Baget-Bozzo, "Contro giganti ciechi," *rocca* 15 November 1983. For specific antinuclear activities of Sicilian feminists, see chapter 16, this work. For the Italian peace movement after installation of the missiles at Comiso in February 1984, see "I missili sono qui ma il movimento non si arrende," *com-nuovi tempi*, 16 February 1984. For a call (by peace committees of northern Italy) to all Italian committees, see "imac '83," *il manifesto*, 3 May 1984, urging all Italian committees to coordinate nationally and with other European countries to sustain the peoples of El Salvador and Nicaragua against "aggression of U. S. imperialism," to implement direct action to promote the departure of Italy from Nato, to encourage all popular measures of objection of conscience on the ground of self-determination against nuclear weapons. Resistance at Comiso took a variety of forms; see booklet of Bertolt Brecht cultural association, Comitato Unitario per il disarmo e la pace Comiso, *Il riarmo: una lucida follia* (Comiso, 1983). Among the many publications of the Cudip peace organization at Comiso, see *Alternativa Comiso*, June, 1983; among the many women's groups working for disarmament at Comiso, see leaflets of la ragnatela (the spider web), whose projects have included purchasing the land where the missiles were placed (see "Un metro quadro di pace," *pace e guerra*, 4 August 1983). See chapter 16. The best source for the Italian peace movement in 1985 is *Pace in Movimento*, a new publication of all Italian peace committees published at Rome. See "Assemblea nazionale del pacifismo di base," May 1985.

16. *femminismo inedito: differenze:* unedited feminism: differences

1. Spotts and Wieser, *Italy*, chap. 14.
2. *noidonne, supplemento*, March 1983.
3. Ibid.
4. Ibid. For background to women's demands for justice in many areas, see Giuliane Dal Pozzo et al., *Cosa loro. e tutto vero, verissimo e non e tutto. testimonianze-denunce al tribunale 8 marzo* (Rome, 1980). Includes reference to medical "violence in white shirt."
5. *noidonne, supplemento*, March 1983.
6. Ibid.   7. Ibid.
8. See Alessandro di Loreto and Giancarlo Storto, *Casa: un problema per la sinistre* (Rome, Perugia, 1980).
9. Ibid.
10. Maria Rosa Cutrufelli, *Le donne protagoniste*. Also, *Lega nazionale delle cooperative: la sua storia, la sua immagine, la sua politica* (Rome, 1983); Onelio Prandini, *La cooperazione* (Rome, 1982); Romolo Menighetti, "La terza via italiana: autogestione," *rocca*, 15 January 1982. There are more than 120,000 coops in Italy, most in the North, although a good many have recently been built in the South. See *Cooperazione italiana*, weekly bulletin of the *Lega nazionale delle cooperative italiane* (Rome).

11. "Comunicazione speciale delle donne della cooperativa 'la casa matta' di Milano," *noidonne, supplemento,* March 1983.
12. Ibid.
13. Ibid. In the 1970s and 1980s, Italian women consciously aligned their movement with peasant women of the third world. Italian feminist perspective is close to the programs of the United Nations, supplemented by the conviction that laws do not by themselves change women's condition if women remain in a subaltern role economically. "For women emigrants to the city in the third world, a minimal concession is made to them to enter commerce, selling food, handicrafts, domestic service. Or prostitution." At Rome an Italian association for development (Aidos) has launched a campaign for development from women's perspective, emphasizing women's coops. This subject was brought before the women's world conference marking the end of the United Nations decade of women at Nairobi, Kenya, in July 1985.
14. "Più donne che uomini," *sottosopra, fascicolo speciale,* January 1983 (Milan).
15. Ibid.
16. Ibid. With different implication but a similar tone, see Christiane Collange, *Voglio tornare a casa: il riposo della guerriera dopo 10 anni di battaglie femministe* (Milan, 1979). See journal of Milanese feminists, *Via Dogana,* September 1983. See also Ludovica Ripa di Meana, "Confessioni/le donne del post-femminismo raccontano il loro disincanto," *l'Europeo,* September 1984.
17. *sottosopra,* January 1983.
18. Ibid.   19. Ibid.
20. Ibid. For a philosophical discussion of the concept of difference, see "Figure della differenza," *aut aut,* March–June 1981.
21. Coordinamento per l'autodeterminiazione della donna, Catania, "donne e disarmo: una parola in più," *Rassegna stampa per 8 marzo 1983, incontro internazionale Comiso* (a collection of newspaper articles recounting the history and activities of the Catanese feminist committee).
22. A good discussion of the code of honor can be found in Richard Gambino, *Blood of My Blood: The Dilemma of the Italian Americans* (New York, 1974). See "L'uomo di Pazienza—The Ideal of Manliness," 128 ff. Also, "The Problem of the Mafia Image," 274 ff.
23. See Lucia C. Birnbaum, "Earthmothers, godmothers, and radicals: the inheritance of Sicilian American women," *Marxist Perspectives,* Spring, 1979. A good contemporary evaluation of the social and economic condition of the South is "The mezzogiorno: a word of warning," *notizie dall'Italia* (Fondazione Giovanni Agnelli), November 1984. Referring to the south of Italy as the "cradle of great civilizations," the article states that it is today "a ruin, a collection of failed initiatives, a heap of illusions that have cost millions (and have made some people very rich) but the hoped-for progress has never reached the honest Southerners." The historical context for the passionate intensity of Sicilian feminists is suggested in the history recounted in this article of poverty, quashed hopes, emigration, many governmental plans for improvement, yet the "disparity between North and South is still obvious." Legislation to continue the thirty-four-year-old Cassa per il Mezzogiorno was voted down July 1984. This article, written for the northern newspaper *la stampa* and reprinted by the Agnelli Foundation's newsletter, does not mention the deleterious effects of Nato missiles at Comiso. See Bibliographical Essay, this work.

24. See Birnbaum, "Earthmothers, godmothers, and radicals."

25. Ibid.   26. Ibid.   27. Ibid.

28. See Maria Rosa Cutrufelli, *Disoccupata con onore: lavoro e condizione della donna* (Milan, 1975). See also Ann Cornelisen, *Women of the Shadows* (New York, 1976), and a book of photographs by Denise Jacobs and Rean Mazzone, *Donna in sicilia* (Palermo, 1978). Two indispensable studies are S. Mafai *et al.*, *Essere donne in Sicilia*; and Simonetta Piccone Stella, *Ragazze del sud* (Rome, 1979)

29. See Cutrufelli, *Disoccupata.*

30. Birnbaum, "Earthmothers, godmothers, and radicals." For feminism from the perspective of southern women, see Maria Teresa Giannelli, *Il sud delle donne. diario di una ricerca* (Milan, 1981).

31. Birnbaum, "Earthmothers, godmothers, and radicals." See also Cutrufelli, *Disoccupata.*

32. Interviews, 1982.

33. Coordinamento per l'autodeterminazione della donna, Catania, "donne e disarmo: una parola in più," *Rassegna stampa per 8 marzo 1983, incontro internazionale Comiso.*

34. Ibid. Feminist efforts to dismantle the nuclear base at Comiso were within a context of similar activity by a variety of people. See Denise Jacobs, ed., *No ai missili, no alla guerra, documenti sulla manifestazione dell'11–10–1981 a Comiso* (Palermo, 1982) The cudip peace office at Comiso publishes pamphlets and a newsletter; see *nove giorni di lotta per la sospensione della base della morte. per il disarmo, la pace, la libertà dei popoli. Comiso 29 aprile–7 maggio 1982* (Comiso, 1982). Associazione culturale B. Brecht, *Prima che sia troppo tardi* (Comiso, 1982). Cudip, *Lettera aperta al presidente del consiglio dei ministri* (Comiso, 1981); see *bollettino* of Cudip, Comiso. There is a large literature of groups involved in demonstrations at Comiso; e.g., lega per il disarmo unilaterale, "International antimilitarist nonviolent march, Catania-Comiso, December 25–January 2, 1983"; Raffaele Luise, "Una croce al Magliocco," *pace e guerra*, 14 April 1983; "Convegno di Bozze 82. Ragusa; invece dei missili una nuova cultura di pace," *com-nuovi tempi*, 9 May 1982. For Italian anxiety about being a nuclear target, see "Italia ora H," *l'Espresso*, 4 July 1982. "Rapporto sulla guerra atomica nel nostro paese: attacco al nord," *l'Espresso*, July 1982. See also newsletter of World Student Christian Federation, Europe Office. Convegno Ecumenico Internazionale, "Fede e impegno per la pace," Federazione delle Chiese Evangeliche in Sicilia e della Commissione pace e disarmo delle Chiese Battiste, Metodiste e Valdesi. Comiso 1983 (Catania 1983). See Rome journal *lotta per la pace;* e.g., "A Comiso per difenderela pace" (7/8 1983).

35. Coordinamento per l'autodeterminizazione della donna, Catania, "donne e disarmo."

36. Ibid.   37. Ibid.   38. Ibid.   39. Ibid.   40. Ibid.

41. Ibid.   42. Ibid.   43. Ibid.

44. "Comiso," *il manifesto*, 13 March 1983.

   See "un albero della pace dalle Alpi alla Sicilia," *noidonne, supplemento*, February 1984, for the telephone tree devised by the women's group at Comiso, la ragnatela, to coordinate initiatives of Italian women against the nuclear base. Adriana Zarri, "Lettera aperta a la giuria del tribunale di Ragusa," *rocca*, 1 May 1984 is a discussion of the trial of the twelve women (from Germany, Denmark, Ireland, Britain, Holland, and Italy) who protested nonviolently at Comiso, were arrested, tried, and the non-Italians expelled from Italy. Zarri said that these women had understood that the nuclear base at Comiso is not an Italian matter, nuclear death is "universal."

45. "Oggi molta gente del mondo nega la cultura di guerra e le armi di ogni contrada che porta in grembo," *il manifesto*, 22 October 1983.

46. Leaflet, women's peace committee-Rome, 22 October 1983.

17.   *io sono mia/siamo in tante:*
I am my own person/we are many

1. Patrizia Magli, "Riconoscimento e differenza: i paradossi del marginale," *i nuovi paradigmi della cultura 'frammentata': una mappa del sapere degli anni 80,* convegno pro civitate christiana, Assisi, 3–8 December 1983. See Magli, *Corpo e linguaggio* (Rome, 1980).

2. Aldo Garzia, "L'unità nazionale ha interroto il trend storico del voto italiano, il Pci che sale, la Dc che scende," *pace e guerra*, 30 June 1983. See *Italy in Transition: Conflict and Consensus,* ed. Peter Lange and Sidney Tarrow (Bournemouth, Great Britain, 1983). For a glimpse of the decentralized socialism envisioned by feminists, the new left, left catholics, and the independent left who supported the Pci in 1983 and 1984, see *Quale socialismo? dibattito aperto,* including essays of Luigi Pintor, Gianni Baget-Bozzo, Giulio Girardi, Lidia Menapace, Rossana Rossanda *et al.* (Assisi, 1980).

3. The May 12, 1985, administrative elections placed the Dc in first place (ca. 34%, with the Pci dropping back to 30%). A preelection analysis written by Rina Gagliardi ("Le tre carte nel gioco delle regione," *il manifesto*, May 9, 1985) puts election results into perspective. She pointed out that the Dc secured 36.8% of the vote in 1980; three years later, the Dc vote had fallen to 32.9%. The Pci received 29.9% in regional elections of 1983 and thereafter 34.5% at the European elections. Sicily did not vote on May 12, leaving the southern question hanging in Italian politics.

4. Franco Bassanini *et al.,* "L'Italia postdemocristiana," *pace e guerra*, July 1983. For a contemporary peasant perspective on "l'alternativa," see Carlo Consiglio, *Una società a misura di natura* (Catania, 1981), a series published by Pr which aims to rediscover the "real socialism" of the beginning of the twentieth century in Italy grounded on a peasant culture described as "anarchic, autonomous" and unbureaucratized. For a feminist interpretation of "l'alternativa," see Antonella Nappi, *L'alternativa: esperienze di autonomia, identità femminile e nuovi rapporti sociali* (Milan, 1983). For a left catholic and marxist interpretation of "l'alternativa," see Roger Garaudy's best seller on self-managed socialism grounded on a religious consciousness, *L'alternativa: cambiare il mondo e la vita* (Assisi, 1980), 78, 84, 87, 91, 93, 101–3, 107, 112, 127.

5. Luciana Castellina, "La campagna è noiosa? No. io mi diverto," *pace e guerra*, 23 June 1983. See Bassanini *et al.,* "L'Italia postdemocristiana."

6. For the "changed Pci," see Pia Bruzzichelli, "Il dibattito aperto dal XVI congresso del Pci," *idoc*, April 1983. Diana Johnstone, "Idealism bolsters communist party," *In These Times*, 6–12 April 1983.

For an evaluation of the June 1984 elections, see Ruggero Orfei, "Elezioni: non esistono più posizioni di rendità," *rocca*, 15 July 1984. Orfei pointed out that the Pci by 1984 in its slight voter preponderance over the Dc had gathered the new left electorate of Pdup while the Psi appeared to be in decline; the salient fact is that Italian voters are no longer "married" to a particular party. Claudio Bascape, "Dal voto prospettive diverse," in the same issue of *rocca*, explored the ideological issues involved in the June 1984 elections: opposition to European missiles and growth of the greens in the European parliament.

7. Ida Dominijanni, "Donne/Pci: dagli anni 70 agli 80, un passaggio difficile," *il manifesto*, 2 March 1984. Ida Dominijanni, "VII conferenza. donne comuniste. il disagio diventa conflitto. prima va cambiato il partito," *il manifesto*, 4 March 1984. Norma Rangeri, "Roma VII conferenza delle donne comuniste. Berlinguer accolto come un divo, 'adotta' le donne e sgrida il partito," *il manifesto*, 6 March 1984.

8. For the women's group in parliament, see "Alla camera e al senato, vinta la diffidenza dei parlamentari, è nato il 'gruppo' delle donne comuniste," *la repubblica*, 18 November 1983. The number of women in the Italian parliament is smaller than the cultural influence women have exercised on Italian politics; ca. 30 percent of the members of the Italian parliament are communists; approximately 6 to 7 percent of this number are women. In addition to women communists, there are feminists in other parties.

9. Ida Dominijanni, "Se ben che siamo donne," *il manifesto*, 6 March 1984.

10. Ibid.

11. Paolo Spriano, "Gli anni di Berlinguer," *Rinascità*, 20 October 1984. See Ugo Faller, *Berlinguer: il marxismo in doppiopetto* (Milan, 1976). See "Berlinguer e l'ansia dei poveri," *com-nuovi tempi*, 24 June 1984 for a left catholic view of Berlinguer, whose death, it was felt, affected those "without voice": workers who paid for the economic crisis, unemployed young people, and immigrants from countries of the third world. See, "'Enrico Enrico,' il saluto della piazza. Migliaia di piccoli cortei a Roma: le stazioni, Botteghe oscure, San Giovanni," *il manifesto*, 14 June 1984, "Berlinguer è morto. Quel filo tra 'compromesso' e alternativa," *l'Unità*, 11 June 1984.

12. Comunità di animazione cristiana, Formia, *giovani e politica. inchiesta con gli studenti medi superiori di Formia, com-nuovi tempi, supplemento* no. 19, 25 May 1980.

13. Arci, *Il grande Karl*, with a hundred 'unedited' photos of the 'family of Carlo Marx' (Rome, 1983). See cartoons 6, 13, 27, 47.

14. *noidonne*, December 1983.

15. Ibid.

16. Rossana Rossanda, "Due orbite" in "La barba del profeta," *noidonne*, December 1983.

17. Anna Maria Crispino, "La barba del profeta," *noidonne*, December 1983.

18. Ibid.

19. Lidia Menapace, "Cosa vuol dire essere comunisti oggi," seminario organizzato dal comitato regionale del Pdup del Lazio, Rome, 10 November 1983.

20. Acquaviva, "Utopia francescana e utopia del '68" in *Francesco*. See also "Eulogy to madness" in "presentazione"; Luigi Bettazzi, "La 'pazzia' della pace"; Anna Portoghese, "Una svolta profetica e istuzionale"; Luigi Ciotti, "I 'nuovi' lebbrosi"; Bianca Fornari, "Chiara e Jacopa: il femminile nell'uomo votato al vangelo"; Giannino Piana, "Francesco e la donna: una provocazione salutare."

21. Acquaviva, "Utopia francescana," in *Francesco*.

22. Annamaria Guadagni, "Le cattoliche alla riscossa," *noidonne*, November 1983.

23. Grazia Francescato, "Tra donne e politica," *donne e politica* May–August 1982.

24. Ibid. See comments by Giglia Tedesco, Giancarla Codrignani, Elena Marinucci. See also Claudio Calvaruso, *La società emergente tra utopia e consenso* (Assisi, 1977), 134.
25. Massimo Cacciari, "Frammentazione della cultura contemporanea: crisi della metafisica dello stato"; Seminario di Studio, Pro Civitate Christiana, Assisi, *I nuovi paradigmi della cultura 'frammentata'; una mappa del sapere degli anni 80,* 3–7 December, 1983, Assisi. See also Giulio Girardi, "La politica fra realismo e utopia," seminario, Assisi, 3–7 December 1983. See special issue of *rocca,* 1–15 February 1984, "I nuovi paradigmi della cultura contemporanea: una mappa del sapere degli anni 80." See also Franco Ferrarotti, "La revoluzione è femmina" (the gender of the revolution is female) in *Come muore una classe dirigente* (Rome, 1980).
26. See editorial, *noidonne,* October 1983, "La donna che vuole essere dio" (the woman who wants to be God).
27. Ibid.
28. Andrew M. Greeley, "Not as Pawns of the Church," *New York Times,* 12 August 1984. See Marie-Dominique Chenu, "Preti-operai. hanno saltato il muro ma il muro resta," *rocca,* 1 June 1984. See Giovanni Bianchi and Renzo Salvi, "I nuovi cattolici oltre il dissenso e oltre le sette," *rocca,* 15 December 1983; Giancarlo Zizola, "Il settembre nero di papa Wojtyla," *rocca,* 15 September 1984; "E dopo Boff, l'Europa," *lettere, com-nuovi tempi,* 2 December 1984; "Boff, sant'Uffizio e teologia della liberazione," *com-nuovi tempi,* 16 September 1984.
29. Beth Maschinot, "Catholic Church. Vatican backlash hits nuns' independence on abortion," *In These Times,* 15–19 January 1985. For an Italian left catholic view of what contemporary papal intransigence connotes, see Giancarlo Zizola, "Religione e politica: una nuova pace costantiniana," *rocca,* 1 January 1985, in which he suggests that the movements (visible in the U. S. as well as in Italy) "for a new peace between church and society, of Reagan and Wojtyla" will be a precarious peace because it connotes "the last defense that the empire hopes to construct against the new barbarians," against "the threat of the poor and to gain time." See Malachi Martin, *Rich Church, Poor Church* (New York, 1984), pt. 4. See Francesco Alberoni, "Il papa e le donne," *la Repubblica,* 8 December 1983.
30. Annamaria Guadagna, "Berlinguer," *noidonne* July 1984.
31. Ibid.
32. Giorgio Galli, *Storia del socialismo italiano* (Rome, Bari, 1980). 330–37.
33. Ibid.   34. Ibid., 334–36.   35. Ibid., 336–37.
36. Ibid., dedication. Whether or not there will be a new witch hunt in Italy in the eighties is as yet unclear. There is evidence of a backlash against women, from condemnations of the pope to the October 1984 mutilation of the sexual violence bill in the house to new activity by right-wing terrorists (the bomb in the train tunnel at Christmas 1984) to sensational exposés of the contemporary condition of the *casa della donna* at Rome that had once been the center of Italian feminism to numerous pronouncements that the women's movement is dead (see "Has silence fallen on the Italian Feminist Movement?" *notizie dall'Italia,* Fondazione Giovanni Agnelli, May 1984).

Feminists abandoned the *casa della donna* in March 1983; subsequently it became a refuge for homeless, famished women, some of them recently released from prison or asylums. Newspaper articles publicized discoveries of drugs, prostitution, theft at the *casa.* See "L'ex roccaforte delle femministe, al Governo Vecchio, trasformata in una scuola di violenza. tutte donne. un'assassina il capo," *il Messagero*, 18 September 1984. "Eroina e prostituzione nella ex Casa delle donne," *la Repubblica*, 18 September 1984.

For the upheaval over the manhandling of the sexual violence bill by the camera, see "Femministe e sinistra deluse la loro legge ha un marchio dc," *la Repubblica*, 20 October 1984. Feminists of independent collectives are particularly enraged; polemics have erupted. See, "Le femministe tornano all'assalto del 'maschio politico,'" *Corriere della Sera*, 13 January 1985. During a debate sponsored by Arci on the sexual violence bill, Pci men were criticized by feminists of independent collectives for trying to manipulate the women's movement. Rino Serri (of the Pci central committee) was devastatingly criticized by a militant feminist whom he had known intimately (Serri could not speak about the sexual violence bill, said the feminist—in what may be the ultimate Italian insult— because he did not know how to make love). Serri wrote a letter to the *Corriere della Sera* on 17 January 1985, "Maschilismo, Pci e donne 'separate'," avowing his continued support for the law punishing sexual violence.

There are advances among the setbacks; a parliamentary committee on male/ female equality recommended a constitutional amendment clarifying the language of original articles on equality. A rewritten Article 36 holds implication of payment for housework: "every worker, man or woman, has the right to recompense" ("Como l'uomo e la donna diverranno 'più pari'," *Corriere della Sera*, 15 November 1984).

37. . . . daddy enjoys and momma works . . . daddy eats *fagioli* and momma worries about the children."

38. Marina Bacchetti, ed., *Nella donna c'era un sogno . . . canzoniere femminista* (Milan, 1976). See "Dirindina la malcontenta" (20); "Siamo in tante" (130); "Se ero io" (32). See also "Siamo in tante . . . la condizione della donna nelle canzoni popolari e femministe," ed. Yuki Maraini (Rome, 1975).

39. We are many, we are more than half
    we have always been in this humanity.
    We are many, we are more than half
    but we count for nothing in this society.

    And if we are separate each in her house
    then we are exploited and without liberty
    and if we hide each of us in our cell
    we waste our life which will soon end.

    We are many, we are more than half . . .

    But if we unite and breathe deeply
    then we shall see others and recognize ourselves
    we have a hope that all can change
    and we say 'basta' to this old reality.

    We are many, we are more than half. . . ."

See also *Canzoni italiane di protesta 1789/1974 dalla rivoluzione francese alla repressione cilena*, ed. Giuseppe Vettori (Perugia, 1974); *Canti popolari italiani: una suggestiva raccolta dei folk italiano della tradizione contadina alla nuova realta operaia* (Perugia, 1974); Luigi Infantino, *Sicilia amara e duci: raccolta di canti Siciliani* (Milan, 1967)

afterword

1. *Dal movimento femminista al femminismo diffuso*, ed. Laura Grasso and Annarita Calabro (Milan, 1985). See review "Ciascuna a suo modo: Una ricerca sul femminismo in Lombardia dal '65 agli anni '80," *il manifesto*, 8 May 1985.
2. Sandro Medici, "La pizza con la ricotta: La circoscrizione più piccola è antinucleare e pacifista. Parla la presidentessa," *il manifesto*, 6 May 1985.
3. "Demetra," *noidonne*, May 1984.

glossary

aggiornamento: The orientation of vatican council II, (1963–65), proposing to bring the catholic church up to date, or to make it relevant to the twentieth century.

autogestione: Self-management. The term has antecedents in Gramsci's encouragement of factory councils and holds connotations of libertarian socialism. For feminism, the term is given immediate meaning in the phrase "l'utero è mio e me lo gestisco io" (It is my uterus and I will manage it).

autonomous feminists: Militant Italian feminists of the seventies who in describing themselves as "autonomous" differentiated themselves from those feminists in the Pci and Dc whose organizations, particularly *Unione donne italiane* (Udi) and *Centro italiano femminile* (Cif), held an auxiliary status in the parties. Udi effected its autonomy of the Pci in 1982 and Cif women by the 1980s tended to identify with other women rather more than with their party.

bandiera rossa: The red flag of communism.

case della donna: Women's houses which were created after 1976, first at Rome, then all over Italy. They served as women's refuges, as well as political, educational, and social centers.

cdb (comunità di base): Italian base communities where men and women live in accordance with an unedited reading of the judeo-christian gospel. They are close to Italian liberation theology and are a major source of feminist support.

consultori: Women's health clinics where women can talk with other women and secure help for birth control, abortion, and other matters.

democratic centralism: Traditional principle of communist parties. Debate among party members in formulation of policy is considered the democratic aspect. Centralism is demonstrated in obligatory obedience of party members to final decisions of central committee. This principle was a major target of new left criticism in Italy after 1968; it was reformed in the Pci congress of 1983 and in party actions which recognized the integrity of different perspectives and different strategies.

dopoguerra: The postwar era in Italy, 1945–1968, a political climate of cold war currents and an intellectual atmosphere of neorealism in films and novels.

doppia militanza: the "double militancy" of women who simultaneously work for feminist concerns and also in parties, unions, movements, and institutions where men are dominant.

inedito (unedited): A word that came to be used in the nineteen-seventies to refer to an unmediated view of the gospel, of marxism, of feminism, and of other matters. The term connotes direct democracy, direct experience, and trust in individual conscience. For feminists the antinomian implications of the term are modified; moral judgments are made by looking inward, but also by looking at others.

integralismo: The Italian religious and political assumption before vatican council II and the political confrontations of 1968 that unity is imposed from the top—by the church or by the party. Debate on feminist issues after 1968 challenged the integralism of the church (imposing doctrine on its communicants) and the integralism of the party (imposing its definition of marxism on party members) and was informed by the competition between the church and the party for precedence. In 1985 the Pci has relinquished aspirations to integralism by supporting feminists and new left dissenters on its ballots and stipulating that party members need not be marxists and may be practicing catholics. The church, in its condemnations of liberation theology, birth control, abortion, premarital sex, homosexuality, and women in the priesthood has apparently not given up aspirations toward *integralismo*.

one-hundred-and-fifty-hour classes: Stipulation in labor union contracts of the 1970s that enabled workers, unemployed people, and housewives to take 150 hours of free classes; women often used the option to take women's studies classes.

lo strappo: The Pci rupture of remaining ties with the communist party of the Soviet Union in December 1981, accusing the soviets of lack of representative institutions, of closed hierarchical structures, of perpetuating the "false idea" that the Soviet Union is a model for socialism, instead of recognizing that socialism is a "historical process developing on a world scale in the most diverse ways."

gli ultimi (or, in women's translation, *le ultime*): Refers to the "least" or the "last" in the judeo-christian gospel. For the new left and for feminists the term referred to all marginal people: the elderly, children, the handicapped, the mentally ill, drug addicts—and the poor of the South of the globe.

"violento in camice bianco" (violent in white shirts): A term that arose in the March 8, 1980, Italian women's tribunal denouncing the violence of doctors and psychologists toward women.

bibliographical essay

Feminist research in general, and this manuscript in particular, is rather more horizontal than vertical. This essay is to be read together with sources cited in the text and in the notes and should be regarded as an exploratory guide to the continuing Italian feminist cultural and political revolution.

her story

history of Italian feminism

Italian research in the history of Italian feminism is evaluated by Franca Pieroni Bortolotti in "A Survey of Recent Italian Research on the History of Feminism," *The Journal of Italian History* 1 (Winter 1978). Indispensable for the historiography of Italian feminism are the journals *donnawomanfemme, memoria,* and *noidonne.* Pathbreaking works in the history of Italian women are Franca Pieroni Bortolotti, *Alle origini del movimento femminile in italia (1848–1892)* (Rome, 1963), and Anna Maria Mozzoni, *La liberazione della donna,* ed. Franca Pieroni Bortolotti (Milan, 1975). See also Camilla Ravera, *Breve storia del movimento femminile in Italia* (Rome, 1978). For the women's movement in Sicily, see Jole Calapso, *Donne ribelli: un secolo di lotte femminili in Sicilia* (Palermo, 1980).

Italian feminists in the context of European history

For Italian feminists in the context of European history, see Natalie Zemon Davis, "La storia delle donne in transizione: il caso europeo," *donnawomanfemme,* April–June 1977. Davis's *Society and Culture in Early Modern France* (Stanford, California, 1965) is an example of distinguished European feminist history. See also *La stregoneria in Eu-*

ropa, ed. Marina Romello (Bologna, 1975); Jane Slaughter and Robert Kern, *European Women on the Left: Socialism, Feminism, and the Problems Faced by Political Women, 1880 to the Present* (Westport, Connecticut, 1981); Louise Tilly and Joan Scott, *Women, Work and the Family* (New York, 1978); Charles Tilly, Louise Tilly, and Richard Tilly, *The Rebellious Century, 1830–1930* (Cambridge, Mass., 1973); Chapter 3, "Italy," in Eleanor S. Riemer and John C. Fout, *European Women: A Documentary History, 1789–1945* (New York, 1980); and Carol R. Berkin and Clara M. Lovett, eds., *Women, War, and Revolution* (New York, 1980). A useful bibliographical guide to sources in English for recent Italian history is Peter Lange, *Studies on Italy, 1943–1975: Select bibliography of American and British materials in Political Science, Economics, Sociology and Anthropology* (Turin, 1977), especially chapters 4 and 5, "The Family" and "Women."

global feminist studies

In addition to Italian feminist studies cited throughout the text, global feminist studies may be sought in the pages of *Signs, donnawomanfemme, Feminist Studies*, and other such journals. A select list of studies in the English language that have been important to this writer (and that will help the reader to locate the author on the landscape of feminist historiography) include: Simone de Beauvoir, *The Second Sex* (first published 1952; New York, 1974); *Feminist Theory: A Critique of Ideology*, ed. Nannerl O. Keohane, Michelle Z. Rosaldo, and Barbara C. Gelpi (Chicago, 1981); Dorothy Bryant, *Miss Giardino* (Berkeley, Calif. 1978); Angela Davis, *Women, Race and Class* (New York, 1981); Natalie Zemon Davis, *Society and Culture in Early Modern France* (Stanford, Calif., 1965); Barbara Ehrenreich and Deirdre English, *For Her Own Good: 150 Years of the Experts' Advice to Women* (Garden City, N. Y., 1979); Elizabeth Schussler Fiorenza, *In Memory of Her: A Feminist Theological Reconstruction of Christian Origins* (New York, 1983); Clare Fischer, *Breaking Through: A Bibliography of Women and Religion* (Berkeley, Calif., 1980); Susan Griffin, *Woman and Nature: The Roaring Inside Her* (New York, 1978); Paule Marshall, *Praisesong for the Widow* (New York, 1984); Kate Millett, *Sexual Politics* (New York, 1971); *This Bridge Called My Back: Writings by Radical Women of Color*, ed. Cherrie Moraga and Gloria Anzaldua (Watertown, Mass., 1981); Robin Morgan, ed., *Sisterhood is Global: The International Women's Movement Anthology* (Garden City, N. Y., 1984); Tillie Olsen, *Tell Me a Riddle* (New York, 1956); Adrienne Rich, *Of Woman Born* (New York, 1976); *On Lies, Secrets, and Silence: Selected Prose 1966–1978* (New York, 1979); Michelle Zimbalist Rosaldo and Louise Lamphere, *Women, Culture and Society* (Stanford, Calif., 1974); Ruth Rosen, *The Lost Sisterhood: Prostitution in America, 1900–1918 (Baltimore, Md., 1982);* Sheila Rowbotham, *Women, Resistance and Revolution: A History of Women and Revolution in the Modern World* (New York, 1972); and *Hidden From History: Rediscovering Women in History from the Seventeenth Century to the Present* (London, 1973); Sheila Rowbotham, Lynne Segal, and Hilary Wainwright, *Beyond the Fragments: Feminism and the Making of Socialism* (London, 1979); Dale Spender, *Man Made Language* (London, 1980); and Alice Walker, *You Can't Keep a Good Woman Down: Stories* (New York, 1981).

earth mothers, goddesses, and godmothers

archeological studies

Archeological studies are indispensable for women's history. An excellent guide to the archeology of Sicily is Margaret Guido, Sicily: An Archeological Guide: The Prehis-~ toric and Roman Remains and the Greek Cities (New York, 1967). See also Eugenio Manni, Sicilia pagana (Palermo, 1963).

women's place in world religions

For women and religion, see G. Quispel, Gnosis als Weltreligion (Leiden, 1951); and Hans Jonas, The Gnostic Religion (Boston, 1958). See also Philip E. Slater, The Glory of Hera: Greek Mythology and the Greek Family (Boston, 1968); Elaine Pagels, The Gnostic ✓ Gospels (New York, 1979); and Elizabeth Schussler Fiorenza, In Memory of Her: A Feminist Theological Reconstruction of Christian Origins (New York, 1973).

Italian studies of earth mothers, goddesses, and matriarchy

Italian studies of earth mothers, goddesses, and matriarchy include Pietro Angelini, Le cattive madri: l'emarginazione della donna e il mito 'maschile' del matriarcato (with the writings of Kant, Hegel, Bachofen, Morgan, Engels, Bebel, Freud, Horney, Jones, Adler, Stekel, Michelet, Fromm, Campbell, Lederer, Bermann) (Rome, 1974); and Eva Cantarella, L'ambiguo malanno: condizione e immagine della donna nell'antichità greca e romana (Rome, 1981); see chapter 1, "Il matriarcato tra preistoria, mito e storia." The conflicting emotions evoked by earlier and later mothers for contemporary Italian feminists are suggested by Angela Cattaneo and Silvana Pisa in L'altra mamma: la maternità nel movimento delle donne: fantasie, desideri, domande e inquietudini, con un commento di Laura Grasso (Perugia, 1979).

women in antiquity and today

For women in antiquity, see Sarah Pomeroy, Goddesses, Whores, Wives and Slaves: Women in Classical Antiquity (New York, 1975); cf. Susan Moller Okin, Women in Western Political Thought (Princeton, N.J., 1979); and Sarah B. Pomeroy, "A Classical Scholar's Perspective on Matriarchy," in Liberating Women's History: Theoretical and Critical Essays, ed. Berenice A. Carroll (Urbana and Chicago, 1976). The classic study of matriarchy is available in English as Myth, Religion, and Mother Right: Selected Writings of J. S. Bachofen, With a preface by George Boas and an introduction by Joseph Campbell (Princeton, N. J., 1967). See also Erich Neumann, The Great Mother: An Analysis of the Archetype, trans. Ralph Manheim (Princeton, N. J., 1955); and Michael Grant, Myths of the Greeks and Romans (New York, 1962). Early, and controversial, studies of prechristian women include Helen Diner, Mothers and Amazons: The First Feminine History of Culture (originally published 1965; New York, 1973); and Robert Graves, The White Goddess: A Historical Grammar of Poetic Myth. (New York, 1948). For an indispensable contemporary study, see The Politics of Women's Spirituality: Essays on the Rise of Spiritual Power within the Feminist Movement, ed. Charlene Spretnak (New York, 1982). The C. G. Jung Institute of San Francisco holds a considerable library of papers that relate to the topic; see Ute Dieckmann, M.D.; Katherine Bradway, Ph.D.; and Fareth Hill, M.S.W.; Male and female, feminine and masculine (1974); Katherine Bradway, Villa of Mysteries: Pompeii Initiation Rites of Women (1982); Jane H. Wheelwright, A.L.A., Women and Men (1978). An excellent study of the relevance of goddesses to women today is Jean Shinoda Bolen, M.D., *Goddesses in Everywoman* (San Francisco, 1984). A valuable contemporary sociological study is Robert N. Bellah and Phillip E. Hammond, *Varieties of Civil Religion* (San Francisco, 1980), chapter 4, "The Five Religions of Modern Italy."

godmothers and their lore

folklore as a source

The possibilities of folklore as a source for women's history are shown in the Giuseppe Pitré library, *Biblioteca delle tradizioni popolari siciliane*. The span of the collection is suggested in a partial list of Pitré writings reprinted in Palermo in 1978: *Proverbi motti e scongiuri del popolo; Giochi fanciulleschi siciliani; I studi di leggende popolari in Sicilia; Spettacoli e feste popolari siciliane; Fiabe novelle e racconti popolari siciliani* (vols. 1 and 2), *Proverbi siciliani*. Important Pitré studies are those on dialect, e.g., *Grammatica siciliana* (reprinted Palermo, 1979); on food: *O mangi questa minestra . . .* (reprinted Milan, 1979); and on death: *. . . O salti questa finestra* (Milan, 1979). Among his many works, *Le parità morali* (1883) by Serafino Amabile Guastella is most helpful for peasant beliefs and customs; see also his *Vestru: Scene del popolo siciliano* (1882; reprint ed. Ragusa, 1973). Salvatore Salomone-Marino, *Costumi ed usanze dei contadini in Sicilia* (Palermo, 1879) is an indispensable source. See Santi Correnti, *Storia di Sicilia come storia del popolo siciliano* (Milan, 1982); and *Leggende di Sicilia e loro genesi storica* (Milan, 1975); Giuseppe Cocchiara, *Preistoria e folklore* (Palermo, 1978) and his *Storia del folklore in Italia* (Palermo, 1981); C. Alberto Garufi, *Ricerche sugli usi nuziali del medioevo in Sicilia* (Palermo, 1980). "Il vespro" is a series of reprints of folk studies; e.g., Giuseppe Pitré, *Le lettere le scienze e le arti in Sicilia* (Palermo, 1979), and *Il vespro siciliano nelle tradizioni popolari nella sicilia* (Palermo, 1979); S. Salomone-Marino, *Le reputatrici in Sicilia nell'età di mezzo e moderna* (Palermo, 1979); Franco Mistrali, *Storia popolare della rivoluzione di Sicilia e della impresa di Giuseppe Garibaldi* (Palermo, 1979); Antonino Cutrera, *I ricottari (la mala vita di Palermo)* (Palermo, 1979); and Francesco Tarducci, *La strega l'astrologo e il mago* (Palermo, 1980). For a semiotic and anthropological approach to the folk tradition, see Antonino Buttita, *Semiotica e antropologia* (Palermo, 1979). Other studies include Giorgio Santangelo, *Letteratura in Sicilia da Federico II a Pirandello* (Palermo, 1941); G. Ragusa Moleti, *Il signor di Macqueda* (Palermo, 1881; reprint ed. 1980); *400 indovinelli siciliani raccolti da Carmelo Assenza* (Ragusa, 1972); Santo Rapisarda, *Raccolta di proverbi siciliani ridotti in canzoni* (Catania, 1924; reprint ed. Catania, 1979); and Emanuele Scalici, *La mafia siciliana* (a nineteenth-century study reprinted in Palermo, 1980). The popular Sicilian legend *La baronessa di Carini* was cast as a play by Alceste de Cenzo and reprinted in Palermo, 1971. For witchcraft, see Elsa Guggino, *Magia in Sicilia* (Palermo, 1978). See also the collection of writings of the folklorist Giuseppe Cocchiara, *L'eterno selvaggio*, ed. Antonino Buttita (Palermo, 1972). For Italian cultural anthropology, see *Appunti per la storia dell'antropologia culturale* (Rome, 1981). The journal of anthropological studies in Sicily is *uomo e cultura* (Palermo).

literature that taps folklore beliefs

For literature that taps folklore beliefs, see the novels of Giuseppe Verga. His stories "Nedda" and "La lupa" may be found in Giovanni Verga, *Tutte le novelle*

(Rome, 1975); in English, they are published as Giovanni Verga, *The She-Wolf and Other Stories*, trans. Giovanni Cecchetti (Berkeley and Los Angeles, 1958). Verga's masterpiece, *I malavoglia*, is available in many editions. An edition with biography and bibliography is *I malavoglia* (Rome, 1939; reprint ed. 1975). For didactic literature couched as fables, the works of Luigi Capuana are important. In addition to the many editions of *C'era una volta* published in the 1880s and 1890s, see *Versi giovanili* (reprint ed. Catania, 1978; *Giacinta: commedia in 5 atti* (1879; reprint ed. Catania 1980); *Il marchese di Roccaverdina*, with biographical essay and bibliography (Rome, 1974). See also Marina Warner, *Sola fra le donne: Mito e culto di Maria Vergine* (Palermo, 1976). For the modern period, a highly valuable work is Giuseppe Tomasi di Lampedusa, *Il gattopardo* (1957; reprint ed. Milan, 1983). For contemporary appreciation of the role of peasant women in Italian history, see "Gli uomini eravamo noi donne" (We women were the men), *Corriere della Sera*, 17 January 1985, an interview with Nuto Revelli, whose *L'anello forte* (Milan, 1985) is a collection of contemporary interviews with peasant women.

the southern question

Gramsci

A good beginning to this subject is Antonio Gramsci, "The southern question," in *The Modern Prince and Other Writings* (New York, 1957). See also Leonardo Sciascia, *La Sicilia come metafora* (Rome, 1979).

history of Sicily

For the history of Sicily, see Denis Mack Smith, *Storia della Sicilia medievale e moderna*, 3 vols. (Rome-Bari, 1976); also available in English, this history of Sicily builds on M. I. Finley's *Ancient Sicily, Medieval Sicily: 800–1713*, and *Modern Sicily: after 1713* (New York, 1968). Research in Sicilian history is facilitated by these important studies: Vladimoro Agnesi, *Alla scoperta della Sicilia antica* (Palermo, 1979); Eugenio Manni, *Sicilia pagana* (Palermo, 1963); Michele Amari, *Storia dei musulmani di Sicilia* (1872; reprint ed. Catania, 1983); Umberto Rizzitano, *Storia e cultura nella Sicilia saracena* (Palermo, 1941); Giuseppe De Pasquale, *L'islam in Sicilia* (Palermo, 1941); Vladimoro Agnesi, *Breve storia dei normanni in Sicilia* (Palermo, 1941); Guido Di Stefano, *Monumenti della Sicilia normanna* (Palermo, 1955); Claudio Meldolesi, *Spettacolo feudale in Sicilia* (Palermo, 1941); Steven Runciman, *The Sicilian Vespers* (London and New York, 1958); Carmelo Trasselli, *Siciliani fra quattrocento e cinquecento* (Messina, 1981); Fernand Braudel, *The Mediterranean and the Mediterranean World in the Age of Philip II* (New York, 1972); Gino Stefani, *Musica e religione nell'Italia barocca* (Palermo, 1975); Virgilio Tritone, *La società siciliana sotto gli spagnoli e le origini della questione meridionale* (Palermo, 1978); Michele De Sangro, *I borboni nel regno delle due Sicilie* (1884; reprint ed. Bologna, 1979); Francesco Brancato, *Storiografia e politica nella Sicilia dell'ottocento* (Palermo, 1941); Francesco Renda, *Baroni e riformatori in Sicilia sotto il ministero Caracciolo (1786–1789)* (Messina, 1974); Giovanni Russo, *Baroni e contadini* (Rome-Bari, 1979); *Il sud nella storia d'Italia: antologia della questione meridionale* (Bari, 1981); Francesco De Stefano, *Storia della Sicilia dall'XI al XIX secolo* (Bari, 1977); Santi Correnti, *La Sicilia del cinquecento: il nazionalismo isolano* (Milan, 1980); Santi Correnti, *La Sicilia del seicento: società e cultura* (Milan, 1976); and Gaetano Falzone, *La Sicilia tra il sette e l'ottocento* (Palermo, 1965). Two helpful syntheses are Salvatore Francesco Romano, *Breve storia della Sicilia: momenti e problemi della civiltà siciliana* (Turin 1964); and Santi Correnti, *Storia e folklore di Sicilia* (Milan, 1975). For the perseveration of prechristian beliefs among first- and second-generation Italian Americans and the connection of the primordial mother and peasant woman ritual for exorcising *mal occhio* see Lawrence Di Stasi, *Mal Occhio: The Underside of Vision* (Berkeley, Calif., 1981). See Lucia Chiavola Birnbaum, Sicilian Women on the Eve of Emigration: Images in the Literature of Verga, Capuana, Pitré, and Sicilian Folklore, paper delivered at the conference of the California chapters of the American Studies Association, San Jose State University, 25 February 1979; and Lucia Chiavola Birnbaum, Political Economy of Oppression and Folklore Nurturing Rebellion: Sicily in the 1890s, paper delivered at the spring conference, West Coast Association of Women Historians; Mills College, Oakland; 21 April 1979. For emigration, see *Movimento operaio e socialista: Dall'Italia alle Americhe: Storie di emigranti e immagini dell'emigrazione* (Turin, 1981).

For Sicilian peasant socialist leagues in the 1890s, see Francesco Renda, *I fasci siciliani 1892–94* (Turin, 1970); *I fasci siciliani* (2 volumes) by Giuseppe Giarizzo *et al.* (Bari, 1975, 1976); and Giuseppe Casarrubea, *I fasci contadini e le origini delle sezioni socialiste della provincia di Palermo*, 2 vols. (Palermo, 1978). This subject is of high interest to the Italian left today; research is proceeding town by town in Sicily; e.g., Enzo Barnaba, *I fasci siciliani a Valguarnera* (Milan, 1981); and Giuseppe Micciche, *I fasci dei lavoratori nella Sicilia sud-orientale*, con documenti (Ragusa, 1981). An excellent 1976 summary of the southern problem is Francesco Renda, *Il movimento contadino in Sicilia e la fine del blocco agrario nel Mezzogiorno* (Bari, 1976). An important study in English is Jane Schneider and Peter Schneider, *Culture and Political Economy in Western Sicily* (New York, 1976). Charles Tilly, Louise Tilly, and Richard Tilly, *The Rebellious Century, 1830–1930* is valuable for Italian social movements. For the period prior to Sicilian emigration to the new world, see Donna R. Gabaccia, *From Sicily to Elizabeth Street, Housing and Social Change among Italian Immigrants, 1880–1930* (Albany, N. Y., 1984).

For Italian religious millenarianism and socialist activism, see E. J. Hobsbawm, *Primitive Rebels: Studies in Archaic Forms of Social Movements in the Nineteenth and Twentieth Centuries* (New York 1959), chapter 6, "Millenarianism III: The Sicilian Fasci and Peasant Communism." For a contemporary Italian study of this subject, see R. Cipriani, G. Rinaldi, and P. Sobrero, *Il simbolo conteso: simbolismo politico e religioso nelle culture di base meridionali* (Rome, 1979).

the woman question

history of the feminist/socialist argument

For the feminist/socialist argument a good historical analysis from the perspective of a critical contemporary Italian feminist is that of Maria Antonietta Macciocchi, "Quelques themes autour du marxisme et des femmes" in *Les femmes et leurs maitres* (Paris, 1978). A definitive logical analysis of the issue by a U. S. feminist scholar is that of Catherine A. MacKinnon, "Feminism, Marxism, Method, and the State: An Agenda for Theory," in *Feminist Theory: A Critique of Ideology*, ed. Nannerl O. Keohane, Michelle Z. Rosaldo, and Barbara C. Gelpi (Chicago, 1981). Also see *Women and*

Revolution: A Discussion of the Unhappy Marriage of Marxism and Feminism, ed. Lydia Sargent (Boston, 1983); *Women and Communism: Selections from the Writings of Marx, Engels, Lenin and Stalin* (Westport, Conn., 1973); Batya Weinbaum, *The Curious Courtship of Women's Liberation and Socialism* (London, 1978); M. Jane Slaughter, "Feminism Socialism: Theoretical Debates in Historical Perspective," *Marxist Perspectives*, Fall 1979; *Women and Revolution: A Discussion of the Unhappy Marriage of Marxism and Feminism*, ed. Lydia Sargent, South End Press Political Controversies Series, no. 2 (Boston, 1983). For the subject in its Italian context, see Teresa Noce, *Gioventù senza sole* (Rome, 1973); "Organizing a women's union, Italy, 193)" in Riemer and Fout, *European Women*; and Annamaria Galoppini, *Il lungo viaggio verso la parità: i diritti civili e politici delle donne dall' unità ad oggi* (Bologna, 1980). Very important is Anna Maria Mozzoni, *La liberazione della donna*, ed. Franca Pieroni Bortolotti (Milan, 1975). Also see E. M. Standing, *Maria Montessori: Her Life and Work* (New York, 1957).

Italian anarchism

For Italian anarchism, see James Joll, *The Anarchists* (New York, 1964). For a contemporary new left evaluation of anarchism, see *Reinventing Anarchy: What are Anarchists Thinking These Days?* ed. Howard J. Ehrlich *et al.* (London and Boston, 1979.) For contemporary Italian anarchism, see *bollettino del centro di documentazione anarchica* (Rome, 1983). For Italian feminist anarchism, see Maria Occhipinti, *Una donna di Ragusa* (Milan, 1957); Adele Cambria, *Marx: la moglie e la fedele governante* (Padua, 1980); *Il Lenin delle donne: dalla castrazione amorosa alla violenza terrorista* (Padua, 1981); and *Amore come rivoluzione: tre sorelle per un rivoluzionario: le lettere inedite della moglie e delle cognate di Antonio Gramsci*, con un testo teatrale, "Nonostante Gramsci" (Milan, 1976).

women's early socialist tradition

For an early women's socialist tradition, see Anna Maria Mozzoni (cited above) and works of Rosa Luxemburg, Clara Zetkin, and Alexandra Kollontai. See Marmo Mullaney, *Revolutionary Women: Gender and the Socialist Revolutionary Role* (New York, 1983); and Cathy Porter, *Alexandra Kollontai: The Lonely Struggle of the Woman Who Defied Lenin* (New York, 1980). Related to this topic are Esther Kingston-Mann, *Lenin and the Problem of Marxist Peasant Revolution* (New York, 1983); Raya Dujanayevskaya, *Rosa Luxemburg: Women's Liberation and Marx's Philosophy of Revolution* (Atlantic Highlands, N. J., 1982); *A Reader of Self-Governing Socialism*, vol 1, ed. Branko Horvat, Mihailo Markovic, and Rudi Supek (White Plains, N. Y., 1975); Alexandra Kollontai, *Love of Worker Bees* (Chicago, 1977). See also Rose Glickman, *Russian Factory Women* (Berkeley, Calif., 1984). Giorgio Galli, *Storia del socialismo italiano* (Rome-Bari, 1980) is indispensable, as is Camilla Ravera, *Breve storia del movimento femminile in Italia* (Rome, 1978).

women, Gramsci, and Italian communism

For Antonio Gramsci, see *The Modern Prince and Other Writings* (New York, 1957); *Selections from the Prison Notebooks*, ed. and trans. Quintin Hoare and Geoffrey Nowell Smith (New York, 1971); Martin Clark, *Antonio Gramsci and the Revolution that Failed* (New Haven, 1977); Giuseppe Fiori, *Antonio Gramsci: Life of a Revolutionary* (New York, 1973); Hugues Portelli, *Gramsci e la questione religiosa* (Milan, 1974); Anne Showstack Sassoon, *Approaches to Gramsci* (London, 1982); John Cammett, *Antonio*

Gramsci and the Origins of Italian Communism (Stanford, Calif., 1967); and Eugene Genovese, "On Antonio Gramsci," *studies on the left* 7 (1967). In Robert N. Bellah and Phillip E. Hammond, *Varieties of Civil Religion* (San Francisco, 1980), see discussion of Gramsci in chapter 4, "The Five Religions of Modern Italy."

women and Italian fascism and antifascism

For Italian fascism, see "Italy" in *The Rebellious Century, 1830–1930* by Charles Tilly, Louise Tilly, and Richard Tilly (Cambridge, Mass., 1975); Alexander De Grand, *Italian Fascism: Its Origins & Development* (Lincoln, Nebraska, 1982; and Palmiro Togliatti, *Lectures on Fascism* (New York, 1976). Fascist documents are reprinted in Charles F. Delzell, *Mediterranean Fascism, 1919–1945* (New York, 1970). See also Herman Finer, *Mussolini's Italy: A Classic Study of the Non-communist One-party State* (first published 1935; reprint ed. New York, 1965). Richard Webster, *The Cross and the Fasces* (Stanford, Calif., 1960), is valuable as are Roland Sarti, ed., *The Ax Within: Italian Fascism in Action* (New York, 1974); and Giorgio Bassani, *Il giardino dei Finzi-Contini* (Turin, 1962). See also Denis Mack Smith, *Mussolini: A Biography* (New York, 1983).

For Italian women and fascism, see Annamaria Galoppini, *Il lungo viaggio verso le parità* (Bologna, 1980); and Paola Di Cori, "Storia, sentimenti, solidarietà nelle organizzazioni femmini cattoliche dall'età giolittiana al fascismo" in *donnawomanfemme*, January–June 1979. Also Maria Antonietta Macciocchi, *La donna 'nera', 'consenso' femminile e fascismo* (Milan, 1976); Victoria De Grazia, *The Culture of Consent: Mass Organization of Leisure in Fascist Italy* (Cambridge, 1981); Camilla Ravera, *Breve storia del movimento femminile in Italia* (Rome, 1978); Jole Calapso, *donne ribelle: un secolo di lotte femminile in Sicilia* (Palermo, 1980); Lucia Chiavola Birnbaum, Italian women and fascism, paper delivered at session on Resistance and Revolution, Conference of the Western Association of Women Historians; Mills College; Oakland, California; 12 May 1985; Denis Mack Smith, *Mussolini: A Biography* (New York, 1983); Victoria De Grazia, "Il fascino del priapo: Margherita Sarfatti biografa del duce," *memoria*, June 1982; Iris Origo, *An Italian War Diary, 1943–1944* (1947; reprint ed. Boston, 1984). Elio Vittorini, *In Sicily* (New York, 1949); Ignazio Silone, *Fontamara* (1934); *Bread and Wine* (1936); and *School for Dictators* (1938); Frank Rosengarten, *The Italian Antifascist Press, 1919–1945* (Cleveland, Ohio, 1968); James D. Wilkinson, *The Intellectual Resistance in Europe* (Cambridge, Mass., 1981); and Ivo Herzer, Italy and the Jews, World War II, paper delivered at the Conference of the American Italian Historical Association; Washington D. C.; 11 November 1984. Primo Levi's true story about Jewish partisans and the Jews of Italy, *If Not Now, When?* (New York, 1985), is valuable. For women, see *Noi Donne, 1944–45, ristampa* (Rome, 1978) and issues of *Noi Donne* thereafter.

women partisans and world war II

For Italian women during world war II, see Camilla Ravera, *Breve storia*, "il secondo Risorgimento," (cited above) and Iris Origo, *An Italian War Diary, 1943–1944* (1947; reprint ed. Boston, 1984). Also of interest are Jane Slaughter, Women's Politics and Women's Culture: The Case of Women in the Italian Resistance, a paper read at the Sixth Berkshire Conference on the History of Women, 3 June 1984, Smith College, Northampton, Massachusetts; *L'Udi: laboratorio di politica delle donne: idee e materiali per una storia* by M. Michetti, M. Repetto Alaia, and L. Viviani (Rome, 1985); Margherita

Repetto Alaia, The Unione Donne Italiane: Women's Liberation and the Italian Workers Movement, 1945–1980, a paper read at the Sixth Berkshire Conference on the History of Women, 3 June 1984, Smith College, Northampton, Massachusetts; Adriana Sartogo, ed., *Le donne al muro: l'immagine femminile nel manifesto politico italiano 1945/77* (Rome, 1977); and Annamaria Galoppini, *Il lungo viaggio verso la parità: i diritti civili e politici delle donne dall'unita ad oggi* (Bologna, 1980). Togliatti's speeches on women are reprinted in *The Communist Parties of Italy, France, and Spain: Postwar Change and Continuity: A Casebook*, ed. Peter Lange and Maurizio Vannicelli (Birmingham, England, 1981). See too Roberto Battaglia, *Storia della resistenza italiana* (Turin, 1964), Vincenzo Mauro, *Lotte contadine e repressione nel Sud* (Milan, 1979); Ignazio Silone, *Fontamara* (1934); *Bread and Wine* (1936); *The School for Dictators* (1938); and *The Seed Beneath the Snow* (1942); and James Wilkinson, *The Intellectual Resistance* (cited above).

women and the *dopoguerra*
For the postwar period, see *L'Udi: laboratorio di politica* (cited above) and Margherita Repetto Alaia, "The Unione Donne Italiane . . . 1945–1980" (cited above). Also see Miriam Mafai, *L'apprendistato: le donne italiane nel dopoguerra* (Rome, 1979); James D. Wilkinson, *The Intellectual Resistance* (cited above), chapter 8, "A season of hope"; Joseph La Palombara, *Interest Groups in Italian Politics* (Princeton, N. J., 1964); Carlo Levi, *Cristo si è fermato a Eboli* (Rome, 1945); Paul Ginsborg, "The Communist Party and the Agrarian Question in Southern Italy, 1943–48," *History Workshop*, Spring, 1984; and Giuliana Saladino, *Terra de rapina: come un contadino siciliano può diventare bandito* (Turin, 1977).

women and postwar literature
Women may be studied in the literature of the period. For the resistance and postwar period, see Elsa Morante, *Un scandalo che dura di diecimili anni* (Turin, 1974). For a partisan who became a new left theorist after 1968, see Rossana Rossanda, *Un viaggio inutile: o della politica come educazione sentimentale* (Milan, 1981). See the collection of postwar stories by Italo Calvino, *Difficult Loves*, trans. William Weaver *et al.* (San Diego, New York, and London, 1984). Alberto Moravia's treatment of women was criticized by feminists of the seventies and eighties as sexist; see his novel, *La romana* (first published in 1947; Milan, 1980). The Works of Natalia Ginsburg offer a cultural history of Italy from the forties to the eighties—with acuity about women/men relationships. For 1942 to 1968 see *La strada che va in citta* (Turin, 1942); *E stato cosi* (Turin, 1947); *Valentino* (Turin, 1957); *Ti ho sposato per allegria e altre commedie* (Turin, 1966). *The Advertisement* (1968) may be found in the anthology, *Plays by and about Women*, ed. Victoria Sullivan and James Hatch (New York, 1973). Later works are cited below. Ginzburg was born in 1916 in Palermo; she is, in the eighties, an independent left member of the Italian parliament.

women and postwar politics
For politics in the postwar era, see Francois Goguel, *Christian Democracy and France* (first published in 1952; reprint ed. South Bend, Indiana, 1969); J. Derek Holmes, *The Papacy in the Modern World, 1914–1978* (New York, 1981); Ravera, *Breve storia* (cited above); Grant Amyot, *The Italian Communist Party: The Crisis of the Popular Front Strategy* (New York, 1981); Frederic Spotts and Theodor Wieser, *Italy: A Difficult De-*

mocracy (New York, 1986). Possibly the best interpreter of the christian democrats is Gianni Baget-Bozzo, a priest who shifted from catholic activism in the Dc to liberation theology and the political left. See his *Il partito cristiano e l'apertura a sinistra: la Dc di Fanfani de Moro, 1954–62* (Florence, 1977); *Questi cattolici, la Dc, la Chiesa, la coscienza religiosa davanti alla crisi contemporanea* (Rome, 1979); and *Tesi sulla Dc: rinasce la questione nazionale* (Bologna, 1980).

women and postwar religion

For religion and women in the postwar era, see Jean Marie Aubert, *La donna: antifemminismo e cristianesimo* (Assisi, 1978); Giancarlo Zizola, *L'utopia di Papa Giovanni* (Assisi, 1974); and *The Documents of Vatican II*, sixteen official texts promulgated by the ecumenical council from 1963 to 1965, Walter M. Abbott, S. J., general editor (Piscataway, N. J., 1966). See also Giulio Girardi, *Credenti e non credenti per un mondo nuovo* (Assisi, 1969); *donna, cultura e tradizione*, a cura di Pia Bruzzichelli e Maria Luisa Algini (Milan, 1976); and Julien Travers, *10 donne nonconformiste* (Bari, 1968).

women and Italian society and politics to 1968

On women and Italian society and politics before 1968, see Gian Enrico Rusconi and Sergio Scamuzzi, "Trend Report—Italy: An Eccentric Society" in *Italy Today: An Eccentric Society* (International Sociological Association, 1981); Grant Amyot, *The Italian Communist Party: The Crisis of the Popular Front Strategy* (New York, 1981); S. S. Acquaviva and M. Santuccio, *Social Structure in Italy: Crisis of a System* (Boulder, Col., 1976); Ann Cornelisen, *Strangers and Pilgrims: The Last Italian Migration* (New York, 1980); and Giorgio Galli and Alessandra Nannei, *Il capitalismo assistenziale: ascesa e declino del sistema economico italiano, 1960–1975* (Milan, 1976). Indispensable are the works of Pier Paolo Pasolini: *Le ceneri di Gramsci: poemetti* (Turin, 1957; reprint ed. Turin, 1981), and *Una vita violenta* (Rome, 1959). From a similar perspective but with a woman's eye, see Dacia Maraini, *La vacanza: l'adolescenza di una donna-oggetto* (Milan, 1962), and *L'eta del malessere* (Turin, 1963).

Italian feminism—cultural and political revolution

post-1968 politics and feminist manifestos

For the extraparliamentary left after 1968, see Luigi Bobbio, *Lotta continua: storia di una organizzazione rivoluzionaria: Dalla fondazione del partito al congresso di 'autoscioglimento' di Rimini* (Rome, 1979). For Pdup, the best source is the newspaper *il manifesto*. A good collection of interviews on new left topics is *Le interviste del manifesto, 1971/ 1982*, ed. Marco Calabria, Michele Melillo, and Gianni Riotta (Rome, 1983). Herbert Marcuse, *One Dimensional Man: Studies in the Ideology of Advanced Industrial Society* (Boston, 1964), was influential in Italy.

A good collection of source materials on feminist manifestos, demonstrations, and writings after 1968 is Anna Riva, *La rabbia femminista* (Rome, 1981). A significant early collection of manifestos is Carla Lonzi, *Sputiamo su Hegel: La donna clitoridea e la donna vaginale, e altri scritti di rivolta femminile* (Milan, 1974). See also Luisa Abba et al., *La coscienza di sfruttata* (Milan, 1972), and Lieta Harrison, *La donna sposata: mille mogli accusano* (Milan, 1972).

For the political context of Italian feminism after 1968, see Frederic Spotts and Theodore Wieser, *Italy: A Difficult Democracy* (New York, 1986), and Joanne Barkan,

Visions of Emancipation: The Italian Workers' Movement since 1945 (New York, 1984). Also helpful are Yasmin Ergas, "1968–79—Feminism and the Italian Party System: Women's Politics in a Decade of Turmoil," *Comparative Politics*, April 1982; Giuseppe Di Palma, *Surviving Without Governing: The Italian Parties in Parliament* (Berkeley and Los Angeles, 1977); and *Italy in Transition: Conflict and Consensus*, ed. Peter Lange and Sidney Tarrow (Bournemouth, England, 1980).

contemporary Italian feminism

Sources for Italian feminists after 1968 include Annamaria Galoppini, *Il lungo viaggio verso la parità: i diritti civili e politici delle donne dall'unità ad oggi* (Bologna, 1980); chapter 7, "L'attuazione della costituzione"; Adriana Sartogo, ed., *Le donne al muro: l'immagine femminile nel manifesto politico italiano, 1945/77* (Rome, 1977); *il mio segno. la mia parola. rabbia, amore, confessioni, appuntamenti, disegni nella casa della donna in via del governo vecchio* (Rome, 1979). An early anthology of feminist writings is that edited by Lidia Menapace, *Per un movimento politico di liberazione della donna: saggi e documenti* (Verona, 1972); this is an important source because it contains essays by U. S. and other world feminists, as well as a provocative essay by Menapace suggesting that emancipation is not an adequate feminist aim and an encounter between U. S. feminist Betty Friedan and Italian feminists that highlights differing assumptions. A study that places Italian feminists in European context is Vera Squarcialupi, *Donne in Europa* (Rome, 1979). Rossana Rossanda, *Le altre: conversazioni a Radiotrè sui rapporti tra donne e politica, libertà, fraternità, uguaglianza, democrazia, fascismo, resistenza, stato, partito, rivoluzione* (Milan, 1979), is indispensable for the political and cultural thought of Italian feminism. See Adriana Seroni, *La questione femminile in Italia, 1970–1977* (Rome, 1977). Other important feminist studies include *Essere donna in Sicilia* by Simona Mafai *et al.* (Rome, 1976); Gigliola Lo Cascio, *Occupate e casalinghe* (Rome, 1979); Maria Rosa Cutrufelli, *L'invenzione della donna: miti e tecniche di uno sfruttamento* (Milan, 1974); *Disoccupata con onore: lavoro e condizione della donna* (Milan, 1975); *Le donne protagoniste nel movimento cooperativo* (Milan, 1978); *Economia e politica dei sentimenti* (Rome, 1980); and Bernardi *et al.*, *La casalinga di Cristo* (Rome, 1976). See the collection of documents in *La politica del femminismo: il movimento femminista, l'Unione della donne italiane, le forze politiche di sinistra di fronte al femminismo nei documenti, 1973–76* (Rome, 1978). Also see Erica Scroppo, *Donna privato e politico: storie personali di 21* ✓ *donne del Pci* (Milan, 1979); *Lessico politico delle donne: teorie del femminismo* (Milan, 1978); *care compagne: il femminismo nel Pci e nelle organizzazzioni di massa*, ed. Laura Lilli and Chiara Valentini (Rome, 1979); *Sesso amaro: trentamila donne rispondono su maternità, sessualità, aborto*, ed. Fausta Cecchini *et al.* (Rome, 1977); *La politica del femminismo: il movimento femminista, l'Unione della donne italiane, le forze politiche di sinistra di fronte al femminismo nei documenti, 1973–76* (Rome, 1978); and Simonetta Piccone Stella, *Ragazze del sud* (Rome, 1979). For health clinics and the abortion campaign, see Liliana Barca *et al.*, *Chi ha paura del consultorio* (Rome, 1981) and *Aborto: Norme per la tutela sociale della maternita e sull'interruzione volontaria della gravidanza* (Perugia, 1978). See the Rai television program on the history of feminism published by Ginevra Conti Odorisio, *Storia dell'idea femminista in Italia* (Rome, 1980), and a social anthropological study of women in the city by Matilde Callari Galli, *Il tempo delle donne* (Bologna, 1979). Among memoirs, see Laura Gemini, *Dossier di una femminista*

(Milan, 1973). For collections of interviews with feminists, see Guido Gerosa, *Le compagne: venti protagoniste delle lotte del Pci dal Comintern a oggi narrano la loro storia* (Milan, 1979). For a collection of documents, see *Per l'emancipazione della donna: 3 anni di lavoro, di dibattito, di lotta*, ed. Sezione Femminile del Pci (Rome, 1976), which is particularly good for differing views of feminism held by women within the Pci. The best source for Italian feminism and the antinuclear movement is "Donne e disarmo: una parola in più," Rassegna stampa per 8 marzo 1983, Coordinamento per l'autodeterminazione della donna, Catania. Also see Lucia C. Birnbaum, "Earth-mothers, Godmothers, and Radicals: The Inheritance of Sicilian American Women," *Marxist Perspectives*, Spring 1979. Feminist journals cited in the text are indispensable for understanding the Italian movement.

left catholicism, liberation theology, feminist theology

For postconciliar ferment among left catholics, protestants, and Jews, one should see *L'altra chiesa in Italia*, edited by Arnaldo Nesti (Rome, 1970). The ferment was visible in scholarly studies of witchcraft; e.g., Carlo Ginzburg, *The Night Battles: Witchcraft and Agrarian Cults in the Sixteenth and Seventeenth Centuries*, trans. John and Anne Tedesci (Baltimore, Md., 1983). This book was published in Italy as *I benedanti: stregoneria e culti agrari tra cinquecento e seicento*, Milan, 1983. Reflecting the ecumenical spirit is a work written by the Commissione del Sinodo delle chiese valdesi e metodiste, *I matrimoni interconfessionali tra cattolici ed evangelici in Italia* (Turin, 1982). An important historical enterprise stimulated in Italy by postconciliar thinking is the study of beliefs; see Costantino Cipolla with the collaboration of Stefano Martelli, *Marxismo e religione nella cultura operaia* (Bologna, 1983). Among regional studies, see Mario Farinella, *I cattolici siciliani dopo il concilio* (Palermo, 1967). The spirit influenced literary criticism as well, see "Italo Svevo: l'inquietudine del nostro tempo," seminario di studio, Assisi, 23–26 October 1980, ed. Rosa Brambilla (Assisi, 1981). Among historical studies of relations between catholics and communists, see Carlo Felice Casula, *Cattolici-comunisti e sinistra cristiana (1938–1945)* (Bologna, 1976); Lorenzo Bedeschi, *Cattolici e comunisti: dal socialismo cristiano ai cristiani marxisti* (Milan, 1974); Giuseppe Pirola and Gian Luigi Brena, *Movimenti cristiani di sinistra e marxismo in Italia* (Assisi, 1978). For catholic studies of "christian feminism," see Francesco M. Cecchini, *Il femminismo cristiano* (Rome, 1979). For a feminist doctoral dissertation on catholics and communists, see Margherita Repetto (Alaia), "Il movimento dei cattolici comunisti, problemi storici e politici", *i quaderni della rivista trimestrale*, June 1977, rewritten for the feminist journal *donnawomanfemme* as "Movimento di emancipazione e organizzazioni femminili cattoliche", Spring 1981, in an issue of the journal entirely devoted to the ideology and politics of the church (also in this issue, see P. Bruzzichelli, "Papa Wojtyla: il fascino del maschio-padre"; L. Menapace, "Le scelte politiche della Chiesa"; G. Codrignani, "La pratica referendaria davanti alla donna: la posizione della Chiesa"). For John Paul I, see *Illustrissimi: Letters from Pope John Paul I*, by Albino Luciani (Boston, 1976). For a cleric who has received papal censure, see Hans Kung, *Does God Exist? An Answer for Today* (Garden City, N. Y.). For critical clerics inside the church, see the journal *dimensioni sacerdotali*.

Italian literature of left catholicism ranges from anthologies emerging from work-shops to publications of *comunità di base* and studies of liberation theology. A sampling of this literature: M. Gozzini *et al., I cattolici e la sinistra: dibattito aperto,* ed. Salvatore Imbarrato (Assisi, 1977); Pirola and Brena, *Movimenti cristiani* (Assisi, 1978); *Cristiani di base oggi: atti del VI convegno nazionale delle comunità cristiane di base* (Rome, 30/31 October and 1 November 1982); Rafael J. Kleiner, *Gruppi di base nella chiesa italiana* (Assisi, 1978); Ettore Masina *et al., Linee di un catechismo per l'uomo d'oggi,* 2 vols. (Assisi, 1971, 1973). Among cdb publications, see comunità di San Paolo in Roma, *Il cristiano e la sessualita: un contributo di base al sinodo sulla famiglia* (Rome, 1980). For an example of a cdb approach to the bible, see Bruno Corsani, *Atti degli apostoli è lettere* (Turin, 1978) and Ortensio da Spinetoli, "Non tutto il vangelo è vangelo: la formazione dei vangeli: introduzione a Matteo," *quaderni di esodo* no. 5. (Livorno, 1977). For a memoir of a cdb poet, see Franco Barbero, *Gli anni dell'impotenza mistica e politica* (Pinerolo, 1982). Some base communities remained in the church: see *Comunità ecclesiali di base: utopia o realta?* ed. Alfonso Gregory (Assisi, 1977). Sandro Magister, "Come ai tempi di Frate Leone," *l'Espresso,* 2 May 1982 is an analysis of a census of cdb sponsored by the Agnelli Foundation. In the South, analogous to cdb are *comunità ecclesiale di base,* with convergence of clerics and parishioners on issues like "neofemminismo." (see chapter 13, this work).

For liberation theology read by Italians, a sampling includes the works of Giulio Girardi cited in chapter 6, Gustavo Gutierrez, *Teologia della liberazione* (Lima, 1971, Brescia, 1972); *Religione oppio o strumento di liberazione? scritti di Gustavo Gutierrez, Rubem Alves Hugo Asmann sulla 'teologia della liberazione'* (Rome, 1972); Alfredo Fierro, *Introduzione alle teologie politiche* (Assisi, 1977); Leonardo Boff, *Teologia della cattività e della liberazione* (Brescia, 1976); L. Boff *et al., Quale preghiera?* (Assisi, 1976); Ernesto Cardenal, *Grido: salmi degli oppressi,* ed. Giuseppina Pompei (Assisi, 1979); and *Sandino: il padre della guerriglia,* ed. Sergio Ramirez (Assisi, 1978). Two volumes in English that indicate the contours of liberation theology are Gustavo Gutierrez, *The Power of the Poor in History* (1928; reprint ed. Maryknoll, New York, 1983) and Leonardo Boff, *Liberating Grace,* trans. John Drury (Maryknoll, N. Y., 1979). See also Dorothy Soelle *et al., The Challenge of Liberation Theology: A First World Response,* ed. Brian Mahan and L. Dale Richesin (Maryknoll, N. Y., 1981). Writings of major Italian liberation theologians are cited in the text.

For Italian feminist theology, a European anthology that includes historical documents on women and religion is Julia O'Faolain and Lauro Martines, eds., *Not in God's Image: Women in History from the Greeks to the Victorians* (New York, 1973). An Italian synthesis of biographies and documents from the fourteenth to the seventeenth centuries is Marcello Craveri, *Sante e streghe: biografie e documenti dal XIV al XVII secolo* (Milan, 1980), an evocative study that compares saints and witches. An important work sponsored by the cittadella christiana at Assisi was Kari Elisabeth Borresen, *Natura e ruolo della donna in Agostino e Tommaso d'Aquino* (Assisi, 1979). Franca Long and Rita Pierro, *L'altra metà della chiesa: essere femministe e cristiane* (Rome, 1981), is a study of feminist theology by a waldensian and a catholic believer grounded on John XXIII's definition of the church as the people of God in history. The book exemplifies the pattern of Italian feminists crossing religious lines, in this case catholicism, protestantism, and judaism (see essay, "La donna nella societa ebraica"). See also Edith Bruck, "Gli ebrei come le donne: un plurale oltraggioso," in *noidonne,* August 1982. See the chapter "Le comunità primitiva" in Marina Terragni,

Vergine e piena di grazia: la donna secondo la pubblicistica di santa romana chiesa (Milan, 1981). See also "Femminismo e teologia," *quaderni di agape* (Turin, 1981) for essays by European and U. S. feminist theologians. For feminist theology, see Roberta Fossati, *e Dio creò la donna: Chiesa, religione e condizione femminile* (Milan, 1977); also the continuing column of Adriana Zarri in *rocca*, and her *I guardiani del sabato: riflessioni sulla chiesa italiana dopo il referendum sull'aborto (com-nuovi tempi*, 1981); also Zarri's *nostro signore del deserto: teologia e antropologia della preghiera* (Assisi, 1978). Compare Rosemary Radford Ruether, *Sexism and God-Talk: Toward a Feminist Theology* (Boston, 1983); Mary Daly, *Beyond God the Father: Toward a Philosophy of Women's Liberation* (Boston, 1973); *The Church and the Second Sex* (New York, 1975); *Gyn/Ecology: The Metaethics of Radical Feminism* (Boston, 1979); *Pure Lust: Elemental Feminist Philosophy* (Boston, 1984); and Elizabeth Schussler Fiorenza, *In Memory of Her: A Feminist Theological Reconstruction of Christian Origins* (New York, 1983). For Teresa, see Rosa Rossi, *Teresa d'Avila: Biografia di una scrittrice* (Rome, 1983), and *St Teresa of Avila: Collected Works*, 2 vols. (Washington, D. C., 1976 and 1980). See also Lucia Chiavola Birnbaum, *La religione e le donne sicule americane* (Modica Alta, 1982), Arnaldo Nesti, *Una cultura del privato: morfologia significato della stampa devozionale italiana* (Turin, 1983), Gabriele De Rosa, *Chiesa e religione popolare nel mezzogiorno* (Rome-Bari, 1978), G. Guizzardi *et al., Chiesa e religione del popolo: analisi di un'egomonia* (Turin, 1981), and Vittorio Lanternari, *Movimenti religiosi di libertà e di salvezza dei popoli oppressi* (1960; reprint ed. Milan, 1974, 1977).

Significant journals for left catholicism in the 1970s and 1980s include *com-nuovi tempi, rocca, idoc,* and *bozze.* See "Against abortion in defense of the law," *com-nuovi tempi* supplement, 1981, and Daniele Menozzi, "La Chiesa e i poveri nella storia . . ." and "La ratifica del Concordato: documenti," *bozze 84*, September/October 1984. For a feminist left catholic critique of the image of women in catholic journals, see Giancarlo Codrignani, "L'immagine femminile dei giornali cattolici," *donne e politica*, May–June 1981. *Famiglia Cristiana*, the widely read conservative catholic family journal, used the language of crisis in the 1981 environment of heated discussion of the referendum on abortion, describing the family as the place women realize themselves as wives and mothers and as a healthy cell in a sick society.

For the convergence of left catholicism with the Italian new left, see "Cristiani impegnati per l'alternativa" *com-nuovi tempi* supplement, June 1983. For an evaluation of the liberal spirit in postconciliar catholicism, see Thomas Sheehan, "Revolution in the Church," a review essay on Hans Kung, *Eternal Life: Life After Death as a Medical, Philosophical, and Theological Problem* (New York, 1984), *New York Review of Books*, 14 June 1984.

unpaid housework

For the literature of unpaid housework, the significant study is Mariarosa Dalla Costa, *Potere femminile e sovversione sociale* (Padua, 1972). See also "Lavoro/non lavoro: per un economia politica della liberazione della donna," *donnawomanfemme*, July–December 1979, and *Le operaie della casa*, ed. collettivo internazionale femminista (Padua, 1975). The best analysis in English is that of Nona Glazer-Malbin, "Housework," a review essay in *Signs*, Summer 1976. See also Glazer, "The Invisible Intersection: Involuntary Unpaid Labor Outside the Household and Women Workers,"

Center for the Study, Education and Advancement of Women, University of California (Berkeley, Calif., 1982). Also see Susan Strasser, *Never Done: A History of American House-work* (New York, 1982), and Alice Kessler-Harris, *Out to Work: A History of Wage-Earning Women in the United States* (New York, 1982). See *Women and Work: Problems and Perspectives,* ed. Rachel Kahn-Hut, Arlene Kaplan Daniels, and Richard Colvard (New York, 1982). Proceedings of the important international conference on women's work in Turin in 1984 are published as *Produrre e riprodurre, cambiamenti nel rapporto tra donne e lavoro: primo convegno internazionale delle donne dei paesi industrializzati promosso dal movimento delle donne di Torino* (Turin, 1984). See also the sources cited in chapter 10 of this work.

women and the political parties

See *Italy at the Polls, 1979: A Study of the Parliamentary Elections* (Washington, D.C. and London, 1981), particularly the analysis of the Dc (chapter 3), of the Pci (chapter 4), of the Psi (chapter 5), of the smaller parties (chapter 6). Karen Beckwith's essay, in this volume, "Women and Parliamentary Politics in Italy: 1946–1979," is indispensable. For feminism and Italian party politics, Yasmin Ergas, "1968–79—Feminism and the Italian Party System: Women's Politics in a Decade of Turmoil," *Comparative Politics,* April 1982, is highly valuable. For the Pci, see *The Politics of Eurocommunism: Socialism in Transition,* ed. Carl Boggs and David Plotke (Boston, 1980). For the Pci at a local level, see Max Jaggi, Roger Muller, and Sil Schmid, *Red Bologna* (London, 1977). For the Pci and the catholic church, see "The Church & the Party: Documents on the Catholic-Communist Dialogue in Italy," *Marxist Perspectives,* Fall 1979. For the Dc, see works by Baget-Bozzo cited above. A good commentary on the period by a columnist in *Corriere della Sera* can be found in Alberto Ronchey, *Diverso parere: Le opinioni sui temi piu scottanti del nostro tempo a confronto con la verifica dei fatti e la critica dei lettori* (Milan, 1983). See Diana Johnstone, "Communist Party Scraps Soviet Model," *In These Times,* 20–26 January 1982, and "Italy: Communists Turn to a 'Third Way'," *In These Times,* 31 March–6 April 1982.

women's studies in Italy

A guide to the literature of women's studies in Italy may be found in the library of *donnawomanfemme* (Via S. Benedetto in Arenula, 00186 Roma). A guide to women's centers in Italy, each of them with libraries of women's studies, may be secured from *noidonne,* at the address above. An excellent synthesis of the subject is the essay of Sara Poli, History and future of women's higher education and women's studies in Italy, delivered at the Sixth Berkshire Conference on the History of Women, Northampton, Massachusetts, 2 June 1984.

Major centers of women's studies outside the universities include the center of historical studies of the Feltrinelli foundation at Milan, the fondazione basso in Rome, and centers of documentation at Bologna and Mestre. Many of these are financed by regional governments and administered by women. Griff (group for the study of the family and the feminine condition) at Milan conducts courses for workers throughout the area. Similar institutions at Trent, Padua, and elsewhere offer seminars open to the public. See lists of doctoral dissertations that refer to women, a widening field that extends from historical and sociological studies of popular culture to linguistics, philosophy of language, and feminine language.

feminist manifestos as primary sources

Carla Lonzi, *Sputiamo su Hegel: La donna clitoridea e la donna vaginale: e altri scritti di rivolta femminile* (Milan, 1974), is the significant early manifesto. Anna Riva, *La rabbia femminista* (Rome, 1981), is an excellent collection of documents. See also Luisa Abba et al., *La coscienza di sfruttata* (Milan, 1972); Adriana Sartogo, ed., *Le donne al muro: L'immagine femminile nel manifesto politico italiano 1945/77* (Rome, 1977); and Annamaria Galoppini, *Il lungo viaggio verso la parita: I diritti civili e politici delle donne dall'unita ad oggi* (Bologna, 1980). Lidia Menapace, *Per un movimento politico di liberazione della donna: Saggi e documenti* (Verona, 1972), is an important collection of essays. Vera Squarcialupi, *Donne in Europa* (Rome, 1979), puts the subject in European context. A Rai television program that focused on the history of feminism has been published as Ginevra Conti Odorisio, *Storia dell'idea femminista in Italia* (Rome, 1980); a social anthropological study of women in the city is Matilde Callari Galli, *Il tempo delle donne* (Bologna, 1979). A memoir is Laura Gemini, *Dossier di una femminista* (Milan, 1973). Collections of interviews include Guido Gerosa, *Le compagne: Venti protagoniste delle lotte del Pci dal Comintern a oggi narrano la loro storia* (Milan, 1979), and Laura Lilli and Chiara Valentini, *care compagne: il femminismo nel Pci e nelle organizzazioni di massa* (Rome, 1979) A good collection of documents may be found in *Per l'emancipazione della donna: 3 anni di lavoro, di dibattito, di lotta*, ed. Sezione Femminile del Pci (Rome, 1965). A helpful chronology may be found in "Sessant'anni: il nostro cammino" in *donne e politica* January–February 1981.

feminist biographies as cultural history

A sampling of Italian women's studies includes feminist biographies that are also cultural history: e.g., Amelia Camboni, *I figliastri di Dio* (Rome, 1981). Widely read novels like Alba de Cespedes, *Quaderno proibito* (Milan, 1967), touched feminist themes: a woman of middle age began writing a journal and began to see the crisis in relations between women and men: "We have become so alienated from each other that we cannot see one another and we walk alone." Joyce Lussu, a partisan, wrote an autobiographical novel that was a feminist parable: *Padre, padrone, padreterno* (Milan, 1976) is a story about "slaves and matrons, peasant women and ladies of the manor, witches and women merchants, women proletarians and bosses." Lussu criticizes left parties for myopia about women and criticizes women for interpreting feminism in a simplistic manner. Lussu's best-selling book pointed to the strain of women's resistance deriving from prechristian beliefs through witches, healers, and peasant women. The former partisan advised younger women that class as well as gender was central, that ladies of the manor behaved differently from peasant women, and that the heritage of history had bequeathed a problematic high valence to the subject of sex.

specialized feminist studies

For an anthology addressed to high school students, see Serena Castaldi and Liliana Caruso, *L'altra faccia della storia (quella femminile)* (Florence, 1975). For a doctoral dissertation, see Serena Castaldi, *Femminile pateriale: vicende del femminino fra matriarcato e patriarcato* (Milan, 1978). For feminist poetry, see *Donne in poesia: antologia della poesia femminile in Italia dal dopo guerra ad oggi*, a cura di Biancamaria Frabotta con una nota critica di Dacia Maraini (Rome, 1977). Lino Prenna, *Antropologia della coniugalità: corpo e sentimento* (Rome, 1980), traces the history of sexuality from primitive christianity to contemporary masculine and feminine attitudes; for sociology, see Marisa Ferrari Occhionero, *Verso una sociologia della donna* (Rome, 1979). *Il problema 'donna' soggettivita psico-sociale e identità sessuale*, ed. Carlamaria Del Miglio and Laura Fedeli, is a collection of theoretical papers on the social psychological relationship between women's ego and the collective. *Donnawomanfemme* is the best source for Italian feminist theory; e.g., "il luogo delle ipotesi: feminismo e conoscenze," *donnawomanfemme*, Winter 1981. Branches of Udi also published theoretical papers: e.g., *la dimensione donna: educazione sessuale e divisione dei ruioli*, a cura dell' Udi di Ferrara (Padua, 1976). Dwf sometimes decentralizes its editorial functions; e.g., see *luna e l'altro*, a supplement to *donnawomanfemme*, Spring 1981, a reprint of a women's journal whose publication had been blocked. For Italian feminist poetry, see *Donne in poesia: antologia della poesia femminile in Italia dal dopoguerra ad oggi*, ed. Biancamaria Frabotta (Rome, 1976). Sara Poli has translated U.S. feminist writers, notably Tillie Olsen (*Tell Me A Riddle* and *Silences*), and interviewed a number of U.S. feminist activists for Italian newspapers, notably Grace Paley.

Concern about the children was evident in many Italian feminist studies. Elena Gianini Belotti, *Dalla parte delle bambine: l'influenza dei condizionamenti sociali nella formazione del ruolo femminile nei primi anni di vita* (1973), which reached its twentyfourth edition by 1978, was probably critically important in projecting the importance of environment in fixing characteristics of male and female. Belotti, a Montessori teacher, emphasized the importance of drawing from each child her or his fullest potential. *Noi donne* gave copies of Danielle and Emmanuelle Flamant-Paparatti, *Emanuele: infanzia di una donna*, prefazione di Elena Gianini Belotti (Rome, 1979), a study in a similar vein, to its subscribers in 1980.

For health clinics, see Liliana Barca *et al.*, *Chi ha paura del consultorio* (Rome, 1981). For interruption of pregnancy, see *Aborto: Norme per la tutela sociale della maternia e sull'interruzione volontaria della gravidanza* (Perugia, 1978).

cultural and political backdrop to feminism, 1970s and 1980s
cultural backdrop

For the cultural backdrop of the seventies, see the writings of Natalia Ginzburg, especially *Vita immaginaria* (newspaper articles written from 1969 to 1974); *Le voci della sera*, ed. Sergio Pacifici (Turin, 1961; New York, 1971); *Mai devi domandarmi* (Rome, 1970), and *Famiglia* (Turin, 1977).

Perhaps more than elsewhere, psychoanalytic theory has been indispensable to Italian women's studies. The accepted Freudian view is that of Juliette Mitchell in *Psicoanalisi e femminismo: Freud, Reich, Laing e altri punti di vista sulla donna* (Turin, 1976). Mitchell states that Freudianism is not a recommendation of a patriarchal society, but an analysis of one. "The particular task of psychoanalysis is to decipher how we acquire our heritage of the ideas and laws of human society within the unconscious mind." See *differenze 11* of the gruppo donne e psicanalisi, Rome. Michel Foucault influenced Italian feminist thinking of the late 1970s and 1980s. Foucault's ideas were regarded as an implicit critique of the Pci, not only because Foucault was among the French intellectuals who published a criticism of the Italian communist party for advocating severe measures against violent revolutionaries, but because Foucault drew unsettling connections between politics and sexuality: "When I think of the mechanics of power, I think of its capillary form of existence, of the extent to which power seeps into the very grain of individuals, reaches right into their bodies, permeates their gestures, their posture, what they say, how they learn to live and work with other people" (quoted in Alan Sheridan, *Michel Foucault: The Will to Truth* [London and New York, 1980], 217).

Biancamaria Frabotta, a feminist poet and literary critic who reflected the interests of Italian cultural feminists, was indebted to Foucault, to international feminist theories, and to the French psychoanalyst Luce Irigaray. The wider implications of sexuality are explored by Irigaray in *Questo sesso che non è un sesso* (Milan, 1978). Cultural feminists emphasized women's literature; see a television series published as *letteratura al femminile: itinerari di lettura: a proposito di donne, storia, poesia, romanzo* (Bari, 1980). Cultural feminists were critical of the Pci although they generally voted for the party after 1981. Perhaps the best sources of Italian cultural feminism are the programs of Centro culturale Virginia Woolf. Among feminist dissenters, see the works of Maria Antonietta Macciocchi: *Pour Gramsci* (Paris, 1974); *Letters from Inside the Italian Communist Party to Louis Althusser* (London, 1973); *Les Femmes et Leurs Maitres* (Paris, 1978); *La Donna Nera* (Milan, 1978). On her return to Italy, Macciocchi identified politically with the radical party (Pr).

political backdrop

The best synthesis of the political history of the seventies and eighties is Frederic Spotts and Theodor Wieser, *Italy: A Difficult Democracy* (New York, 1986). For the Dc, the works of Gianni Baget-Bozzo are valuable; see his *Il partito cristiano e l'apertura a sinistra: la Dc di Fanfani di Moro 1954–1962* (Florence, 1977); *Questi cattolici: la Dc, la Chiesa, la coscienza religiosa davanti alla crisis contemporanea* (Rome, 1979); and *Tesi sulla Dc: rinasce la questione nazionale* (Bologna, 1980). Leonardo Sciascia, *L'affaire Moro* (Palermo, 1978), is important for the independent radical perspective. See Aldo Garosci et al., *Communism in Western Europe* (Ithaca, N. Y., 1951; reprint ed. 1971); Carl Marzani, *The Promise of Eurocommunism* (Westport, Conn., 1980); *The Politics of Eurocommunism: Socialism in Transition*, ed. Carl Boggs and David Plotke (Boston, 1980); Max Jaggi, Roger Muller, and Sil Schmid, *Red Bologna* (London, 1977); and "The Church and the Party: Documents on the Catholic-Communist Dialogue in Italy," *Marxist Perspectives*, Fall 1979. See also Giuseppe Di Palma, *Surviving Without Governing: The Italian Parties in Parliament* (Berkeley and Los Angeles, 1977), and Peter Lange and Sidney Tarrow, eds., *Italy in Transition: Conflict and Consensus* (Bournemouth, England, 1980).

feminist culture

Indispensable is *Il mio signo. la mia parola: rabbia, amore, confessioni, appuntamenti, disegni nella casa della donna in via del governo vecchio* (Rome, 1979). See *Contro la violenza sessuale: le donne, la legge: Incontro aperto didonne: atti del convegno tenuta a Milano, 27–28, 1979*; Maria Rosa Cutrufelli, *Economia e politica dei sentimenti* (Rome, 1980), *Le donne protagoniste nel movimento cooperativo* (Mi.·ın, 1978), *L'invenzione della donna: miti e tecniche di uno sfruttamento* (Milan, 1974), and *il cliente: inchiesta sulla domanda di prostitu-*

zione (Rome, 1981). See also Chiara Saraceno, *Uguali e diverse* (Bari, 1980); Radiotelevisione italiana, *Le reazioni di un campione di pubblico al programma 'storie allo specchio'* (Rome, 1981); *Agenda '82: Spacca la mela* (Rome, 1982); *Il diario delle lune, 1982* (Rome, 1982); *L'orsaminore: mensile di cultura e politica*; and *programmi, Centro culturale Virginia Woolf*. Dacia Maraini, *A memoria* (Milan, 1968), and *Memorie di una ladra* (Milan, 1972), are valuable. Also see Maraini's theatrical works: *La famiglia normale, Il ricatto a teatro, Recitare e Venere, Viva l'Italia, La donna perfetto, Dialogo di una prostituta con un cliente, Suor Juana, Manifesto dal carcere, Don Juan,* and *I sogni di Clitennestra*. Recent novels include *Storia di Piera* (Milan, 1980) and *Lettere a Marina* (Milan, 1981). Works by Oriana Fallaci include *Letter to a Child Never Born*, trans. John Shepley (New York, 1978); *A Man: A Novel* (New York, 1980); and *Interview with History* (Boston, 1977).

catholic culture and feminism

Catholic culture and feminism is perhaps best studied in conference proceedings of the catholic women's organization Cif. See Cif convegno regionale, *La donna oggi: realtà e prospettive* (Palermo, 1978), and Cif convegno regionale, *Più spazio alla donna, per una famiglia nuova, per una società piu umana* (Palermo, 1981). See also La federazione italiana donne arti professioni affari, *quarant'anni di vita associativa 1930–1970* (Naples, 1970); *il focolare, mensile della famiglia*; and *la lucciola*. Other variables in the change in the collective consciousness are suggested in these works: Umberto Cerroni, *Il rapporto uomo-donna nella civiltà borghese* (Rome, 1975); Giovanni Cesareo, *La contraddizione femminile* (Rome, 1977); Umberto Eco, *Sette anni di desiderio, cronache 1977–1983* (Milan, 1983); Franco Ferrarotti, *Una teologia per atei* (Rome, 1983); Joanne Barkan, *Visions of Emancipation: The Italian Workers' Movement Since 1945* (New York, 1984); and *Operai senza politica: il caso Moro all Fiat e il 'qualunquismo operaio': Le risposte degli operai allo Stato e alle Br registrate ai cancelli della Fiat durante i 55 giorni del rapimento di Aldo Moro*; ed. Brunello Mantelli and Marco Revelli (Rome, 1979).

For the reach of *comunità di base*, see "Come ai tempi di Frate Leone," *L'Espresso*, 2 May 1982. For the contemporary Italian belief in nonviolence, see *La strada è un'altra: dati e riflessioni per un'alternativa alla violenza*, a cura del gruppo ecclesiale "giovani zona 2" di Roma e di G. Martina e D. Mongillo (Assisi, 1981). For the 1981 peace demonstration, see "Siamo oggi a Roma . . . ," *com-nuovi tempi*, 22 November 1981 and "Essere per la pace non è solo essere contro la guerra," *rocca*, 15 November 1981. For the wide implications of Italian thinking on peace, see Luciana Castellina, Biagio De Giovanni, and Valdo Spini, "Terzo mondo e questione cattolica nel dibattito sulla terza via," *idoc*, March–April 1982. See Giulio Girardi for the meaning of violence in Italian liberation theology; e.g., "In principio era la violenza" in *rocca*, September 1983. Journals whose main theme is nonviolence include *azione nonviolenta; rivista mensile edita dal movimento nonviolento* and *alternativa nonviolenta* (see speciale "Fame," 1983). *Cristiani nonviolenti*, a journal of Italian protestants, emphasizes dialogue, non-cooperation, and civil disobedience grounded on conscience. (See October 1983 issue). See Lucia Chiavola Birnbaum, "European disarmament movement; the next steps," *journal of women and religion*, Winter 1982; Mario Pancera, *Conversazione con Bettazzi: la rivoluzione cattolica* (Vicenza, 1978); Italian Christian Workers Associations (Acli) *Before all else, peace* (Rome, 1983); *Casa: un problema per la sinistra*, a cura di

Alessandro di Loreto e Giancarlo Storto (Rome and Perugia, 1980); Maria Rosa Cutrufelli, *Le donne protagoniste nel movimento cooperativo: la questione femminile in un'organizzazione producttiva democratica* (Milan, 1978); Lega nazionale delle cooperative, *la sua storia. la sua immagine. la sua politica* (Rome, 1983); and Onelio Prandini, *La cooperazione* (Rome, 1982). The Milanese feminist journal *sottosopra* is indispensable. See also *noidonne*, *effe*, *donne e politica*, and others mentioned in the text. Also see Lucia Chiavola Birnbaum, "Earthmothers, godmothers, and radicals: the inheritance of Sicilian American women," *Marxist perspectives*, Spring 1979.

violence and peace

The best source for the independent political position of people in the peace movement was *pace e guerra*, until it ceased publication in 1983. A good source of independent left thinking on violence and peace is *bozze* (e.g., Fabrizio Mastrofini, "La bomba come cosa visibile e nascosta," May/August 1984). *Bozze* is also a good source of left catholic thinking on contemporary issues; e.g., Daniele Menozzi, "La Chiesa e i poveri nella storia: Dalla povertà delle origini al dividendo sulle tasse"; and "La ratifica del Concordato: documenti," September/October 1984). The wide range of principles encompassed in the Italian peace movement is suggested in "Alcune considerazione sul movimento per la pace," *il manifesto*, 4 January 1985, in which Peppe Sini, of the committees for peace of Viterbo, recommends to all Italian peace committees the unifying theme of peace/democracy/human rights, with a program of constructing a "new model of development" coordinated by movements of liberation. The peace movement touches catholics inside and outside the church. See Laura Barone, "Necessita di una pedagogia della pace" in *il focolare*, September/October 1984; Barone, a Cif activist, urges a revision of school curricula to emphasize peace not war.

In addition to sources on the Italian peace movement cited in the text, see "I missili sono qui ma il movimento non si arrende," *com-nuovi tempi*, 16 February 1984. For a call by peace committees of northern Italy to all Italian committees, see "imac '83," *il manifesto*, 3 May 1984, which urges all Italian committees to coordinate nationally and with other European countries to sustain the peoples of El Salvador and Nicaragua against "aggression of U.S. imperialism," to take direct action to promote the departure of Italy from NATO, and to encourage all popular measures of objection of conscience on the ground of self-determination against nuclear weapons. Resistance at Comiso has taken a variety of forms; see the booklet of the Bertolt Brecht cultural association, comitato unitario per il disarmo e la pace Comiso, *Il riarmo: una lucida follia* (Comiso, 1983). Among the many publications of the Cudip peace organization at Comiso, see *Alternativa Comiso*, June 1983; among the many women's groups working for disarmament at Comiso, see the leaflets of *la ragnatela*, whose projects have included purchasing the land where the missiles were placed (see "Un metro quadro di pace," *pace e guerra*, August 1983.

the woman question and the southern question in Italy

social and economic condition of the South

A good contemporary evaluation of the social and economic condition of the South is "The mezzogiorno: A word of warning," *notizie dall'Italia*, Fondazione Giovanni Agnelli, November 1984. For contemporary studies of the southern question, see Francesco Renda, *Il movimento contadino in Sicilia e la fine del blocco agrario nel mezzogiorno* (Bari, 1976); Pio La Torre, *Comunisti e movimento contadino in Sicilia* (Rome, 1980); Rosario Villari, *Mezzogiorno e democrazia* (Bari, 1978); Anton Blok, *The Mafia of a Sicilian Village, 1860–1960: A Study of Violent Peasant Entrepreneurs* (New York, 1974); *La Sicilia alla svolta degli anni '80*, a cura di Alfredo Galasso (Milan, 1981); and E. Macaluso, *La Sicilia e lo stato*, intervista a cura di Vittorio Nistico (Milan, 1979).

cultural history of Sicily

For contemporary cultural history of Sicily, see the works of Ignazio Buttita, *Il poeta in piazza* (Milan, 1974); *Lo faccio il poeta* (Milan, 1972,); *La peddi nova*, prefazione di Carlo Levi (Milan, 1963,); and *La paglia bruciata, racconti in versi* (Milan, 1968). See the works of Leonardo Sciascia, particularly *la Sicilia come metafora*, intervista di Marcelle Padovani (Rome, 1979); *Candido: ovvero un sogno fatto in Sicilia* (Turin, 1977); *Dalle parti degli infedeli* (Palermo, 1979), and *A ciascuno il suo* (Turin, 1966). See the Introduction, this work. See also the works of Danilo Dolci, a prophet of nonviolence and peasant responsibility: *Conversazioni* (Turin, 1962), *Racconti siciliani* (Turin, 1963), *Report from Palermo* (New York, 1961), *Inventare il futuro* (Bari, 1968), and *A New World in the Making*, trans. R. Munroe (New York, 1965). See also Maria Rosa Cutrufelli, *Disoccupata con onore: lavoro e condizione della donna* (Milan, 1975); Denise Jacobs and Rean Mazzone, *Donna in Sicilia* (Palermo, 1978); "un albero della pace dalle Alpi alla Sicilia," *noidonne* supplement, February 1984. For southern interest in retaining the values of the peasant tradition, see Nicola Zitara, "Da Marx al meridione" in *quaderni di cultura contadina*, *quaderni calabresi*, June 1983: "Marx is alive in our consciousness even when we deny him," because he represents the idea of revolution, "even when we mean by this a radical but peaceful change of society." ..."Without Marx we would not have discovered our southern condition." Contemporary southern cultural and political consciousness has engendered keen interest in the *fasci siciliani* of the 1890s (see chapter 1, this work) and in the southern land occupations of the postwar era (see chapter 5, this work). See also Emanuele Amodio, *Oppressione e cultura sulla produzione culturale subalterna* (Catania, 1980). Regional consciousness has stimulated interest in preserving dialects; see "Questioni del dialetto", *quaderni de "Le ragioni critiche" 2, atti del convegno di studi sul dialetto siciliano Pachino, 29, 30, 31 maggio 1981* (Catania, 1981). For historians of Sicilian peasant culture, the casa-museo founded by Antonino Uccello at Palazzolo Acreide is a unique re-creation of a peasant home with actual artifacts.

Italian feminism and changing interpretations of Marxism

For the study of Marx today, see *The History of Marxism*, Vol. one: *Marxism in Marx's Day*, ed. Eric J. Hobsbawm (Bloomington, Ind., 1982). In David McLellan, *Marxism after Marx: An Introduction* (Boston, 1979), see chapter 1, "The Contribution of Engels," for a contemporary evaluation of Engels's essay *Origin of the Family, Private Property and the State*, a study indebted to Bebel's *Women under Socialism* (1883) which is now regarded as a racist disregard of Asia and Africa. For an example of the candid atmosphere of the Italian left in the 1980s, see the account of the Pci conference commemorating the twentieth anniversary of Togliatti's death. In the newspaper *il manifesto* (whose new left party members are, in the eighties, supported on Pci lists), the founder of the modern Pci is irreverently described in a headline as "Togliatti, un liberal-staliniano" (*il manifesto*, 28 December 1984). In addition to the unedited views of Marx presented in this text, see an Italian new left and ecological view of Marx by Michelangelo Notarianni, "Non celebriamo Marx. Non si può pacificarlo nel pantheon della cultura. Le sue domande oggi diventano una sola. Perchè la merce produce guerra?" (We do not celebrate Marx.... Why does production produce war?), *pace e guerra*, 17 March 1983. On the other hand, there were in the eighties many analyses of the compatibility of marxism with Italian left catholicism; see Biagio De Giovanni, "Marx oltre i marxismi," *bozze*, March–April 1983 ("The nucleus of elementary truth in the thinking of Marx was that history is the contrast between the oppressed and oppressors and that history could be changed.... it is necessary to liberate Marx from marxisms"). See Italo Mancini, "Il dibattito acceso dal centenario: il principio di Marx e il cristianesimo," *bozze*, May/August 1983 ("Today marxism no longer has a country because it is present in all countries"). See also Franco Angeli, *Lineamenti: quale marxismo oggi* (Milan, 1983). The complex role of belief in contemporary Italy is explored in "Operai cultura religione," a review essay by Roberto Cipriani of three books: Costantino Cipolla, *Religione e cultura operaia* (Brescia, 1981); Massimo Conte et al., *Cultura operaia nel mezzogiorno: sindacato dei consigli e modelli culturali, una ricerca sui delegati di fabrica* (Rome, 1983); and Costantino Cipolla con la collaborazione di Stefano Martelli, *Marxismo e religione nella cultura operaia* (Bologna, 1983). Cipriano refers to Togliatti's view that the aspiration toward a socialist society could be facilitated among people who have a religious faith—in the religious consciousness itself, outside institutional religion—and awakened by the problems of today's world. Cipriano also referred to Pier Paolo Pasolini, who said before he died in 1975 that neither the vatican nor the Pci understood this. An article by Giovanni Bianchi and Renzo Salvi, "Quandro crollano gli scaffali" in *rocca*, 15 June 1984, explores this subject among Italian youth; the authors suggest that a religious consciousness outside the institution of the church may be studied in the activism of Italian youth in movements against violence, in work for an ecological perspective in problems of underdevelopment, in work on the drug problem, and in opposition to nuclear weapons. See "I giovani tra continuità e rinnovamento," *comnuovi tempi*, 22 July 1984. See also Roger Garaudy, *L'alternativa: cambiare il mondo e la vita* (Assisi, 1980); Elsa Morante, *Aracoeli*, trans. William Weaver (New York, 1984); Arci, *Il grande Karl*, with a hundred "unedited" photos of the "family of Carlo Marx" (Rome, 1983); and Sabino Acquaviva et al., *Francesco un "pazzo" da slegare* (Assisi, 1983). See also Giorgio Galli, *Storia del socialismo italiano* (Rome-Bari, 1980); *Nella donna c'era un sogno . . . canzoniere femminista*, ed. Marina Bacchetti (Milan, 1976); *Canzoni italiane di protesta 1789/1974 dalla rivoluzione francese alla repressione cilena*, ed. Giuseppe Vettori (Perugia, 1974; *Canti popolari italiani: una suggestiva raccolta dei folk italiano della tradizione contadina alla nuova realtà operaia* (Perugia, 1974); and Luigi Infantino, *Sicilia amara e duci: raccolta di canti Siciliani* (Milan, 1967).

Index

343